A Pentecostal Reads

The Book of Mormon

A Literary and Theological Introduction

A PENTECOSTAL READS
THE BOOK OF MORMON

A LITERARY AND THEOLOGICAL INTRODUCTION

JOHN CHRISTOPHER THOMAS

CPT Press
Cleveland, Tennessee

A Pentecostal Reads the Book of Mormon
A Literary and Theological Introduction

Published by CPT Press
900 Walker ST NE
Cleveland, TN 37311
email: cptpress@pentecostaltheology.org
website: www.pentecostaltheology.org

Library of Congress Control Number: 2015951054

ISBN-13 9781935931553

Cover Image
Minerva Teichert (1888-1976), Love Story, 1949-1951, oil on masonite, 36 x 48 inches. Brigham Young University Musuem of Art, 1969.

DEDICATION

Madeline Danielle Scaperoth

CONTENTS

Afterword

PREFACE

My initial encounter with the Book of Mormon came in January 1974 as a result of a visit to Temple Square in Salt Lake City, Utah. The college touring choir of which I was a member was in the midst of a trip across the United States, from Cleveland, Tennessee to California and back again. Having visited the impressive Mormon Tabernacle, complete with a demonstration of its acoustic sophistication, we stopped by the Visitors Center before continuing our tour. After the orientation presentation, some of us accepted a complementary copy of the Book of Mormon, which had the iconic blue cover with the angel Moroni appearing on it. Little did I know that the reception of this copy would be the first of numerous encounters with this distinctive book and a variety of people for whom it would function as Scripture.

The next few years would be marked by my becoming acquainted with Mormonism through extended conversations with LDS (Latter Day Saint) missionaries (some of whose names I still can recall), literature written to respond to the claims of Mormonism, a graduate course on Mormon history from its beginnings through the events of Nauvoo, Illinois (including the death of Joseph Smith and his brother Hyrum in the Carthage Jail in Carthage, Illinois), visiting various historic Mormon sites (Harmony, PA; Palmyra, Manchester, the Hill Cumorah, and Fayette, NY; Kirtland, OH; Monongahela, PA; Nauvoo and Carthage, IL; Lamoni, IA; Independence, Richmond, Far West, Liberty, and Adam-ondi-ahman, MO; and Salt Lake City and Provo, UT), extensive reading of a variety of studies devoted to Mormonism more generally and the Book of Mormon more specifically by authors both friendly and unfriendly to its claims, and a graduate level reading course on the Book of Mormon itself. As this journey began I could not have imagined that I would one day author a monograph-length study devoted to the Book of Mormon. But as I write the words of this Preface, it now seems quite natural and fitting that I would eventually do so.

There are, of course, a number of people who contribute to the production of a book aside from the writer and in this case my level of indebtedness is great indeed. A number of people have kindly read drafts of the manuscript at various stages and have spared me from numerous errors of all sorts. Any errors that remain are not theirs but my own. It should also be noted that not all readers of the manuscript agree with everything that appears here. Consequently, they should not be held accountable for its contents.

A few people have actually read almost the entire manuscript. This short list begins with my friend and former student at the Pentecostal Theological Seminary, Derrick Harmon, who offered enthusiastic support for the project, suggested numerous improvements to the text, and functioned as a frequent dialogue partner about all manner of things Book of Mormon. A couple of readers, who desired to remain anonymous, have offered detailed responses to the manuscript and answered hundreds of questions. Their genuine interest in my reading of the Book of Mormon as an 'outsider' encouraged me throughout. They have spared me from many grammatical and theological embarassments – but perhaps not all!

A host of individuals have read specific sections of the manuscript, providing the kind of critical engagement sorely needed all along the way. Dale E. Luffman kindly arranged for me to study the Book of Mormon with him at graduate level, opened many doors for me in the Community of Christ branch of the restoration tradition, and read portions of the manuscript making helpful suggestions. His own monograph on the book continues to be one of the best explorations of the theology of the book available. John Turner has proven to be an invaluable dialogue partner, as we would often trade drafts of our almost simultaneously written books for the other to read. His expertise and wise counsel have improved the work at many points. Charley Harrell has been a valued sounding board for me on all manner of theological issues related to the Book of Mormon. I hate to think what it would have been like to write the theology chapters without his *This Is My Doctrine* and our frequent engagements via Skype and in person. Brian Hauglid facilitated my work by making study space available for me at the Maxwell Institute, arranging accommodation, and inviting me to give two public lectures at Brigham Young University during my stays. Brian also facilitated times of interaction with a number of significant dialogue partners whilst I was in Utah. He too has read sections of my work making helpful observations along the way, helping me understand better the issues I was investigating. D. William Faupel has read the chapters devoted to Pentecostalism and the Book of Mormon. I have profited both from his expertise and friendship over the years.

Rachel Killebrew generously opened the Community of Christ archives to me, making possible a first hand examination of the Printer's Manuscript of the Book of Mormon, as well as other significant artifacts and archival materials. Robin Jensen kindly arranged for a first hand examination of the Original Manuscript of the Book of Mormon in Salt Lake City as well as answering a variety of questions related to the Book of Mormon and its reception history. Later, Robin also invited me to give a seminar on my research for the scholars working at the Church History Library in Salt Lake City. I am indebted to these individuals for the warm hospitality they extended to me during my stays in their respective locales. Being able to examine the earliest extant manuscripts of the Book of Mormon added significantly to my research and engagement with the text. I offer my heart-felt thanks to them both for the splendid opportunities they afforded me, understanding well how rare such access is, owing to the fragile nature of the manuscripts.

Gratitude is here expressed to Clyda Ludlow and the Brigham Young University Museum of Art for granting permission for the use of Minerva Teichert's 'Love Story' that graces the cover of this volume; to Lachlan Mackay, Rachel Killebrew, the Community of Christ, and the Lynn Smith family for granting permission for the use of the David Hyrum Smith's 'The Vision of Lehi'; and to Donna Poulton for arranging use of the photograph of Reuben Kirkham's 'Alma Baptizing in the Waters of Mormon'. The images that appear in this volume were supplied by these individuals and/or institutions.

Special thanks are also offered to John Hilton III and Morgan Davis for cheerfully securing many articles and book chapters beyond my reach. Ben Huff generously added me to the program of a Society of Mormon Philosophy and Theology Conference at Utah Valley University in 2013 to offer my first paper on the Book of Mormon and arranged for a plenary session devoted to my work on the program of a Society of Mormon Philosophy and Theology Conference at Brigham Young University in 2015. These opportunities stand as a nice inclusion around the work. Finally, I would be remiss not to mention Eric Eliason, one of the first scholars from BYU that I met all those years ago, whose engagement and encouragement have meant much to me. I imagine neither of us could have envisioned where our initial meeting would wind up taking us.

Closer to home, I want to offer my sincere appreciation to Mark L. Williams, Presiding Bishop of the Church of God, and R. Lamar Vest, President of the Pentecostal Theological Seminary, with whom I consulted during the course of the writing of this book. Their personal encouragement and spiritual support have meant much to me during the writing of the volume.

It has been one of the blessings of my life to work within two communities of faith that inform all that I do, the Pentecostal Theological Seminary in Cleveland, Tennessee and the Woodward Church of God in Athens, Tennessee. Each of these communities of faith contributes more to me than anyone will ever know. The provisions of the Clarence J. Abbott Chair of Biblical Studies underwrites and makes possible my research projects and I am happy to offer thanks to the President and Board of Directors of the seminary for this on-going support. My friend, Old Testament colleague, and co-conspirator in a variety of ventures, Lee Roy Martin, contributes much to me at various levels. His interest in this and other projects is a constant source of strength and encouragement. It is one of the blessings of my life to be able to work with him on a daily basis. His contributions to the production of this volume are many and are too numerous to be listed here. For all these things I say thanks.

As ever, the people who contribute the most to my scholarly activites are my family. My parents continue to be sources of spiritual and emotional strength for me and my family. My wife Barbara is the hardest working person I have ever known, whose labor has made possible my own academic pursuits. Her contributions to this project have been no less significant than to the other pursuits. Specifically, she has shouldered more burdens than ordinary owing to my absences that this research entailed. She has willingly agreed to the many 'detours' from a pre-arranged journey we took owing to our close physical proximity to some significant site or person I needed to visit. My daughters, Paige Thomas Scaperoth and Lori Thomas Brown, and their husbands, David Scaperoth and Chad

Brown, continue to bring great joy to Barbara and me. Their interest in this project was great and I enjoyed very much indeed our numerous conversations about 'Project M', as this research soon became known in the family!

This book is dedicated to our granddaughter, Madeline Danielle Scaperoth, who has brought unimaginable joy and love to us as we see her grow and develop. Her young life has coincided with the period during which this project was researched and written. I hope that one day she will know of my love for her in part by means of this token of dedication.

INTRODUCTION

As has oft been observed, one does not have to have read the Book of Mormon to have an opinion about it.[1] In point of fact, opinions about the Book of Mormon often have little to do with the book itself. There have even been long stretches of time when some of those for whom the book functions as Scripture paid comparatively little attention to it in their worship services, theology, and teachings.

Book of Mormon studies as a discipline is complicated by the fact that it is not altogether clear who qualifies as a Book of Mormon scholar, that is to say, who has a right to comment on it. An argument could be made that scholars of the Ancient Near East are those most qualified, as the book makes claims to be of ancient origin, written originally in 'Reformed Egyptian'. Given the book's detailed comments on the Americas, perhaps historians of the Americas are best prepared to study it and offer comment. Since the book emerged during the early nineteenth century, one could argue that historians of the Americas of that era are those best suited to offer informed comment. Owing to the fact that the earliest extant manuscripts of the book appear in English, perhaps those with English literature sensibilities would prove to be the best commentators. Owing to the theological claims and biblical texts that appear in it, perhaps theologians or biblical studies scholars have contributions to make.

A review of monograph length studies reveals that representatives from nearly all these disciplines (and more) have tried their hand at an examination of the book. As one would expect, most of

---

[1] Thomas F. O'Dea, *The Mormons* (Chicago: University of Chicago Press, 1957), p. 26.

these attempts have come from those for whom the book functions as Scripture. Until recently, very few scholars from outside the LDS family of churches have given significant attention to the Book of Mormon or even Mormonism(s) more generally. But, to quote Bob Dylan from decades ago, 'The times they are a-changin', as more and more 'Gentiles' are devoting scholarly attention to this book and its peoples.[2] At the same time, there are voices emerging from within the somewhat cloistered world of Mormon Studies that acknowledge the need of and issue an invitation for more scholarly work to be done by those from outside the tradition(s) in order to make Mormon Studies a more mainstream discipline, as new, and sometimes fresh, eyes read the texts and history sacred to the LDS family of churches.

This book finds its place somewhere within this broader context. Despite the plethora of studies devoted to the Book of Mormon, few of them address many of the questions (at least under one cover) that I brought to this text, for many of the works are primarily interested in whether or not the Book of Mormon is historically true or false, verifiable or not. The purpose of this volume is to acquaint its (mainly non-Mormon) readers with the book while offering engagement from a Pentecostal perspective. That said, it should be noted that my primary interests are literary and theological, with significant interest in reception history. Historical interests are secondary and make their appearance mainly when considering the knotty issue of origins. Thus, this book seeks to treat the Book of Mormon primarily from literary, theological, and reception history perspectives. It seems that despite the variety of books devoted to it, the Book of Mormon has only recently begun to receive the kind of literary and theological analyses that can become the basis for a variety of other investigations and perhaps move the conversations beyond the apologetically driven issue of historicity.[3]

The following chapters are divided into six parts, which are unequal in terms of length. Part One of the volume is devoted to mat-

---

[2] One thinks of John G. Turner's recent magnificent biography of Brigham Young as an example. Cf. John G. Turner, *Brigham Young: Pioneer Prophet* (Cambridge, MA: Belknap Press, 2012).

[3] Cf. Mark D. Thomas, *Digging in Cumorah: Reclaiming Book of Mormon Narratives* (Salt Lake City: Signature Books, 1999), and esp. Grant Hardy, *Understanding the Book of Mormon: A Reader's Guide* (Oxford: Oxford University Press, 2010).

ters of structure. Specifically, this first part seeks to identify the overall structure of the book by means of literary markers within the text itself. This initial exploration is followed by Part Two that seeks to describe in some detail the actual contents of the book, topics that often receive only passing attention even in works that set out as their stated aim to examine such issues. Attention is given to textual indicators that serve to guide readers through the narrative. Part Three of the study is devoted to an exploration of the theology of the Book of Mormon. More than a comparison of the book's theological orientation with that of the Bible, as numerous works have offered, this part of the study seeks to identify the major theological emphases that emerge from the pages of the Book of Mormon itself and offer some reflection upon them. Part Four of the monograph is an examination of the book's impact on followers and opponents alike, as well as the imprint it has left on music, art, and a couple of examples of disastrous interpretations of the book. Part Five seeks to place the Book of Mormon and Pentecostalism into dialogue by identifying historical figures that anticipated the movement or functioned as early leaders in the Pentecostal movement whose paths crossed those for whom the book functioned as Scripture, by examining references in the pages of early Pentecostal periodical literature to the Book of Mormon and the movement(s) it spawned, and by comparing the Book of Mormon with the theological heart of the Pentecostal tradition. Part Six, the final section of the study, takes up the issues of the book's origins. This part begins with locating and engaging the earliest story of origins offered by Joseph Smith, turns to identifying the complications with this standard story, and concludes by offering a taxonomy of the various responses to these complications offered by a variety of interpreters. A bibliography of works cited concludes the study along with indices of texts and authors. As should be apparent, this particular outline mirrors the way in which I tend to approach biblical texts, as one trained in biblical studies. Beginning with the text as we have it, moving to an analysis of its theology, identifying a text's reception history, reflecting on the text's theological significance for Pentecostal theology, and finally to matters of origins, or provenance, my methodological approach seeks to privilege the text and engage it before entertaining arguments of origins which often are much less clear. Consequently, my approach does not make my lit-

erary and theological engagement with the Book of Mormon dependent upon issues related to the book's origins. Rather, these
analyses are pursued independently from the issues of origins. As a
result, my references to 'readers' in the first three parts of the monograph are normally to readers implied by the narrative in the Book
of Mormon. Actual readers are much more the focus of attention in
the section devoted to reception history. Though such a methodological approach is quite a departure from the standard way the
Book of Mormon is often studied – and will perhaps take some getting used to, I believe it has gifts to give and fruit to bear – not least
of which is the chance for those who may disagree about issues of
origins to have candid, constructive conversations about a number
of literary and theological aspects of the book before parting company – if such be the case – over differences of opinion with regard
to the book's origins.

As is perhaps well known, the Book of Mormon first appeared
in print in 1830, with a copyright date of 1829. The culmination of a
nearly two-year period of 'translation', editing, and publishing, the
appearance of the Book of Mormon was met quite early by both
severe criticism from opponents and unbridled praise from the adherents it quickly gathered. The work purports to be a historical
account covering a period of nearly a thousand years, detailing the
history of the descendants of one Lehi, who is said to have left Jerusalem shortly before its fall to the Babylonians and who jour-
neyed to the Americas around 600 BCE. The story concludes with
the destruction of the Nephites (descended from Lehi's son Nephi)
and the surviving Lamanites (descended from Lehi's son Laman),
with a description of resurrection appearances by Jesus Christ to the
Nephites in North America after his ascension in Galilee. This account claims to have been taken from engraved plates, written in
'Reformed Egyptian', prepared (with some abridgement) by a Nephite father and son, Mormon and Moroni, plates eventually
'found' and 'translated' by one Joseph Smith, Jr.

Two handwritten manuscripts used by Smith and his various
scribes survive in part or in whole. The manuscript known as the
'Original Manuscript' is housed in the church historian's office of
the Church of Jesus Christ of Latter-day Saints in Salt Lake City,
Utah. About 25-30% of the book is preserved in this manuscript.

The manuscript known as the 'Printer's Manuscript' is housed in the archives of the Community of Christ in Independence, Missouri. The entire Book of Mormon is contained in this manuscript. Both of these documents were utilized, to one extent or another, in setting the type in the publication of the 1830 edition of the Book of Mormon.

For the most part, quotations of the Book of Mormon in this study will follow the 1830 edition with modern (LDS) versification added as an aide to the reader.

PART ONE

THE STRUCTURE OF THE BOOK OF MORMON

Part One of this book is devoted to an examination of the overall structure of the Book of Mormon. It will give attention to the way in which Mormon and Moroni contribute to the book's structure as well as to the contributions of three sets of chronological indicators around which the book appears to be structured. Such structural indicators can in turn serve as guides that help the readers make their way through the whole. Throughout much of this monograph there is an emphasis upon how the readers would experience the Book of Mormon. As noted in the Introduction, in this chapter references to readers are to readers implied by the text. Thus, much of the volume is devoted to constructing readers envisioned by the text. When reference is made to actual historical readers, such will be noted.

.

1

THE STRUCTURE OF THE BOOK OF MORMON

Though it contains a variety of literary forms (epistle, sermon, prophetic oracle, testimony, etc.), unlike the Bible, the Book of Mormon is for the most part one extended narrative comprised of various books. Thus, at one level, identifying the book's structure could be thought of as arranging the book's contents in the order in which they occur in the volume. Such an arrangement would look like the following:

The Title Page
The First Book of Nephi
The Second Book of Nephi
The Book of Jacob
The Book of Enos
The Book of Jarom
The Book of Omni
The Words of Mormon
The Book of Mosiah
The Book of Alma
The Book of Helaman
The Book of Third Nephi[1]
The Book of Fourth Nephi
The Book of Mormon
The Book of Ether
The Book of Moroni

---

[1] In the 1830 edition of the Book of Mormon, Third and Fourth Nephi appeared as the Book of Nephi, the Son of Nephi, Who Was the Son of Helaman, followed by the Book of Nephi, Who Is the Son of Nephi, One of the Disciples of Jesus Christ.

Mormon and Moroni

However, a closer examination reveals that the macro-structure of the narrative takes shape around the central writers/editors, Mormon and Moroni, as their names occur in strategic locations throughout the book.[2] For example, both names appear on the title page, where the Book of Mormon is described as 'an account written by the hand of Mormon, upon the plates taken from the plates of Nephi' and as 'sealed by the hand of Moroni and hid up unto the Lord, to come forth in due time by the way of Gentile'.[3] Such prominence leads the readers to expect that both figures will have more than passing significance in the pages to follow.

Such expectancy is not disappointed, for after the first six books (that come from the small plates of Nephi), covering some 146 pages in the 1830 edition, an entire book is devoted to the Words of Mormon. In these words the readers once again find reference to Moroni as well,

> And now I, Mormon, being about to deliver up the record which I have been making, into the hands of my son Moroni, behold have witnessed almost all the destruction of my people, the Nephites. And it has been many hundreds of years after the coming of Christ, that I deliver these records into the hands of my son (Words of Mormon 1-2).

Whereas the preceding narrative (1 Nephi – Omni) has given the impression of chronological movement from the narrative's beginning – devoted to Lehi's departure from Jerusalem before its destruction by the Babylonians, down to the events associated with Amaleki, the Words of Mormon break this narrative development, jumping ahead many hundred years after the coming of Christ. In

---

[2] Hardy (*Understanding the Book of Mormon*) is not far from this idea when he suggests that the primary structural aspects of the book are the narrators: Nephi, Mormon, and Moroni. Though he does not appeal to such as evidence, his proposal, too, has the advantage of the inclusion of Nephi on the title page along with Mormon and Moroni.

[3] Unlike most modern editions of the Book of Mormon, the books in the 1830 edition are divided into long chapters without versification. Following the lead of John Turner, in this work I cite the chapter and verse divisions of contemporary LDS versions, primarily owing to the demographics of readership, whilst seeking to retain the language and grammar of the 1830 edition.

point of fact, Mormon's words come from the perspective of the book's anticipated end, which includes the complete destruction of the Nephite people. This perspective lends a certain credibility to Mormon's words for the readers, for he apparently knows his people's entire history from beginning to end. Mormon goes on to locate his readers within his own editorial work. At this point he looks back on his work from the plates of Nephi and his locating additional plates containing a 'small account of the prophets, from Jacob down to the reign of this king Benjamin' (Words of Mormon 3). But he also gives the readers an orientation to what lies ahead. Much of the rest of Mormon's work will come from the abridgement of other plates of Nephi. Thus, Mormon speaks authoritatively to the readers about their location or progress within the broader narrative. He also provides a transition with regard to the account of king Benjamin, who was introduced near the end of the book immediately preceding the Words of Mormon (Omni 23) and who is taken back up in the book that immediately follows the Words of Mormon (Mosiah 1.1-6.5).

Mormon makes another appearance within the broader narrative in 3 Nephi 5.10-20, where he steps out of the narrative with claims that he has made a record on plates from the plates of Nephi, that he is 'a disciple of Jesus Christ, the Son of God', that his small record runs from the time Lehi left Jerusalem 'even down until the present time', that his record is 'just and true', and that he is a true descendant of Lehi. With these words, Mormon reassures his readers of the trustworthiness of his account for it includes 'things which I have seen with my own eyes'. Mormon reappears near the end of 3 Nephi (26.8-13),[4] where he again underscores his role in the writing of these records specifically with regard to the words and actions of Jesus in his appearance to those in the Americas. Here Mormon makes clear that he recorded only those things not forbidden by the Lord to be recorded. In 4 Nephi (23) Mormon briefly reappears, it seems as a guarantor who testifies of the way in which the people multiplied, became exceedingly rich, and prospered in Christ.

---

[4] Actually, the words of Mormon mark the conclusion of each major section of 3 Nephi at 5.10-20, 10.11-19, 26.8-13, and 28.13-30.2.

As the story of the Nephites and Lamanites draws to a conclusion, Mormon and Moroni once again figure prominently, this time in a book that bears the name, the Book of Mormon. Mormon begins this book by once again emphasizing his role as eyewitness to many of the things he records and tells the readers something of his call to this task. For when Mormon was but ten years old, Ammaron, who himself had become the guardian of the sacred records (4 Nephi 48-49), recognized that Mormon was a 'sober child, and … quick to observe' and instructed him that when he is twenty-four years old to go to the land Antum, to a hill called Shim, and retrieve the plates of Nephi and engrave upon them all the things that you observe about your people (Book of Mormon 1.4). At the age of fifteen Mormon writes that he was visited of the Lord (1.15) and owing to his stature was made the leader of the Nephites in their on-going struggle against the Lamanites (2.1). Whilst fighting near the location of the hidden plates of Nephi, Mormon retrieved the plates and made a full record of all the wickedness and abominations according to the instructions he had received from Ammaron (2.17-18). As the fighting intensifies Mormon goes back to the hill Shim and retrieves all the plates Ammaron hid there (4.23). As he grows old Mormon hides all the plates, save the few he entrusts to his son Moroni (6.6) who leads the Nephite army (6.12). Upon the death of Mormon at the hands of the Lamanites, Moroni writes in his father's stead (8.1) and purposes to hide the records in the earth (8.4), a promise on which he is said to make good (8.14), pronouncing a blessing on whoever brings them to light (8.16).

But before the solitary Moroni completes his task, he gives an account of the Jaredites in the Book of Ether taken from the twenty-four plates found by the people of Limhi (Ether 1.1-6). In his abbreviated account Moroni recounts the history of this people who came to the Americas at the time of the events surrounding the Tower of Babel.

Finally, whilst attempting to avoid death at the hands of the Lamanites, Moroni offers his final words and (the final words of the entire Book of Mormon) in the book that bears his name. After recording instructions on a variety of ecclesiological matters (Moroni 1.1-6.9), Moroni and Mormon stand together at the conclusion of the entire Book of Mormon. Here Moroni includes additional words from his father (Moroni 7.1-48), as well as two epistles from

Mormon to Moroni (Moroni 8.1-30; 9.1-26). And as death draws near for Moroni, he bids farewell with an expectation of resurrection (Moroni 10.34).

It is difficult to underestimate the structural significance of Mormon and Moroni for the book, for not only do they appear together as an inclusio around the entire narrative, but they also appear (often together) at a variety of strategic locations throughout, orienting the readers as to their own location in the broader composition, apprising them of the specific plates and records being relied upon, and assuring the readers of the trustworthiness of the accounts. In each case it seems that Mormon, Moroni, or both appear when the narrative introduces a new set of plates from which the record is drawn. Thus, standing at the beginning (the Title Page), at the end of the small plates of Nephi, at the end of the other plates of Nephi, and on either side of the plates found by the people of Limhi, Mormon and/or Moroni appear as structural markers for the readers, providing recognizable landmarks to guide them. In this light, the structure of the book might be represented in the following way:

The Title Page: Mormon and Moroni
The First Book of Nephi
The Second Book of Nephi
The Book of Jacob
The Book of Enos
The Book of Jarom
The Book of Omni
The Words of Mormon
The Book of Mosiah
The Book of Alma
The Book of Helaman
The Book of Third Nephi
The Book of Fourth Nephi
The Book of Mormon
The Book of Ether
The Book of Moroni

Chronological Indicators

The strategic appearances of Mormon and Moroni throughout the narrative are not the only keys to the structure of the book. Another set of clues comes in the form of chronological and/or temporal indicators found in various sections of the book. Whilst a variety of temporal indicators occur at any number of points in the book which denote the reign of a specific king, the ministry of a certain prophet, the amount of time war or peace lasted, or simply the passage of time, there are three major sets of chronological indicators that give the narrative a sense of movement and contribute to a sense of the book's macro-structure.[5]

From very near the book's beginning, time begins to be measured based upon the number of years that have passed from the moment Lehi left Jerusalem. There are seventeen such indicators scattered throughout the Book of Mormon. They appear in the following order:

Number of Years Since Lehi Left Jerusalem	Book of Mormon Location
600	1 Nephi 10.4
8	1 Nephi 17.4-5*
(600)	1 Nephi 19.8
30	2 Nephi 5.28
40	2 Nephi 5.34*
(600)	2 Nephi 25.19
55	Jacob 1.1
179	Enos 25
200	Jarom 5*
238	Jarom 13*
276	Omni 3*
282	Omni 3*
320	Omni 5*
476	Mosiah 6.4
509	Mosiah 29.46
600	3 Nephi 1.1
609	3 Nephi 2.6

* Indicates that the formula used to designate this passage of time was something like 'when x number of years had passed away'.

---

[5] Cf. John R. Pratt, 'Book of Mormon Chronology', *Encyclopedia of Mormonism* (New York: MacMillan, 1992), I, pp. 169-71.

A number of aspects of this list are worthy of comment. First, it is significant that this means of reckoning is anticipated by or begins with a prophetic word from Nephi that 'even six hundred years from the time that my father left Jerusalem, a Prophet would the Lord God raise up among the Jews; yea, even a Messiah; or, in other words, a Saviour of the world' (1 Nephi 10.4). Not only are the readers put on notice that a Messiah would arise six hundred years after the departure of Lehi from Jerusalem, but they are also led to expect that this remarkable event would serve as one of the culminating purposes of the story carefully being recorded in the plates. Such notice would perhaps create within the readers an anticipation that this period of time would somehow be marked in the narrative that at this point lies ahead. Second, the fact that this notice is reiterated twice more (1 Nephi 19.8 and 2 Nephi 25.19) indicates something of the significance attached to this measurement of time. Third, though the first indicator that time was being marked in this manner does not include the phrase 'from the time that my father left Jerusalem', the observation that this company of folk sojourned for eight years in the wilderness (1 Nephi 17.4) could hardly be understood in any other way. Fourth, it is noteworthy that an example of this means of calculating time appears at least once in every book in the Book of Mormon save the Words of Mormon, Alma, Helaman, 4 Nephi, the Book of Mormon, Ether, and Moroni. In other words, this chronological indicator appears in every book that comes from the small plates of Nephi as well as 3 Nephi. Thus, the calculation does not appear in the works of the editors/compilers (Words of Mormon, Book of Mormon, and Moroni), nor in the chronologically misplaced Ether. As for the lack of a referent in 4 Nephi, it should be noted that the six hundred years were completed by the time of 3 Nephi 1.1. Fifth, it appears that this means of marking chronological progression (since Lehi left Jerusalem) goes a long way toward holding the book together for its readers while conveying a sense of progress.

The absence of this means of calculation in Alma and Helaman is explained, in part, by the appearance of a second means of calculation, where the readers are told that the reign of the judges commences (Mosiah 29.44). Shortly thereafter, the readers learn that five hundred and nine years had passed since Lehi left Jerusalem (Mosiah 29.46) and that the reign of the kings over the people of

Nephi ended with the death of Alma (Mosiah 29.47), an event with which the book of Mosiah ends. In the first verse of the next book, Alma 1.1 – a book devoted to the son (Alma) of the deceased high priest and church founder by the same name, the readers are introduced to the next means of marking chronological progression when they are told, 'Now it came to pass that in the first year of the reign of the Judges over the people of Nephi ...' This means of calculation, which dominates the book from this point on in Alma and Helaman – even extending into the first part of 3 Nephi – chronicles the passing of 100 years in which the judges reigned. The references occur in the following texts illustrated by the chart on the next page.

A review of these texts reveals a number of relevant details. First, it is significant that the reign of the judges covers 100 years exactly. The readers are reminded of this fact by the running calculation of the reign of the judges. In addition, they would pick up on the fact that before the reign of the judges commences, the last mention of the calculation that dates the passage of time from when Lehi left Jerusalem stood at 509 years (Mosiah 29.46). The next occurrence of this means of calculation does not occur until 3 Nephi 1.1, where the readers are told that it had been 600 years since Lehi had left Jerusalem, and the 91st year of the reign of the judges, reminding the readers that a Messiah was to be born 600 years after Lehi left Jerusalem. After the 100 year reign of the judges has been completed (3 Nephi 2.5), the readers learn that it had been 609 years since Lehi had left Jerusalem (3 Nephi 2.6), exactly 100 years. Second, although the 100 year reign of the judges is clearly an important means of calculation, not all 100 years are specifically mentioned. In point of fact, only 90 of the 100 years are explicitly mentioned with ten years left unspecified (years 3, 4, 12, 13, 32-35, 55, 70, 73). These omissions are an interesting phenomenon given the fact that some verses describe the passing of multiple years (Alma 50.24; Helaman 3.2; 3.19; 4.5; 11.36; and esp. 3 Nephi 2.4), while still others describe the passage of succeeding years one verse after another (Helaman 3.1-3, 32-33, 36-37; 4.4-5, 8-10; 6.13-16; 11.5-6, 21-24, 35-37; 16.10-13; 3 Nephi 1.27-28), making clear that their primary function in many of these cases is to remind the hearers of where they find themselves in the 100 year reign. Third, the rapidity with which years 87 through 100 occur may well generate within the

Number of Years in the Reign of the Judges	Book of Mormon Location	Number of Years in the Reign of the Judges	Book of Mormon Location
1	Alma 1.1, 2; 17.6	54	Helaman 4.1
2	Alma 1.23	56	Helaman 4.4
[5]	Alma 1.33; 2.1; 3.25	57	Helaman 4.5
6	Alma 4.1	58	Helaman 4.5, 8
7	Alma 4.5	59	Helaman 4.8
8	Alma 4.6, 9, 10	60	Helaman 4.9
9	Alma 4.11, 20; 8.2	61	Helaman 4.10, 17
10	Alma 8.3; 10.6; 14.23; 15.19	62	Helaman 4.18; 6.1
11	Alma 16.1, 9	63	Helaman 6.6
14	Alma 16.12, 21 [17.4]	64	Helaman 6.13
15	Alma 28.7, 9, 10	65	Helaman 6.14
16	Alma 30.2, 4	66	Helaman 6.15
17	Alma 30.5	67	Helaman 6.16, 32
18	Alma 35.13; 43.3, 4; 44.24	68	Helaman 6.33, 41
19	Alma 45.2, 20; 49.1, 29	69	Helaman 7.1
20	Alma 50.1, 16	71	Helaman 10.19
21	Alma 50.17, 23	72	Helaman 11.1
22	Alma 50.24	74	Helaman 11.5
23	Alma 50.24	75	Helaman 11.6
24	Alma 50.25, 35, 40	76	Helaman 11.17, 21
25	Alma 51.1, 12, 37	77	Helaman 11.21
26	Alma 52.1, 14	78	Helaman 11.22
27	Alma 52.15, 18	79	Helaman 11.23
28	Alma 52.19; 53.23	80	Helaman 11.24
29	Alma 57.6; 58.38	81	Helaman 11.35
30	Alma 59.1	82	Helaman 11.35
31	Alma 62.12; 62.39	83	Helaman 11.36
36	Alma 63.1, 3	84	Helaman 11.36
37	Alma 63.4, 6	85	Helaman 11.37
38	Alma 63.7, 9	86	Helaman 13.1; 16.9 [400 years before smitting 13.9]
39	Alma 63.10, 16	87	Helaman 16.10
40	Helaman 1.1, 13	88	Helaman 16.11
41	Helaman 1.14, 34	89	Helaman 16.12
42	Helaman 2.1, 12	90	Helaman 16.13, 24
43	Helaman 3.1	91	3 Nephi 1.1
44	Helaman 3.2	92	3 Nephi 1.4, 26
45	Helaman 3.2	93	3 Nephi 1.27
46	Helaman 3.3, 18	94	3 Nephi 1.28
47	Helaman 3.19	95	3 Nephi 2.1
48	Helaman 3.19, 22	96	3 Nephi 2.4
49	Helaman 3.23, 32	97	3 Nephi 2.4
50	Helaman 3.32	98	3 Nephi 2.4
51	Helaman 3.33	99	3 Nephi 2.4
52	Helaman 3.36	100	3 Nephi 2.5
53	Helaman 3.37		

readers an anticipation of the conclusion of this time period and the onset of the next.[6] Fourth, at first glance it appears that certain specific years are canonically out of place. For example, the fifth year of the reign is referenced in Alma 1.33; 2.1, before the third year, mentioned in Alma 3.25. Although years 26 (Alma 52.1, 14), 27 (Alma 52.15, 18), 28 (Alma 52.19; 53.23), 29 (Alma 54.1; 55.35), and 30 (Alma 56.1) are introduced in what might be the expected canonical/chronological order, they are later reintroduced, as if for the first time in the narrative: 26 (Alma 56.7, 9, 20), 27 (Alma 56.20), 28 (Alma 57.5), 29 (Alma 57.6; 58.38), and 30 (59.1). A closer examination reveals that these latter 'misplaced' dates, though not the former, are actually accounted for by a flashback technique where a letter by Helaman is being cited. Fifth, the significance of this means of calculation is made clear when the reign of the judges comes to an end in 3 Nephi 2.5, for in the very next verses the readers learn both that it has been 609 years since Lehi left Jerusalem (3 Nephi 2.6) and nine years since the sign of Christ's coming into the world has occurred (3 Nephi 2.7).

The readers are informed that at this point the Nephites began to reckon time from the coming of Christ (3 Nephi 2.8). And with this means of calculation in hand, the readers will find their way chronologically throughout the rest of the book with numerous reminders of where they find themselves in the meta-narrative of the Book of Mormon. These markers appear in the following locations illustrated by the chart on the next page.

An examination of this list reveals several significant details. First, although this means of calculation indicates that 420 years will have passed between the appearance of the sign of Christ's coming and Moroni's last recorded words, only 71 of those years are specifically mentioned, a move more reminiscent of the first means of calculation than the second. Second, again such omissions are an interesting phenomenon given the fact that some verses describe the passing of multiple years (3 Nephi 5.7; 6.4; 7.23; 4 Nephi 1, 6, 14, 41; Book of Mormon 2.28), while others describe the passage of succeeding years one verse after another (3 Nephi 2.18-19; 4.4-5,

---

[6] As Hardy (*Understanding the Book of Mormon*, p. 103) observes, '... there is a sense of momentum that builds when the year markers come faster as the narrative gets closer to Jesus' appearance among the Nephites'.

Time Counted from the Pre-diction of the Birth of Jesus	Book of Mormon Location	Time Counted from the Prediction of the Birth of Jesus	Book of Mormon Location
600 Before	1 Nephi 10.4; 19.8; 2 Nephi 25.19	59	4 Nephi 6
Many Hundred years before	Jacob 4.4	71	4 Nephi 14
400 Before	Alma 45.10	72	4 Nephi 14
1	3 Nephi 1.1	79	4 Nephi 14
9	3 Nephi 2.8	100	4 Nephi 14
11	3 Nephi 2.10	194	4 Nephi 21
13	3 Nephi 2.11, 13, 16	200	4 Nephi 22
14	3 Nephi 2.17, 18	201	4 Nephi 24
15	3 Nephi 2.19	210	4 Nephi 27
16	3 Nephi 3.1	230	4 Nephi 34
17	3 Nephi 3.22	231	4 Nephi 35
18	3 Nephi 4.1, 4	244	4 Nephi 40
19	3 Nephi 4.5, 15	250	4 Nephi 41
20	3 Nephi 4.15	260	4 Nephi 41
21	3 Nephi 4.16	300	4 Nephi 45
22	3 Nephi 5.7	305	4 Nephi 47
23	3 Nephi 5.7	320	4 Nephi 48
24	3 Nephi 5.7	326	Mormon 2.2
25	3 Nephi 5.7	327	Mormon 2.3
26	3 Nephi 6.1, 4	344	Mormon 2.15
27	3 Nephi 6.4, 9	345	Mormon 2.16
28	3 Nephi 6.9	346	Mormon 2.22
29	3 Nephi 6.10	349	Mormon 2.28
30	3 Nephi 7.13	350	Mormon 2.28
31	3 Nephi 7.14, 21	360	Mormon 3.4
32	3 Nephi 7.23	361	Mormon 3.7
33	3 Nephi 7.23	362	Mormon 3.8
34	3 Nephi 8.5; 4 Nephi 1	363	Mormon 4.1
35	4 Nephi 1	364	Mormon 4.7
36	4 Nephi 2	366	Mormon 4.10
37	4 Nephi 4	367	Mormon 4.15
38	4 Nephi 5	375	Mormon 4.16
39	4 Nephi 6	379	Mormon 5.5
41	4 Nephi 6	380	Mormon 5.6
42	4 Nephi 6	384	Mormon 6.5
49	4 Nephi 6	400	Mormon 8.6
51	4 Nephi 6	420	Moroni 10.10
52	4 Nephi 6	Many Hundreds of Years After	Words of Mormon 2

15-16; 6.9-10; 7.13-14; 4 Nephi 1-2, 4-6, 21-22, 34-35, 47-48; Book of Mormon 2.2-3, 15-16; 3.7-8; 4.15-16; 5.5-6). Third, some of the omissions are startling. For example, the 200 years after the coming of Christ, perhaps the 'golden age'[7] of the peoples described in the book, are narrated in a mere 21 verses (4 Nephi 1.1-22)![8] Fourth, while other omissions are puzzling, the repetition of the 71 years specifically mentioned have a way of driving home for the readers the significance of the sign of Christ's coming for the book as a whole, a not wholly unexpected phenomenon owing to all the predictions of his coming found within the book. Fifth, this means of calculation, as the others before it, reminds the readers of where they find themselves in this final period of time to be recorded. Owing to the post-destruction perspective found in the Words of Mormon, the readers would know full well that this is the end of the epoch, as time runs out for the Nephites.

As revealed in the accompanying chart on the next page, it is clear that the three primary modes of marking chronology in the book work together to guide the reader through its contents. Since the first two chronological markers conclude at the same time and since their conclusions overlap with the beginning of the final marker, it may be suggested that the period of overlap is a most important time in the book's plot. It is not surprising then that this remarkable convergence takes place in and around the coming of Christ as described in 3 Nephi, indicating the significance of these events in the book's narrative.

Conclusion

As has been seen, the readers of the Book of Mormon are assisted in their journey by means of the significant role played by the editors in the structure of the book itself and the three sets of chronological indicators that guide the readers from very near the narrative's beginning to its conclusion as Moroni signs off. Such literary markers go some way toward ensuring that the readers do not become too disoriented and lose their way during their journey through the Book of Mormon.

---

[7] For this designation cf. Chris B. Hartshorn, *A Commentary on the Book of Mormon* (Independence, MO: Herald Publishing House, 1964), p. 417.

[8] Hardy, *Understanding the Book of Mormon*, p. 107.

Chronological Indicators Viewed Together

Books	1 Ne.	2 Ne.	Jacob	Enos	Jarom	Omni	WMormon	Mosiah	Alma	Helaman	3 Ne.	4 Ne.	Mormon	Ether	Moroni
Lehi	8	30, 40	55		179	200, 238 276, 282, 320		476, 509			600, 609				
									1-39	40-90	91-100				
Christ											1-34	34-320	326-400		420

PART TWO

THE CONTENT OF THE BOOK OF MORMON

This Part of the book is devoted to an extensive examination of the content of the Book of Mormon. Specifically, it seeks to acquaint readers with the book's basic storyline as well as identify the literary markers around which the individual books are structured. In turn, such structural indicators are utilized to explicate the meaning of the text as it stands. Avoiding hypothetical constructions against which to read the text, this Part strives to approach the text on its own terms, allowing its own narrative structure to emerge in order to inform the readers implied by the text of its contents.

2

THE TITLE PAGE

The first thing the reader encounters in the Book of Mormon is the book's title page containing some 272 words. While the title page of many books is relatively unimportant, this title page is actually a significant part of the book for it was claimed to have been translated from the plates near the end of Smith's 'translation' work[1] and contains important information for the book's readers. In point of fact, the title page provides a description of the book's origins as well as contents and means of production. The Book of Mormon, so the title page reveals, is 'an account written by the hand of Mormon, upon plates taken from the plates of Nephi', who is the book's primary narrator. The plates are a record of the Nephites and the Lamanites, a remnant of the House of Israel, to whom the book is written. The audience also includes Jew and Gentile. The book was 'written by way of commandment, and also by the Spirit of Prophesy [*sic*] and Revelation'. It was written and sealed up so that it would 'come forth by the gift and power of God unto the interpretation thereof'. It was eventually 'sealed by the hand of Moroni, and hid up unto the Lord, to come forth in due time by the way of the Gentile; the interpretation thereof by the gift of God'. The book also contains the Book of Ether, 'a Record of the People of Jared, which were scattered at the time the Lord confounded the language of the people when they were building a tower to heaven'. The whole is offered to convince 'the Jew and Gentile that Jesus is the Christ, the Eternal God, manifesting himself to all nations'. Curiously, the title

---

[1] Hardy, *Understanding the Book of Mormon*, p. 325 n. 20.

page concludes with this caveat, 'And now if there be fault, it be the mistake of men; wherefore condemn not the things of God, that ye may be found spotless at the judgment seat of Christ'.

Armed with this brief orientation, and assurance of the book's divine origin, the reader is prepared to begin the journey through the Book of Mormon.

3

1 NEPHI

The journey proper begins with the first book found in the Book of Mormon, a twenty-two chapter book called the First Book of Nephi that covers about 45 pages in the 1830 edition containing some 26,498 words. Owing to a significant structural marker in the text, it appears that the book falls into three major parts, each of which concludes with the phrase, 'And thus it is. Amen' (1 Nephi 9.6; 14.30; and 22.31).[1] Based on the strategic locations of this phrase, a tripartite structure emerges consisting of the following blocks of text:

Part One – Lehi and his Sons (1.1-9.6)

Part Two – Nephi Becomes a Spirit Empowered Spokesperson (10.1-14.30)

Part Three – Nephi Leads the Community (15.1-22.31).[2]

---

[1] Though Brant A. Gardner notes that the phrase is an 'obvious closing statement', he does not explore its structural significance, mentioning only its relationship to the theme of prophecy (*Second Witness: First Nephi* [ACCBM 1; Salt Lake City: Greg Kofford, 2007], p. 186).

[2] At first glance the two part structure proposed by Noel B. Reynolds ('Nephi's Outline', *BYU Studies* 20.2 [1980], pp. 131-49) appears to provide a helpful way to identify the book's structure, but upon closer examination it falters at a couple of significant points. First, Reynolds builds his division, in part, on the occurrences of the phrase 'And thus it is. Amen.' at the end of each of his two major sections. Unfortunately, he does not account for the other occurrence of this phrase in 14.30, which on its own suggests a tripartite division instead of a bipartite one. Second, despite the numerous parallels Reynolds points out between the two parts, chs. 1-9 and 10-22, his chiastic outlines for each section at times appear to work only after the text has been manipulated by omission of

When the contents of **Part One** (1.1-9.6) are examined in narrative order, the readers would likely be impressed by the amount of space devoted to the records and/or plates associated with Nephi. The book's initial words focus on Nephi's record keeping, the origins of the records, their trustworthiness, and his immediate role in making them (1.1-3). The readers would also likely be struck by the amount of space devoted to Nephi's father, Lehi. His experience of the Spirit (1.4-17) becomes the basis of his prophesying to the Jews in Jerusalem about the coming destruction of that city (during the first year of Zedekiah's reign), 'the coming of a Messiah', as well as 'the redemption of the world' (1.18-20). When his prophetic work is met with mocking, Lehi is directed to take his family (Sariah, his wife, and Nephi's elder brothers Laman, Lemuel, and Sam) into the wilderness (2.1-7) – leaving their gold, silver, and precious things behind – taking nothing with him, a move which Laman and Lemuel murmur against (2.8-15),[3] but which Nephi embraces and is blessed as a result (2.16-24).

Nearly the whole of 1 Nephi 3.1-5.22 is devoted to the obtaining of the brass plates of Laban by Nephi and his brothers, the consequences of such an acquisition, and the contents of the plates. Lehi's command (based upon the Lord's command via a dream) stands behind the quest to acquire the brass plates from their relative Laban. It would take Nephi and his brothers three attempts to retrieve successfully the plates of Laban. In their first attempt Laman, chosen by lot, went to Laban's house and desired from him the plates, which among other things contained the genealogy of Lehi. Laman's attempt met with Laban's anger, with the result that Laman fled from his presence, determined to return to his father in the wilderness (3.11-14). But Nephi persuaded his brothers to make a second attempt owing to the fact that if they had to leave the country these records would prove instrumental in their children learning the language of their fathers and the words spoken by the mouths of the holy prophets. Gathering up their gold, silver, and

certain verses. The chiastic structure proposed by John W. Welch ['Chiasmus in the Book of Mormon', in N.B. Reynolds (ed.), *Book of Mormon Authorship: New Light on Ancient Origins* (Provo, UT: BYU Religious Studies Center, 1982), pp. 33-52], suffers from a similar weakness.
[3] Gardner observes, 'With these verses Nephi sets up the major conflict within the new colony. Laman and Lemuel are murmurers, doubters, and troublemakers.' *Second Witness: First Nephi*, p. 91.

precious things they returned to Laban to request the plates. But Laban lusted after their property seeking it for himself. Leaving their property behind, they once again fled into the wilderness (3.15-27). After again encouraging his murmuring brothers to make yet a third attempt to secure the plates of brass from Laban, Nephi caused his brothers to hide while he went on alone. Coming upon Laban, who had fallen down drunk, Nephi took Laban's sword as he was constrained by the Spirit to kill Laban – a prompting that Nephi resisted. A second time the Spirit instructed Nephi to kill Laban, who had been delivered into Nephi's hands. In addition to the command, Nephi remembered that Laban had desired to kill Lehi's sons, had refused to hearken to the commandments of the Lord, and had taken away their property. The third time the Spirit commanded Nephi to kill Laban, who had been delivered into his hands, Nephi took Laban by the hair of the head and smote off his head with Laban's own sword. Dressing as Laban and speaking in the voice of Laban, Nephi commanded Laban's servant to follow him and carry the plates of brass outside the treasury (4.1-29). The servant of Laban, whose name was Zoram, would wind up joining the brothers in the wilderness.

When the brothers were reunited with the rest of the family, the contents of the plates were revealed as containing the five books of Moses, the prophecies of the holy prophets down to those of Jeremiah, and the genealogy of Lehi's fathers, who were descendants of Joseph, the son of Jacob. Thus the commandments of the Lord could be preserved for the children of Nephi and his brothers (5.10-22). References to Nephi's initial work of writing down the things of God in his records/plates (6.1-6) and the two sets of plates for which he is responsible (9.1-6), surround the content of the final section of Part One, again indicating the significance which records/plates hold (and will hold) in this narrative.

Later, Lehi instructs the brothers to return to Jerusalem once again, this time in order to bring Ishmael and his family into the wilderness, an action that results in a rebellion in the wilderness against Nephi (and Lehi) by Nephi's brothers Laman and Lemuel, as well as Ishmael, Ishmael's wife, and his three daughters (7.1-22). Lehi's other major activity in Part One is the recounting of his extensive Dream of the Tree and his preaching of the need for faithfulness on the part of Laman and Lemuel (8.2-38). The phrase 'And thus it is. Amen.' indicates that Part One of 1 Nephi has come to a conclusion.

When the contents of **Part Two** (10.1-14.30) are examined in narrative order, it becomes clear that this entire portion of 1 Nephi is devoted to establishing Nephi as an authorized, Spirit-inspired spokesperson, as his father before him. As this part begins, the readers are told that Nephi will now begin an account of his own proceedings, reign, and ministry. Yet, the first things to be described are not Nephi's own proceedings, reign, and ministry, but rather things that concern his father and brothers. As such, this section might be taken as an unnecessary diversion away from the stated purpose, but a closer examination of these verses reveals that this further description of Lehi's message serves as a transition that gives way to an account of Nephi's own Spirit-inspired activity. One could say that in some ways Nephi's activities are rooted and grounded in that of his father. When the readers first make their way to this portion of 1 Nephi, they have a rather high opinion of Nephi, especially when compared to his brothers, but there is still some distance between their opinion of Nephi and that of Lehi. However, in this section Nephi is transformed before their eyes into an authorized, Spirit-inspired spokesperson like his father.[4]

The readers learn that not only does Lehi prophesy about the destruction of Jerusalem, the exile of its people, and the return of the captives to 'the land of their inheritance' (10.2-3), but he also goes on to predict the coming of a Messiah within 600 years,[5] 'a Savior of the world', a 'Redeemer of the world' (10.4-6). He predicts the coming of a prophet to prepare the way for this Messiah (10.7-

---

[4] This observation appears to be in keeping with Gardner's comments on the purpose of 1 Nephi, 'The story begins with Lehi as his clan's patriarch and the prophet; but as the story develops, the prophetic mantle shifts to Nephi's shoulders as does the leadership role'. *Second Witness: First Nephi*, p. 48. Gardner goes on to argue that the phrase, 'dwelt in a tent', is a literary marker used three times in 1 Nephi (2.15; 10.16; 16.6) to designate the end of a unit of text. He proposes that in 10.16 the phrase 'marks a shifting focus in the narrative. We begin with Lehi, move to a unit including Lehi and Nephi, and continue to the third unit that focuses on Nephi alone. All of these things happened as Lehi "dwelt in a tent".' Whether or not one assigns the same interpretive significance to this phrase as does Gardner, it is clear that he sees a similar development of plot as here suggested.

[5] Gardner describes 1 Nephi 10.4 as 'the essential baseline for calculating dates in the Book of Mormon' (*Second Witness: First Nephi*, p. 188).

10), the fact that this Messiah will be slain, and will be preached to the Gentiles who will receive 'the fullness of the Gospel' (10.11-15).

The magnitude of such things, revealed by the power of the Holy Ghost, created within Nephi a desire to know such Spirit-inspired mysteries for himself (10.17-22), something for which he prays. In his subsequent conversation with the Spirit, Nephi sees the same tree as had Lehi and asks for its interpretation (11.1-12). By means of an angelic guide, Nephi is then given a panoramic view of prophetic history to include a remarkably detailed vision of Jesus Christ (who is named in 1 Nephi 12.18 [in the 1830 edition]) in the old world (11.13-36) and his appearance in the new world (12.1-12), the unbelief and war that will result amongst Lehi's descendants (12.13-23), the great and abominable church (13.1-9), the arrival of Gentiles in the promised land/new world (13.10-19), and Gentiles with the record of the Jews (13.20-29). He is also told about the restoration of the Gospel (13.30-37), sees additional records come forth (13.38-41), is assured that Gentiles can repent (13.42-14.7), sees the wrath of God poured out on the wicked (14.8-17), and even sees the Apostle John (14.18-30). In other words, by means of his encounter with the Spirit, Nephi sees more of redemptive history unfold before his eyes in astonishing detail than any Spirit-inspired spokesperson before him (in the Hebrew Bible or 1 Nephi to this point), uniquely qualifying him for his task as well as underscoring the truthfulness of the events described in the plates that follow (cf. esp. 14.30). And with this, the phrase 'And thus it is. Amen.' occurs, indicating the close of Part Two of 1 Nephi, leaving the readers with an intense level of expectancy for that which follows.

As the readers make their way from the contents of **Part Two** of 1 Nephi to **Part Three** they discover that their high level of expectancy with regard to Nephi is not disappointed for at this point he begins to rival his father Lehi as Spirit-inspired spokesperson, even serving as the interpreter of his father's hard sayings for his brothers. This interpretive work includes the meaning of the allegory of the Olive Tree (15.12-20) as well as the meaning of the tree, the rod, and the river (15.21-36). All of this takes place between references to hard sayings (15.3 and 16.1-6), indicating that Nephi now possesses the Spirit-given abilities to understand such mysteries. Significantly, Nephi's own Spirit-inspired activity is bounded on either side by the phrase, 'Now, all these things were said and done

as my father dwelt in a tent in the valley which he called Lemuel'
(10.16; 16.6), suggesting that, though present, Lehi is no longer the
center of Spirit-inspired activity in this section. This message is further reinforced by the fact that after Nephi, his brothers, and
Zoram take as wives the daughters of Ishmael, it is noted, 'And thus
my father had fulfilled all the commandments of the Lord which
had been given to him' (16.8). Though Lehi will continue to have a
major role in hearing the voice of the Lord and offering commands
based upon such divine directives, these words suggest that more
and more Nephi will stand at center stage with the future of the
book focusing more exclusively upon his activities.

The next section of Part Three is concerned almost wholly with
the group's travels in the wilderness, an undertaking commanded by
Lehi when the voice of the Lord next speaks to him (16.9). During
this sojourn the readers are told of a brass ball of 'curious work-
manship' that acted as a compass of sorts, directing the travelers in
the right direction (16.10-16). They also learn that Nephi breaks his
steel bow causing the group much hardship, owing to a lack of
food. This event leads to more murmuring, so much so that even
Lehi joins in (16.20) – though he will eventually enquire of the Lord
and be humbled (16.24-25). Other noteworthy events include an
account of the death of Ishmael (16.33-34), father-in-law of all (or
most at any rate!), the resulting murmuring and rebellion (16.35-39),
and the trip to a Place called Bountiful, owing to its much fruit
(17.1-6).

The next major section of Part Three focuses almost completely
on the preparation and sailing of a ship to the new world. The section commences when Nephi is commanded to build a ship (17.7-
16), an event that leads to even more murmuring by his brothers
(17.17-22). Warning his brothers by means of a recounting of Israel's history (17.23-47), Nephi commands them to stop their murmuring, a command accompanied by a divine sign (17.48-55). The
construction of the ship is next described (18.1-8), where it is
learned that Lehi and Sariah have two additional sons – Jacob and
Joseph, as well as a description of sailing to the promised land
(18.9-25), which included more murmuring against, even physical
persecution of, Nephi.

The final section of Part Three is devoted to Nephi's accounting
of the making and purpose of two sets of plates (19.1-7), the first

apparently consisting of the prophecies of Christ (19.8-21), the second consisting of prophecies from Isaiah 48-49 (1 Nephi 19.22-21.26). The section concludes with Nephi offering an interpretation of the words of Isaiah (and Zenos) for his brethren (22.1-31), which consists of warnings about future judgments, the great and abominable church, and a final word about the truthfulness of the plates, singling out himself and his father as examples of those who have testified and taught. As with the previous major parts, Part Three also concludes with the phrase 'And thus it is. Amen.' (22.31).

4

2 NEPHI

The readers' journey continues with the second book found within the Book of Mormon, a thirty-three chapter book called the Second Book of Nephi that covers about 63 pages in the 1830 edition containing some 30,789 words. The structure of this book, though somewhat obvious, is not highlighted by the same kind of literary markers as is 1 Nephi. However, the reader is not left without assistance but can detect the structure based upon the overall movement of the narrative. An examination of 2 Nephi reveals that the book may be divided into five major parts:[1]

Part One – Lehi's Farewell Discourse (1.1-4.12)

Part Two – The Rejection of Nephi by his Brothers (4.13-5.34)

Part Three – Jacob's Discourse (6.1-10.25)

Part Four – Nephi Cites the Words of Isaiah as Witness of
        Christ – Isaiah (11.1-24.32)

Part Five – Nephi's concluding Prophecies and Words of
        Explanation (25.1-33.15).

When the contents of **Part One** of 2 Nephi (1.1-4.12) – Lehi's farewell discourse – are laid out in narrative order, three things become clear about this section. First, there is an explicit contrast between Jerusalem and the land of promise in which they now dwell.

---

[1] For a similar division of the book cf. Brant A. Gardner, *Second Witness: Second Nephi-Jacob* (ACCBM 2; Salt Lake City: Greg Kofford, 2007), p. 15.

On the one hand, Jerusalem, mentioned five times in this section, is the place from which they have been brought (1.1) owing to the warning to flee (1.3). Lehi knows from a vision that Jerusalem has been destroyed and that they too would have perished had they remained there (1.4). Further, it is those from Jerusalem about whom Lehi has received the promise that if they keep God's commandments they will prosper (1.9). On the other hand, the land of promise is that which Lehi's descendants have obtained (1.3, 5). It is a choice land, above all others, an inheritance, covenanted to Lehi's children forever (1.5), a land kept from the knowledge of other nations (1.8). But if Lehi's people transgress God's commandments, other nations will be brought in and Lehi's people will lose their inheritance (1.10-11). Second, the divinely sanctioned transfer of charismatic leadership from Lehi, who prophesies 'according to the workings of the Spirit' (1.6), to Nephi, through whom the Spirit of the Lord spoke during their epic experiences (1.27), is underscored.[2] In fact, if not for Nephi, Lehi's descendants would have perished in the wilderness (1.24); thus, Nephi should be obeyed. Third, a tension exists between Lehi's repeated calls for faithfulness on the part of his hearers, often with the refrain 'arise from the dust' (1.14, 21, 22), and the implicit inevitability of their disobedience (1.10-23).[3]

The rest of Part One is devoted to Lehi's words to a variety of his descendants and those under his care. First, he addresses Laman, Lemuel, and Zoram, making clear the absolute necessity of listening to Nephi (1.28-32). Second, Lehi speaks to Jacob (2.1-13) his 'firstborn in the wilderness' (2.1-2, 11) who will dwell safely with his brother Nephi (2.3). Lehi's words to Jacob give way to a somewhat extended discussion of the atonement (2.11-13) which is based on a theology of opposition, the idea being that life itself consists of a necessary interdependency of opposites upon one another – all things must be held together as one: good and bad, righteousness and wickedness, etc. Third, in his exhortation to all his sons (2.14-30), Lehi extends his explanation of opposition to explain the necessity of the fall on the part of Adam and Eve after creation, oth-

---

[2] A possibility mentioned, but not developed, by Frederick W. Axelgard, '1 and 2 Nephi: An Inspiring Whole', *BYU Studies* 26.4 (1986), p. 59, though cf. p. 62.

[3] On Lehi's resignation to this fate cf. Gardner, *Second Witness: Second Nephi-Jacob*, p. 30.

erwise everything would have stayed in its original created state – in a state of innocence – with no children born, an idea Lehi sums up in 2.25, 'Adam fell that men might be; and men are, that they might have joy'. The human being has the power of choice, enabling a choice of liberty and eternal life or captivity and death (2.27).

Fourth, in his last words to Joseph (3.1-25), Lehi pronounces blessings upon 'my last born ... born in the wilderness of my afflictions'. His last born, Joseph, will keep the commands of the Holy One of Israel and be faithful to his brother Nephi. These words of blessing are followed by extensive citation of the prophetic words of the Patriarch Joseph, apparently cited from the Brass Plates,[4] where a lineage is claimed from the Patriarch to Lehi, who is a descendant of Joseph, to Joseph (Lehi's son), to a future seer who shall be 'great like unto Moses' named Joseph, whose father will also be named Joseph! He will be an instrument in the hands of God and his work will bring God's people to salvation. The physical connection between all these Josephs is made clear in part by the fact that the phrase 'the fruit of thy/the loins' appears some seventeen times in this chapter! In the next two verses (4.1-2), Nephi adds his own voice in affirming the prophecies of his father noting that they are written upon the Plates of Brass. Fifth, Lehi blesses the sons and daughters of Laman and Lemuel in turn (4.3-9), exhorting them unto faithfulness and exonerating them from any curse placed upon them owing to the fault of their parents. Lehi's blessing will ensure that they never perish and that God will be merciful to them forever (4.7). Sixth, Lehi blesses the sons of Ishmael, Levi's son Sam, and all Sam's household. With 'the Spirit of the Lord' in him until the end, Lehi waxes old, dies, and is buried (4.10-12).

In **Part Two** of 2 Nephi (4.13-5.34) the readers encounter the aftermath and various responses to Lehi's farewell discourse in the light of his death, providing the basic trajectory for much of that which follows in the Book of Mormon. First, not surprisingly, Laman, Lemuel, and the sons of Ishmael are angry with Nephi for the words that his father spoke and the words that Nephi spoke, words written on his other plates (4.13-14). Second, within this con-

---

[4] A suggestion made by Hardy, *The Book of Mormon: A Reader's Edition*, p. 68 n. b on 3.6.

text of opposition, Nephi records a psalm that exhibits a number of inter-textual connections with what has preceded and with a number of biblical texts (4.15-35). The psalm alternates between Nephi's admission about his struggle with sin, his remembrance of God's deliverance from various situations (previously described in 1 Nephi), his prayers for deliverance from his enemies (i.e. his brothers Laman, Lemuel, and the sons of Ishmael), and his affirmations of praise. One of the effects of this psalm on the reader is that it offers in summary form the story of 1 Nephi that precedes, implicitly reminding the readers of Nephi's divinely appointed role in these events.

Third, owing to the hatred, murmuring, and opposition of his brothers, who planned to murder their younger brother, Nephi cried unto the Lord and like his father before him was warned by the Lord to flee into the wilderness for his/their preservation. This Nephi does with all 'those who believed in the warnings and revelations of God' (5.6), specifically Zoram, Sam, Jacob, Joseph, and Nephi's sisters. This wilderness period results in a new corporate identity – the place where they camped was named Nephi while the group became known as Nephites (5.8-9). Both these events serve to heighten still further the profile of Nephi for the readers. Owing to their obedience to the judgments, commandments, and statutes of the Lord, the Nephites prospered and multiplied, even building a temple in many respects like that of Solomon's (5.10-18). Those who oppose Nephi are first named Lamanites during this period (5.14). Not surprisingly, the Nephites seek to make Nephi king, an honor he declines. Fourth, for their disobedience and disregard for the words of Lehi, the Lamanites are cut off from the presence of God and cursed. Remarkably, those so cursed had to this point possessed white, exceedingly fair, and delightsome skin, but from this point on were cursed with the skin of blackness making them loathsome to God's people, the Nephites (5.21-23)! Furthermore, they become idle, full of mischief and subtlety, a scourge to the Nephites. Fifth, Nephi consecrated Jacob and Joseph as priests and teachers over the land of his people, leading to lives 'lived after the manner of happiness' (5.26-28). Sixth, a final section is devoted to Nephi's words about making additional plates and engraving them at the direction of the Lord (5.29-33). Ominously, though only *forty years pass*, already there are wars and contentions with Nephi's brothers (5.34).

In **Part Three** of 2 Nephi (6.1-10.25) the readers encounter the words of Jacob, the son of Lehi, most recently consecrated as a priest and teacher over the people. Though clearly in a subordinate position to Nephi his brother, Jacob's words carry divine authority for he is called of God and ordained by holy order (6.2). Apparently, over the previous ten years Jacob has spoken many words to the Nephites, including the words of his father and everything from the creation of the world (6.3). In the first section of Part Three (6.1-8.25), Jacob offers two extensive quotations from the prophet Isaiah with some comment (including words of hope for Gentiles who do not unite with that great and abominable church). These quotations are offered owing to the similarities of the situations of Israel at the time of Isaiah and the Nephites at this point in the narrative. Jacob notes that these texts might be likened to them and their situation. As had Lehi, Jacob sees a vision of the destruction of Jerusalem and the return from exile, which allows him to offer appropriate comment upon the text cited, Isa. 49.22-26, before reading to them Isa. 50.1-52.2 (2 Nephi 7.1-8.25).

The second section of Part Three (9.1-54), though addressing a variety of issues, appears in some ways to be held together by the words 'the Holy One of Israel', which appear some fourteen times in this chapter, after occurring only four times previously in 2 Nephi (1.10; 3.2; 6.10 [2x]). This section begins with Jacob's explanation that to fulfill the merciful plan of the Creator a resurrection of the dead is necessary, for aside from the resurrection there would be no way the corruptible could put on incorruption. The readers learn that 'the infinite atonement' demands a resurrection, lest those who die become like the devil (9.1-16). Here 'the Holy One of Israel' is identified as the deliverer from death (9.11), who has the power of the resurrection (9.12). Such reflection prompts a hymn to 'the Holy One of Israel', offered by Jacob, which focuses upon God's greatness and mercy, the righteous faithful who will inherit his kingdom prepared before the foundation of the world, as well as God's mercy and his deliverance from the devil, death, hell, and eternal punishment (9.17-19). Here, 'the Holy One of Israel' is identified as the one to whom the saints belong – those who have believed in him (9.18), and as the God who is great in mercy (9.19).

This hymn gives way to more reflection on the resurrection and the commands to insure that one is not damned. This includes belief in 'the Holy One of Israel' (9.23) who speaks these things (9.24). Jacobs' words continue with a series of ten woes tied to particular obstacles/sins that could keep the readers from being delivered from that 'awful monster the Devil' (9.25-38). Here, the mercies of 'the Holy One of Israel' are once again underscored (9.25) and he is called the God of restoration, the one who gives breath (9.26). The final portion of this section (9.39-54) appears structured around several uses of the phrase, 'O, my beloved brethren', or one very much like it, followed by the imperatives 'remember' (9.39), 'give ear' (9.40), 'come' (9.41), 'remember' (9.44), 'turn away' (9.45), and 'remember' (9.52), as Jacob returns to many of the ideas found within the woes in his warnings to his people about the grave consequences of sin, reminding that God has promised that he would preserve them and that in future generations they shall become a righteous branch (9.53). Here, 'the Holy One of Israel' is closely connected to his 'greatness' (9.40), is identified as the 'keeper of the gate' (9.42) and as the one who provides spiritual nourishment that does not perish (9.51).

In the third section of Part Three (10.1-25) Jacob concludes his words by focusing on the restoration of Israel – which comes by way of Christ (10.1-8a), the Gentiles, and the Americas – the land of inheritance (10.8b-19). Jacob's address concludes with words of exhortation to lay aside sin and be reconciled to God for 'he remembereth us also' (10.20-25). In this conclusion, the previously mentioned themes of the grace of God, the power of the resurrection, the power of the atonement, and the eternal kingdom of God converge.

Finally, after hearing the words of Lehi and Jacob, in **Part Four** of 2 Nephi (11.1-24.32) the readers again encounter Nephi, who reappears stating his desire to write many words of Isaiah (Isa. 2.1-14.32) 'for my soul delighteth in his words' (2 Nephi 11.2), as he seeks to liken Isaiah's words to his people. Significantly, this introductory section (11.1-8) is dominated by the phrase 'my soul delighteth', which occurs five times in these eight verses. The predicates of this phrase include: 'his words' (11.2), 'in proving ... the coming of Christ' (11.4), 'in the covenants' (11.5), 'in his grace' (11.5), and 'in proving ... that save Christ should come, all men must perish' (1.6). The remainder of Part Four is given over to the Isaianic quotes, which focus on judgment and restoration, with not a few passages of messianic significance owing in part to the frequency with which many of them show up in various New Testament documents.

In **Part Five** of 2 Nephi (25.1-33.15) the readers continue to encounter the words of Nephi, which cover a variety of issues. In the first section of Part Five (25.1-27.35), Nephi proceeds with his own prophecy (25.7), though with the words of Isaiah never far away. Among other things Nephi prophesies about Christ and the Jews (25.9-19), Christ and the Book of Mormon (25.20-23), Christ and the Law of Moses (25.24-30), Christ and the Nephites (26.1-11), and Christ and the Gentiles (26.12-13). This section continues with a turn toward the eschatological where attention is given to the Lehites in the last days – drawing heavily on Isa. 29.3-5 (2 Nephi 26.14-19); the Gentiles and their many false churches in the last days (26.20-33); those Gentiles and Jews who fight against Zion in the last days – drawing heavily on Isa. 29.6-10 (2 Nephi 27.1-5); the appearance of the Book of Mormon in the last days – drawing heavily on Isa. 29.11-12 (2 Nephi 27.6-23); and an extensive quotation with regard to the last days from Isa. 29.13-24 (2 Nephi 27.24-35).

In the second section of Part Five (28.1-32) Nephi revisits the topic of corrupt churches in the last days. Among the things for which such churches will be known is their denial of miracles to God (28.6), their excessive pride, being lifted up, and puffed up (28.11-14), and their false teachings. 'That great and abominable church, the whore of all the earth' reappears with the promise of its demise (28.18). The section concludes with a series of woes, warning the readers about the consequences of a variety of activities (28.24-32).

The third section of Part Five (29.1-14) is devoted to a discussion of the extent and identity of Scripture. Here the taunt, 'A Bible! A Bible! We have got a Bible, and there cannot be any more Bible' (29.3, cf. also v. 6) prepares the readers for the fact that there is more scriptural revelation to come forth than the Bible.[5] This un-

---

[5] Cf. Paul C. Gutjahr, *The Book of Mormon: A Biography* (Lives of Great Religious Books; Princeton: Princeton University Press, 2012), pp. 35-36.

derstanding is summed up in the words, 'And because that I have spoken one word, ye need not suppose that I cannot speak another; for my work is not yet finished; neither shall it be until the end of man …' (29.9b). Not only will God speak to the Nephites and they will write it (the Book of Mormon) and to the House of Israel and they will write it (the Bible), but he will also speak to 'all the nations of the earth and they will write it' (29.12). The Jews, Nephites, and the Lost Tribes of Israel will one day have access to one another's words (or books of scripture).

In the fourth section of Part Five (30.1-18) Nephi prophesies about the future declaration of the Gospel of Jesus Christ to 'our seed', which eventually results in the darkness falling from their eyes and 'they shall be a white and delightsome people' (30.6). The Jews scattered upon the face of the earth who believe shall also 'become a delightsome people' (30.7). Such thought again leads Nephi to draw upon an extended passage from Isaiah (11.4-9) that envisions the restoration of God's people upon the earth (2 Nephi 30.8-15), before he concludes this portion of his words.

The readers would likely be surprised by the fact that despite Nephi's words, 'And now, my beloved brethren, I must make an end of my sayings' (30.18), he continues to write. The fifth section of Part Five (31.1-32.6) is devoted, in large part, to 'the doctrine of Christ' which focuses on Nephi's prophecy with regard to the fore-runner of Jesus and the way in which those with 'real intent' may follow the commands given by the Father by repenting, being bap-tized in the name of Christ, and then receiving the Holy Ghost – speaking with the 'tongue of angels' (31.4-13). Such obedience ne-cessitates endurance until the end, in order to 'be saved in the king-dom of God' (31.21). The power of the Holy Ghost enables one to speak with the tongue of an angel, which are the words of Christ (32.2-3), which words one should feast upon!

The sixth and final section of Part Five (32.7-33.15) consists of Nephi's admonitions to pray for understanding (32.7-9), a final af-firmation of the truthfulness of his record (33.1-9), and his final farewell (33.10-15), which focuses upon his admonition to believe in Christ and his words. For those who believe, his farewell is tem-porary – until that great day shall come, but for those who do not believe his farewell is an everlasting farewell (33.14).

5

JACOB

The readers' journey continues with the third book found within the Book of Mormon, a seven-chapter book called the Book of Jacob – the brother of Nephi – that covers some 21 pages in the 1830 edition containing some 9,476 words. Like 2 Nephi, the broad structure of Jacob can be observed based on the overall movement of the narrative, as well as occasional transitional indicators. Broadly speaking, Jacob falls into four major parts:

Part One – Transition to Jacob and Transition in Leadership (1.1-14)

Part Two – Jacob's Temple Discourse (1.15-3.14)

Part Three – Jacob and the Plates, Jacob's Prophetic Knowledge of Christ and the Jews, and the Allegory of the Olive Tree (4.1-6.13)

Part Four – Sherem, the Lamanite Conflict, and Jacob's Farewell (7.1-27).

As the readers make their way to this book they immediately become aware of the prominent role Nephi plays. Perhaps most obvious is the fact that the book's title in the 1830 edition makes clear Jacob's relationship to Nephi, as 'the Brother of Nephi' follows 'the Book of Jacob'. It might also become evident to the readers that the Book of Jacob's location after Nephi means that Nephi's extensive words in 2 Nephi (11.1-33.15) are literally surrounded by words of Jacob, in 2 Nephi 6.1-10.25 and in the Book of Jacob. Structurally, such a literary enfolding suggests the significance of the former for the latter. Nephi will also be mentioned near the book's conclusion (7.27), so that in some ways Nephi also enfolds the Book of Jacob.

Part One of the Book of Jacob (1.1-15) introduces the readers to two significant transitions from 2 Nephi. The first section of Part One (1.1-8) locates Jacob both chronologically – it has been *55 years since Lehi left Jerusalem* (1.1) – and vocationally – his relationship to the plates. Not only is Jacob given charge of the plates, but he is also commanded by Nephi to write upon them (1.2), not a history of the people of Nephi, but preaching, revelation, and prophesying (1.3-4). Specifically, Jacob is concerned to persuade his people 'to come unto Christ' (1.7) and 'not to rebel against God' (1.8). The second section of Part One (1.9-14) informs of Nephi's anointing a man to be king and ruler in his stead as civil leader. So loved was Nephi that those men who reigned were referred to by the people as 'Second Nephi', 'Third Nephi', etc. (1.11). At this point, the death of Nephi is mentioned (1.12). Something of Nephi's legacy is revealed by the fact that Jacob calls his followers Nephites, that is, those who were not Lamanites, but were either friendly to the people of Nephi or are the people of Nephi (1.13-14).

Part Two of the Book of Jacob (1.15-3.14) is devoted to an extensive discourse offered by Jacob in the Temple. Section one of Part Two (1.15-19) is a narrative introduction. Here the readers learn that chronologically these events occur under the reign of the second king and that the hearts of the people of Nephi had begun to harden, making them susceptible to three wicked practices: desiring many wives and concubines, searching for much gold and silver, and being lifted up in pride (1.15-16). Jacob's actions are based upon the Lord's directive, his role as one consecrated a priest and teacher (along with his brother Joseph) by the hand of Nephi, and the fact that the blood of the people would be upon him if he did not teach them (1.17-19). As the discourse proper begins in section two of Part Two (2.1-11), Jacob expresses how his task grieves him (2.6, 7) owing to the wickedness and abominations of their hearts, which have caused many wounds – a form of the word 'wound' appearing six times in two verses (2.8-9). Section three of Part Two (2.12-22) offers warnings of riches and pride, admonishing the readers 'to do good; to clothe the naked, and to feed the hungry, and to liberate the captive, and administer relief to the sick, and the afflicted' (2.19), before turning to their 'grosser crime'.

Section four of Part Two (2.23-3.14) focuses squarely on such 'grosser crimes' – the taking of many wives and concubines. This practice Jacob describes as 'whoredoms', 'abominations', and 'wickedness', which 'wound' the tender 'daughters of my people', 'your tender wives', creating 'mourning' and 'sobbing' amongst them, owing to the men's 'bad examples', which cause 'many hearts' to die, being 'pierced with deep wounds' (2.23-35). Not even the Lamanites, who 'are cursed with a sore cursing', are guilty of such acts – that is, 'are not filthy like unto you' (3.3)! Owing to the fact that the Lamanites keep this command, they will not be destroyed (3.5-7). In point of fact, if the Nephites do not repent the Lamanites' skin will be whiter than theirs (3.8)! Owing to their own filthiness, the Nephites should no longer revile the Lamanites owing to the darkness of their skin (3.9). Jacob continues to speak against fornication and lasciviousness (3.12), but has only recorded one-hundredth of these events, for they are too numerous to be written on the plates called the plates of Jacob, made by the hand of Nephi. However, many of them are recorded on the larger plates (3.13-14). The words, 'And I make an end of speaking these words' (3.14b) mark the end of Part Two.

Part Three of the Book of Jacob, the most extensive portion of this book (4.1-6.13), focuses upon the purpose of the plates which Jacob keeps (4.1-3), Jacob's prophetic knowledge of Christ, the atonement of Christ, the resurrection (4.4-11), and Jacob's prophetic knowledge that the Jews will reject the stone they might have built upon as the foundation. Yet, as the readers are told, the Jews will eventually build upon this foundation (4.12-18). The latter observation leads Jacob to unfold this mystery in some detail by recounting Zenos' Allegory of the Olive Tree (5.1-6.13). The readers would already be acquainted with the prophet Zenos, to whom reference has been made and also from his prophetic words quoted in 1 Nephi 19.10-21 from the brass plates. Here, Jacob cites Zenos' words about 'the Olive Tree'.

This extended discourse likens the House of Israel unto a tame olive tree that began to decay as it grew old. In order to save the tree, the master of the 'vineyard' instructs his servants to care for it so that it might grow young and tender branches; a result that eventuates although the main top of the tree began to perish (5.2-6). Next, the master instructs that branches from a wild olive tree be grafted into the tree and that the young and tender branches be planted 'whithersoever I will' (5.7-14). The result of such activity was that the wild olive branches brought forth good fruit like the natural branches brought forth. In fact, the master concludes that if not for such grafting the tree would have perished. The natural branches planted in the nethermost places also brought forth good fruit (5.15-28). As time passed, the wild branches had the effect of taking over the roots so that they now brought forth bad fruit, as did the natural branches in the nethermost places (5.29-46). The distress of the master at such a turn of events is conveyed by his words, 'it grieveth me' (vv. 7, 13, 32, 47), and the question, 'What more could I have done for my vineyard?' (vv. 41, 47, 49), both of which appear several times in the story. The master then instructs that both the natural branches and the wild branches be grafted back into the mother tree in order to save the roots (5.47-59). Such radical actions work, with good fruit being produced and the mother tree saved. So successful were these actions that the natural branches and the wild branches 'became like unto one body' with their fruit being equally good (5.60-74). The story takes on an eschatological feel as early as v. 62 (cf. also vv. 29 and 47), where references to 'the end draweth nigh' and 'the last time' begin to appear and continue to the story's end (vv. 62, 63, 64, 71, 75, 76), language that describes the final gathering of both good and bad fruit at the end, when the vineyard itself will be burned with fire (5.75-77).

As Part Three concludes, Jacob does not offer an explanation of the story as much as he validates its truthfulness, prophesying by means of Zenos' allegory that its contents will come to pass for the Lord will remember both roots and branches (6.1-4). Jacob's final words in Part Three (6.5-13) focus upon his desire and attempt to bring his readers to repentance, those who have been nourished by 'the good word of God'. Specifically, he asks how they can reject the many, many prophetic words spoken concerning Christ. To do so will result in shame and awful guilt before the judgment bar of God. Thus, repentance is the only way to obtain eternal life. Jacob signs off with the ominous farewell, 'Finally, I bid you farewell, until I shall meet you before the pleasing bar of God, which bar striketh the wicked with awful dread and fear. – Amen' (6.13), bringing Part Three to a close.

Part Four of the Book of Jacob (7.1-27), with which the book concludes, consists of three sections. Section one of Part Three (7.1-23) tells the story of a certain Sherem[1] who comes among the people of Nephi preaching that there 'should be no Christ', overthrowing 'the doctrine of Christ', and leading their hearts away (7.2-3a). So ambitious was Sherem that he even desired to shake Jacob in his faith – the same Jacob who had seen so many revelations and had been ministered to by angels (7.3b-5). Sherem went so far as to say that Jacob, and by implication all those who prophesied as he, taught blasphemy – for no one can tell of the things to come (7.7). In his response, Jacob drives home the point that the Scriptures truly testify of Christ and his work. In response to Sherem's request for a sign, Jacob says, 'And thy will, O Lord, be done, and not mine' (7.14), at which point the power of God comes upon Sherem, who falls to the earth. After many days Sherem requests the opportunity to address all the people, at which point he rejects his earlier teaching, confessing and testifying to the truth. Having said these things 'he gave up the ghost' (7.15-20). The result of this incredible turn of events was that the people fell to the ground, overcome by the power of God that had come down upon them (7.21). They were restored, searched the Scriptures, and listened to Sherem no more (7.23). At this point, perhaps the readers realize that Sherem is a representative of all those who reject the prophecy of Zenos, Isaiah, Lehi, Nephi, and Jacob.

Section two of Part Four (7.24-25) implies that one of the results of the Nephites' spiritual restoration were numerous attempts to reclaim and restore the Lamanites to the truth. However, the Lamanites' delight in wars and bloodshed and their eternal hatred of the Nephites meant that these efforts were in vain. Ironically, one of the results of this failed attempt was the militarization of the Nephites.

Section three of Part Four (7.26-27) is devoted to Jacob's farewell. He concludes his story of the Nephite sacred history in poetic form where he essentially sums up, not only the story of the Ne-

---

[1] Though often referred to as 'Sherem the Antichrist' in secondary literature, Sherem is never called 'Antichrist' in this passage, but 'thou art of the Devil' (7.14).

phites to this point in the narrative, but also their bleak future that awaits narration:

> That the time passed away with us,
> and also our lives passed away,
> like as it were to us a dream,
> we being a lonesome and a solemn people,
> wanderers, cast out from Jerusalem;
> born in tribulation, in a wilderness,
> and hatred of our brethren, which caused wars and contentions;
> wherefore, we did mourn out our days (7.26b).

The final part of section three provides a description of Jacob's formal transfer of the plates to his son Enos, relaying the commands that he himself had received from Nephi. Jacob concludes by bidding his 'Brethren, adieu' (7.27).

6

ENOS

The readers' journey continues with the fourth book found within the Book of Mormon, a one-chapter book called the Book of Enos that covers 3 pages in the 1830 edition containing some 1,209 words. In fact, it is the first of four, one-chapter books the readers will encounter in succession. The book itself has a relatively clear structure.

Enos Narrates his Experience of Forgiveness (vv. 1-8)

Enos Intercedes for the Nephites (vv. 9-10), Lamanites, and the Preservation of the Nephite Records (vv. 11-18)

Enos Prophesies and Testifies to the Nephite and Lamanite Peoples (vv. 19-24)

Enos Bids Farewell (vv. 25-27)[1]

As the book opens, Enos makes mention of the words of his father and their influence upon him, though oddly Enos never names his father, Jacob. Ostensibly, in this short book Enos' desire is to recount his wrestling with God before the remission of his sin (v. 2). The reader has no way of knowing that this modest objective

---

[1] Thomas' observation (*Digging in Cumorah*, p. 136) that the Book of Enos is structured around the three occurrences of the prayer of faith recorded in the book – 'for himself, for his people, and for his enemies' – does not seem to take into sufficient account Enos' entreaties with regard to preserving the Nephite records and his subsequent prophesying and testifying to the Nephites and the Lamanites. Though Thomas does acknowledge the significance of the later theme, it does not seem to rise to the level of structural significance for him.

holds the key for all that follows. For in the word 'wrestling', Enos introduces the readers to the first of a number of visceral and/or affective words that permeate this brief document. At the same time, his reference to 'remission of sins' anticipates the theme that, in many ways, will drive the rest of the narrative. Whilst hunting for beasts in the forests, the words of his father concerning 'eternal life' and the 'joy of the saints' sunk deep into his heart (v. 3). Reference to 'the joy of the saints' would perhaps remind the readers of the promise that the joy of the saints should be forever (2 Nephi 9.18) and of the happiness prepared for them (2 Nephi 9.43), despite the fact that several texts have reference to the saints' suffering and martyrdom (1 Nephi 13.5 [2x], 2 Nephi 26.3 [2x]). Other previous references to the saints have occurred in 1 Nephi 14.12, 14; 15.28; 2 Nephi 9.19. At any rate, such recollections appear to have touched Enos deeply as he uses the language of 'my soul hungered', 'kneeled', 'cried … in mighty prayer … all day long', at night 'I did raise my voice high that it reached the heavens' (vv. 3-4) and to describe his entreaties for his soul. In response, Enos hears a voice saying, 'Enos, thy sins are forgiven thee, and thou shalt be blessed' (v. 5), the first of several times God or Christ speaks or will speak to Enos in the book (cf. vv. 5, 8, 10, 12, 15, 18, 27). Enos takes the voice as coming from God and felt his guilt swept away, as God cannot lie (v. 6). Enos does enquire as to how this is accomplished (v. 7). Again God speaks to Enos. It is his faith in Christ – whom he has never before heard – that has made him whole (v. 8). On the one hand, this verse introduces a most significant term in the book, as 'faith' will appear ten times in its twenty-seven verses. On the other hand, despite Jacob's many recorded words about Christ, apparently he never spoke to Enos about him.

As a result of this divine encounter, Enos became concerned for the welfare of his Nephite brethren, pouring out his whole soul to God on their behalf, to which God responds that he will visit them according to their diligence in keeping his commandments (vv. 9-10). These words result in Enos' unshaken faith in the Lord and he begins to struggle long for his brethren the Lamanites (vv. 10-11). After Enos prays and labors with all diligence, God again speaks to him. The divine words appear clear enough, 'I will grant unto thee according to thy desires, because of thy faith' (v. 12). But rather than asking the Lord for the conversion of the Lamanites, Enos prays that if the Nephites fall into transgression and are destroyed and the Lamanites survive, that God would ensure the preservation of a record of his people, a record he will mention four times in this section (vv. 13, 14, 15, 16). Despite Enos' faith and God's offer to grant his desires, Enos makes clear that at present there is no hope for a Lamanite conversion. In fact, the Lamanites hate the Nephites so much that they would not only destroy them if they had the chance, but their records as well (v. 14). Yet again the Lord speaks to Enos, assuring him that his request is in accord with that of his fathers (cf. 2 Nephi 29.2), whose faith is like that of Enos (v. 18).

True to his word, Enos prophesies and testifies to the Nephite people (v. 19), who in turn join him in seeking to turn the Lamanites back to true faith in God. However, such efforts were in vain owing to the recalcitrance of the Lamanite people. Specifically, their refusals resulted from their hatred of the Nephites, their evil nature making them 'wild and ferocious, and a bloodthirsty people, full of idolatry and filthiness, feeding upon beasts of prey … And many of them did eat nothing save it was raw meat' (v. 20). In contrast to their nomadic life, the Nephites seem to be praised for their agrarian lifestyle (v. 21). Such an uncharitable description of the Lamanites might speak to the readers in two ways. First, Jacob's words of condemnation of the Nephites, owing to the filthiness of taking many wives and concubines, would no doubt be felt all the more in the light of the Lamanites thorough-going wickedness. Second, it might strike the readers as a bit odd that the Lamanites would appear to be condemned for 'feeding upon beasts of prey', owing to the fact that the Book of Enos commences (v. 3) with Enos in the forests hunting beasts (apparently for food),[2] and condemned for eating raw meat, as the readers would likely remember where Nephi recounts that he and the others in the wilderness 'did live upon raw meat' (1 Nephi 17.2). But despite Enos' efforts and those of many other Nephite prophets, there was nothing that

---

[2] Brant A. Gardner (*Second Witness: Enos through Mosiah* [ACCBM 3; Salt Lake City: Greg Kofford, 2007], p. 16) explains such a tension as not a condemnation of hunting *per se* but rather the condemnation of a lifestyle that is the opposite of the Nephites. 'The Lamanites are "wild and ferocious" because they hunt and eat animals that are also "wild and ferocious" (beasts of prey). Lamanites are wild. Nephites are civilized.' From a narrative perspective it is not clear that the text can bear the weight of this interpretation. Gardner goes on to question whether 'the Lamanites actually ate raw meat' though acknowledges this possibility.

could turn the Lamanites to the fear of the Lord. In point of fact, Enos would testify of seeing wars between the Nephites and Lamanites in his lifetime (vv. 22-24).

In Enos' farewell, with which the book concludes, a) he locates his life chronologically – *one hundred and seventy-nine years have passed (since Lehi left Jerusalem)*, b) he testifies of his life's work – preaching about Christ his Redeemer, and c) he describes his anticipated reception by Christ, 'Come unto me, ye blessed, there is a place prepared for you in the mansions of my Father' (vv. 25-27). A final 'Amen' marks the formal conclusion of this short book.

7

JAROM

The readers' journey continues with the fifth book found within the Book of Mormon, a one-chapter book called the Book of Jarom that covers 2 pages in the 1830 edition containing some 773 words.[1] This is the second of four one-chapter books that the readers encounter in this portion of the Book of Mormon. The book may be structured around six short sections, which begin and end with discussions of the plates.

Jarom and the Plates (vv. 1-2)

Spiritual Condition of Jarom's People (vv. 3-4)

The Development of the Nephite and Lamanite Peoples (vv. 5-9)

The Spiritual Labor of Prophets, Priests, and Teachers (vv. 10-12)

Chronological Location (v. 13)

Jarom's Farewell and the Plates (vv. 14-15)

As the book opens, Jarom identifies himself as writing a few words according to the commandment of his father, whom he identifies as Enos, in order that a genealogy of his people might be kept (v. 1). Jarom's writing on the small plates is for the benefit of the Lamanites, perhaps suggesting to the readers that the Lamanites are

---

[1] Making it the shortest book in the Book of Mormon. Cf. Hartshorn, *A Commentary on the Book of Mormon*, p. 175.

now understood to outlast the Nephites.[2] Jarom is reluctant to record any of his prophesying or revelations, as in his estimation they would contribute little to the plan of salvation as previously elaborated (v. 2).

The situation faced by Jarom is in some ways dire because most, but not all, of his people exhibit hardness of hearts, deafness of ears, blindness of minds, and stiffness of necks.[3] But God is 'exceedingly merciful' and not all the Nephites are without faith (vv. 3-4).

Despite the words of the previous verse, Jarom notes that *in the two hundredth year of their new world existence*, the Nephites had kept the law of Moses, the Sabbath day, and avoided blasphemy. 'They were scattered upon much of the face of the land' as were the Lamanites, who were the more numerous of the two groups. Unlike the Nephites, the Lamanites 'loved murder and would drink the blood of beasts', clear violations of the law of Moses (vv. 5-6).[4] Despite the numerous attacks of the Lamanites, the Nephites were able to withstand them, owing to the fact that the Nephite 'kings and leaders were mighty men in the faith of the Lord', who taught the people the ways of the Lord and fortified their cities (v. 7). As a result, the Nephites multiplied exceedingly, and, somewhat surprisingly given the rebuke found in Jacob (Jacob 2.12-24), they became exceedingly rich from gold and silver, being prosperous in all manner of craftsmanship which helped them withstand the Lamanites in accordance with the words spoken to their fathers, 'That inasmuch as you keep my commandments, ye shall prosper in the land' (vv. 8-9).

The prophets seem to have kept the Nephites properly oriented, reminding them of the connection between falling into transgression and being destroyed (v. 10). In point of fact, the prophets, priests, and teachers labored diligently teaching the people to keep the law of Moses and persuading them to look forward to the Mes-

---

[2] Terryl L. Givens (*The Book of Mormon: A Very Short Introduction* [Oxford: Oxford University Press, 2009], p. 86) notes, 'By the time his (Enos') son Jarom writes, the writing on the wall is all too apparent. While dutifully maintaining the family genealogy, Jarom simply assumes that he is really writing for "the benefit of our brethren the Lamanites," though he still uses the first person plural (1:2).'

[3] Hartshorn, *A Commentary on the Book of Mormon*, p. 175. *Contra* Gardner, *Second Witness: Enos through Mosiah*, p. 27.

[4] Gardner, *Second Witness: Enos through Mosiah*, p. 29.

siah, believing in him as though he had already come (v. 11). Both of these activities kept the Nephites from destruction, continually stirring them to repentance (v. 12).

Unfortunately, in the chronological location of Jarom – *after two hundred and thirty eight years had passed* – there is found testimony of wars, contentions, and dissensions for much of this time (v. 13).

Jarom's farewell communicates three things. First, he did not write more owing to the smallness of the plates. Second, for those interested, the wars of the people have been engraved elsewhere in the writings for the kings (v. 14). Third, Jarom delivers the plates into the hands of his son Omni so that they might be preserved according to the commandments of his fathers (v. 15). Perhaps in this section the readers would pick up on the fact that this brief book is enveloped by references to the plates. The book concludes with no mention made of Jarom's death.

8

OMNI

The readers' journey continues with the sixth book found within the Book of Mormon, a one-chapter book called the Book of Omni that covers three and a half pages in the 1830 edition containing some 1,468 words. This is the third of four, one-chapter books that the readers encounter in this portion of the Book of Mormon. Unlike its predecessors, the Book of Omni does not consist of the words of one writer but five. Thus, the book might conceivably be structured around the individual writers: Omni (vv. 1-3), Amaron (vv. 4-8), Chemish (v. 9), Abinadom (vv. 10-11), and Amaleki (vv. 12-30), the most prolific of the six. However, such a structure is complicated by the text itself as two textual indicators suggest. First, the phrase, 'And I make an end' is strategically located at four places within the book (vv. 3, 9, 11, and 30, where 'and I make an end of my speaking' occurs). Second, the amount of space devoted to Amaleki is disproportionate in comparison with the other writers named in the book, suggesting that his words need more structural recognition than simply a listing of his name. Together, these indicators suggest the following structure:

Omni (vv. 1-3)

Amaron and his brother Chemish (vv. 4-9)[1]

---

[1] Significantly, Amaron and Chemish are the only brothers in Omni entrusted with the task of writing on the plates. The other writers are father and son combinations, which may go some way toward explaining why the phrase, 'And I make an end' does not conclude the words of Amaron, but the words of

Abinadom (vv. 10-11)

Amaleki on Mosiah and Zarahemla (vv. 12-23)

Amaleki Transfers the Plates to Benjamin (vv. 24-26)

Amaleki on Expeditions to the Land of Nephi (vv. 27-30a)

Amaleki's Farewell (v. 30b)

The first figure to appear is Omni, for whom the book is named, who describes that he was commanded by his father, Jarom, to write something on the plates to preserve 'our' genealogy (v. 1). Not only did Omni faithfully fulfill this duty, but he also fought successfully (v. 2), despite 'many seasons of serious war, and bloodshed', to preserve the Nephites from the Lamanites. Though a self-confessed wicked man – not having kept the statutes and commandments of the Lord as he ought – Omni nevertheless kept the plates according to the commandments of his fathers, conferring them upon his son Amaron. Omni's words include two references to his chronological location, *two hundred seventy-six years have passed* and *two hundred eighty-two years have passed*, both in v. 2. The phrase, 'And I make an end', concludes the book's opening section (v. 3).

Though Amaron claims to write few words in the book of his father, who is unnamed, he does include four significant details. First, he provides his chronological location, *three hundred twenty years had passed*, continuing to orient the readers as to their location within the book's broader narrative. Second, Amaron reveals that the 'more wicked part of the Nephites were destroyed' by the hand of the Lord owing to their lack of obedience, with Amaron citing the negative version of Jarom 9b, 'That inasmuch as ye will not keep my commandments, ye shall not prosper in the land' (Omni 6).[2] Third, the Lord did deliver the righteous Nephites out of the hands of their enemies. Fourth, Amaron delivered the plates to his brother Chemish (v. 8), without the customary words of conclusion, 'And I

Chemish, suggesting that the work of the two brothers is to be seen together. Gardner (*Second Witness: Enos through Mosiah*, p. 41) observes, 'Other than Nephi himself, Amaron is the only writer on the small plates to pass them horizontally to a brother rather than vertically to a son'.

[2] Gardner (*Second Witness: Enos through Mosiah*, p. 40) notes, 'In Ammaron's account, the negative promise has been applied: "the Lord did visit them in great judgment"'.

make an end'. In many ways, Chemish's few words in the same book with his brother's serve almost exclusively as a testimony to Amaron's writing activity, perhaps assuring the readers of the trustworthy nature of the those things written upon the plates in the possession of the writers here surveyed.[3] Specifically, Chemish claims to have seen the last words that Amaron wrote, that it was written with Amaron's own hand, and that it was written on the day that Amaron delivered them (the plates, though previously reference was made to 'the same book') to him on the day that he wrote, and that this is the manner in which such Nephite records were kept – in accordance with the commandments of their fathers. Perhaps Chemish's testimonial character explains why Amaron and Chemish are treated together in this section. Significantly, Chemish does not describe entrusting the plates to another. The phrase 'And I make an end' concludes this section of the book (v. 9).

In the next verse (v. 10), Abinadom introduces himself as the son of Chemish. Like Omni, Abinadom saw much war between the Nephites and Lamanites, with Abinadom having taken the life of many Lamanites himself in defense of his brethren (v. 10). Noting that the history of this people is engraved upon the plates that the kings possess, Abinadom confesses that he knows of no revelation nor prophecy written during these years (v. 11). Significantly, as Chemish before him, Abinadom does not describe entrusting the plates to another. The familiar phrase 'And I make an end' concludes this section of the book as well (v. 11e).

At this point, the readers become acquainted with the primary writer in the Book of Omni, Amaleki – the son of Abinadom. The first section of Amaleki's words is devoted to Mosiah, who was made king over Zarahemla (vv. 12-23). The readers would quickly recognize that Mosiah's introductory inscription has numerous parallels to the lives of Lehi and Nephi.[4] For Mosiah is warned that he should flee out of the land (of Nephi on this occasion) and go into

---

[3] Givens (*The Book of Mormon: A Very Short Introduction*, p. 9) observes that such activities as these serve 'to reinforce more dramatically the efficacy of the imposed obligation to maintain intact the line of transmission, the authentication of provenance, of the sacred records'. Though Givens' point is offered in support of the plates' historical reliability, the readers implied by the text are, no doubt, drawing similar conclusions on the narrative level.

[4] Gardner, *Second Witness: Enos through Mosiah*, pp. 44-45.

the wilderness (v. 12). His obedience results in those who hearkened to the voice of the Lord going with him,[5] being 'led by many preachings and prophesyings', being admonished continually by the word of God and led by the power of his arm, resulting in their relocation in the land of Zarahemla (v. 13). Owing to the similarities between Mosiah, Lehi, and Nephi, the readers' level of expectancy is no doubt very high at this point. Their expectations are not frustrated, for Mosiah discovers that the people of Zarahemla had themselves come out of Jerusalem at the time of Zedekiah, the king of Judah who was taken into Babylonian captivity (vv. 14-15). This numerous people, who had many wars and contentions, had no records, which resulted in a corruption of their language, a language Mosiah could not understand, and the loss of their theological identity – 'they denied the being of their Creator' (v. 17). Mosiah remedies this situation by teaching them his language, with Zarahemla then giving them a genealogy of his fathers from memory, resulting in the uniting of the people of Zarahemla and the people of Mosiah, with Mosiah appointed as king (vv. 18-19). Following this, a stone with engravings was brought to Mosiah who interpreted them 'by the gift and power of God'. The contents revealed an account of Coriantumr and his slain people, who had been discovered by the people of Zarahemla 'nine moons' before Coriantumr's death. It is discovered that his parents had come at the time of the tower of Babel event, but he alone remained; the bones of his people are 'scattered in the land northward' (vv. 20-22). This first section of Amaleki's words concludes with his claims that he was born during the reign of Mosiah, seeing his death, and lived during the reign of his son Benjamin (v. 23), to which his attention turns in the second section of his words.

As others before him, Amaleki witnesses 'a serious war and much bloodshed between the Nephites and the Lamanites' during the days of King Benjamin, but the king drove the Lamanites out of the land of Zarahemla (v. 24). Becoming old and having no seed, Amaleki transfers oversight of the plates to King Benjamin who was a 'just' man. This transfer came with the intent of 'exhorting all men to come unto God, the Holy One of Israel, and believe in

---

[5] Hartshorn (*A Commentary on the Book of Mormon*, p. 178) observes that the phrase 'as many as would hearken', which appears twice, may suggest that not all responded to the 'preachings and prophesyings'.

prophesying, and in revelations, and in the ministering of angels, and in the gift of speaking with tongues, and in the gift of interpreting languages in all things which is good' (v. 25), all things which have earlier been identified as part of God's salvific activity. Amaleki desires that his people would partake of the salvation of Christ and the power of his redemption, 'offering your whole souls', continuing in prayer and fasting, and enduring until the end (v. 26).

The third section of Amaleki's words concern those who attempted to return to the land of Nephi to possess the land of their inheritance, but were all destroyed, save fifty who returned to the land of Zarahemla. Others went out into the wilderness including Amaleki's brother, who have not been heard from since (vv. 27-30).

In his farewell, Amaleki acknowledges his nearness to death and the fact that the plates entrusted to him are now full (v. 30b). The phrase 'And I make an end of my speaking' concludes both this section and the book as a whole (v. 30c). With this, the readers reach a significant moment in the narrative for, among other things, the plates are full.

9

THE WORDS OF MORMON

The readers' journey continues with the seventh book found within the Book of Mormon, a one-chapter book called the Words of Mormon that covers two pages in the 1830 edition containing some 889 words. This is the fourth of four one-chapter books the readers encounter in this portion of the Book of Mormon. This short book may be structured in the following way:

Mormon Speaks from and of the Future (vv. 1-2)

Mormon Explains his Spirit-Directed Choice of Plates (vv. 3-8)

The Plates of Nephi and the Rest of Mormon's Presentation (vv. 9-11)

King Benjamin and the Slaying of the Lamanites (vv. 12-14)

False Christs, False Prophets, False Preachers, and False Teachers Are Punished, Peace in the Land Is Once Again Established (vv. 15-18)

Despite the fact that Mormon has earlier appeared in the content of the Title Page, his appearance here in the Words of Mormon (vv. 1-2) is unexpected and abrupt, having an almost 'whiplash' effect on the readers. For whereas the preceding narrative (1 Nephi – Omni) has given the impression of chronological movement from Lehi's departure from Jerusalem down to the events associated with Amaleki, the Words of Mormon interrupt this narrative development, jumping ahead many hundred years after the coming of Christ, an event only prophesied to this point in the narrative.[1] In point of fact, Mormon's words come from the perspective of the book's anticipated end, his personal witnessing of the near total destruction of his people, the Nephites, and his supposition that his son Moroni, to whom he will entrust the plates, will witness the entire destruction of his people. This perspective lends a certain credibility to Mormon's words for the readers, as Mormon now locates them within his own editorial work.

In the second section of the Words of Mormon (vv. 3-8), Mormon recounts his previous abridgement of the plates of Nephi down to the reign of King Benjamin and his discovery of the plates that contain a small account of the prophets from Jacob to King Benjamin and the words of Nephi, which contain prophecies of the coming of Christ, many of which have been fulfilled by Mormon's time.[2] Deciding to include the contents of this second set of plates as well, Mormon finds that he does so for a wise purpose as the Spirit makes clear, for the Lord knows all things and knows why this inclusion is important. As for Mormon's own desires, they are for his brethren to come again to the redemption of Christ and once again be 'a delightsome people'.

In the third section of the Words of Mormon (vv. 9-11), Mormon describes his plan to finish out his record based upon the (small) plates of Nephi. He traces the transmission of the plates from Amaleki to Benjamin – who puts them with the other plates, their transmission from generation to generation until they finally reach the hands of Mormon, whose desire – like Lehi, Nephi, and Enos before him – is that they may be preserved from this time forward, a preservation he is convinced will happen, records from which his people and brethren shall be judged 'at the last great day'.

The fourth section of the Words of Mormon (vv. 12-14) focuses almost exclusively upon King Benjamin's leadership in the battles of his armies with the Lamanite armies, destroying many thousands of them, and driving them out of all the lands of their inheritance.

---

[1] Hardy (*Understanding the Book of Mormon*, p. 90) calls the Words of Mormon, 'an urgent time capsule from the future dropped into the narrative at about 200 BC.

[2] Gardner (*Second Witness: Enos through Mosiah*, p. 76) notes, 'While the writers had only anticipated the coming of Christ, Mormon knows that he came and fulfilled the prophecies'.

The final section of the Words of Mormon (vv. 15-18) testifies to the punishment – according to their crimes – of false Christs, false prophets, false preachers, and false teachers, who arose in the Nephites' midst.[3] King Benjamin, a holy man who reigned in righteousness, with the assistance of the holy prophets spoke 'the word of the Lord with power and authority'. 'King Benjamin, by laboring with all the might of his body and the faculty of his whole soul and also the prophets, wherefore, they did once more establish peace in the land' (v. 18).

Mormon's words here bring a great deal of clarity to the readers as they now learn that the prophecies in the narrative that have indicated the complete destruction of the Nephites and the survival of the Lamanites indeed point to just such an unpleasant end for his people. His authoritative speech both interprets the past and points to the future, all the while underscoring the importance of the preservation of the plates with which he has been entrusted and upon which he works. Unbeknownst to the readers at this point, the 'Words of Mormon' provides a transition with regard to king Benjamin, who was introduced near the end of Omni (1.23) and whose reign will be further documented in the book that immediately follows, the Book of Mosiah (1.1-6.5).

---

[3] Richard Dilworth Rust, (*Feasting on the Word: The Literary Testimony of the Book of Mormon* [Salt Lake City: Deseret Book Co and FARMS, 1997], p. 21) identifies the Lamanites as external enemies and the false Christs, false prophets, false preachers, and false teachers as internal enemies.

10

MOSIAH

The readers' journey continues with the eighth book found within the Book of Mormon, a twenty-nine chapter book called the Book of Mosiah that covers 68 pages in the 1830 edition containing some 32,408 words. This is the first of the books of the abridgement attributed to Mormon that the readers encounter.

In some ways the Book of Mosiah has a very meandering, even abrupt, structure and style with duplicate accounts of the same events, retrospective retellings of the same stories, and proportionately little attention given to Mosiah in the vast preponderance of chapters. Though the structure of the book could be set forth in numerous ways, depending on which events are seen to be dominant and defining – of which there are many – the book appears to be structured around the reigns of various kings. The dominant structure takes shape around King Benjamin and his son King Mosiah, who is introduced at the beginning of the book (1.2, 10, 18; 2.1, 30), begins to reign and gives a command around which much of the remainder of the book is concerned (6.3-7; 7.1-3), and reappears as a major figure in the last five chapters of the book (25.1-29.47). Thus, although other royal and prophetic figures play a not insignificant role in the book, narratively speaking it becomes clear that Mosiah is the character around which the book takes shape. On this view, the book may be structured broadly into eight parts:[1]

---

[1] Despite the scholarly questions with regard to the book's original composition etc., from the very first edition of the Book of Mormon, the Book of Mosiah has appeared as a distinct book within the larger volume with direct connections

Part One – King Benjamin's Reign, His Sons, His Farewell
    Speech, His Successor, and His Death (1.1-6.7)

Part Two – King Mosiah Begins his Reign (7.1-8.21)

Part Three – The Record of Zeniff (9.1-10.21)

Part Four – 'Wicked' King Noah and the Prophet Abinadi
    (11.1-19.24)

Part Five – King Limhi (19.25-22.15)

Part Six – Alma and his People (23.1-24.25)

Part Seven – King Mosiah and Alma Establish a People and a
    Church (25.1-28.9)

Part Eight – King Mosiah's Farewell (28.10-29.47).

Part One of the Book of Mosiah (1.1-6.7) is bounded on
either end by the observation that there was no contention amongst
the people. In Benjamin's case it is observed 'there was no more
contention in all the land of Zarahemla, among all the people who
belonged to King Benjamin', so that he 'had continual peace all the
remainder of his days' (1.1) – the triple use of 'all' in these statements underscoring completeness in each case. This part ends with
the observation that there was no contention for the first three
years of Mosiah's reign (6.7), the limited nature of this contention-
free period being evident. Part One also begins and concludes with
brief narratives (1.1-8; 6.1-7), while an extended farewell speech
stands at the section's center (2.1-5.15). The fact that Part One recounts Benjamin's farewell is revealed by reference to his soon ap-

to that which precedes and follows. Cf. the discussion in Gary L. Sturgess, 'The
Book of Mosiah: Thoughts about Its Structure, Purposes, Themes, and Authorship', *Journal of Book of Mormon Studies* 4.2 (1995), pp. 107-35. Two pieces of evidence give one pause as to Mosiah's original composition. First, it lacks a head
note or summary of the book's content, a most unusual occurrence in the Book
of Mormon where larger books occur (at least those attributed to Mormon's editorial work). Second, in the Printer's Manuscript of the Book of Mormon it appears that what proves to be the first chapter was originally marked as chapter
three. Cf. the facsimile of this passage in Royal Skousen and Robin Scott Jensen
(eds.), *Printer's Manuscript of the Book of Mormon: 1 Nephi 1 – Alma 35* (Vol. 3.1 of
the Revelations and Translations series of The Joseph Smith Papers; Dean C.
Jessee, Ronald K. Esplin, and Richard Lyman Bushman [eds.], Salt Lake City:
Church Historian's Press, 2015), p. 252. Cf. also Gardner, *Second Witness: Enos
through Mosiah*, p. 97.

proaching death that punctuates this portion of the book at various points (1.9; 2.26, 28; 6.5).

The first section of Part One (1.1-18) acquaints the readers with King Benjamin's sons (Mosiah, Helorum, and Helaman) and their education in the languages of Benjamin's fathers, so that they would be men of understanding, knowing the prophecies 'spoken by the mouths of their fathers' (1.2). Specifically, they are taught about the 'true' records (1.3, 6 [2x]), the brass plates (1.3 [3x]; 4), the engravings (1.4), and the plates of Nephi (1.6), all of which contain the mysteries of God (1.3, 5). Obviously, a great deal of emphasis is placed upon the role and function of the plates at the beginning of this book. With his own death approaching, Benjamin turns to one of his sons, Mosiah, commissioning him to serve as king in Benjamin's place, an eventuality that will be announced formally at a gathering of all the people. Promising the people that he will give them a name that will distinguish them from all others (1.11-12), Benjamin gave Mosiah 'charge concerning the records which were engraven on the plates of brass; and also, the plates of Nephi; and also, the sword of Laban, and the ball or director' (1.16).

The second section of Part One (2.1-6.3), the longest section of this portion of Mosiah, is devoted to Benjamin's farewell speech. The narrative introduction (2.1-8) describes the enormous response of the people to the announcement that the king was to speak. Having brought animals for sacrifice, according to the law of Moses, they pitched their tents, family by family, around the temple awaiting the King's words, words that would be delivered from a tower constructed for just this occasion owing to the crowd. The speech may be divided into four distinct subsections (2.9-42; 3.1-27; 4.4-30; 5.6-15), with each subsection concluding with a warning from Benjamin.

King Benjamin begins by promising to reveal to his readers 'the mysteries of God' (2.9), then recounts the details of his reign as their servant – a service performed in order that he might answer God with a clear conscience – whilst encouraging them to be servants of one another (2.15-26). Completing the description of his reign and transfer of the kingship to Mosiah (2.27-30), he concludes this subsection by warning the readers to remember that those who keep the commandments of the Lord will be happy and prosper, whilst those who do not will experience torment and everlasting judgment (2.31-41).

In the next subsection of his farewell speech (3.1-27) Benjamin narrates words that have come to him by an angel from God. The first portion focuses upon explicit words about numerous aspects of the coming of Jesus Christ, the Son of God – his life of miraculous activity, atoning death, and resurrection (3.1-15). Here, Benjamin makes clear the necessity of repentance and faith for salvation and the remission of sins. The king emphasizes that Moses and the holy prophets foretold many things about Christ's coming. The second portion of these angelically mediated words (3.16-23) focuses exclusively upon the fall of Adam and the atoning blood of Jesus using the imagery of children as a model of how one must come to Christ the Lord – Christ being the name Benjamin had earlier (1.11-12) promised to give his people. The third portion of this subsection (3.24-27) concludes with a warning that his people avoid at all costs the drinking of damnation unto their souls that will result in their eternal torment. So effective were Benjamin's words that when he looked up from speaking he saw that the people had fallen to the earth owing to the fear of the Lord, crying out for mercy, for application of the atoning blood of Christ, for forgiveness of sin, and for the purification of their hearts. Afterwards, the Spirit of the Lord came upon them, filling them with joy, remitting their sins, giving peace of conscience, and faith 'in Jesus Christ who should come' (4.1-3).

The third subsection of Benjamin's speech (4.4-30) calls the readers' attention to the central aspect of the people's salvation, with emphasis placed upon the atonement that has been 'prepared from the foundation of the world' (4.4-8) – the phrase 'prepared from the foundation of the world' occurring twice in the middle of the first portion of this sub-section (4.6, 8). In the next portion Benjamin calls upon his hearers to 'believe' (4.9 [4x], 10 [2x]), to be assured of their 'remission of sins' (4.11, 12), to have joy and rejoice (4.11, 12), to love and care for one another (4.13, 14), to teach their children to walk in truth – loving and serving one another (4.15), and to 'succor' those in need, sharing their substance, looking upon the beggar with sympathy (4.16). This final instruction leads to an extensive admonition on the relationship between caring for beggars and the beggarly identity of everyone in need of forgiveness of sin (4.17-30). Specifically, 'I would that ye should impart of your substance to the poor, every man according to that which he hath, such as feeding the hungry, clothing the naked, visiting the sick and administering to their relief, both spiritually and temporally ...' (4.26), connecting this practice to the reception of the forgiveness of sin. But such imparting of one's substance must be done in wisdom and order, 'for it is not requisite for a man to run faster than he has strength' (4.27). The admonition concludes with a warning that the listeners must be careful to watch themselves until the end of their lives lest they perish (4.28-30). Once again, the effect of the king's words was met with conviction and acceptance, resulting in a change of heart, great joy, and the people's entering into a covenant with God (5.1-5).

In the fourth subsection (5.6-15), Benjamin draws his speech to a close by focusing upon the implications of taking the covenant – they have become children of Christ, the name by which they are called, the name that Benjamin has revealed to them. He urges them to steadfast loyalty and diligence.

The conclusion of Benjamin's farewell speech is followed by his taking down the names of all those who entered into the covenant with God, that is those who took upon themselves the name of Christ. At this point, Benjamin consecrates Mosiah as king before dismissing the people back to their own houses (6.1-3). The final verses of this subsection (6.4-7) describe Mosiah's age – thirty, his chronological location – *four hundred and seventy-six years since Lehi left Jerusalem*, and Benjamin's death – three years after Mosiah began his reign. Mosiah taught his people to till the earth, something he himself did so as not to be 'burdensome' to the people. The subsection and Part One conclude with the words, 'And there was no contention among all his people for the space of three years' (6.7c).

Part Two of the Book of Mosiah (7.1-8.21) begins by reminding the readers of the three contention-free years with which Mosiah's reign begins and then describes Mosiah's first action as king – the sending of twelve strong men to Lehi-Nephi to enquire as to what had happened to their brothers who had earlier disappeared there – according to Omni 29-30 (Mosiah 7.1-6). Led by Ammon, 'a strong and mighty man', the men went down into the land of Nephi, were discovered, thrown into prison, and brought before King Limhi, the son of Noah, the son of Zeniff, to be questioned.

When Ammon revealed that they had come to learn the fate of Zeniff and his people, Limhi 'was exceeding glad' for he now knew that his brethren were alive and well in the land of Zarahemla. Revealing that he and his people were slaves to the Lamanites, paying heavy tribute to them, Limhi expressed that it would be better to be the slaves of the Nephites than the Lamanites (7.7-16). The next day Limhi addressed his people summarizing the history of his people, describing their disobedience as the reason for their predicament, and urging repentance as the way to deliverance (7.17-33). When asked by the king to speak, Ammon told them of his brethren in Zarahemla, describing their journey as well as rehearsing the last words of King Benjamin (8.1-4). Next, twenty-four plates of pure gold filled with engravings were brought to Ammon, plates that had come from a land that Zeniff's people had found, a land covered with the bones of men and beasts, as well as ruins of buildings. Limhi had hopes that Ammon could translate the plates and, though he could not, Ammon told him of a 'seer' who by the use of 'interpreters' could so translate, acknowledging that a seer is greater than a prophet for a seer is a revelator and a prophet. Book of Mormon readers, of course, would likely suspect that reference is being made to Mosiah who earlier is said to have translated certain stone engravings (Omni 20-22). Limhi was ecstatic at such news (Mosiah 8.5-21).

At this point the narrative diverts to tell the stories of the past that are of relevance to Limhi and his people, Ammon and his people, and the readers of the Book of Mormon more generally. In point of fact, the diversion is so extensive that it is not until Mosiah 21.28 that the story line of Ammon and Limhi resumes.[2]

This diversion begins in **Part Three of the Book of Mosiah (9.1-10.22)** with a detailed recounting of the record of Zeniff. Not only is this Part identified in a headnote in the 1830 edition of the Book of Mormon as coming from Zeniff, but the first person singular voice also indicates that the record is being recounted by Zeniff himself. The record of Zeniff begins with the initial expedition Zeniff and his brethren make to spy out the Lamanites, a trip that resulted in internal fighting, dividing fathers and sons and brothers, causing a return to the land of Zarahemla (9.1-2). But Zeniff was

---

[2] Hardy, *Understanding the Book of Mormon*, p. 198, n. a.

'over-zealous' to possess the land so that he and those desirous to go went again into the wilderness, this time making contact with the Lamanite king, who gave Zeniff and his people the land of Lehi-Nephi, which they began to repair and in which they began to prosper. But 'the cunning and craftiness of King Laman' would work against them to bring them into eventual bondage (9.3-10). After thirteen years, King Laman began to stir up his people that they might contend with Zeniff's people, eventuating in an attack upon Zeniff's people which they repelled, killing three thousand and forty-three Lamanites, driving them out of the land, while losing two hundred seventy-nine of their own brethren (9.11-19). Zeniff next describes his preparations for additional attacks by the Lamanites and the prosperous nature of his people's life together – living in continual peace for twenty-two years (10.1-5). After the death of King Laman, his son who inherited his rule began to stir up his people against Zeniff's people, leading an attack against them. Zeniff conveys something of the Lamanites' ferocity in two ways. First, he gives a physical description of them as having shaven heads and being naked except for a leather girdle about their loins (10.8). Second, Zeniff recounts the grievances of this 'wild', 'ferocious', and 'blood-thirsty' people, which notably rehearses the history of Lehi's descendants from the Lamanite perspective. They were forced to leave Jerusalem owing to the iniquities of their fathers, were wronged in the wilderness by their brethren, wronged while crossing the sea, wronged because of Nephi's leadership in the land, and wronged by his taking the plates of brass when he departed. Thus their children were taught hatred so that they should 'murder', 'rob', 'plunder', and 'destroy' the Nephites. In this way King Laman deceived Zeniff into coming into his country to destroy him and his people (10.11-18). Yet, Zeniff led them to military victory yet again, returning to their previous way of life (10.19-21). Zeniff's brief farewell (10.22) consists of an acknowledgement of his old age, a conferral of the kingdom upon one of his sons, a final word about his record, 'therefore, I say no more', and a final word of blessing, 'And may the Lord bless my people. Amen.'

Part Four of the Book of Mosiah (11.1-19.24), the book's longest division, is devoted primarily to 'wicked' King Noah and the prophet Abinadi. This part begins with Noah commencing his reign as king following the death of his father (11.1) and concludes with

Noah's untimely death (19.23-24). Interestingly enough, the voice of narration changes from first person, as in the record of Zeniff, to third person in this portion of Mosiah. The first section of Part Four (11.1-19) indicates that unlike his father, Noah did not keep the commandments of the Lord, instead walked after his own desires, took many wives and concubines, performed abominable acts, taught his people to sin, and committed 'whoredoms and all manner of wickedness' (11.1-2). He imposed a twenty percent tax on his people, dismissed his father's consecrated priests, and appointed those who were lifted up in pride and themselves had wives and concubines (11.3-7). King Noah built many spacious buildings, placed his heart upon his riches, spent his time in riotous living – becoming 'a wine-bibber and also his people' (11.8-15). As his father before him, he had battles with the Lamanites, who sought to destroy them owing to their long-standing hatred. Rather than giving thanks to God when victorious, Noah and his people were filled with pride about their strength, delighted in blood, all because of their wickedness (11.16-19). The second section of Part Four (11.20-12.16) introduces the prophet Abinadi who began to prophesy, condemning the people's 'abominations', 'wickedness', and 'whoredoms', foretelling that they would soon be brought into bondage owing to their culpability, inasmuch that Noah and the people sought to take him (11.20-29). The second section continues (after two years had passed) with the return of Abinadi and his, as yet unheeded, more detailed prophesies of destruction: unless they repent they will be utterly destroyed off the face of the earth, but will leave a record (12.1-8). In response, Abinadi is arrested and handed over to the king (12.9-16).

Section three of Part Four (12.17-17.20) is devoted to Abinadi's trial before King Noah. The King's priests begin Abinadi's interrogation, which is a ruse to cross him so that they might accuse him, by asking him to explain the meaning of the words recorded in Isa. 52.7-10 (Mosiah 12.17-24). Abinadi responds by charging the priests with pretending to teach and to understand prophesying, thereby perverting the ways of the Lord (12.25-27). When the priests respond that they teach the law of Moses, Abinadi asks how they can teach it if they do not keep it, as they 'commit whoredoms' and spend their 'strength with harlots'. To the priests' insistence that salvation comes via the law of Moses, Abinadi challenges them as to whether they have kept the commandment with regard to the prohibition against idolatry, answering for them, 'Nay, ye have not ... Nay, ye have not' (12.28-37). When they seek to take him to kill him, Abinadi rebukes them owing to the fact that he has not yet delivered the message that the Lord sent him to deliver (13.1-6a). Then Abinadi offers an extensive message with occasional rhetorical questions. Here he addresses: the ten commandments (13.6b), the time when it will not be expedient to keep the law of Moses owing to the atonement which God himself will make (13.27-32), the many prophecies about Christ – drawing heavily on Isa. 53.1-12 (Mosiah 13.33-14.12), the identification of Christ as the Father and the Son who has 'broken the bonds of death' drawing on catch words/phrases from Isaiah 53 (Mosiah 15.1-9), identifying the seed of Christ drawing on catch words/phrases form Isaiah 53 (Mosiah 15.10-18), the first resurrection including a quotation of Isa. 52.8-10 (Mosiah 15.19-31), and redemption and judgment in Christ which has been spoken of as if he had already come (16.1-14). Running throughout this section is the idea that many of these things spoken are types and shadows of that which is to come. One of Abinadi's significant results is the conversion of one Alma, a descendant of a Nephite priest, who believed Abinadi's words, and then had to flee owing to the wrath of the king. During his time in hiding, Alma wrote down all the words he had heard from Abinadi (17.1-4). After three days in prison, Abinadi is brought back before King Noah who pronounces judgment upon him. Though Abinadi's final words to the king made him afraid to kill the prophet, Noah was agitated by his priests to kill Abinadi anyway. So Abinadi was bound and scourged, 'even to death', and subjected to death by flames of fire. Abinadi's last words were words of judgment that Noah's people would suffer afflictions in the future for 'God executeth vengeance upon those that destroy his people' (17.5-20).

Section Four of Part Four (18.1-35) is devoted to the activity of Alma, who had earlier been described as believing Abinadi's words and even going so far as to write them down. Alma's reappearance at this point means that the death of Abinadi is surrounded by narratives devoted to Alma (17.1-4; 18.1-35), indicating a very close connection between the person and mission of Abinadi and the person and mission of Alma. First, the readers are introduced to Alma's escape from the servants of Noah, his repentance of sins and iniquities, and his private teaching of the words of the prophet Abinadi to all those who would listen. Specifically, he taught them of things to come, including the resurrection of the dead, the redemption of the people, and Christ's death, resurrection, and ascension. Many believed his words and they gathered to hear his words at a place called Mormon that had a large fountain of water (18.1-6). Second, all those who proclaimed their belief were baptized in the Waters of Mormon, apparently the first baptisms to be described in the Book of Mormon. The first person to be baptized by Alma was Helam. The following baptismal formula was uttered by Alma over Helam:

> Helam, I baptize thee, having authority from the Almighty God, as a testimony that ye have entered into a covenant to serve him until you are dead as to the mortal body; and may the spirit of the Lord be poured out upon you; and may he grant unto you eternal life, through the redemption of Christ, which he hath prepared from the foundation of the world (18.13).

After these words 'both Alma and Helam were buried in the water', resulting in their being filled with the spirit. That day Alma baptized two hundred four individuals, but he was only buried in the water with Helam. They were filled with grace as a result (18.7-16). Third, those baptized by Alma constituted 'the Church of God or the Church of Christ', with Alma ordaining one priest per every fifty to preach and teach, to have no contention with one another but to have 'one faith and one baptism'. The priests were to be self-supporting, the people giving temporally and spiritually to all those in need. This activity resulted in a poetic or hymnic stanza:

> And now it came to pass that all this was done in Mormon;
> yea, by the waters of Mormon,
> in the forest that was near the waters of Mormon;
> yea, in the place of Mormon,
> the waters of Mormon,
> the forest of Mormon,
> how beautiful are they to the eyes of them
> who came to the knowledge of their redeemer;
> yea, and how blessed are they,
> for they shall sing to his praise forever (18.17-30).

Fourth, eventually the activities of Alma and his people were discovered so he led his four hundred and fifty souls into the wilderness (18.31-35).

Section Five of Part Four (19.1-24) recounts the arising of a strong man named Gideon who swore that he would kill King Noah (19.1-8), the enslavement of Noah's people by the Lamanites (19.9-15), the reintroduction of King Noah's son Limhi (19.16), and the death of Noah (19.17-24).

Part Five of the Book of Mosiah (19.25-22.15) is devoted primarily to the rise and reign of King Limhi after his father's death. In section one of Part Five (19.25-29), Limhi, having the kingdom of his father 'conferred upon him by the people', negotiated the payment of tribute to the Lamanite king and established a period of peace for two years. Section two of Part Five (20.1-21.17) records Limhi's numerous conflicts with the Lamanites, the first of which was precipitated by rebel priests of King Noah who kidnapped 24 daughters of the Lamanites as wives for themselves. Convinced that this action was the work of Limhi and his people, the Lamanite king attacked them, losing his life in the process. When Limhi discovers the reason for the attack by the Lamanites, Gideon remembers the renegade priests and reminds Limhi of them, enabling Limhi to pacify the Lamanite king, sparing Nephite lives (20.1-26). Other conflicts were owing to the oppressive conditions of the Nephites under Lamanite rule, with the Lamanites victorious in each battle that resulted (21.1-12). But the Lord slowly heard the cries of the Nephites, softening the hearts of the Lamanites to ease the Nephite burdens. As they began to prosper, Limhi commanded the men to care for the needs of the many widows and orphans among them (21.13-17). Section three of Part Five (21.18-27) takes the readers back to where this action begins, revealing that the reason Ammon and his brethren were discovered in the first place was owing to Limhi's guards keeping vigilant lookout for the renegade priests. Mistaking Ammon and his brethren for the rebel priests, Limhi has them imprisoned with the intent to punish them by death (21.18-24). The other bit of information revealed in this retrospective portion of the book is that Limhi had himself earlier sent several men into the wilderness to search for the land of Zarahemla. Becoming lost they stumbled upon the ruins of a city covered with dry bones, bringing a record of these people 'engraven on plates of ore' (21.25-

27). At this point, the storyline broken off in 8.21 picks back up with reference to Limhi's joy at hearing from Ammon the news that there was one who could interpret the plates, King Mosiah who had a gift from God. Limhi and Ammon's joy is tempered by sorrow for those who had been slain and those who had departed. Since Ammon's arrival, King Limhi made a covenant with God desiring baptism and planning for an escape from the hands of the Lamanites (21.28-36). At the encouragement of Gideon, King Limhi sent an abundance of wine to the Lamanite guards at the back pass of the back wall. When they were drunk, the king directed his people to take their possessions and escape into the wilderness, finally arriving in the land of Zarahemla where they joined Mosiah's people, becoming his servants. Mosiah received them and their records with joy, whilst the Lamanites who followed them became lost in the wilderness (22.1-16).

Part Six of the Book of Mosiah (23.1-24.25) is devoted to an account of Alma and his people. Warned by the Lord that the armies of King Noah were in pursuit, Alma and his people escaped into the wilderness a journey of eight days, where they come upon a beautiful and pleasant land that they began to till and upon which they began to build buildings (23.1-5). When the people sought to make Alma their king he declined, reminding the people of the iniquity of King Noah. Rather, Alma served as their high priest, 'being the founder of their Church', having consecrated all their priests and teachers (23.6-18). As they began to prosper exceedingly in the land called Helam the Lord decided to chasten them, as an army of Lamanites overcame them and at Alma's prompting the people gave over the land of Helam, enslaving themselves (23.29-30). Whilst searching for the people of Alma, the Lamanites found the renegade priests in the wilderness who had stolen their daughters. Prepared to kill them, the Lamanites relented on account of their daughters' pleas for mercy (23.30-35). Deceived by the king of the Lamanites, Alma and his brethren were subjected to the rulership of Amulon, the leader of the renegade priests of King Noah. The Lamanites consolidated the lands and delighted in all manner of wickedness and plunder, except amongst their own (24.1-7). Suffering under the tyranny of Amulon, Alma and his people cried unto the Lord who supernaturally sustained them in the midst of their burdens (24.8-15). Owing to their faith and patience, the Lord delivered them by causing a deep sleep to come upon the Lamanites and after a twelve days' journey in the wilderness they came to the land of Zarahemla and were received also by King Mosiah (24.16-23).

Part Seven of the Book of Mosiah (25.1-28.9) recounts the re-appearance of King Mosiah and his work with Alma to establish a people and a church. The first section of Part Seven (25.1-14) begins with Mosiah calling all the people together, with more people of Zarahemla than any other peoples present. They gathered in two bodies, the people of Nephi and the people of Zarahemla (25.1-2). Mosiah then had the records of Zeniff and the account of Alma read to the assembled peoples (25.3-6), readings that resulted in wonder and amazement amongst the hearers as they vacillated between joy and sorrow at the goodness of God and the suffering and/or unbelief of their brothers (25.7-11). At this point the children of Amulon and his brethren, who had kidnapped the daughters of the Lamanites, being displeased with the conduct of their fathers, renounced the names of their fathers taking upon themselves the name of Nephite and all the people of Zarahemla were joined to the Nephites, as the kingdom was conferred only upon the descendants of Nephi (25.12-13).

The second section of Part Seven (25.14-24) consists of Alma's preaching repentance to and faith on the Lord. Alma then baptized King Limhi and his people who were desirous of baptism in the manner that he had baptized those at the Waters of Mormon, each of whom now belonged to the Church of God owing to their belief on the words of Alma (25.14-19). In addition, King Mosiah gave Alma the authority to establish churches throughout Zarahemla and 'power to ordain priests and teachers over every Church' (24.19). Though there were (seven) different bodies owing to the great numbers, 'they were all one Church; yea, even the Church of God' (25.20-22). Section three of Part Seven (26.1-39) narrates the rise of a group of young individuals who did not believe the traditions of their fathers, nor the resurrection of the dead, nor the coming of Christ. Not being half as numerous as the people of God, these unbelievers rejected baptism, deceived many, and committed many sins (26.1-6). Deeply troubled by this turn of events, and instructed by King Mosiah to render judgment in this matter, Alma enquired of the Lord. In response to this enquiry Alma received a personal divine blessing, a reaffirmation of the way in which baptism and proper belief constitutes one's participation in the church, and direction as to the eternal destiny of those who refuse baptism and repentance. Though longsuffering in granting forgiveness to those who repent, 'whosoever will not repent of his sins the same shall not be numbered among my people' (26.7-33). Thus, Alma administered the church based upon these divine instructions (26.34-39).

Section four of Part Seven (27.1-28.9) recounts the way in which King Mosiah brings an end to the persecution suffered by the church at the hands of unbelievers, instructs that there should be 'equality among all men', and that every man including priests and teachers should 'labor with their own hands for their support'. Such admonitions resulted in peace and prosperity and near universal expansion amongst the people (27.1-7). Next it is learned that part of the persecution experienced by the church apparently came from the sons of Mosiah and Alma – the son of Alma – who were numbered amongst the unbelievers. They, unlike their fathers, were wicked and idolatrous destroying the church of God. But an angel of the Lord appeared to them in a cloud, with a voice like thunder, causing the earth to quake and all those present to fall down. Specifically, the angel called Alma by name asking him why he was persecuting the church of God, informing him of the many prayers that had been offered on his behalf, and instructing him to remember how God had delivered his ancestors (27.8-17). The effects upon Alma were immediate. Being left weak and not able to speak or to move his hands, he was carried and laid before his father, who called for prayer and fasting for his son. Upon his recovery, Alma confessed to the great multitude assembled that he had repented, had been redeemed, and born of the Spirit (27.18-31). This encounter also resulted in Alma and the sons of Mosiah – Ammon, Aaron, Omner, and Himni – going throughout all Zarahemla preaching what they had seen and heard, seeking to repair all the injuries to the church for which they were responsible (27.32-37). Not content with this activity, the sons of Mosiah asked their father for permission to go and evangelize amongst the Lamanites to 'cure them of their hatred' and to prevent their enduring eternal torment. Instructed by the Lord to let them go, for many would believe on their words and have eternal life, Mosiah granted their request. And so they went – as the words of Mormon instruct the readers that an account of Mosiah's sons' activities will be given later (28.1-9).

Part Eight of the Book of Mosiah (28.10-29.47) is devoted to Mosiah's farewell. The farewell is signaled by the observation that since Mosiah's sons had gone to convert the Lamanites, 'King Mosiah had no one to confer the kingdom upon, for there was not any of his sons who would accept the kingdom' (28.10). Thus, he began to gather all the records engraven on the plates of brass, the plates of Nephi, all the things he recorded, and the plates of gold found by the people of Limhi, the latter which he began to translate owing to the great anxiety of the people (28.11-12). By means of 'two stones fastened into the two rims of a bow', prepared from the beginning, handed down through the generations by the preservation of God for interpreting languages, Mosiah as 'seer' translated the records – for 'whosoever has these things is called "seer," after the manner of old times' (28.13-16). The translated plates revealed the story of a destroyed people originally from the time of the tower (of Babel), a story that stretches all the way back to the creation of Adam. The contents generated much sorrow but also conveyed wisdom. Just as an account of the evangelistic efforts of the sons of Mosiah are promised to the readers, so are the contents of these plates (28.17-19).

Standing near the middle of the farewell is a description of King Mosiah conferring all the plates and records upon Alma – the son of Alma – commanding him to keep and preserve them as well as to keep a record of the people himself and to pass it on to a future generation as has been the practice since the time of Lehi (28.20).

The final section of Mosiah's farewell is devoted to an account of the transition from Mosiah's leadership to that of Alma, the son of Alma (29.1-47). When the people express their preference for Aaron, Mosiah's son, to serve as their next king – as Mosiah had asked for the people to express their preference for king – Mosiah was unable to grant their desire as Aaron had gone to convert the Lamanites and had already declined such a potentiality as had his brothers (29.1-3). In a written document which Mosiah had circulated amongst his people, he warned against the appointment of another king owing to the possibility that any king so appointed could turn out to be a wicked ruler, mentioning King Noah specifically, 'for ye cannot dethrone an iniquitous king save it be through much contention, and the shedding of much blood'. Rather, Mosiah encourages them to choose judges that are accountable to the laws given by your fathers, as they will be judged by a higher judge (29.4-36). Convinced by Mosiah's words, a king whom they loved very much, the people appointed Alma as the first chief judge, with his father Alma conferring the office upon him giving him charge over all the affairs of the church. Alma walked in the ways of the Lord and there was continual peace in the land. With this, the transition was made from leadership by kings, to leadership by judges. The transition became complete with the death of Alma, the founder of the church, at the age of 82 and the death of Mosiah at the age of 63 in the 33rd year of his reign. This transition took place *509 years after Lehi left Jerusalem* (29.37-47).

11

ALMA

The readers' journey continues with the ninth book found within the Book of Mormon, a sixty-three chapter book called 'the Book of Alma, the Son of Alma' that covers 186 pages in the 1830 edition and contains some 88,358 words, making it the longest individual book in the Book of Mormon. This is the second of the books that the readers encounter of the abridgement attributed to Mormon. The Book of Alma continues the story that leaves off in Mosiah with attention initially focused on Alma, the first of the judges to rule the Nephites.

Like Mosiah, the Book of Alma has somewhat of a meandering structure and style, with duplicate accounts of the same events, and retrospective retellings of the same stories. But as one delves deeper into the book a certain narrative structure emerges. While there are numerous ways to outline the Book of Alma, literarily and theologically the book may be divided into eight parts:[1]

Part One – Alma Faces Opposition from Nehor, Priestcraft, Amilici, as well as the Lamanites, and He Resigns his Judgeship to Preach (1.1-4.20)

Part Two – Alma Preaches and Establishes the Church (5.1-16.21)

Part Three – The Ministry and Preaching of the Sons of Mosiah amongst the Lamanites (17.1-29.17)

---

[1] For a similar, though not identical, division of the text cf. Hardy, *Understanding the Book of Mormon: A Reader's Guide*, p. 106.

Part Four – The Activities of an Anti-Christ Named Korihor,
and Alma's and Amulek's subsequent Mission
amongst the Zoramites (30.1-35.14)

Part Five – Alma's Instruction to his Sons (35.15-42.31)

Part Six – The Sons of Alma Preach and Moroni Leads the
Nephites (43.1-44.24)

Part Seven – Alma's Last Prophecy and Death, Helaman and
Moroni Lead the Nephites in Various Military
Engagements (45.1-62.52)

Part Eight – The Records Are Transferred to Shiblon and then
Helaman's Son (Helaman) and the Nephites are
Victorious in the Final Battle Described in the
Book of Alma (63.1-17).

It should also be observed that in this book the readers are assisted
by the recounting of the first thirty-nine years of the reign of the
judges, of which Alma is the first. The fact that such a large book is
devoted to such a short period of time – on average nearly five pages in the 1830 edition are devoted to each year – would suggest to
the readers that the period described in Alma would be a most significant one with very important events described therein.

Shortly after being told that during Alma's reign as judge there
was 'continual peace through the land' (Mosiah 29.43), the readers
might be a bit shocked to learn in **Part One** of the Book of Alma
(1.1-4.20) that a variety of conflicts face Alma even in *the first year of
his reign!* The first section of Part One (1.1-15) describes the conflict
represented by a large and strong man, later identified as Nehor,
who was brought before Alma for judgment owing in part to his
unorthodox teaching. Two points are specifically mentioned: Nehor
believed that every priest and teacher should be supported by the
people and that all humankind will be saved at the last day and have
eternal life (1.3-4). His preaching had such an enormous impact on
the church of God he was eventually withstood by Gideon (of Mosiah 22.3-9 fame). But Nehor was stronger and killed the older Gideon with the sword (1.7-9). For this murder Nehor was brought
before Alma for judgment. Alma indicates that Nehor had introduced priestcraft among the people for the first time. The readers
would know that earlier, priestcraft was defined as men who preach
in order to get gain and praise for themselves (2 Nephi 26.29) and

who would be responsible for the crucifixion of Christ (2 Nephi 10.5). But it was for slaying the righteous Gideon that Alma, based on the law established by Mosiah, assigned the death penalty to Nehor, who confessed shortly before he died that his own teaching was contrary to the word of God (Alma 1.12-15).

The second section of Part One of the Book of Alma (1.16-33) documents that the spread of priestcraft throughout the land led to a persecution of the church of God by those who did not belong to the church of God – a division caused by attitudes toward wealth and riches (1.16-24), *during the second year of the reign of the judges*. But as the priests left their labor to impart the word of God to the people, they showed their equality by imparting their substance and not wearing costly apparel. This attitude was found among the church so much so that they did not turn away anyone in need away (1.25-30). They prospered with abundance more so than those outside the church who indulged in sorceries, idolatries, idleness, babblings, envyings, strife, wearing costly apparel, being lifted up in pride, lying, and thieving (1.31-33).

Section three of Part One (2.1-3.27) introduces, *in the fifth year of the reign of the judges*, an individual named Amlici, who was 'after the order of the man who slew Gideon by the sword' (Nehor) and desired to be king over the people, but was not elected by the people as such (2.1-7). Stirring up the people, a group later known as the Amlicites made him their king, resulting in a war with Alma and the Nephites, with 12,562 Amlicites falling in battle, while 6,562 Nephites died (2.8-19). This battle was followed by one in which the Amlicites were joined by the Lamanties, but the Nephites again prevailed with Alma personally slaying Amlici (2.20-3.3). Taking on the appearance of the Lamanites in dress and markings, the Amlicites fulfill the promises of the Lord with the curse of dark skin falling on them as it had the Lamanites (3.4-19). While the Amlicites mark themselves with a red mark on their foreheads, God marks them with dark skin. In still another battle a number of Lamanites fall to the Nephites (3.20-27).

The subject changes in section four of Part One (4.1-20), *in the sixth year of the reign of the judges*, from wars to the establishment of the church, with Alma baptizing in the waters of Sidon, ironically the same waters into which the corpses of the Lamanites and Amlicites had been cast (2.34; 3.3)! Alma's ministry was so effective that, *in the seventh year of the reign of the judges*, 3,500 souls were united to the church of God and were baptized (4.1-5). But once again, already by *the eighth year of the reign of the judges* the church was torn apart by pride resulting from their riches, flocks, and costly apparel, with these sins so characterizing their lives that such activities became a stumbling block to those outside the church (4.6-10). Owing to the great wickedness of the church and the extreme economic inequalities *in the ninth year of the reign of the judges* Alma was led to appoint Nephihah as the chief judge, with Alma resigning his post in order to retain the title and function of high priest and to preach to the people. This transition took place by 'the spirit of revelation and prophecy' (4.11-20).

Part Two of the Book of Alma (5.1-16.21) recounts Alma's preaching ministry and the establishment of the church. Section one of Part Two (5.1-6.6) gives an account of Alma's preaching at Zarahemla as well as the establishment of the church, including baptizing in the waters of Mormon. Using dozens of rhetorical questions Alma encourages his hearers to remember a variety of things related to their salvation and the deliverance of their fathers in order to repent to be saved (5.1-32). Appealing to the call of the good shepherd, he urges repentance lest their rejection of his call reveals that they are children of the devil (5.33-42). Bearing testimony to those things spoken to 'our fathers', the truthfulness of Alma's words is underscored by several appearances of the word 'true' and its cognates – a testimony offered to encourage the hearers to 'repent and be born again' (5.43-49). The call to repentance is further underscored by a fourfold reference to the words of the Spirit (5.50-52). The sermon concludes with a warning to those who persist in wickedness (5.53-57) and an assurance that those who respond to the good shepherd can be baptized unto repentance and partake of the fruit of the tree of life (5.57-62). After the sermon the establishment of the church in Zarahemla is further described with priests and elders being ordained by the laying on of hands (6.1-6).

The second section of Part Two of the Book of Alma (6.7-7.27) is devoted to a description of the establishment of the church in Gideon and Alma's preaching there. The mention that the city of Gideon was named for the man whom Nehor killed with the sword keeps the archetypal advocate of priestcraft before the eyes of the readers (6.7-8). This narrative description gives way to a recounting of Alma's sermon. Unlike his sermon to those in Zarahemla, this sermon is filled with hope, optimism, and joy with regard to this church's spiritual situation (7.1-6). Alma gives testimony of the Redeemer who is to come, using language reminiscent of the words of John the Baptist. He goes so far as to name the mother of this Redeemer, Mary – a virgin, who conceived by the power of the Holy Ghost – who will give birth in Jerusalem to the Son of God, who will take upon himself 'the pains and sicknesses of his people', 'loose the bands of death', 'take upon him the sins of his people', and 'blot out their transgressions' (7.7-13). This testimony is followed by exhortations to 'repent', be 'born again', 'be washed from your sins', 'going into the waters of baptism', and 'keeping the commandments of God' (7.14-16). Alma's confidence in their faithfulness is revealed in part by the concentration of 'path' language in 7.17-21 to describe their righteous lives. Alma's farewell includes multiple exhortations to live godly lives with several appearances of the idea of spotless garments (7.22-27).

The third section of Part Two of the Book of Alma (8.1-16.21) briefly recounts Alma's successful preaching to those in Melek, *during the tenth year of the reign of the judges*, where 'they were baptized throughout the land' (8.1-5) and contains an extended discussion of his ministry in Ammonihah (8.6-16.21). After encountering initial rejection and leaving the city (8.6-13), Alma is directed to return to Ammonihah for the inhabitants of the city will perish if they do not repent (8.14-17). Upon his return to the city Alma asks a man for something to eat. This man, Amulek by name, turns out to be a Nephite who hosts Alma – whom he knows to be a holy prophet of God – for many days before preaching repentance to the people whose lives had grown more gross in iniquities. When Alma and Amulek go out to preach, they are filled with the Holy Spirit and given power that makes them invincible to the malicious intents of the people (8.18-32). The initial response of the people is to challenge Alma's authority to preach, asking why they should believe his prophesy of the destruction of the city. The full irony of these words would not be clear to the readers until later in the narrative (9.1-6).

As the people desired to harm Alma by laying hands upon him, he begins to preach, even as the people tried to contend with him.

Reminding his hearers of the numerous things they need to remember but have forgotten, Alma urges them to repent (9.7-12).
Citing words found initially in 2 Nephi 1.20, Alma warns his hearers
that those who remember and keep the commandments will prosper, while those who do not will be cut off from the Lord's presence. If this had been seen among the Lamanites, it would be more
tolerable for them than Nephites who refuse to repent, for the
Lamanites will be sent to them to make war. Owing to the many
blessings, including gifts, tongues, preaching, the Holy Ghost, translation, the Nephites' judgment will be greater than that of the Lamanites (9.13-24). Alma next appeals to the words of an angel who
calls the people to repent and warns that they will reap according to
their works (9.25-30). But Alma's words are met with anger on the
part of his audience (9.31-33).

At this point Amulek preaches to the crowd, recounting his pedigree – all the way back to Joseph, Jacob's son. He then tells of his
rebellion against God and an angel's subsequent preparation of him
to receive the holy man Alma who has blessed his house (9.34-
10.11). After this, lawyers seek to catch Alma and Amulek in their
words (10.12-16), but Amulek knows their thoughts and rebukes
them (10.17-23). However, the words of Amulek are misconstrued
and he is accused of being a child of the devil. One of the foremost
to accuse Amulek is Zeezrom (10.24-32). The observation that the
objective of the lawyers is to get gain leads to an interlude about the
value of Nephite currency (11.1-20). After the interlude Zeezrom
interrogates Amulek, who confronts his accuser with the charge of
lying (11.21-38) and then speaks to him about the resurrection and
the restoration that shall come explaining how the mortal body –
mentioned three times in 11.45 – becomes immortal. Upon hearing
these words the people are astonished while Zeezrom begins to
tremble (11.38-46). Alma also addresses Zeezrom, unfolding the
Scriptures beyond what Amulek could do. Specifically, he too
speaks about the resurrection of the dead and the judgment that is
to follow (12.1-18).

At this point, Antionah, the chief ruler, begins to quiz Alma
about the change from mortality to immortality and the relationship
between Adam and Eve and the fruit of the tree of life and the garden of Eden (12.19-21). In response, Alma explains the plan of redemption and the necessity of the fall in order that there be a pre-

paratory state here on earth (12.22-37). He goes on to describe the way God ordained priests 'after the order of the Son', 'called and prepared from the foundation of the world'. Alma repeatedly makes use of 'holy' language in the description of the origins and nature of the priesthood that is founded in the Only Begotten Son. Melchizedek is offered as an example of one who took upon himself the high priesthood forever, who himself preached repentance to his people (13.1-20). The sermon closes with an urgent call for repentance and an emphasis upon the soon coming of the Lord (13.21-31).

Even as many believed – repenting and searching the Scriptures – Alma and Amulek were bound with strong cords and taken before the chief judge of the land and accused of a variety of offenses caused by their words. The accusations were so outrageous that Zeezrom was astonished and confessed, 'Behold, I am guilty, and these men are spotless before God', as he pled for them (14.1-7). Those in Ammonihah who believed the word of the Lord were brought together, including wives and children, and cast into the fire to die before the eyes of Alma and Amulek, who were constrained by the Spirit not to intervene (14.8-13). Afterwards, Alma and Amulek were smitten by the chief judge, thrown into prison, beaten, spat upon, starved, and stripped of their clothing (14.14-22). After much suffering, Alma and Amulek broke their cords, at which point an earthquake rent the walls of the prison in 'twain', with many falling to the ground. As Alma and Amulek left the prison unhurt, but apparently still naked, great fear struck the people who fled from their presence (14.23-29).

Departing from the city they went to the land of Sidom where they were reunited with those believers who escaped from the land of Ammonihah (15.1-2). In Sidom, Zeerom lay ill, burning with a fever and in great distress owing to his role in the recent events in Ammonihah. Calling for Alma and Amulek to come to him he declared his faith in Alma's words that tied healing to redemption. Zeezrom was healed according to his faith, with Alma baptizing Zeezrom, who preached from that time forward to the people (15.3-12). Word of these remarkable events spread throughout the land of Sidom, where Alma established the church complete with teachers and elders and many were baptized (15.13-14). Meanwhile, the hard-heartedness of those at Ammonihah had not dissipated, as their alignment with the profession of Nehor continued (15.15-19). *In the eleventh year of the reign of the judges* the Lamanites overran and destroyed the city of Ammonihah and took its people captive. At the instruction of Alma, Zoram, the chief captain of the armies of the Nephites, and his two sons, Lehi and Aha, retrieved all the Nephites taken, with not one soul lost. The carnage of the fall of Ammonihah resulted in the place being referred to as the Desolation of Nehors, 'for they were of the profession of Nehor, who were slain and their lands remained desolate' (16.1-12).

The peace that followed (*until the fourteenth year of the reign of the judges*) allowed space for the church to be established, with no inequality amongst them and the Spirit poured out on all (16.13-17). The priests preached against all sorts of vices and predicted the coming of the Son of God to the Lehites after his resurrection in the old world (16.18-21).

Part Three of the Book of Alma (17.1-28.13) is devoted to the ministry and preaching of the sons of Mosiah amongst the Lamanites. In section one (17.1-4) of Part Three, as Alma was making his way to the land of Gideon he encountered the sons of Mosiah who were returning from a fourteen year ministry amongst the Lamanites, many of whom, owing to the teaching of these brothers, came to the knowledge of the truth. They were extraordinary teachers who possessed the spirit of prophecy and revelation (17.1-4). Last mentioned in Mosiah 28.9, these sons turned down leadership of their father's kingdom, entered into the wilderness, fasted and prayed much, were comforted by the Spirit, and reassured with the Lord's promise, 'I will make an instrument of thee in my hands unto the salvation of many'. With these words of promise they separated from one another and went to evangelize the Lamanites, who were described as 'wild', 'hardened', 'ferocious', who delighted in murdering, robbing, plundering, with their hearts set upon riches, gold, silver, and precious stones. They did not labor with their own hands, they worshipped idols, and they bore the curse of God (17.5-17).

In section two of Part Three (17.18-19.36), Ammon, the chief son, went to the land of Ishmael, where he was bound and taken to King Lamoni, who instead of killing him made of Ammon a servant. Ammon served the king faithfully, defending his flocks, cutting off the arms of his adversaries, appendages that were subsequently carried to the King (17.18-39). Ammon engages Lamoni about the Great Spirit, and eventually teaches him the Gospel (18.1-39). Believing Ammon's words, King Lamoni began to cry out to the Lord for mercy, then fell to the earth as though dead, being lifeless for two days and two nights (18.40-43). Believing that King Lamoni was dead, as they were preparing to take him for burial, the queen, having heard of Ammon, called for him. Ammon assured her that Lamoni was not dead but knew that he was carried away in God, experiencing the light of everlasting life. Believing the word of Ammon, the queen refused Lamoni burial (19.1-10). The next day, at the word of Ammon the king arose and told of his encounter with the Redeemer. At this, both Lamoni and his queen were overpowered by the Spirit, falling down. As Ammon gave thanks to God, overpowered with joy, the king's servants who witnessed these events all fell to the ground as well (19.11-16). However, one Lamanitish woman named Abish, who had been converted many years before, knew these phenomena to be the result of the power of God. Thus, she went from house to house gathering the people. But when they saw that Ammon was a Nephite, some of the people began to murmur. One person went so far as to try to kill Ammon with a sword, but fell down dead himself. And there was great contention among them (19.17-27). In the midst of this contention, Abish touched the hand of the queen, who stood and exclaimed, 'O blessed Jesus, who has saved me from an awful hell! O blessed God, have mercy on this people!' She also spoke many words the people did not understand, an apparent glossolalic utterance. When she touched Lamoni's hand he arose and taught the words he heard from Ammon to those gathered. Ammon too ministered to them and many believed and were baptized with a church established (19.28-36).

Section three of Part Three (20.1-30) recounts how despite Lamoni's invitation to meet his father, the voice of the Lord revealed to Ammon that his brothers (Aaron, Muloki, and Ammah) were in prison in the land of Middoni. Upon hearing this news from Ammon, Lamoni organized the trip and accompanied Ammon (20.1-7). On their way they encountered Lamoni's father, who was the king over all the land. Being angry with his son about not attending the feast and being in the company of a Nephite, 'one of the children of a liar', he tried in vain to get Lamoni to slay Ammon, but his son refused. Filled with anger, Lamoni's father attempted to kill his son but was prevented from doing so by Ammon. Understanding that he was powerless to harm Ammon and that Ammon had prevented him from killing his innocent son – perhaps losing his soul in the process – Lamoni's father granted the release of Ammon's brothers and granted that Lamoni could rule his own kingdom without supervision. True to his word, the brothers of Ammon were released from prison where they had suffered hunger, thirst, and all kinds of afflictions (20.8-30).

Section four of Part Three (21.1-25.16) is devoted for the most part to the activity of Mosiah's son Aaron. Aaron's journey took him to a place called 'Jerusalem' by the Lamanites where he not only encountered Lamanites, but also Amalekites and Amulonites who possessed harder hearts that the Lamanites. Preaching in their synagogues – built according to the instructions 'of the order of the Nehors' – Aaron was mocked. Having little missionary success there, he departed for a village called Ani-Anti, where he joined his brothers Muloki and Ammah in preaching (21.1-11). The story of the imprisonment and subsequent release of Aaron and his brethren in Middoni by Lamoni and Ammon is retold, with the additional note that those delivered were fed and clothed upon their release (21.12-14). Led by the Spirit they next preached in every synagogue of the Amalekites and assemblies of the Lamanites (where admitted), bringing many to the truth (21.15-17). At this point, Ammon and Lamoni return to the land of Ishmael where Lamoni built synagogues and Ammon preached to the people of King Lamoni (21.18-23).

Meanwhile, Aaron and his brethren preached in the land of Nephi, gaining admittance to the house of Lamoni's father, the king over all the land except for the land of Ishmael. Explaining that God is the Great Spirit about whom the king had been troubled, beginning with creation Aaron explained the plan of redemption to the king. At this point the king prays:

O God, Aaron hath told me that there is a god; and if there is a god, and if thou art god, wilt thou make thyself known unto me, and I will give away all my sins to thee, and that I may be raised from the dead, and be saved at the last day (22.18).

Praying for forgiveness as Aaron directed, the king bowed down and was struck down as if he were dead (as Lamoni before him). When his queen heard of these events she was angry and desired that Aaron and his brethren be slain. However, the reluctance of the servants caused the queen herself to be afraid. At this point Aaron put forth his hand and raised the king from the earth, who began to minister to all and his household was converted, prompting the king to ask Aaron and his brethren to preach the word to the gathered multitude, a proclamation the king sent throughout the entire land (22.1-35).

This encounter led the king of the Lamanites to issue a proclamation protecting Aaron, Omner, Himni, and any of their brethren in order that they might preach unhindered, convincing the Lamanites that the Nephites are their brothers and that they desist from various sinful activities (23.1-2). This proclamation resulted in Aaron and his brethren preaching throughout the land (the lands of Ishmael, Middoni, Shilom, and the cities of Nephi, Lemuel, and Shimnilom) with many of the Lamanites brought to the knowledge of the truth, though not the Amulonites. The fruit of the Lamanites' repentance was the putting down of the weapons of their rebellion against God and their brethren. So complete was the conversion of the king and his people that they desired to have a name that would distinguish them from their Lamanite brethren. In consultation with Aaron and their priests they were called Anti-Nephi-Lehies,[2] they became friendly with the Nephites, and the curse of God followed them no more (23.3-18).

When the Amalekites discovered that not all the Lamanites had converted, they stirred up the unconverted Lamanites to rebel against the Lamanite king and to attack Anti-Nephi-Lehi's people. The king, who would die within a year, named Lamoni's brother Anti-Nephi-Lehi as king. Seeing the nature of the Lamanites' preparation for war, Ammon called a council to determine how they might defend themselves against the Lamanites. Astonishingly, not one person amongst all those converted would take up arms against their brethren nor prepare for war (24.1-6). The theological justifi-

---

[2] Rust (*Feasting on the Word*, p. 145) suggests that the etymology of the word 'anti-' conveys the sense of 'against' or 'opposite' as in a 'reflection in a mirror', thus here meaning 'a similarity or likeness' – signifying something of 'the Lamanites' desire to be like the prophet-fathers Nephi and Lehi'.

cation of their decision is made clear in King Anti-Nephi-Lehi's address that follows:

> I ... thank my God, that ... we have been convinced of our sins, and of the many murders we have committed ... since God hath taken away our stains, and our swords have become bright, then let us stain our swords no more with the blood of our brethren ... for perhaps, if we should stain our swords again they can no more be washed bright through the blood of the Son of our great God, which shall be shed for the atonement of our sins. And now, my brethren, if our brethren seek to destroy us, behold, we will hide away our swords, yea, even we will bury them deep in the earth, that they might be kept bright, as a testimony that we have never used them, at the last day; and if our brethren destroy us, behold, we shall go to our God and shall be saved (24.7-16).

Moved by these words, the Anti-Nephi-Lehies buried their weapons deep in the earth as a testimony to God as, 'they buried the weapons of war, for peace' (24.17-19). As the Lamanites came down upon them, the Anti-Nephi-Lehies came out to meet them, prostrated themselves, and called upon the Lord. When 1,005 had been slain and the Lamanites saw all this, they cast down their own weapons and more than 1,000 were brought to salvation that day, but none of the Amalekites or Amulonites – those after the order of Nehor – were among them. In frustration about their actions against their own brothers, some of the unconverted Lamanites sought to take out their vengeance upon the Nephites, but they were driven out and/or slain by the Nephites (24.20-25.3).

Almost all of those who died were the descendants of Amulon and his brethren, who were priests of Noah, a number of whom died by fire. In this, Abinadi's words (Mosiah 13.10) came to pass about the descendants of the priests of Noah dying by fire. Many of the rest began to disbelieve the traditions of their fathers and believe in the Lord. As the Lamanites could not withstand the Nephites they began to join themselves to the people of God, the people of Anti-Nephi-Lehi, burying their weapons of war, as had their brethren, becoming righteous people, keeping the commandments and statutes of the Lord. They kept the law of Moses as a type of the coming of Christ, relying on the spirit of prophecy (25.4-16).

Section Five of Part Three of the Book of Alma (25.17-26.37) finds the sons of Mosiah reunited and rejoicing over their experience. Ammon, Aaron, Omner, Himni, and their brethren rejoiced exceedingly because the Lord granted to them all they asked in the evangelism of their Lamanite brethren verifying his word in every particular (25.17). At this point Ammon began to exhort his brethren to rejoice and sing owing to the great deliverance of the Lamanties out of the darkest abyss into the marvelous light of God – an event thought almost unbelievable when they set out on this mission (26.1-9). When Aaron cautioned Ammon about not getting too carried away 'unto boasting', Ammon rejoiced all the more, boasting in the Lord who had accomplished these great things, bringing thousands of souls to repentance. Reminding his brethren of the way they were laughed at to scorn by their fellow Nephites who preferred to take up arms against the Lamanites, Ammon again underscores the way in which God extended his mercies amongst the Lamanites. The fruit of their labors is seen by the fact that their converts would prefer to lay down their lives rather than take up arms against their brethren – a love so great that it has never been seen among the Nephites! 'God is mindful of every people, whatsoever land they may be in … his bowels of mercy are over all the earth' (26.10-37).

Section Six of Part Three of the Book of Alma (27.1-28.14) recounts the preservation of the Anti-Nephi-Lehies and their incorporation into the Nephites. The anger of the Amalekites continued to wax strong against the Anti-Nephi-Lehies, so much so that they attacked them once more and again the Anti-Nephi-Lehies refused to take up arms allowing themselves to be slain. Moved with compassion Ammon negotiated for the Anti-Nephi-Lehies to go down to the Nephites (27.1-15). During this time Ammon and his brethren met Alma. The joy of their reunion was so great that Ammon was overcome and fell to the earth (27.16-19). The Nephites received the Anti-Nephi-Lehies, giving them as an inheritance the land of Jershon, in exchange for Anti-Nephi-Lehi support for the Nephite army. They became known as the 'people of Ammon', being numbered amongst the people of Nephi, never again taking up arms against their brethren, being 'a zealous and beloved people, a highly favored people of the Lord' (27.20-29). After the church was established in Jershon the Lamanites again attacked, with tens of thousands slain and scattered abroad. Even amongst the Nephites there was great mourning over the losses the battle brought (28.1-13), as *the fifteenth year of the reign of the judges* came to a close.

Section Six concludes Part Three of the Book of Alma (29.1-17) and consists of words that reflect upon the recent missionary successes. Significantly, the identity of the speaker is not altogether clear. Though generally attributed to Alma, the immediate antecedent is Ammon and his brethren (28.8), to whom the narrative eventually returns (30.20; cf. also the immediate mention of 'the people of Ammon' when these words conclude in 30.1). The words themselves focus on the desire of the speaker to trumpet forth a call for repentance to every soul on the face of the earth. Careful not to overstep the place appointed him by God, the speaker does glory in what he has been commanded to do, the repentance resulting from his being an instrument in the hands of God, and the joy such repentance brings to his soul. However, such joy is not restricted to his own success but is fuller owing to the success of his brethren who have gone up to the land of Nephi (29.1-17). Such a sentiment fits well with Ammon's earlier response to Aaron's caution (26.10-37). Whatever the identity of the speaker, the readers would no doubt be reminded of Ammon's earlier words.

Part Four of the Book of Alma (30.1-35.14) is devoted to the activities of an Anti-Christ named Korihor, and Alma's subsequent mission amongst the Zoramites (30.1-35.14). In the first section of Part Four of the Book of Alma no sooner are the readers told of continual peace throughout all the land during *the sixteenth and seventeenth year of the reign of the judges* (30.1-5) than they learn of the arrival and activities of an Anti-Christ named Korihor. Though other figures are sometimes referred to by commentators on the Book of Mormon as Anti-Christ figures, this is the first and only individual in the book actually called an Anti-Christ. Korihor's message consisted of preaching against the prophecies concerning the coming of Christ and that there could be no atonement for the sins of men. The result of his preaching was an increase in wickedness and whoredoms for he argued that when a man died 'that was the end thereof'. When Korihor preached in Jershon the people of Ammon bound him and took him before Ammon the high priest, who expelled Korihor from the land (30.6-21).

Moving to the land of Gideon, Korihor was taken bound to a high priest and chief judge named Giddonah who challenged him about speaking against the prophecies of the holy prophets. Korihor argued that the people were in bondage owing to the traditions of their fathers, that Giddonah could not know if the ancient prophecies were true, that children are not guilty owing to the transgression of a parent, and that it was impossible to know if there would be a Christ who would be slain for the sins of the world. Seeing his obstinacy, the officers brought Korihor before Alma and the chief judge, where Korihor continued in his claims, now charging that the priests and teachers glutted themselves on the labors of the people (30.21b-30). Bitterly denying this last charge, Alma begins an interrogation of Korihor, charging that he has a lying spirit. When Korihor asked for a sign, he was struck dumb. Unable to speak, Korihor wrote a confession about how the devil appeared to him in the form of an angel and taught him what to say. Refusing to pray for the removal of this curse, Alma turned Korihor out to a life of begging for his food – serving as a sign to all the people. Eventually joining the Zoramites, Korihor was trodden down by them until he was dead (30.31-60).

The second section of Part Four of the Book of Alma (31.1-35.14) is devoted to Alma's mission amongst the Zoramites. After Korihor came to his end, word came to Alma that a man named Zoram and his followers, the Zoramites, who had separated themselves from the Nephites, were leading the people to bow down to dumb idols. Thus, Alma took Ammon, Aaron, Omner, Amulek, Zeezrom, and two of his sons, Shiblon and Corianton to preach to the Zoramites (31.1-11). Upon arrival they discovered that the Zoramite synagogues had a place built up in the center, above the heads of the other worshippers upon which there was room for only one person. The prayer uttered from there was one that focused upon the rejection of the traditions of their brethren (the Nephites), the affirmation of the eternality of God as spirit, the fact that there shall be no Christ, and that they had been the elect of God. Each worshipper uttered the identical prayer and after returning to their homes never spoke of God again until the next week when they assembled (31.12-23). These things grieved Alma's heart greatly for he saw their love of gold, silver, fine goods, costly apparel, ringlets, bracelets and that they were filled with pride. Therefore, Alma cried out to the Lord asking that he and those with him would have success in bringing these souls again to God. And when he 'clapped' his hands upon them, they all were filled with the Holy Spirit (31.24-38).

So they went out and preached in synagogues, houses, and streets where they found success with the poor who had been cast out of the synagogues because of the coarseness of their apparel, being regarded as filthy. Such 'poor in heart' ones came to Alma prepared to hear the word (32.1-6). Thus, Alma directs his words to them saying that God is not worshipped in synagogues alone nor worshipped only once a week. Underscoring the need for humility, Alma encourages those who humble themselves, repent of their sins, believe the word of God, and are baptized without stubbornness of heart – who have faith without the need for a sign (32.7-20).

Alma continued his preaching by offering the Zoramites an opportunity to participate in an experiment of faith in which the mercy of God is foundational, with his word being given to everyone, men and women and even children (32.21-23). The word is compared to a seed, which when received (though not with perfect knowledge) increases faith for it enlightens understanding. In like manner the growth of the seed reveals that it is good seed. Ultimately growing into a tree, one who believes can pluck and partake of the tree of life (32.24-43). In response to Zoramite questions about how they might obtain this fruit, Alma points them to the words of the ancient prophet Zenos noting the many locations in which God responded to his prayers, 'because of thy Son' (33.1-11). Pressing the Zoramites on to faith in the Son of God, Alma cites the words of Zenock and then refers to the type Moses raised in the wilderness for the healing of those who looked upon it as pointing to the Son of God who would suffer and die to atone for sins, rise again, bring the resurrection to pass, and judge at the last day. Thus, Alma closes with an appeal to the Zoramites to plant the seed of Christ in their hearts, nourishing it by their faith, and letting it become a tree, springing up into everlasting life – 'And even all this you can do if ye will' (33.12-23).

When Alma ceased speaking, his missionary partner Amulek began to teach the Zoramites. Rehearsing some of the words of Alma, Amulek gives his own testimony with regard to the coming of Christ among the children of men to atone for the sins of the world, for 'an infinite and eternal sacrifice' is a necessity. Such a sacrifice fulfills the law of Moses in every jot and tittle (34.1-16). In the light of this plan of redemption, Amulek gives a visceral appeal to the Zoramites to pray in all places and at all times, being certain to accompany their prayers with caring for the needy, naked, sick, and afflicted, lest their prayers reveal them to be hypocrites (34.17-29). Amulek concludes his words by calling upon the Zoramites to repent without procrastination, for the same spirit that possesses one's body at death possesses one's body afterward. It is essential that they remember these things, not deny the coming of Christ, not contend anymore against the Holy Ghost, take upon themselves the name of Christ, humble themselves, live in thanksgiving daily, exhort the brethren, be watchful, have patience, and endure afflictions (34.30-41).

After these words the missionaries went into the land of Jershon, amongst the people of Ammon, while most of the Zoramites were angry not hearkening to the words of the missionaries. Those who believed in the words spoken by Alma and his brethren were cast out of their land and went to the land of Jershon. While the chief ruler of the Zoramites was breathing out threats against those who had departed, all the poor of the Zoramites came over and were given lands for their inheritance (35.1-9). Mingling with the Lamanites, the Zoramites made war against 'the people of Ammon' and the Nephites *in the eighteenth year of the reign of the judges*. With this, Alma, Ammon, their brethren, and the two sons of Alma returned to the land of Zarahemla, having been God's instruments in bringing many Zoramites to repentance. With an inheritance in the land of Jershon, the converted Zoramites took up arms to defend themselves (35.10-14).

Part Five of the Book of Alma (35.15-42.31) consists of Alma's instruction to his sons, Helaman, Shiblon, and Corianton, beginning with a narrative introduction that describes Alma's grief and the sorrow of his heart owing to the iniquity of his people. Thus, he caused his sons to gather in order that he might give each one separately an individual charge (35.15-16). The first section of Part Five (36.1-37.47) recounts Alma's words to Helaman. Beginning with the challenge that the extent to which Helaman and the Nephites (note the plural 'ye') keep the commandments of God, to that extent they will prosper in the land. Underscoring the necessity of remembering

God's deliverance of their fathers, Alma rehearses to Helaman his conversion. While caught in the torment of the memory of his sins Alma's mind went to his father's prophesying 'the coming of one Jesus Christ, a Son of God, to atone for the sins of the world', thoughts which lead to his conversion and a vision of Lehi, God sitting upon his throne, and countless numbers of angels praising God. So that from that day on Alma worked without ceasing to bring souls to repentance, the fruit of such labors being visible before them. Again Alma testifies of his own remembrance of the experience of their father, reminding Helaman of the correlation between keeping the command of God and prospering in the land (36.1-30).

At this point, Alma entrusts the sacred records to Helaman with the command that Helaman continue to keep a record of the Nephites. This conferral would be an act that the readers might take as signaling Alma's impending death, as such is often the context for the transfer of the sacred records in the book. The brass plates conferred contain an account of the holy scriptures and are said to have already convinced many of the error of their ways, including many thousands of the Lamanites, and may yet bring many thousands more Lamanites and even Nephites to repentance. After still again reminding Helaman of the correlation between keeping the command of God and prospering in the land, Alma indicates that through these plates God will show forth his power to future generations – even the restoration of many thousands of Lamanites (37.1-20). In addition to these records, Alma speaks of the 24 gold plates (found by the people of Lemhi) and charges his son to preserve the interpreters, as well as preparing for him a stone for revelation/interpretation. Helaman is to keep their secret plans of oaths and covenants from the people, writing only of their wickedness, murders, and abominations (37.21-31). This prohibition is followed by admonitions to preach repentance, teach humility and to withstand temptation and not be weary in well doing, to remember to keep the commandments of God, to cry out to God, and to counsel with the Lord in doing all things (37.32-37).

The conclusion of Alma's words to Helaman makes reference to the ball, compass, or director, calling it 'Liahona'. Unfortunately, those entrusted with this small means (of marvelous works) were slothful and forgot to exercise it, losing their way in the wilderness by not following its direction. It functions as a type, Alma says, of the words of Christ that will take them to a far better land of promise. And with this, Alma bids this son farewell (37.38-47).

The second section of Part Five (38.1-15) is an account of Alma's words to his son Shiblon. Beginning with words about the correlation between keeping the commands of God and prospering in the land, Shiblon is praised for his steadiness and faithfulness unto God, which brings Alma great joy. Shiblon's many sufferings, endured with great patience, were made known to Alma by the Spirit of God – the same Spirit that sent an angel to Alma who confronted him face to face, resulting in Alma's cry for mercy. In abbreviated form, Alma testifies to Shiblon of his conversion. Underscoring the fact that the only means for salvation is through Christ, Alma closes his words to Shiblon with a series of instructions about avoidance of pride, overbearance, idleness, and praying as the Zoramites. Rather, Alma instructs his son to seek forgiveness for unworthiness and to show mercy to others. And with these words Alma bids farewell to Shiblon (38.1-15).

The third section of Part Five (39.1-42.31) contains Alma's words to his son Corianton, the longest of these three addresses, ostensibly because Corianton did not give heed to Alma's words, even going after the harlot 'Isabel'. What's more, apparently Corianton has come close to committing the unpardonable sin – denying the Holy Ghost after it has once had a place in him (as a believer). Alma urges his son to repent and forsake his sins and the lusts of his eyes, for his bad example has led many of the Zoramites away from the faith. After this rather extensive opening (39.1-14) Alma addresses a variety of theological issues each of which begins with an expression of Alma's perception that the topic at hand troubles Corianton's mind.

First, Alma speaks to Corianton about the certainty of the coming of Christ to take away the sins of the world. Corianton's mission is to prepare the minds of the people to prepare their children to hear the word at the time of his coming. These things have been made known beforehand owing to the fact that all deserve to hear the plan of redemption (39.15-19).

Second, Alma takes up the issue of the resurrection of the dead, another topic he perceives to be troubling Corianton's mind. The timing of the resurrection of the dead, though unknown by mortals,

will take place after the coming of Christ with a space of time existing between death and the resurrection. Concerning the state of the
soul between death and the resurrection, an angel has revealed the
answer to Alma. 'The spirits of all men, whether they be good or
evil, are taken home to that God who gave them life.' Those who
are righteous are taken to a state of happiness called paradise, while
those who are evil are cast out into outer darkness until the time of
the resurrection. Such a state should not be confused with the resurrection, which is a reuniting of the body and the soul, though the
timing of the resurrection of the wicked is not clear. Of the resurrection Alma concludes, 'The soul shall be restored to the body, and
the body to the soul; yea, and every limb and joint shall be restored
to its body; yea, even a hair of the head shall not be lost; but all
things shall be restored to their proper and perfect frame'. The
righteous shall shine forth in the kingdom of God while the unclean
will 'drink the dregs of a bitter cup' (40.1-25).

A third thing that Alma perceives to be troubling Corianton's
mind is the plan of restoration. According to Alma, restoration is
requisite with the justice of God. All things must be restored to
their proper order, even as every part of the body shall be restored
to itself. This restoration includes the judging of individuals according to their works. Those whose lives are good will be raised to endless happiness, but no one will be raised from sin to happiness for
the carnal state is contrary to the nature of happiness. Thus, Corianton is urged to be righteous, just, and merciful for it will be reward-
ed to him. Restoration is to bring back again, so if one does good,
one will receive a reward in keeping with one's life, 'for that which
ye do send out shall return to you again' (41.1-15).

The fourth thing apparently troubling Corianton's mind is taken
up next: the justice of God and the punishment of the sinner (42.1-
14). The discussion begins with an appeal to Eden, explaining that if
Adam had quickly eaten from the tree of life there would have been
no space for repentance and the plan of salvation would have been
frustrated. But having been cut off from God both temporally and
spiritually, humanity entered into a preparatory state. The plan of
redemption was dependent upon their repentance, which itself was
dependent upon an atonement for the sins of the world (42.15-28).
With the knowledge conveyed by Alma, Corianton is encouraged to
be troubled no longer and to deny the justice of God no longer, for

Corianton has been called to preach to the people – a mission Alma blesses (42.29-31).

Part Six of the Book of Alma (43.1-44.24) briefly describes Alma's sons preaching and more extensively Moroni leading the Nephites in battle against the Lamanites. The section begins with a short acknowledgement that both the sons of Alma and Alma himself went forth preaching among the people – preaching the word 'according to the spirit of prophecy ... after the holy order of God' (43.1-2).

At this point the narrative shifts back to the subject of wars between the Nephites and the Lamanites *in the eighteenth year of the reign of the judges* left off at 35.13. The non-converted Zoramites had by this time become Lamanites and began to come upon the Nephites who had to prepare for war. Zerahemnah, the leader of the Lamanties, appointed chief captains from the Amalekites, who had a more wicked and murderous disposition than the Lamanites, and from the Zoramites. The Nephites in turn were trying to preserve their lands, people, and religious freedom. The people of Ammon (the Anti-Nephi-Lehis), who had sworn off bearing arms against their brethren were still dedicating a large portion of their substance to the support of the Nephite armies, upon whom all the fighting fell. Meanwhile the Lamanites – made up of the children of Laman, Lemuel, Ishmael, and all those who dissented from the Nephites, namely the Amalekites, Zoramites, and the descendants of the priests of Noah – gathered for war (43.3-15).

The chief captain of the Nephite war effort was a twenty-five year old man named Moroni, who so out-prepared the Lamanites that the Lamanites were exceedingly afraid of the Nephite armies. Seeking to ambush Moroni's army, the Lamanites sought to circle around the Nephite forces through the wilderness. Warned both by his spies and the word of the Lord from Alma, Moroni knew his opponents' intent and thought it no sin to defend his people by 'strategem'. Having divided his army he awaited the Lamanite attack (43.16-33). When the battle began the fighting was fierce, with the Lamanites fighting like 'dragons'. But the Nephites were fighting for a better cause, so that not being guilty of the first offense, they defended their families, lands, rights, and religion (43.34-47). Eventually overcoming the Lamanites, who outnumbered the Nephites two to one, Moroni commanded a cease to the shedding of Lamanite blood (43.48-54). Making an offer of peace to Zerahemnah, Moroni's offer was rejected. In fact, Zerahemnah was so angry with Moroni that he rushed forward trying to kill him, but one of Moroni's soldiers smote with the sword cutting Zerahemnah's scalp loose. Placing the scalp on the point of his sword he warned all the Lamanites that they would fall to the earth if they did not depart with a covenant of peace. Wounded, Zerahemnah still stirred up his soldiers to fight, prompting Moroni to order their destruction. Finally, when Zerahemnah saw that all was about to be lost, he cried out to Moroni that he was prepared to covenant that they would come to war no more – at which point Moroni caused the work of death to cease. So many died in this battle that they were not numbered and many corpses were thrown into the waters of Sidon. With this Alma's record in the Plates of Nephi ends (44.1-24).

Part Seven of the Book of Alma (45.1-62.52) focuses upon Alma's last prophecy and his death, as well as Helaman and Moroni leading the Nephites in various military engagements. The first section of Part Seven (45.1-24) recounts Alma's last prophecy to Helaman, Alma's last blessing and departure from Zarahemla, and the missionary efforts of Helaman and his brethren. Alma's last prophecy is made in private to Helaman *in the nineteenth year of the reign of the judges* with explicit instructions not to make it known but to write it down only. The reason for such an instruction is because Alma prophesies that 400 hundred years after the coming of Christ the Nephites will become extinct owing to their unbelief, lasciviousness, and all manner of iniquities. Those now numbered amongst the Nephites will no longer be so, save a few disciples. Such an unexpected turn of events casts a shadow over all that follows, for the readers from this point forward know that as far as the Nephites are concerned their fate is sealed! It would also come as a bit of a shock that before the coming of Christ even occurs, an event long prophesied in the Book of Mormon, the ultimate disappointing fate of the Nephites is revealed, a prophecy that in some ways would seem to undermine the significance of Christ's coming for the Nephites, as not even his coming to them can save them from such a fate!

After this prophecy Alma blesses Helaman, his other sons, and the earth for righteousness' sake, but ominously warns of the curse that will come upon the land owing to the wickedness done upon it, 'for the Lord cannot look upon sin with the least degree of allowance'. After blessing the church Alma departed from the land of Zarahemla and was never heard from again. The assumption of the writer(s) of the Book of Alma is that, like Moses, Alma was received by the spirit of the Lord (45.15-19). Despite the work of Helaman and his brethren in declaring the word, establishing the church, and appointing priests and teachers over the churches, a dissension arose at the instigation of those not giving heed to Helaman and his brethren – those who were proud owing to their great riches (45.20-24).

The second section of Part Seven (46.1-51.37) is devoted to recounting a series of events in the Amalickiahite wars against the Nephites. The leader of those angry with Helaman and his brethren was a large and strong man named Amalickiah, who desired to be king and used flatteries to gain the support of various followers (46.1-10). When Moroni heard of this situation he was angry and rent his coat, writing upon a piece of it the words, 'In memory of our God, our religion and freedom, and our peace, our wives, and our children'. He then fastened this piece of cloth onto a pole calling it the 'Title of Liberty' and prayed for the cause of Christians and the freedom of the land. Moroni then waved this 'Title of Liberty' amongst the people as a rallying call for those who would maintain this title, to which a number of individuals came running, casting their garments at Moroni's feet, and promising that if they should prove unfaithful in their commitment to God that they should be rent even as they had rent their garments (46.11-27).

When Amalickiah saw that the Nephites outnumbered them, and that his people were doubtful about their own cause, he led them away into the land of Nephi. But Moroni followed them into the wilderness to cut them off, putting to death any of the Amalickites who would not enter into a covenant of peace. Following this, Moroni planted the standard of liberty amongst the Nephites: the standard being displayed from every tower in the land (46.28-41).

Meanwhile, Amalickiah and some of his men escaped to the land of Nephi and enlisted the support of the king of the Lamanites to do battle with the Nephites, but the king's followers greatly feared going into battle. Frustrated with this turn of events, the king gave Amalickiah command of that part of his army. Thus, Amalickiah, who all the while desired to dethrone the Lamanite king, set about to gain favor with the Lamanite army. He also made entreaties to a rival king, Lehonti, to meet with him and convinced this king of his support, becoming Lehonti's second in command. Having one of his servants poison Lehonti by degrees, Amalickiah became leader in his stead. Returning to the Lamanite king under the pretense of peace, Amalickiah's servants killed the king by stabbing him in the heart. Pretending to be upset at the king's death, Amalickiah led the Lamanites, conquered the Lamanite city called Nephi, and took the wife of the fallen king as his own wife. At this point in the narrative the composition of the Lamanites is again delineated as composed of the Lamanites, Lemuelites, Ishmaelites, and dissenters from Nephi, who became wilder, more wicked, and ferocious than the Lamanites – entirely forgetting the Lord their God (47.1-36).

Amalickiah wasted little time in consolidating his power as king, inspiring his followers against the Nephites as he desired to be king over all the land. Hardening the Lamanites' hearts and blinding their minds, he appointed Zoramite chief captains over his army. But Moroni fortified the Nephite positions by erecting small forts, throwing up banks of earth, building walls of stone, and placing most of his soldiers in their weakest fortifications, seeking to protect liberty, lands, wives, children, and peace (48.1-10).

The magnitude of Moroni's work caused his extraordinary skills to be praised at this point in the text. Not delighting in taking blood, he was a man of perfect understanding who defended his people, his rights, his country, and his religion even to the loss of blood. As the relationship between keeping the commandments of God and prospering in the land is once again raised, Moroni is described in glowing, almost hyperbolic terms – if all men were as him the very gates of hell would have been shaken – the devil would never have power over the hearts of men – he was a man like unto Ammon – even the other sons of Mosiah – like unto Alma and his sons. Neither is Helaman excluded from extraordinary praise for he preached and baptized, his words causing many to humble themselves (48.11-20). But despite their desire for peace, the fact that they did not delight in the shedding of blood, and their sorrow for having to take up arms, the Nephites were eventually compelled to contend with their brethren the Lamanites. For the Nephites could not stand aside so long as there were those who kept the commandments of God and prospered in the land (48.21-25).

When the armies of the Lamanites finally decided to attack the Nephites they expected easy victories owing to the previous condition of the city of Ammonihah and the city of Noah. But Moroni's fortifications were so extraordinary, being of a nature never known amongst the sons of Lehi before, instead of experiencing easy victories over the Nephites, the Lamanite armies suffered catastrophic defeats. In the battle of the city of Noah, all the Lamanite chief captains and more than one thousand of their men were slain, while not a single Nephite was killed, though about fifty were wounded. When word of the results of the battle reached King Amalickiah, who was himself born a Nephite, he cursed God and swore that he would drink Moroni's blood, while the Nephites thanked the Lord their God for his matchless delivering power (49.1-30).

Despite such victories Moroni did not stop making preparations for war but constructed a series of high and strong towers (*in the twentieth year of the reign of the judges*) that their opponents could not reach and from which the Nephites could cast stones down upon their opponents. Moroni united Nephite holdings from east to west in a straight line and cut off the strongholds of the Lamanites. Further, the Nephites began construction of the cities named Moroni, Nephihah, and Lehi (50.1-16). As a result, *in the twenty-first year of the reign of the judges* the people of Nephi prospered greatly in accord with the promise to those who keep the commandments of God (50.17-22a), while thousands of their wicked brethren were in bondage, perished, or dwindled in unbelief (50.22b). So prosperous were these times for the obedient Nephites that it was said:

> But behold, there was never a happier time among the people of Nephi, since the days of Nephi, than in the days of Moroni, yea, even at this time, in the twenty and first year of the reign of the judges (50.23).

It appears that the zenith of happiness for the Nephites – at least before the coming of Christ – was reached at this time. Yet, such a statement might generate a question in the minds of the readers about whether Mormon is implying more, since at this point he is apparently looking back on this period from the passage of several centuries. The peace here described would last for the next two years (*the twenty-second and twenty-third year of the reign of the judges*) as well (50.24).

This peace was interrupted not by Lamanite attacks but by an internal dispute over land that bordered the land of Lehi and the land of Morianton. In fact, the inhabitants of the latter invaded the land of the former, whose inhabitants fled to the camp of Moroni. Fearing that Moroni would send his armies upon them, Morianton, the leader of the people of Morianton, devised a plan to flee with his people to the north. Not only had the people of Lehi informed Moroni of Morianton's actions, but one of his maid servants, whom Morianton had beaten much, also fled to Moroni, informing him of Morianton's intentions to flee. As a result, Moroni sent an army led by Teancum who caught up to the Morianton army, slaying Morianton, defeating his army, taking prisoners, and returning to Moroni. At this point the people of Morianton took a covenant of peace, were restored to their land, and were united with the people of Lehi (50.25-36). In this same year Nephihah, the second chief judge, died and his son Pahoran was appointed to fill his seat (50.37-40).

However, *in the twenty-fifth year of the reign of the judges* a controversy broke out over Pahoran's role as chief judge brought by a group who wanted certain laws modified – something Pahoran would not do – wanted Pahoran dethroned, the overthrow of the free government, and the installation of a (Nephite) king. These were called 'King-men'. Those who believed Pahoran should be retained as judge were called Freemen. The issue was settled by the voice of the people, which came in favor of the Freemen, so Pahoran was retained. The agenda of the king-men, primarily those of high birth who sought to rule over the people, was defeated, at least for a time (51.1-8).

Meanwhile, Amalickiah was preparing 'a wonderfully great army' and himself led the army against his enemy Moroni, whose blood he had sworn to drink, an oath taken by his army as well. The readers would be alerted to the connection between Amalickiah's and the intervening Nephite contentions around Pahoran, as this story is surrounded by references to the contentions at the beginning and end of this reference to Amalickiah and his intentions (51.9-12, cf. esp. vv. 9 and 12). When the king-men heard of Amalickiah's preparations for war they were glad in their hearts and refused to take up arms to defend their country – so angry were they with Pahoran. When Moroni became aware of this he was filled with anger and made arrangements with Pahoron to pursue these king-men and either humble them with the sword or compel them to defend their country. In the resulting confrontation, four thousand dissenters were killed by the sword, their leaders were imprisoned, the title of freedom was flown from every tower, while others chose to fight valiantly for their freedom from potential Lamanite bondage (51.13-21). Perhaps the readers would be taken by the difference in response to these who refused to take up arms and the Anti-Nephi-Lehies.

While Moroni was busy sorting out the contention with the king-men the Lamanites invaded and captured the Nephite cities of Moroni, Nephihah, Lehi, Morianton, Omner, Gid, and Mulek (51.22-27). Amalickiah intended to continue his conquest by taking the city of Bountiful, but he encountered the Nephite army led by Teancum, who had killed Morianton earlier. Every one of Teancum's warriors exceeded his Lamanite counterpart in strength and skill of war, so that they killed the Lamanites until dark. At this point, Teancum entered into the Lamanite camp while everyone was sleeping and ran a javelin through the heart of Amalickiah, killing the king without awaking his servants. Returning to camp, Teancum awakened his men, informing them of his actions, and awaited the response of the Lamanites (51.28-37).

The third section of Part Seven (52.1-62.52) continues the emphasis upon the wars with the Lamanites. *In the twenty-sixth year of the reign of the judges*, awakening to the death of their king, the Lamanites sought protection in the city of Mulek. Ammoron, who took the place of his fallen brother Amalickiah, instructed his followers to maintain the cities that they had taken with a great loss of blood (52.1-4). Seeing the strong position of the Lamanites, Teancum decided to wait until Moroni could send a large number of troops to strengthen his army. Moroni sent word that Teancum should keep all the Lamanite prisoners for a future exchange and to fortify the land Bountiful as well as secure the narrow strip of land, but Moroni could not send troops at this time as the Lamanites were at their borders, being harassed by King Ammoron (52.5-14), as *the twenty-sixth year of the reign of the judges ended and into the twenty-seventh year of the reign of the judges.*

When Moroni and his troops finally arrived *in the twenty-eighth year of the reign of the judges* he met with Teancum and the chief captains and planned a deceptive movement, led by Jacob, that drew the

Lamanites out of their fortified city in pursuit of Teancum and his men. As the Lamanites left their posts largely undefended, Moroni and his men seized their city and eventually the Lamanites were trapped between the troops of Moroni and Lehi. The result was a massive battle in which many were killed on both sides and those taken captive exceeded the number of the dead (52.15-40).

The Lamanite prisoners were required to bury their own dead as well as the dead of the Nephites. In addition, they were required by Teancum, at the command of Moroni, to dig a fortification ditch around the city of Bountiful, making it the most 'exceeding strong-hold ever after' (53.1-7). Owing to the fact that the Lamanite armies had gained serious ground over the Nephites, the people of Ammon determined to take up the weapons of war they had earlier renounced. However, Helaman and his brethren persuaded them not to do so, lest by breaking their oath they might lose their souls. But the people of Ammon had many sons who had not taken such an oath, who assembled themselves, took up arms, called themselves Nephites, and were prepared to defend the liberty of the Nephites with their lives. Helaman became the leader of these two thousand stripling soldiers who were exceedingly valiant, courageous, strong, active, and true at all times in whatsoever thing they were entrusted, for they had been taught to keep the commandments of God (53.8-23).

In the twenty-ninth year of the reign of the judges, King Ammoron sent Moroni a letter proposing an exchange of prisoners, which included women and children taken by the Lamanites. In a very threatening response, Moroni proposed that a Nephite man, his wife, and children be exchanged for one Lamanite prisoner, as the Nephites had not taken any women or children as prisoners of war (54.1-14). Taking great offense at Moroni's tone and his theology, Ammoron agreed to Moroni's proposal whilst promising to engage in an eternal war with the Nephites to avenge all the wrongs that had been committed against his people (54.15-24).

King Ammoron's response infuriated Moroni who determined that he would not exchange prisoners unless Ammoron withdraw his purposes. Thus, Moroni caused a search to be made amongst the Nephites for a descendant of Laman. Finding one named Laman, Moroni sent him and a small number of men to the city of Gid where the Nephite prisoners of war were being kept. When

Laman and his men were spotted by the Lamanite guards, he identified himself as a Lamanite who had escaped the Nephites and had
brought some Nephite wine. Upon the insistence of the Lamanite
guards, Laman gave them of his wine. When the guards were drunk,
Laman and his men distributed weapons to all the Nephite prisoners who, rather than escaping, prepared to take the city of Gid from
inside. When the drunkened Lamanites were awakened, they realized that they could not fight the Nephites who had surrounded
them outside the city and who had a formidable fighting force inside the city. Therefore, the Lamanite chief captains brought all
their weapons and laid them at the feet of the Nephites, begging for
mercy. These prisoners were taken into Gid where they worked on
additional fortifications before being dispatched to Bountiful where
they were kept. The fortunes of the Nephite armies increased with
victories and despite Lamanite attempts to get them drunk and take
advantage of them – as they themselves had been conquered – the
Nephites remained strong, keeping the commandments of the
Lord. And Moroni prepared to take the well-fortified city of Morianton, which was continually attracting more and more Lamanite
forces (55.1-35).

The next section of the seventh part of the Book of Alma is devoted to a description of the contents of a letter from Helaman to
Moroni in which Helaman offers a report on the affairs of his people (56.1-58.41). Beginning with an account of the two thousand
striplings (*in the thirtieth year of the reign of the judges*), whom Helaman
now refers to as 'sons', he describes the way they joined forces with
Antipus to assist in the defense of the city of Judea, whose troops
had been reduced owing to the many who died and the fact that the
Lamanites took as prisoners only the chief captains. In point of fact,
the Lamanites were in possession of the cities of Manti, Zeezrom,
Cumeni, and Antiparah. Not only were the spirits of Antipus'
troops strengthened by the arrival of the two thousand fighting
men, but also when the Lamanites saw such reinforcements they
did not come against the city of Judea (56.1-19).

Owing to the fact that King Ammoron ordered his troops to
maintain their fortified cities, the Lamanites did not come out to
fight. During this time Helaman's troops grew to about ten thousand with provisions for them, their wives, and their children
brought by the fathers of the two thousand striplings. Since

Helaman was unable to engage the enemy, he devised a ruse, whereby he would lead his 'sons' toward the Lamanite city of Antiparah, as if carrying provisions to another city. When the superior Lamanite forces followed to overtake them, Antipus and his army would then be dispatched to follow the Lamanites, without being noticed. Thus, a long and speedy chase began until finally Helaman could no longer see the Lamanites in pursuit. Not knowing if Antipus had overtaken the Lamanites, Helaman asked his two thousands 'sons' if they wanted to go into battle against them. Their faith in God's ability to preserve them – taught to them by their mothers – made them fearless though none of them had actually been in battle before! When they arrived at the fight, Antipus and other Nephite leaders had already been slain and the Nephites began to give way. When the two thousand 'sons' entered the fray, Antipus' troops took heart and soon the Lamanites were surrounded with many of them being slain. Therefore, they delivered their weapons to Helaman and themselves as prisoners of war. There were so many prisoners that they were sent back to the land of Zarahemla. Yet, despite such incredible fighting not one soul of the two thousand striplings had fallen in battle. They had all been preserved by the strength of God (56.20-57).

At this point Helaman describes the receipt of a letter from Ammoron who proposed an exchange of the prisoners Helaman had taken in exchange for the city of Antiparah, but Helaman instead insisted on a direct exchange of prisoners, which Ammoron refused. In the meantime, the people of Antiparah fled to other cities and Antiparah fell into Nephite hands (57.1-5). After this, Helaman's army was brought additional provisions and was strengthened by an additional sixty of the sons of the Ammonites who joined his other 'sons'. Surrounding Cumeni they waited on a shipment of Lamanite provisions, which the Nephites took at night upon their arrival. Cut off from their support, the Lamanites began to lose all hope of help, yielding up the city of Cumeni to Helaman. There were so many Lamanite prisoners causing trouble and rebelling that two thousand of them were slain even after their surrender with the rest sent to the land of Zarahemla. Those who were to escort them returned early, the prisoners apparently having escaped. Their return, however, was timely as Ammoron had reinforced his troops and they were fighting fiercely. Only the desperate fighting of the two thousand sixty 'sons' saved the day as they beat back the Lamanites, though the Nephites had suffered great loss (57.6-23). Though one thousand Nephites had been slain and two hundred of the 'sons' had fainted owing to loss of blood, not one soul of Helaman's two thousand sixty was lost even though all suffered many wounds. All were astonished at the miraculous power of God and the faith of these young men (57.24-27). After tending to the wounded and burying the dead, the mystery of the lost prisoners came to light. Gid, the chief captain over this expedition reported that as they made their way to Zarahemla word came from Nephite spies that Helaman was under attack, news that excited the prisoners throwing them into rebellion. Gid and his troops had to kill many of the Lamanites, though some escaped. He then made haste in returning to Cumeni to assist in the fighting (57.28-36).

Next, Helaman describes his desire to take the city of Manti but could not with his small bands nor could he decoy his opponents as he had before. Owing to the numerical and provisional advantages of the Lamanites, Helaman decided to await a new supply of provisions. Despite his embassy to the governor of the land, all Helaman received was some food, but no more fighting men. After many months of being in these difficult circumstances, Helaman and his men cried out to God for strength and deliverance, with these prayers answered in the form of assurances that God would deliver them and would give them great faith to conquer the enemy (58.1-12). Going to the city of Manti, the Nephites camped outside the city so that the Lamanites could see their lack of strength, which led them to plan attacks upon the Nephites. But Helaman divided his troops, sending Gid and Teomner with small numbers of troops secretly into the wilderness with one group on the right and the other on the left. When the Lamanites brought their army out after Helaman with his troops still camped in front of the city, the Nephites retreated into the wilderness, at which point the entire Lamanite army followed them except for a few guards left in the city. Whilst they pursued the Nephites, Gid and Teomner led their troops into Manti, taking the city with little resistance. Realizing what had transpired, the Lamanites fled into the wilderness (58.13-31). Despite the lack of support received, Helaman and his men were determined to hold on in defense of the cities taken. The letter to Moroni ends with a rousing endorsement of the sons of the people of Ammon whose piety and courage continued to inspire – and still not one soul of them had been lost (58.32-41).

When Moroni received Helaman's epistle he was overjoyed owing to the welfare and success of these men, making it known to all his people. He immediately sent an epistle to Pahoran asking for additional men to be sent to Helaman while he made plans to liberate the cities that had been taken by the Lamanites (59.1-4). But as he planned his course of action, Nephihah was attacked and fell to the Lamanites with a great slaughter of its inhabitants. When Moroni learned of this fall he was sorrowful, owing to the wickedness of the people because of the great success of the Lamanites he and his men began to doubt. Angry with the government, he wrote to the governor of the land, Pahoran (59.5-13).

In his caustic epistle Moroni pleads with Pahoran for men and provisions for himself and Helaman. His frustration takes the form of accusing those in leadership with sinning against those defending the nation by being more concerned with their own comfort and power than for those dying to defend their freedom. Accusing the leaders of neglecting the thousands who have died and of contributing to their deaths by not supporting them appropriately, Moroni threatens them with vengeance from God for being derelict in their duties. Placing much blame on the distraction caused by the king-men, he wonders if the leaders are also traitors to the country. Again and again asking for proper support for those defending the liberty of the inhabitants, on two occasions Moroni goes so far as to threaten to come to Zarahemla and set things right with the sword if necessary (60.1-36).

No sooner had Moroni sent his epistle than he received a response from Pahoran. In it Pahoran expresses his grief at the suffering of Moroni and his men and then reveals that he has had to flee from Zarahemla to Gideon owing to a rebellion against him and his leadership. Pahoran has sought to regroup, as daily they are joined by more and more individuals who are opposed to the illegitimate take-over by those in rebellion. They have set over themselves a king who is in league with the king of the Lamanites to defeat Moroni. Not offended by Moroni's strong language, Pahoran invites Moroni with some of his fighting men to come and restore the proper government in Zarahemla, which will ensure support for the fighting men. Thus, Moroni's words, though somewhat misdirected, were accurate, and his willingness to come and enforce proper action with the sword if necessary on the mark (61.1-21).

Upon receiving this epistle Moroni took courage, being filled with joy over the faithfulness of Pahoran, though he mourned that Pahoran had been driven from his rightful judgment seat. Thus, in accord with Pahoran's instruction, leaving Lehi and Teancum in charge of his army, Moroni took a small band of men and marched toward Gideon. Raising the standard of liberty along the way, thousands began to flock to it and the cause it represented. Uniting with the forces of Pahoran they soon outnumbered the forces of Pachus, the king of the dissenters. In the ensuing battle Pachus was slain, his men taken prisoner, and Pahoran restored to his judgment-seat. The men of Pachus and the king-men were tried and put to death (62.1-11).

At the beginning of the thirty-first year of the reign of the judges Moroni immediately caused six thousand men and provisions to be sent to Helaman and another six thousand along with food to be sent to Lehi and Teancum. Moroni and Pahoran then turned their attention to the city of Nephihah, which the Lamanites held. On their way they encountered a large number of Lamanites whom they defeated, taking four thousand prisoners who entered into a covenant that they would never fight against the Nephites again and who were sent to live amongst the people of Ammon. Arriving at Nephihah they set up camp. That night, seeing that the Lamanite troops were clustered together in the east part of the city, Moroni secretly climbed the city wall. Thus, he commanded his troops to climb the walls on the west side and enter the city. When the Lamanites awoke to this sight many of them fled, others were killed, and many were taken prisoner. Not a Nephite soul was lost, and the prisoners petitioned to join the people of Ammon, which they did, relieving the Nephites of the burden of caring for so many prisoners (62.12-29).

Moroni, Lehi, and Teancum pursued the Lamanites and surrounded them at night. Everyone decided to rest except Teancum who was exceedingly angry with Ammoron, who along with his brother Amalickiah, were held responsible by Teancum for the extended war and bloodshed. Having climbed the city wall, he went from tent to tent seeking Ammoron. When he found him, Teancum cast a javelin piercing Ammoron near the heart, as he had Amalickiah earlier (61.33-34). But before he died Ammoron alerted his servants to Teancum's presence, whom they pursued and killed. The next day a mournful Moroni took the city – slaying the Lamanites with a great slaughter (62.30-38).

The war, which lasted many years, had left many hardened; but the afflictions brought on by war had at the same time softened them, making them humble before God. At war's end Moroni retired to his own house, yielding up the command of his armies to his son Moronihah. Helaman returned to preaching, meeting with great success, again establishing the church. Judges and chief judges were chosen. The people of Nephi began to prosper again but were not lifted up unto pride and the Lord did bless them. Helaman died in *thirty-fifth year of the reign of the judges* (62.39-52).

In **Part Eight** of the Book of Alma (63.1-17) the transfer of the sacred records first to Shiblon, then to Helaman's son (also named Helaman), and the victory of the Nephites in the final battle are recounted. *In the thirty-sixth year of the reign of the judges*, Shiblon, a just and upright man, took possession of the sacred things delivered unto Helaman by Alma. In that very year Moroni died (63.1-3). In the next year (*the thirty-seventh year of the reign of the judges*) five thousand four hundred men, with their wives and children, left the land of Zarahemla traveling north on ships built by Hagoth, an exceedingly curious man. The first group returned safely, whilst *in the thirty-eighth year of the reign of the judges* the next set of travellers were never heard from again, presumed drowned (63.4-9). In *the thirty-ninth year of the reign of the judges* Shiblon also died. As his brother Corianton had departed for the north on one of the ships, Shiblon conferred the sacred things to Helaman's son, Helaman (63.10-13). The book closes with a brief account of dissenters who again stirred up the Lamanites, to attack Moronihah and his people, who were beaten back to their own lands, suffering great loss (63.14-16).

12

HELAMAN

The readers' journey continues with the tenth book found within the Book of Mormon, a sixteen-chapter book called the Book of Helaman that covers 44 pages in the 1830 edition and contains some 21,288 words. This is the third of the books the readers encounter of the abridgement attributed to Mormon. The Book of Helaman continues the story that leaves off at the end of Alma.

In this book the readers continue to be assisted by the recounting of the next fifty-one years of the reign of the judges, a means of calculation that began in Alma, bringing the total by the end of Helaman to the first ninety years. In comparison to the Book of Alma, time moves much more swiftly in Helaman, with each year getting less than a page devoted to it on average, whereas in Alma on average nearly five pages in the 1830 edition are devoted to each year. The readers would experience such an increase in pace as indicating a quicker movement to the anticipated coming of Christ, a topic of increasing interest as Helaman unfolds.

On one level the Book of Helaman has a rather straightforward literary structure, consisting of four major parts:

Part One – Disputations, Lamanite Wars, and the Origin of the Gadianton Robbers (1.1-2.14)

Part Two – The judgeships of Helaman and Nephi, the Preaching of Nephi and Lehi, and the Reappearance of the Gadianton Robbers (3.1-6.41)

Part Three – The Prophetic Ministry and Preaching of Nephi,
the Gadianton Robbers, and Mormon's Theological
Reflections on the Hardness of Nephite Hearts
(7.1-12.26)

Part Four – The Ministry of Samuel a Lamanite unto the
Nephites and the People's Refusal to Believe the
Signs and Wonders Given to Them (13.1-16.25).

However, at another level the structure of Helaman is made more
complex by the fact that at strategic locations throughout the book
reference is made to the Gadianton Robbers (2.1-4; 6.16-41; 8.1-9;
11.24-38), with at least one reference to them in each major part of
the book, save the final section. The structure is also made more
complex by the fact that on three occasions the flow of the book is
interrupted or punctuated with significant editorial comments by
Mormon (3.15-17; 4.11-17; 12.1-26).

Part One of the Book of Helaman (1.1-2.10) is divided into
three broad sections. In the first section (1.1-13) the readers are introduced to the fact that in *the fortieth year of the reign of the judges* serious contentions existed amongst the people over the proper succession to the late Pahoran, the chief judge – specifically, which of his
sons (Pahoran, Paanchi, of Pacumeni) should succeed him. Though
Pahoran succeeded his father at the will of the people, he was assassinated secretly by Kishkumen – a follower of Pacumeni, in *the forty-
first year of the reign of the judges.*

At this very time, in the second section of Part One, the Lamanites gathered an innumerable army, led by a large and mighty man
named Coriantumr, a dissenter among the Nephites. Leading the
army with exceedingly great speed, Coriantumr took possession of
the whole city of Zarahemla, slaying all those who opposed them
including Pacumeni the recently seated chief judge. In response,
Moronihah sent Lehi to do battle with Coriantumr, retaking
Zarahemla, even slaying the leader Coriantumr (1.22-33).

The third section of Part One chronicles the origins of the
Gadianton Robbers (2.1-13). In *the forty-second year of the reign of the
judges*, Helaman, the son of Helaman, was appointed by the voice of
the people to fill the judgment-seat. But the same Kishkumen, who
under the direction of his band of brigands had earlier murdered
Pahoran, was intent upon killing Helaman as well. As Kishkumen
made his way to the judgment seat, one of Helaman's servants, dis-

guised as a Gadianton, gave Kishkumen a signal to approach. When they approached the judgment seat, Helaman's servant stabbed Kishkumen in the heart without a sound being made. When Kishumen did not return to his men, Gadianton, the leader of the band of Kiskumen, soon took flight into the wilderness.

Part Two of the Book of Helaman (3.1-6.41) consists of three primary sections, the first of which (3.1-4.26) is devoted to the judgeships of Helaman and Nephi. From *the forty-third year of the reign of the judges* through *the forty-fifth year* there were no contentions amongst the people. But during *the forty-sixth year* contentions and dissensions re-emerged, with many people leaving the land of Zarahemla, traveling to the uninhabited north with the people covering the face of 'the whole earth'. Those in the north lived in tents and houses of concrete, owing to the lack of trees. Those in the south began to ship timber to the north (3.1-12). At this point, Mormon inserts a word about the Nephite records that were being kept (3.13-17), revealing that the records were many, very large, and did not contain a hundredth part of the events of this people. Kept mainly by the Nephites, they were passed from one generation to another, even during the time when the Nephites lost their way spiritually.

Despite great contentions during *the forty-seventh and forty-eighth years of the reign of the judges*, Helaman provided righteous leadership. During this time he named his two sons after the founding fathers Nephi and Lehi (3.18-21). During *the forty-ninth year of the reign of the judges* there was continual peace, aside from the secret combinations that Gadiaton, the robber, had established in various parts of the land. Prosperity was the order of the day with thousands, even tens of thousands joining the church and being baptized – with peace extending into *the fiftieth and fifty-first years of the reign of the judges* (3.22-33). Yet, during this very time pride began to enter the hearts of those who professed to belong to the church of God. But the more humble part of the people often fasted and prayed 'even to the purifying and sanctification of their hearts'. Thus, *the fifty-second year of the reign of the judges* ended in peace aside from the pride owing to riches in the hearts of some. In the next year, *the fifty-third year*, Helaman died and his son Nephi began to reign as chief judge in his stead (3.33-37).

From *the fifty-fourth year of the reign of the judges* through *the fifty-fifth, sixth, and seventh years of the reign of the judges* renegade Nephites convinced the Lamanites to attack and take the land of Zarahemla, which they did, so that by *the fifty-eighth and ninth years of the reign of the judges* they held all the Nephite possessions in the land southward, much of which would be retaken in *the fifty-ninth and sixtieth years of the reign of the judges* (4.1-10). At this point, Mormon explains the reason for the Nephites disastrous defeat – pride of heart, exceeding riches, oppression of the poor, hungry, and naked, denying the spirit of prophecy and revelation, murdering, plundering, lying, stealing, committing adultery, deserting to the Lamanites, and raising contentions (4.11-13).

Despite such great wickedness, the preaching of and military exploits of Moronihah, Nephi, and Lehi brought about great repentance, so that by the end of *the sixty-first year of the reign of the judges* they had regained one-half of their property and lands (4.14-17). During *the sixty-second year of the reign of the judges*, as a result of reflecting on the prophecies of Alma and the words of Mosiah, the Nephites began to understand why they had fallen so far so quickly (4.18-26).

The second major section of Part Two chronicles the preaching of Nephi and Lehi (5.1-6.14). During this same year, Nephi, wearied by the iniquities of his people, delivered his judgment-seat to Cezoram, who was chosen by the evil and stiff-necked people. Nephi would preach for the remainder of his life, as would his brother Lehi (5.1-4). Their activity was spurred on in no small part by their recollection of the words of their father Helaman to remember their heritage – they had been named for their first parents, to remember the words of King Benjamin about the atoning blood of Jesus Christ, to remember Amulek's words that the Lord would surely come to save his people from their sins – not in their sins, and to remember their sure foundation, the rock of the Redeemer, who is Christ, the Son of God. The importance of their remembering is made clear by the fact that a form of the word 'remember' occurs some thirteen times in these eight verses (5.5-13). And remember they did ... preaching with power to the Nephites in Bountiful, Gid, and Mulek, as well as among the Lamanites in the land of Zarahemla, resulting in a widespread confession of sin and baptism unto repentance. In fact, the power of their preaching resulted in the baptism of some eight thousand Lamanites (5.14-19).

But their preaching was not without opposition as Nephi and Lehi were imprisoned by the Lamanite army, being cast into the same prison as Ammon and his brothers were earlier by Limhi. When they were to be executed, a pillar of fire surrounded them, the earth and the walls of the prison shook, and a voice came from above a cloud of darkness confirming their words and calling for repentance – phenomena repeated three times. At this, a dissenting Nephite named Aminadab saw the faces of Nephi and Lehi that shone through the darkness talking to the angels of God. When others saw the same phenomena they asked Aminadab what to do. He then joined his voice with those of Nephi and Lehi instructing the people to repent according to the words of Alma, Amulek, and Zeezrom. As they began to cry out to the Lord, a pillar of fire encircled each one, the Holy Spirit entered their hearts, a pleasant heavenly voice spoke words of peace to them, the heavens opened, and angels ministered to them. In turn, these individuals ministered to their Lamanite brethren, who were convinced to lay aside their weapons of war, their hatred, and the tradition of their fathers – returning the Nephite lands to the Nephites (5.20-51)! Thus, the better part of the Lamanites had become a righteous people, even more righteous than the Nephites who had become hardened, impenitent, and grossly wicked. But the church of God rejoiced at the conversion of the Lamanites and began to fellowship with them. In fact, by the end of *the sixty-third year of the reign of the judges* many of the Lamanites went into the land of Zarahemla and preached to the Nephites with success, going into the land northward with Nephi and Lehi to preach as well (6.1-6). The result of such missionary activity was an unprecedented period of prosperity, free travel, and commerce amongst the Nephites and Lamanites so that *the sixty-fourth and fifth years of the reign of the judges* passed in peace (6.7-14).

The third major section of Part Two of the Book of Helaman (6.15-41) reintroduces the Gadianton robbers. During *the sixty-sixth year of the reign of the judges* Cezoram was murdered while he sat on his judgment seat, with his son being murdered after him (6.15). During *the sixty-seventh year of the reign of the judges* the people grew in wickedness owing to their desire for riches, even committing secret murders. As it turns out, these murderers were a band formed by

Kishkumen and Gadianton. When the Lamanites found that these murderers were present among them they sought to remove them, but many of the Nephites protected them. By means of their secret signs and words they could function in near absolute anonymity. The origin of these secret oaths and activities came from the same one who inspired the murder of Abel and the building of the tower of Babel, that is – the author of sin (6.16-30)! By *the sixty-eighth year of the reign of the judges* the Lamanites grew more and more spiritually, with the Spirit being poured out upon them so much so that they hunted the robbers of Gadianton, preaching the word of God to them until the robbers were destroyed from amongst them. Ironically, during this period the Nephites became more and more wicked, with the Spirit of the Lord withdrawing from them even as they supported the work of the Gadianton robbers (6.31-41).

Part Three of the Book of Helaman (7.1-12.26) is divided into three main sections, the first and most extensive being devoted to the prophetic ministry and preaching of Nephi (7.1-11.23). During *the sixty-ninth year of the reign of the judges* Nephi returned from the land northward to Zarahemla, the land of his nativity, because all his words and prophecies had been rejected. Owing to the exceeding sinfulness of his people, Nephi's heart was swollen with sorrow and he experienced agony of soul. He even desired that he might have been born during the time when his father Nephi first came out of Jerusalem – a desire that must strike the reader as ironic owing to the difficulties encountered by the Jerusalem generation – but resolved himself to being consigned to his own days (7.1-9). Having gone up onto a tower in his own garden that adjoined the highway leading to the chief market, Nephi poured out his heart to God. As a crowd gathered outside the wall, Nephi shared his sorrow, calling for repentance, warning that only scattering and destruction awaited them otherwise. Their rapid fall was owing to their desire to gain riches and fame as well as their willingness to do anything to satisfy their desire for such. So great is their wickedness it will be better for the Lamanites than for them, for the Lamanites are not only more righteous but also have not sinned against the great knowledge given to the Nephites. The Nephites' wickedness and abominations will surely result in them being destroyed from off the face of the earth unless they repent (7.10-29).

Nephi's words provoked a mixed response, with the corrupt judges becoming angry to the point of seeking to incite the people to bring Nephi to them for judgment, whilst some of the people testified to the truthfulness of his words indicating their belief that his prophecies would certainly come to pass (8.1-9). Nephi's response was to preach all the more, citing the example of Moses who caused the Red Sea to swallow up the Egyptians and who spoke of the coming of the Messiah by means of the brazen serpent that was lifted up (8.10-15). Nephi also appealed to the words of Abraham, Zenos, Zenock, Ezias, Isaiah, and Jeremiah – testifying of things from their fathers unto his own time (8.16-23). Owing to the Nephites' lack of belief in the words of their prophets, Nephi tells them they are laying up wrath for themselves on the day of judgment. As a sign of his own authentic role as a prophet in line with the others to whom he appeals, Nephi prophesies that the chief judge has been murdered by the judge's own brother – both of whom belong to the secret band authored by Gadianton (8.24-28).

At the sound of these words five men ran to the judgment-seat to test Nephi's claims, for while they did not believe that he was a prophet, if his words proved true about the death of the chief judge they would believe his other words. Discovering the scene as foretold by Nephi, fear came upon the five that his other words of judgment might be true as well, causing them to quake and fall to the earth. Assuming that these five were the murderers and that God had smitten them for their crime, the gathering crowd bound the five and cast them into prison (9.1-9). Being brought before the judges, these five told of their experience, that they had run ahead to see if Nephi's words were true. The judges, however, were convinced that Nephi had been involved in the murder of the chief judge, despite the protests of the five who were liberated on the day of the chief judge's burial (9.10-18). When arrested, Nephi confronted his accusers with both the revelation of the identity of the murderer – it was Seantum the brother of the chief judge who killed his brother the chief judge Seezoram – and with a strategy to obtain a confession from Seantum, all of which transpired just as Nephi foretold. Thus, some believed on his words and others on the word of the five. Some claimed that Nephi was a prophet, others that he was a god. And there was a division amongst the people as Nephi stood in their midst (9.19-10.1).

Cast down, owing to the burdens of the wickedness of his people, Nephi encountered the voice of God in audible form that pronounced blessing upon him and entrusted him with power over the people (a theme mentioned three times in the span of two verses) to smite the earth except the people repent (10.2-11). Not even pausing to return to his own house, Nephi immediately began to declare the word of the Lord, even though the hearers did not respond. Despite their attempts to seize him, Nephi was transported by the Spirit from their midst and from multitude to multitude to preach. But they hardened their hearts to the point that contentions broke out amongst them so that by *the seventy-first year of the reign of the judges* they had begun to slay one another with the sword (10.12-19).

As such contentions continued for the next two years in *the seventy-fourth year of the reign of the judges* Nephi cried out to the Lord for a famine to commence in the land that would persist into the next year to soften the people's hearts. Thousands perished as a result. Remembering the Lord and the words of Nephi, the judges asked for Nephi to intercede (11.1-9a). Owing to their repentance, Nephi offered a prayer on their behalf, calling upon the Lord by name eight times in the span of seven verses. Thus, in *the seventy-sixth year of the reign of the judges* the famine ended. For the next several years (from *the seventy-sixth through the seventy-ninth year*) peace and prosperity returned with both Nephites and Lamanites belonging to the church, with Nephi and Lehi putting to rest any doctrinal contentions that arose (11.9b-23).

The second section of Part Three of the Book of Helaman (11.24-38) recounts the re-formulation of the Gadianton robbers. During *the eightieth year of the reign of the judges* certain Nephite dissenters and some ethnic Lamanites stirred up other Lamanites and began a war with their brethren, committing acts of murder and plunder before retreating to secret places in the mountains and wilderness. Becoming exceedingly large in a few years' time, they sought out the secret plans of Gadianton and themselves became robbers of Gadianton. They continued this kind of guerrilla warfare into *the eighty-first year of the reign of the judges,* while from *the eighty-second year of the reign of the judges* until *the eighty-fifth year* the people slid further and further into pride and wickedness.

The third section of Part Three of the Book of Helaman (12.1-26) consists of an extensive passage of theological reflection by Mormon on the hardness of Nephite hearts. Though a distinct section of Part Three in terms of content, these words follow immediately on the preceding narrative with no chapter division in the 1830 edition, nor even a sentence division in the Printer's Manuscript. All of this is to say that Mormon's reflections are part and parcel of the account that precedes them. Mormon's words, which seek to explain the hardness of heart of 'the children of men' in the face of God's goodness, is punctuated by the use of the word 'yea' which occurs seventeen times in the first fourteen verses of the section. Despite the Lord's blessings that extend to every part of life, people inevitably harden their hearts and forget the Lord, unless he chastens them with death, terror, famine, and pestilence. There is a certain quickness to do wrong and a slowness to walk in the path of wisdom. Despite their own relative nothingness, they disregard his counsels, counsels that come from the great and everlasting God from whom 'the power of his voice' – mentioned three times explicitly in one verse (!) – creates, shakes, and breaks the whole of the earth (12.1-15). The use of 'yea' gives way to the use of 'behold' in v. 16, as this term appears six times in the next five verses in the description of God's power over the deep, mountains, the earth (which can hide or reveal treasures), and the human being. Mormon's reflections draw to a close by underscoring the blessing that comes upon those who repent, a final warning with regard to the destruction of those who are evil – punctuated by two additional 'yeas' – and the words, 'They that have done good shall have everlasting life; and they that have done evil shall have everlasting damnation'. In a manner reminiscent of 1 Nephi, the words 'And thus it is. Amen' conclude Mormon's reflections (12.16-26).

Part Four of the Book of Helaman (13.1-16.25) describes the ministry of Samuel, a Lamanite prophet unto the Nephites, and the people's refusal to believe the signs and wonders given to them. The first section of Part Four (13.1-39) introduces the prophet and describes his message of warning. In *the eighty-sixth year of the reign of the judges*, whilst the Nephites remained in wickedness, the Lamanites strictly observed the commandments of God according to the law of Moses. At this time there arose a Lamanite prophet, Samuel, who preached to the people in Zarahemla, before being cast out of the city. As he was about to return to his own land, the voice of the Lord instructed him to return to Zarahemla. Prohibited from entering the city Samuel preached and prophesied from the city wall (13.1-4). His message was one of judgment, specifically warning that within four hundred years – explicitly mentioned twice in this section – destruction would fall upon them, unless they were saved by 'repentance and faith on the Lord Jesus Christ, who surely shall come into the world, and shall suffer many things and shall be slain for his people'. Unless repentance occurs, the word of the Lord and the Spirit of the Lord will be withdrawn and destruction by sword and famine will take place. The cities possessed by the Nephites will be destroyed, while their enemies to the fourth generation will live to behold this tragedy (13.5-16). In that day it will be futile to hide their treasures in the earth for they will be found no more, save by the righteous who hide them up unto the Lord. In this way their riches will be cursed because of their iniquities, especially their love of riches (13.17-23). Samuel further condemns his hearers for their rejection of true prophets and their preference for false prophets who speak words palatable to their tastes – 'prophets' they will reward out of their means. As Nephi earlier longed to have lived in the days of his fathers, Samuel's hearers might claim that if they had lived then, they would not have stoned the prophets, but Samuel charges that his hearers are worse than their forebears. Such obstinacy leads Samuel to say:

> O ye wicked and ye perverse generation;
> ye hardened and stiffnecked people,
> how long do you suppose that the Lord will suffer you?
> Yea, how long will you suffer yourselves to be led by foolish and
> blind guides?
> Yea, how long will ye choose darkness rather than light?

But the Lord has already kindled his anger against them, for he has cursed their riches so that they become 'slippery' and cannot be held. When, in their poverty they finally come to their senses and cry out unto the Lord it will be too late to repent: their riches will be gone, they will be surrounded by demons, the angels of those who seek to destroy their souls. 'O ... that you would hear my words', Samuel laments (13.24-39).

The second section of Part Four (14.1-30) is primarily devoted to signs Samuel gives of Jesus' birth and death. With regard to Jesus' birth, Samuel reveals that a sign will be given in five years time that will coincide with the time of Jesus' birth. Specifically, at the time of Jesus' birth there will be light for 'one day and a night and a day, as if there were one day and no night', though they will be able to tell when the sun rises and sets. A new star shall arise, with many signs and wonders in the heavens (14.1-13). Following this, Samuel gives signs associated with Jesus' death, a death that brings about resurrection and redeems all humankind. Specifically, the sun shall be darkened over the face of the whole earth, as will be the moon and stars for the space of three days until his resurrection. During this time thunderings and lightnings will occur for many hours, the earth shall shake and tremble, the rocks shall be rent in twain, and many graves shall be opened yielding up their dead, with many saints appearing. All these signs are for the purpose of generating faith in those who behold them, an eventuality Samuel stresses by underscoring the freedom each individual has to decide how to respond (14.14-31).

In the third section of Part Four (15.1-17) Samuel describes the bleak prospects that await the people of Nephi should they choose not to repent (15.1-3). By contrast, the Lamanites are praised for their diligence in observing the commandments, statutes and judgments of the law of Moses. The remarkable nature of their conversion is evidenced by the fact that they have buried their weapons of war, refusing to take them up again, which they believe would be sinful. In fact, they have been so steadfast in their belief that even if they begin to dwindle in unbelief the Lord shall prolong their days and shall be merciful unto them. Thus it will be better for them than for the Nephites. They will not be utterly destroyed, but as for the Nephites, if they will not repent, they will be utterly destroyed because of the mighty works done among them (15.4-17)!

The fourth section of Part Four of the Book of Helaman (16.1-25) recounts the response of the people who heard Samuel preach from the wall. On the one hand, those who believed his words sought out Nephi confessing to him their sins and expressing their desire for baptism. On the other hand, those who did not believe in Samuel's words were angry and cast stones at him, but he was protected from their attacks by the Spirit of the Lord. When they sought to seize him he jumped off the wall and did flee out of their lands, preaching and prophesying among his own people, never being heard of amongst the Nephites again (16.1-9). From *the eighty-seventh through the eighty-ninth year of the reign of the judges* the people became more hardened. In *the nineteenth year* great signs were given and angels appeared to them but still they hardened their hearts reasoning that while Samuel (and Nephi) may have guessed rightly about certain things it was not possible for these great and marvelous works to come to pass. Specifically they asked why, if there *was* a Son of God, he would only reveal himself in Jerusalem and not to them? They concluded that they would not be able to verify the prophets' words and that the desire of the prophets was to keep them in ignorance. 'Thus, despite the great signs they received, Satan had a great hold on their hearts and they did not believe' (16.10-25).

13

3 NEPHI

The readers' journey continues with the eleventh book found within the Book of Mormon, a thirty-chapter book called 'the Book of Nephi, the Son of Nephi, which was the Son of Helaman' that covers 62 pages in the 1830 edition and contains some 32,357 words. This is the fourth of the books the readers encounter of the abridgement attributed to Mormon. 3 Nephi[1] continues the story that leaves off at the end of Helaman.

While the chronological indicators continue to assist the readers in their journey through the Book of Mormon, in 3 Nephi the two indicators familiar to the readers converge with, and give way to a third indicator, this one based on the birth of Jesus. As the book begins, time moves very swiftly with the passage of about thirty-four years requiring less than twenty pages to recount their passage. But in chapter eight, narrative time comes to a virtual standstill as some twenty-two chapters are devoted to the passage of three days. The reader would likely experience such a continued increase in pace at the book's beginning as reflecting the growing anticipation with regard to the coming of Christ, on the one hand, and the slowing of the passage of narrative time as underscoring the extraordinary importance of Jesus' actions and words whilst on earth, on the other hand.

---

[1] The 'Book of Nephi, the Son of Nephi, which was the Son of Helaman' was first referred to as 3 Nephi in the 1879 LDS version of the Book of Mormon published in Salt Lake City, Utah and Liverpool, England.

Third Nephi has a rather straightforward literary structure, consisting of four major parts each of which conclude with explicit
comments by Mormon:[2]

> Part One – Transmission of the Sacred Records to Nephi, Sam-
> uel's Prophecies Are finally Fulfilled, more Gadian-
> ton Wars, and Mormon's Words (1.1-5.26)
>
> Part Two – Nephite Prosperity, the Unraveling of the Church
> and Government, Nephi's Prophetic Ministry, the
> Signs of Jesus' Death, the Voice of Jesus from
> Heaven, and Mormon's Words (6.1-10.18)
>
> Part Three – Jesus' Ministry and Preaching among the Nephites
> and Mormon's Words (11.1-26.14)
>
> Part Four – Jesus' Final Instructions, His Ministry amongst the
> Nephites, and Mormon's Words (26.15-30.2).

Third Nephi opens with two chronological indicators, the first
of which, *the ninety-first year of the reign of the judges*, continues to lead
the readers through the hundred-year reign of the judges – the
Book of Helaman (16.24) had concluded with *the nineteenth year of the
reign of the judges*. The second chronological indicator, '*six hundred
years from the time that Lehi left Jerusalem*', had last appeared in Mosiah
29.46, '*five hundred and nine years from the time Lehi left Jerusalem*', a reference that had occurred some 230 pages earlier in the 1830 edition
of the Book of Mormon. Part of its significance here is related to its
convergence with the reign of the judges, but its primary impact on
the readers would, no doubt, be the fact that on two previous occasions the Book of Mormon contains predictions that *six hundred
years from the time Lehi left Jerusalem* the Messiah would appear (1
Nephi 19.8; 2 Nephi 25.19). Thus, in 3 Nephi's very first verse, the
readers are informed that they are at the door of this momentous
event. It was in this year that Nephi the son of Helaman entrusted
the Brass Plates and all the sacred records to his son Nephi, who
faithfully kept them (1.1-3).

In *the ninety-second year of the reign of the judges*, although the prophecies of the prophets began to be fulfilled, some challenged those
spoken by Samuel the Lamanite, especially the words with regard to

---

[2] As Hardy (*Understanding the Book of Mormon*, p. 311 n. 12) points out, the
words 'I make an end of my sayings/speaking' occurs in each set of Mormon's
comments.

the day, night, and day that would appear as one long day. These skeptics caused a great uproar, going so far as to set aside a day on which those who believed these traditions should be put to death, except the sign come to pass (1.4-9). Nephi, whose heart was made exceedingly sorrowful, cried out to the Lord all day long, to which the voice of the Lord responded that this sign would be fulfilled on the very next day. When this sign occurred, great fear fell upon those who had not believed. Not only did the sun indeed shine for the prescribed period, but a new star also appeared according to the word of Samuel the Lamanite prophet (1.10-21). As a result, Satan sent forth lies to harden the hearts of the people, but the most part of the people believed and were converted with Nephi the Son of Nephi baptizing those who repented of their sins. There were no contentions except for questions with regard to observance of the law of Moses (1.22-26).

The rest of Part One of 3 Nephi (1.27-5.6) is devoted to events surrounding the activities of the Gadianton robbers. In *the ninety-third year* there was peace except for the Gadianton robbers who dwelt in the mountains and committed many murders. In *the ninety-fourth year* they were joined both by dissenter Nephites and many adult Lamanite children who joined themselves to the robbers. During *the ninety-fifth year* the people began to forget the signs and wonders, hardening their hearts – Satan leading them away from the doctrine of Christ – with such a state of affairs lasting until *the ninety-ninth year* (1.27-2.4). At this point the readers encounter all three means of chronological calculation in the span of three verses: a hundred years had passed since Mosiah was king – the hundred year reign of the judges was now at a close, *six hundred and nine years had passed since Lehi left Jerusalem,* and *nine years had passed since the sign of Christ's birth* was given (2.5-7). From this point the Nephites began to reckon time from the coming of Christ (2.8), a detail that underscores the importance of this event all the more.

Despite the preaching and prophesying amongst them, the people remained in wickedness from the *tenth through the thirteenth year since the coming of Christ,* at which point the activities of the Gadianton robbers were so intense that it was expedient for all the people, both Nephites and Lamanites, to take up arms against them (2.10-11). Interestingly, nothing is said about the pacifistic heritage of the converted Lamanites. Rather, it is simply noted that for the sake of their lives, women and children, their rights to worship, their freedom and liberty, they were compelled to take up arms. Rather than committing the kind of sin they earlier feared if they took up their weapons again, the Lamanites who united with and were numbered amongst the Nephites experienced the removal of their curse with their skin becoming white like the Nephites and their children becoming exceedingly fair (2.12-16). During *the fourteenth and fifteenth years* the Nephites gained, then lost, ground in their battle with the Gadianton robbers (2.17-19).

In *the sixteenth year from the coming of Christ*, Lachoneus, the governor of the land, received an epistle from the governor of the band of robbers (later identified as Giddianhi), seeking to intimidate Lachoneus into surrender owing to the strength of the Gadianton robbers and the many ways in which Lachoneus' people had wronged them. If they would yield up themselves and all they possessed, Giddianhi promises them acceptance not as slaves but as brethren. If not, he promises Lachoneus that he and his people shall become extinct (3.1-10).

Lachoneus was exceedingly astonished by this bold letter and immediately called his people to cry out to the Lord and then sent a proclamation that all his people should gather with their families, livestock, and substance into one central place around which would be constructed fortifications. Reminding the people that they would have no hope for deliverance from the Gadianton robbers without repentance, fear came upon the people and they exerted themselves to do all the words of Lachoneus. Next, chief captains were appointed over the people with Gidgiddoni – who had the spirit of revelation and also prophecy – appointed as the great military commander over them. Though the people desired to confront the Gadianton robbers immediately, Gidgiddoni revealed that now was not the time to attack or else they would fall into the hands of their opponents; rather, they should await an attack by the robbers (3.11-21). Thus, in *the seventeenth year from the coming of Christ* the people responded and moved by the thousands and tens of thousands to the lands of Zarahemla and Bountiful, making weapons of all kinds whilst awaiting their enemy (3.22-26).

In *the eighteenth year from the coming of Christ* the robbers finally attacked, but owing to the fact that there was no game or other food left in the areas deserted by the Nephites the robbers were unable to remain in open battle and had to retreat to the wilderness for support. The Nephites, conversely, had sustenance to survive for seven years (4.1-4)! Thus, Giddianhi made the decision in *the nineteenth year from the coming of Christ* that the robbers should attack, which they did in the sixth month. On that great and terrible day the robbers were attired in lamb-skin about their loins, dyed in blood, with shorn heads, wearing head plates. At their sight the Nephites fell to the ground and called upon the Lord for deliverance from their enemies (4.5-8). However, the armies of Giddianhi mistook the Nephites' action as expressing fear of battle, but the Nephites' feared the Lord. The intensity of the battle is conveyed in part by the triple use of the words 'great and terrible' to describe it – indeed there had never been such a slaughter since Lehi left Jerusalem. In it, the Nephites proved victorious, pursuing their enemies so far as the wilderness, with Giddianhi himself being overtaken and slain, despite his boldness in fighting (4.9-14).

It was not until *the twenty-first year* that hostilities resumed when Zemnarihah, the new ruler of the robbers, commanded that a siege be laid around the Nephite areas, as he assumed that they could soon be deprived of their resources. But owing to the Nephites' stock of provisions, this strategy failed miserably, with the Nephites marching out day and night, cutting off their enemies by thousands and tens of thousands. Eventually the people of Zemnarihah convinced him that they should retreat and head northward, but Gidgiddoni took action to surround them in their retreat, taking many thousands of prisoners, slaying the rest, and hanging Zemnarihah on a tree (4.15-29). As a result of their victories the Nephites praised God mightily, their hearts swollen with joy unto the gushing out of many tears, realizing that their deliverance was the direct result of their repentance. There was not a person amongst the Nephites who failed to believe in the words of all the holy prophets, especially those pertaining to the coming of Christ. 'Therefore they did forsake all their sins, and their abominations, and their whoredoms, and did serve God with all diligence day and night' (4.30-5.3). Those robbers who repented of their sins and entered a covenant that they would murder no more were set at liberty, but those who refused to renounce their evil activity were punished according to the law. Thus an end was put to these murderous activities (5.4-6).

Part One of 3 Nephi closes with some extended words offered by Mormon (5.7-26). Looking back over the first twenty-five years that had passed since the coming of Christ, Mormon reminds his readers that not a hundredth part of the events could be written, though records do exist that contain the proceedings of the people. Mormon underscores yet again that he himself makes a record on plates that he has made with his own hands. He goes on to remind the readers of his pedigree identifying himself with the words, 'And behold, I am called Mormon', after the land of Mormon where the first church was established. 'Behold, I am a disciple of Jesus Christ, the Son of God' who has been called to make a record of these things done from the time Lehi left Jerusalem until the present time. Mormon indicates that he will draw on 'the accounts which have been given to those who were before me' and will conclude with a record of the things he has witnessed with his own eyes (5.7-19). He goes on to say, 'I am Mormon, and a pure descendant of Lehi', who rejoices over the deliverance of his people from Jerusalem and the blessings given unto the house of Jacob. And, despite the fact that the plates have most recently recorded the complete belief on the part of the Nephites, Mormon envisions a time when a remnant of the seed of Joseph will encounter the knowledge of the Lord their God, being gathered from the four corners of the earth. They will know the covenant made with the house of Jacob, that their re-deemer is Jesus Christ, the Son of God (5.20-26).

Part Two of 3 Nephi (6.1-10.18) functions essentially to take the readers from the end of the robbers to the appearance of the resur-rected Jesus. This portion includes recounting a period of Nephite prosperity, the unraveling of the Church and government, Nephi's prophetic ministry that gives way to a description of the occurrence of the signs of Jesus' death, which themselves give way to three en-counters with the voice of Jesus from heaven, and concludes with Mormon's words.

Despite the ominous words of Mormon with regard to the sur-viving remnant at the end of chapter five, Part Two opens with the return of the Nephites to their homes in *the twenty-sixth year*, bringing with them all their possessions including livestock and precious metals. Allowing all robbers, who entered into the covenant to keep the peace, to dwell among them, peace was established in all the land. Throughout *the twenty-seventh and twenty-eighth years* peace, prosperity, and free travel existed (6.1-9). But inevitably, during *the twenty-ninth year* disputes broke out amongst the people over pride produced by great riches, which divided the people according to ranks of those who did and did not have opportunities that wealth afforded. Such inequalities began to break up the church, so that by *the thirtieth year* the whole church was affected, aside from a few of the Lamanite converts who remained steadfast (6.10-16). Owing to the activities of Satan, the people were full of such awful wickedness that they willfully sinned against God (6.15-19). At this time preachers went out boldly testifying about the redemption of the Lord – how Jesus would die for his people and be resurrected – angering the chief judges, high priests, and lawyers, who secretly had these preachers put to death, which in turn resulted in the judges being brought before the governor of the land. But owing to their numerous friends, the evil ones were delivered (6.20-29). Eventually, they destroyed the judgment seat with the people dividing up into tribes, with few righteous people remaining (7.1-8). Ultimately, this 'secret combination' chose a man named Jacob to be their king. Being outnumbered by the various tribes, Jacob commanded that his people should flee to the northern most part of the land and build themselves a kingdom there (7.9-13). During this time the various tribes began to formulate laws not to trespass against one another, but they continued to stone the prophets and cast them from their midst (7.14).

At this point angels continuously appeared to Nephi, who also heard the voice of the Lord. He preached with great power and with great authority, casting out devils, raising his dead brother, performing many more miracles, healing the sick, baptizing all those who repented, and ordaining Nephi's men to minister and baptize unto repentance (7.15-26). Such activities occurred from *the thirty-first to the thirty-third years.*

Upon the passing of the *thirty-third year* people began to look with great earnestness for the sign given by Samuel the Lamanite prophet with regard to darkness covering the earth for a period of three days, though great doubts and disputations remained (8.1-4). In the *thirty-fourth year* a great storm arose that shook the whole of the earth being so violent it changed the whole face of the land, leaving it deformed. The storm, which lasted for three hours, was followed by a period of darkness in which the vapor of darkness could actually be felt! So great were the mists of darkness that no light was possible. For the space of three days the darkness remained causing a regret amongst the people that they had not earlier repented, manifested in their great and terrible howlings (8.5-25).

As events transpire, the readers find themselves at a most momentous location in the Book of Mormon narrative, as a voice from heaven comes that is heard by all the inhabitants of the land. Though not apparent when the voice is introduced, this heavenly voice will be identified as the voice of Jesus. Significantly, this voice is heard before Jesus is actually seen by the Nephites, indicating that his tripartite speech is preparatory to his appearance, both to the characters in the narrative and to the readers who experience it. The first portion of Jesus' words (9.1-12) focus on the destruction that has immediately preceded. The words are punctuated with a refrain occurring in vv. 5, 7, 8, 9, and 11 that underscores the reason for the various destructive acts. The refrain begins either with words something like 'to hide their iniquities and their abominations from before my face' or 'to destroy them from before my face' and concluding with the words 'that the blood of the prophets and the saints shall not come up any more against them'. These refrains occur strategically near the end of the recounting of the destruction of cities in sets of four, excepting the first set of three.

Following immediately on these words with regard to destruction – there is no break in the text – the next words from the heavenly voice are a combination of a merciful call to repentance and words of self-identification. It is here that the speaker of the heavenly voice proclaims, 'Behold, I am Jesus Christ the Son of God'. Reminiscent of the Prologue of John's Gospel,[3] Jesus goes on to speak of himself as creator, his relationship with the Father, and the fact that while he came unto his own he was not collectively received by them, though many did receive him, becoming sons of God. Since redemption comes by him, the law of Moses is fulfilled with no more need for the shedding of blood or other forms of sacrifice. Rather a contrite spirit and broken heart is necessary to be baptized with fire and the Holy Spirit, even as happened to the Lamanites – recounted in Helaman 5, whose belief resulted in this

---

[3] Cf. Nicholas J. Frederick, 'Line Within Line: An Intertextual Analysis of Mormon Scripture and the Prologue of the Gospel of John' (PhD dissertation, Claremont Graduate School, 2013).

very thing, though they did not know what had happened. This portion ends as it began with a merciful call to repentance (9.13-22).

These astonishing words left the hearers silent for the space of many hours. Then Jesus reminds them that, despite the destruction that has fallen upon them, he stood ready to receive them – with the phrase 'how oft have I gathered you as a hen gathereth her chickens under her wings' occurring four times in the space of three verses. At the conclusion of these words the people began to weep and howl over the loss of their family and friends. At the end of the three days of darkness and the trembling of the earth, their weeping, mourning, and wailing give way to praise and thanksgiving to the Lord Jesus Christ, their Redeemer (10.1-10).

Part Two of 3 Nephi concludes, as had Part One, with words from Mormon (10.11-19). On this occasion Mormon focuses upon the fulfillment of the words spoken by the prophets, reminding the readers that those who were saved – who received the prophets – were not affected by the destruction that had been unleashed. He uses the preface, 'And now, whoso readeth, let him understand' to draw the readers' additional attention to the certainty that all these prophecies have been fulfilled. Mormon underscores this point still further by appealing to the prophecies of Zenos, Zenock, and Jacob, written on the plates of brass brought from Jerusalem. He closes his words by giving a preview of the events to be described with regard to Christ's ministry to the Nephites and Lamanites who were spared from destruction.

Part Three of 3 Nephi (11.1-26.14), the most extensive section of the book, is devoted to recounting that which transpired in the first two days of Jesus' three-day appearance amongst the Nephites. On the first day a great multitude gathered at the temple marveling with one another about the changes wrought by the events of the previous days and talking about this Jesus Christ of whom the sign had been given. Whilst conversing they heard a small voice from heaven, the impact of which caused them to quake, piercing their souls, causing their hearts to burn. A second time they heard the voice but did not understand it. The third time they heard the voice and understood the words, 'Behold my Beloved Son, in whom I am well pleased, in whom I have glorified my name. Hear ye him.' Immediately following this instruction they saw a man descending out of heaven, dressed in a white robe, who then stood in their midst.

Whilst they were silently thinking him to be an angel, he stretched forth his hand and identified himself:

> Behold, I am Jesus Christ, whom the prophets testified shall come into the world. And behold, I am the light and life of the world; and I have drunk out of the bitter cup which the Father hath given me, and have glorified the Father in taking upon me the sins of the world, in the which I have suffered the will of the Father in all things from the beginning (11.10-11).

At these words the crowd fell to the earth, but instructing them to arise Jesus invited them to come to him and 'thrust your hands into my side, and also … feel the prints in my hands and in my feet, that you may know that I am the God of Israel, and the God of the whole earth, and have been slain for the sins of the world' (11.13-14). When, one by one, each member of the multitude did just that, and bore record that Jesus is the one of whom the prophets wrote, they cried out praises, falling at Jesus' feet and worshipping him (11.1-17).

When Nephi was called to come to Jesus, he bowed before the Lord, kissing his feet. Arising, he was given the power to baptize after Jesus ascended again into heaven. Others were also called and given this authority by Jesus, who even gave them the words to speak when baptizing – 'Having authority given me by Jesus Christ, I baptize you in the name of the Father, and of the Son, and of the Holy Ghost. Amen' – before immersing the candidate in water. The formula to be used is owing to the fact that 'the Father, the Son, and the Holy Ghost are one' (11.18-28a). After Jesus commands those so chosen to avoid disputations over 'my doctrine' – for the devil is the father of contention – Jesus proceeds to declare unto them his doctrine. Specifically, the doctrine of Jesus focuses on the words 'repent and believe in me … and be baptized in my name', a phrase that occurs three times in the span of four verses. This doctrine enables one to build upon a firm foundation. And with these words Jesus encourages them to declare his words to the ends of the earth (11.28b-41).

Jesus next cries unto the multitude that they should submit to the ministry of the twelve he has chosen to be baptized in water with the promise that he would baptize them with fire and the Holy Ghost (12.1-2). Following this command, Jesus offers an extended sermon (12.3-14.27) that parallels large parts of the Sermon on the Mount almost verbatim.[4] In its narrative context, the sermon follows Jesus' previous words with a systematic exposition on the nature of the Kingdom of God, the fulfillment of the law, the practices of piety, and certain prohibitions and admonitions. For nineteenth-century and modern readers, owing to its nearly unrivaled position in Jesus' teaching in the New Testament, perhaps no other sermon would convey to the readers as clearly the idea that the Jesus who appears to the Nephites and who ministers in the new world is the same Jesus who appeared and ministered in 'Judea' and 'Galilee'.[5] Three aspects of the beatitudes as here given (12.3-12) would likely stand out to the readers. First, the addition of the words 'who come unto me'[6] to the phrase 'blessed are the poor in spirit' would perhaps serve to make clear the way in which Jesus functions as the center of his own proclamation, in keeping with his earlier words. Second, on five occasions the word 'all' is added in several of the beatitudes – 'blessed are *all* the pure in heart' – as a way of underscoring the completeness of Jesus' work. Third, the addition of the phrase 'with the Holy Ghost' to 'they shall be filled' in 12.6 makes explicit the connection between Jesus' earlier words about the Spirit and his words in this sermon.

After the mention of the metaphors of salt and light (12.13-16), in the section devoted to the fulfillment of the law, several differences are noteworthy. First, in making clear the permanence of the law the words 'but in me it hath all been fulfilled' makes explicit the fact that the observance of the law by the Nephites has not been wasted energy but is ultimately connected to Jesus. Second, the previous words are followed up by,

> And behold I have given you the law and the commandments of my Father, that ye shall believe in me, and that ye shall repent of

---

[4] On these similarities cf. the analysis by Ronald V. Huggins, 'Did the Author of 3 Nephi Know the Gospel of Matthew?', *Dialogue: A Journal of Mormon Thought* 30.3 (Fall, 1997), pp. 137-48. Hardy (*Understanding the Book of Mormon*, p. 194) proposes, 'It is therefore fitting that Jesus begins his public teachings among the Nephites with a rendition of the Sermon on the Mount which took as one of its major themes the relationship between the old law and the new'.

[5] Hardy, *Understanding the Book of Mormon*, p. 194.

[6] This phrase appears six times in this sermon in 3 Nephi 12 but not at all in the Sermon on the Mount. On this cf. Hardy, *Understanding the Book of Mormon*, p. 197.

your sins, and come unto me with a broken heart and a contrite spirit … come unto me and be saved; for … except ye shall keep my commandments … ye will in no case enter into the kingdom of heaven

– words that clearly connect the dots as to the relationship between keeping the commandments of the law and Jesus' message of salvation. Third, in words devoted to reconciliation with one's brother, mention of the brother is made explicit, as is the fact that Jesus promises personally to receive such a one, again underscoring Jesus' central role in the entire process (12.24). Fourth, 3 Nephi 12.46-47 contain words that would make clear to the readers that indeed Jesus is the fulfillment of the law and its completion: 'Therefore, those things which were of old time, which were under the law, in me are all fulfilled. Old things are done away, and all things have become new.'[7]

Following Jesus' teaching about giving alms (13.1-4), prayer (13.5-15), fasting (13.16-18), and true treasures (13.19-20), Jesus directly addresses the twelve he has chosen, placing his prohibition against worry in a missionary context (13.25-34). Turning again to the multitude, Jesus gives a prohibition against judging, though discernment is needed so as not to give that which is holy to the dogs (14.1-6). This prohibition is followed by three admonitions: 1) to seek, find, and knock (14.7-12); 2) to enter at the strait gate (14.13, 14); and 3) to beware of false teachers – discerning good fruit from bad (14.15-23). The sermon concludes with a word of warning about the eternal significance of one's response to Jesus' words (14.24-27).

Perhaps by the end of the sermon the readers would recognize that this entire portion has been structured around the alternating appearances of the multitude, on the one hand, and Nephi and/or the 12, on the other hand.

The Multitude	11.1
Nephi and the 11	11.18
The Multitude	12.1
The 12	13.25
The Multitude	14.1

---

[7] Hardy, *Understanding the Book of Mormon*, pp. 197-98.

Thus, this entire section begins and ends with references to the multitudes as the recipients of Jesus' ministry and words. The fact that the middle section is also focused on the multitude would underscore their significance all the more. At the same time, this alternating pattern would prepare the readers for the structure of the words that follow in 15.1-19.14.

Finishing these sayings Jesus again looks around and, focusing his eyes on the *multitude*, speaks to them (15.1-10). Reminding them of the words he taught before he ascended – apparently a reference to his teaching in Judea – he returns to the topic of the law of Moses. Here Jesus makes even clearer his relationship to the law of Moses by saying,

> Behold, I am he that gave the law, and I am he who covenanted with my people Israel; therefore, the law in me is fulfilled, for I have come to fulfill the law; therefore it hath an end … the law which was given unto Moses hath an end in me. Behold, I am the law, and the light … Behold, I have given unto you the commandments; therefore keep my commandments. And this is the law and the prophets, for they truly testified of me (15.5-10).

Turning to the *twelve* Jesus explains their role as light unto this people (of the Americas) and as a remnant of the house of Joseph, a remnant that have been given this land as an inheritance. Jesus makes clear that he has been commanded to tell their brethren in Jerusalem about them, 'other sheep I have, which are not of this fold; them also must I bring, and they shall hear my voice; and there shall be one fold, and one shepherd'. The Jerusalem brethren had misunderstood these words as having reference to the Gentiles, but Jesus' hearers in 3 Nephi 15.21 are identified as those sheep. And Jesus will go to others as well (15.11-16.3). In fact, they are commanded to write down and keep his sayings after he is gone, for when these sayings shall be manifest to the Gentiles, a remnant of the House of Israel will be brought to a knowledge of their Redeemer and will be gathered from the four corners of the earth. When the Gentiles have fallen away, 'I will bring the fullness of my gospel from among them' and 'bring my gospel to the House of Israel'. If the Gentiles repent, they will be numbered among the Lord's people. The gift of this land to the Nephites is seen to fulfill Isa. 52.8-10 (3 Nephi 16.4-20).

Turning again to the *multitude*, Jesus directed the people to their homes to ponder his sayings and to ask the Father to help them understand, preparing their minds for the next day's visitation. But Jesus was moved with compassion for them, his bowels filled with mercy, when he saw that they had sufficient faith that he should heal them. Inviting all the sick – the lame, blind, dumb – to come, he healed them every one, so much so that they bowed before him, kissing his feet, and bathing them with their tears (17.1-10). Commanding that the children be brought to him and that the multitude kneel upon the ground, Jesus groaned in himself, praying to the Father owing to the wickedness of the House of Israel. The people's response to his prayer was to bear record to its marvelous unrivaled nature, being overcome with joy. Owing to their faith, Jesus wept and took their children, one by one, blessed them, and prayed for them. After a second period of weeping he formally presented their children to them. At this, the heavens opened and angels descended out of heaven, encircled the children with fire, and ministered to them. All could bear record to the reality of these events. There were about 2,500 men, women, and children present (17.11-25).

After this, Jesus once again spoke to his *disciples*, commanding them that bread and wine be brought to him. Jesus blessed and gave the bread and wine to the 12. When the disciples had eaten and were filled he charged that they should feed the multitude. After they had eaten, Jesus spoke of one who should be ordained among them to break bread and bless it and give to all who believe and are baptized 'in my name'. By this act they shall always remember Jesus, 'And if you always remember me, ye shall have my Spirit to be with you'. At which point he commanded the disciples to partake and then give to the multitude as well. As Jesus had prayed so shall they pray in church, for he has set an example for them (18.1-16).

Jesus turned again to the *multitude* warning them of Satan's desire to sift them as wheat and encouraging them to pray 'in my name', a phrase that appears four times in the space of five verses. Not only should they pray but they should also meet together often, holding up their light to the world (18.17-25).

Turning again to the *disciples* he solemnly charged that they should not knowingly allow anyone to partake of his body unworthily. Such a one should not be cast out but given space to repent, be baptized 'in my name', and be received (18.26-35). He next touched each of the disciples, speaking to them, giving them the power to give the Holy Ghost. When he had done this, a cloud came and overshadowed the multitude and he departed, ascending into heaven (18.36-39). As the multitude returned to their homes, word went out that they had seen Jesus and that he would appear again tomorrow. The next day, the 12 chosen by Jesus (Nephi, Timothy, Jonas [Timothy's son], Mathoni, Mathonihah, Kumen, Kumenonhi, Jeremiah, Shemnon, Jonas, Zedekiah, and Isaiah) stood in the midst of such a great multitude that they had to be divided into 12 groups. They prayed 'in the name of Jesus' that the Holy Ghost should be given to them and they taught all the things he had taught them. After Nephi was baptized, he baptized all the others Jesus had chosen, after which the Holy Ghost did fall upon them and they were encircled by fire, and angels came out of heaven and ministered to them (19.1-14).

The second major section of Part Three of 3 Nephi is devoted to the second day of Jesus' visitation to the Nephites in the Americas (19.15-26.5), a section, which along with the whole of Part Three concludes with words from Mormon (26.6-14). As angels were ministering to the disciples, Jesus appeared for a second consecutive day to the disciples and the multitude whom he instructed to kneel down in prayer. When the disciples began to pray, they directed their prayers to Jesus, calling him 'their Lord and their God'. Jesus departed from their midst and thanked the Father for giving the Nephite disciples the Holy Ghost. He prayed for them and all those who would believe on their words. When he found the disciples continually praying without ceasing, Jesus blessed them, causing his countenance to shine upon them so that 'they were as white as the countenance and also the garments of Jesus; and behold, the whiteness thereof did exceed all the whiteness, yea, even there could be nothing upon earth so white as the whiteness thereof' (19.25). Such a transformation would likely remind the readers of the Lamanite curse and its removal, which they have encountered from time to time in the Book of Mormon. The transformation here described exceeds that, for it affects those who have not been cursed in such a way; yet their whiteness is incomparable with any other whiteness. It soon becomes apparent that this transformation is closely connected to the disciples' purification for which Jesus thanks the Father, as he prays for them to be one. Returning to them the third time Jesus found them praying 'and behold, they were white, even as Jesus'. This time Jesus' prayer to the Father was of such a marvelous nature that his words could not be written. When he ended his prayer Jesus remarked on their great faith, a faith greater than that among all the Jews, resulting in their seeing greater things than the Jews have seen (19.15-36).

Following this time of prayer Jesus again broke bread, blessed it, and gave it to the disciples to eat, commanding them, in turn, to give to the multitude. In like manner he also gave them wine. Though neither the disciples nor the multitude brought bread or wine, he gave to them saying, 'He that eateth this bread eateth of my body to his soul; and he that drinketh of this wine drinketh of my blood to his soul; and his soul shall never hunger nor thirst, but shall be filled'. When the multitude had eaten and drunk they were filled with the Spirit crying out and giving glory to Jesus (20.1-9).

At this point Jesus began a second major sermon, with the words, 'Behold, now I finish the commandment which the Father hath commanded me concerning this people, who are a remnant of the House of Israel'. Thus the focus of this sermon is on things eschatological. Simply put, when the words of Isaiah are fulfilled, the covenant of the Father will be fulfilled and the Israelite 'remnants' scattered abroad will be gathered from the east, west, south, and north, brought to the knowledge of the Lord who redeemed them. If the Gentiles do not repent they will be judged in accordance with the words of Mic. 4.12-13, 5.8-9. The Lehite remnant will be established in this land as a New Jerusalem. Jesus himself will be in their midst. Identifying himself with the 'prophet like unto Moses', Jesus spells out the promises to the Gentiles including the pouring out of the Spirit upon them, a pouring out that will make them mighty over the House of Israel, whom they will scatter. But when they have received the fullness of the gospel, if they shall harden their hearts Jesus will return their iniquities on their heads. He will remember the covenant he has made to gather his people and give them again the land of Jerusalem for their inheritance (20.10b-29). Jesus goes on to prophesy a time when the fullness of the gospel will be preached to the remnant of Israel and they will believe 'that I am Jesus Christ, the Son of God, and shall pray unto the Father in my name'. He goes further quoting extensively from Isaiah (52.8-10;

52.1-3, 6-7, 11-15), underscoring the theme of Jerusalem as the place to be inhabited by his people (3 Nephi 20.30-46).

The sign Jesus gives that will mark the commencement of his gathering of the House of Israel from their long dispersion is when 'these things that I declare unto you' shall be made known unto the Gentiles (21.2).[8] When this occurs, they shall know the time for the Lord's fulfilling his covenant with Israel is near. Those who in that day will not believe in the words of Christ which shall be brought forth by the Gentiles will be cut off from the covenant people. Jesus then quotes Mic. 5.8-15 at length, some of which (Mic. 5.8-9) appears for a second time in 3 Nephi (20.16-17) with some differences. Specifically, there appears in 3 Nephi 21.14a the phrase, 'Yea, wo be unto the Gentiles except they repent', a phrase that does not occur in Micah. A more extensive addition occurs in 3 Nephi 21.19-20:

And it shall come to pass that all lyings, and deceivings, and envyings, and strifes, and priestcrafts, and whoredoms, shall be done away. For it shall come to pass, saith the Father, that at that day whosoever will not repent and come unto my Beloved Son, them will I cut off from among my people, O House of Israel.

Clearly both changes underscore the point Jesus is making in this section. Such words of warning not withstanding, if the Gentiles will repent and hearken unto the words Jesus has given to the Lehites, Jesus promises to establish his church among them, numbering them among the House of Israel. In fact, they shall assist in building the New Jerusalem and gathering in the scattered remnant. The power of heaven will come down upon them (21.22-25).

Then the work of the Father will commence until the gospel being preached among the Lehite remnant, and the Lord will prepare the way for all his dispersed people to gather to the designated lands of their inheritance. At this point Jesus begins an extensive citation of Isa. 52.12 and 54.1-17, words which deserve the particular attention of Jesus' hearers for they touch all things concerning his people of the House of Israel. Thus, they are to give heed, write down, and

---

[8] Identified by Hardy (*Understanding the Book of Mormon*, pp. 200-201), among others, as the coming forth of the Book of Mormon.

hearken to Jesus' words in order to repent, be baptized, and be saved (3 Nephi 21.26-23.5).

In a section devoted to Jesus' expounding all the scriptures (23.6-13), a reference with which the section begins and ends, Jesus inspects the Nephite records and makes known his desire that other scriptures should be written that have not been. Specifically, he makes reference to the words of Samuel the Lamanite with regard to the resurrection of many saints at the time in which the Father glorified his name in Jesus, which had not been recorded. Such details were then written at Jesus' command. In addition to these words, Jesus commanded that the words of Malachi (3 and 4) also be added (3 Nephi 24.1-25.5), explaining that the Father desired for the Nephites to have such words. Following this, it is noted for a fourth time that Jesus expounded to the multitudes (26.3) – everything from the beginning unto the time he should come in his glory:

> even until the elements should melt away with fervent heat, and the earth should be wrapt together as a scroll, and the heavens and the earth should pass away; and even unto the great and last day, when all people, and all kindreds, and all nations and tongues shall stand before God, to be judged of their works, whether they be good or whether they be evil.

With these words, this eschatological discourse concludes (26.1-5).

As with Parts One and Two, Part Three also concludes with words of Mormon (26.6-14). On this occasion, Mormon underscores the fact that only a hundredth part of the things Jesus spoke is recorded in this book. In point of fact, Mormon had intended to write more but was forbidden to do so by the Lord. His desire in writing these things is that when these words are brought to the remnant of his people by the Gentiles, they shall believe these things. He then offers a summary of what the Lord did during the space of the three days he spent among them. As the readers at this point have only an awareness of the first two days, a sense of anticipation is created as they await a description of the third day's events.

Part Four of 3 Nephi (26.15-30.2) is devoted to a description of Jesus' third visitation to the Nephites in the Americas and Mormon's words with which the book concludes. The first words of Part Four recount Jesus' ascension into heaven with a summary of his activities beforehand which included healing all their sick, lame, blind, deaf, all manner of cures, even raising a man from the dead. The next day (i.e. the third day) as the multitude gathered they witnessed children – even babies uttering such marvelous things that they could not be recorded – perhaps the same children earlier described as being encircled by fire on the previous day. The disciples began to teach those who came to them, baptizing in the name of Jesus, with all those who were baptized being filled with the Holy Ghost. They too saw and heard unspeakable things that cannot be recorded. Significantly, all those 'baptized in the name of Jesus were called the "Church of Christ"' (26.15-21).

When the disciples were gathered in mighty prayer and fasting, for a third day Jesus appeared among them – for a third time, asking what they would have him give them. Their request had to do with what to call this church, for there were disputations about the matter amongst the people. Without uttering the words 'Church of Christ', mentioned at the end of 26.20, Jesus responds that they must take upon themselves the name of Christ, that they are to do everything in his name, and that they are to build upon his gospel, thus the church should bear his name (27.1-12).

The resurrected Jesus next summarizes for his disciples the content of his gospel, with the words 'this is the/my gospel' standing at the beginning and end of this section (27.13-22). Jesus begins with his purpose in coming into the world – sent by the Father to be lifted up upon the cross to draw all men to himself. Following this is the familiar call to repent and be baptized 'in my name', which occurs twice in these verses. Those who do so will be held guiltless before the Father and will be made clean by washing their garments in Jesus' blood. Such ones will be lifted up at the last day.

After instructing the disciples to write all the things they had seen and heard that are not forbidden, Jesus challenges them to be the kind of man he is (27.23-27). Announcing, 'and now I go unto the Father', Jesus reassures the disciples that whatever they ask the Father in Jesus' name they shall receive. At which point he announces that his joy is full owing to the fact that none of the Lehites of this generation will be lost. But just as suddenly, he then declares his sorrow for those of the fourth generation who will be led away captive because of their betrayal of him, words which reminds the readers of the prophecy given by Alma to Helaman (Alma 45.8-14) that the Nephites will one day be annihilated. Though Jesus softens the words of judgment, they would nonetheless likely remind the hearers that despite the threefold heavenly visitation by Jesus himself, the Nephites are doomed to destruction owing to their unfaithfulness, perhaps causing the readers to wonder why Jesus would come to them in the first place rather than their brethren, the Lamanites, who would survive them (27.28-33).

In his final ministry act whilst visiting the Nephites, Jesus repeats his query of 27.2 this time asking his disciples one by one, 'What is it that ye desire of me, after that I am gone to the Father?' Nine of the disciples ask that after lives of ministry they might come speedily to Jesus, a request he answers by assuring them that after they have lived to be 72 years old they will come unto him in his kingdom. When he turns to the other three, they could not put their request into words, for they desired to be like John, the beloved, never tasting death but ministering until Jesus returns in his glory – a request that he grants. Touching each of the nine disciples with his finger – as sign of the Spirit (?) – he departs (28.1-12). As for the three of the promise, the open heavens received them where they saw and heard unspeakable things, experiencing a transfiguration-like event where 'they were changed from this body of flesh into an immortal state, that they could behold the things of God ... whether mortal or immortal' it is not clear. What is clear is that they did minister to all people, uniting many to the church, who believed and were baptized, receiving the Holy Ghost. Despite the opposition of those who did not belong to the church, nothing could prevail against them. Prisons were not strong enough to hold them, nor were pits deep enough to keep them. Three times they were cast into furnaces without harm; twice they were cast into dens of wild beasts but played with the beasts experiencing no harm. They preached unhindered to all the people on the face of the land uniting many to the church (28.13-23).

As with each of the previous three parts of 3 Nephi, Part Four also concludes with words from Mormon, though here the words are more extensive than any of those that have preceded (28.24-30.2). These final words of Mormon in 3 Nephi are divided into two major subsections: the fate and ministry of the three who will never die (28.24-40) and Mormon's final admonitions and warnings with regard to the restoration of the House of Israel and the possible Gentiles' role in these events (29.1-30.2).

Forbidden from writing the names of the three who would never taste death, Mormon claims to have seen them and received ministry from them (28.24-26) – some four hundred years later! These three will appear among the Gentiles and Jews without being known. Ultimately they will minister to the scattered tribes of Israel and all nations bringing many souls to Jesus. They are 'as the angels of God' and when they pray in the name of Jesus to the Father they can show themselves to any person to whom it seems good to do so. They will play a special role in working a great and marvelous work amongst the Gentiles before the judgment day. Wo to those who do not hearken to the words of Jesus and their words – it would be better if they had not been born (28.27-35). Mormon's last words here about the three disciples reveal that he enquired of the Lord as to their physical state and was told that their bodies were changed so that they would not experience death, nor be overpowered by Satan; they were sanctified in the flesh being made holy, not held by the powers of the earth. In this state they will remain until the judgment of Christ (28.36-40).

When the Lord sees fit, these words (the Book of Mormon[?]) shall come to the Gentiles and the readers will know that the covenant concerning the restoration of the remnant of Israel to their lands of inheritance is beginning to be fulfilled. There is no need to imagine that the words of the prophets have been spoken in vain. To underscore this point a series of four woes, three of which are introduced by 'yeas', emphasize that which should be avoided: spurning the doings of the Lord; denying of Christ and his works; denying of revelation, prophecy, gifts, tongues, healings, or the power of the Holy Spirit; or denying of the miracles wrought by Jesus Christ. A final 'yea' warns that the Jews will no longer be made sport of, for the Lord remembers his covenant (29.1-9). Significantly, Mormon's final words in 3 Nephi are an invitation to the Gentiles to hearken to Jesus' words; to turn from their wicked ways; and

come unto me and be baptized in my name, that you may be baptized in my name, and ye may receive a remission of your sins, and be filled with the Holy Ghost, that ye may be numbered with my people who are of the House of Israel (30.1-2).

Given the crucial role to be played by the Gentiles in the restoration, such a conclusion is not a surprising one, for these words were commanded by Jesus that Mormon should speak and write.

14

4 NEPHI

The readers' journey continues with the twelfth book found within
the Book of Mormon, a one-chapter book called the Book of
Nephi, Who Is the Son of Nephi, One of the Disciples of Jesus
Christ, a book that covers five pages in the 1830 edition and contains some 2,222 words. This is the fifth of the books the readers
encounter of the abridgement attributed to Mormon. Fourth
Nephi[1] continues the story that leaves off at the end of 3 Nephi.[2]

After having devoted close to twenty chapters to the activities of
a three-day period, the pace quickens considerably in 4 Nephi
where 286 years are described in a mere five pages! It would not be
going too far to say that in this short book time literally flies by. The
readers could hardly be blamed if they think that the events here
described are not nearly as significant as those described in 3 Nephi.
In point of fact, they may be tempted to take the content of 4
Nephi as somewhat of an afterthought, though it does move them
closer to the end of the narrative and the destruction of the Nephites.[3] The book can be divided into the following sections:

---

[1] 'The Book of Nephi, Who Is the Son of Nephi, One of the Disciples of Jesus Christ' was first referred to as 4 Nephi in the 1879 LDS version of the Book
of Mormon published in Salt Lake City, Utah and Liverpool, England.

[2] Brant A. Gardner, *Second Witness: Fourth Nephi-Moroni* (ACCBM 6; Salt Lake
City: Greg Kofford, 2011), p. 16.

[3] Gardner (*Second Witness: Fourth Nephi-Moroni*, pp. 13, 41) concludes, 'All of 4
Nephi is simply a placeholder between the appearance of the Messiah and Mormon's own story … Fourth Nephi merely fills in the gap between the Savior's
visit and the Nephite annihilation'.

The New Society Established by Jesus (1-18)

The Plates Are Passed from Nephi to his Son Amos, and from Amos to his Son Amos (19-21)

Divisions among the People and Churches as well as the Return of the Gadianton Robbers (22-46)

Ammaron, Constrained by the Holy Ghost, Hides the Sacred Records (47-49)

Remarkably, the structure of 4 Nephi reveals a balance between its two major parts with words about the transfer of the plates standing at the conclusion of each, not unlike the way in which the words of Mormon stand at the conclusion of each major part of 3 Nephi.

During *the thirty-fourth year* since the coming of Christ until the *one hundred tenth year*, the disciples formed the church of Christ, baptizing in the name of Jesus those who truly repented of their sins. So successful were the efforts of the disciples that by *the thirty-sixth year* all the people were converted upon the face of the earth, both Nephites and Lamanites. Having all things in common there was no division. During *the thirty-seventh year*, great and marvelous miracles were done by the disciples; healing the sick, lame, blind, deaf, and all manner of miracles in the name of Jesus. Through *the fifty-ninth year* the Lord caused them to prosper, including the rebuilding of the great city Zarahemla. The people of Nephi did wax strong, multiplying exceedingly fast, becoming exceedingly fair and delightsome, walking after the Lord's commandments – no longer following the law of Moses. By *the hundredth year* all the disciples chosen by Jesus had gone to the paradise of God, save the three who should tarry, with others appointed to take the place of the nine. There were no contentions or wickedness, 'and surely there could not be a happier people among all the people who had been created by the hand of God', a statement that appears to trump an earlier one with regard to the happiness of the Nephites (Alma 50.23). There were no Lamanites 'nor any manner of -ites' for they were one, 'the children of Christ'. During the entire first generation from Christ (through *the hundred tenth year*), there were no contentions; the people were blessed and prospered (vv. 1-18). It might indeed strike the readers as odd that after twenty chapters devoted to Jesus' three-day visitation amongst the people that the effects of his visit are described in a mere eighteen verses.

At this point the readers are informed that Nephi kept the sacred records until his death, with his son Amos then keeping them in his father's stead for eighty-four years. During this time a small group rebelled from the church calling themselves Lamanites. When Amos died in *the hundred fourth year* his son, also named Amos, kept the records in his father's stead, writing in the Book of Nephi (vv. 19-21).

The next major section of this small book chronicles the emergence of a variety of divisions. By the time *two hundred years* had passed, Mormon tells of the people's multiplying and their prospering. By the next year, pride reappeared in the form of costly apparel, fine pearls, and fine things of the world. The people no longer lived in common but divided into classes. Other churches began to be established for the purpose of gain, with the true church of Christ beginning to be denied. In another ten years, many other churches appeared, denying more parts of the gospel. Still another church appeared which denied the Christ, despising the miracles done by the true church of Christ. Despite persecuting the disciples of Jesus who did tarry, their opponents were unable to come against them. Though smiting the people of Jesus, the people of Jesus did not return in kind. By *the year two hundred thirty* unbelief and wickedness was growing year to year. The next year a great division emerged amongst the people along the old lines of the Nephites and Laminates, with those who rejected and willfully rebelled against the gospel being called Lamanites. From *two hundred and forty-four years* until *two hundred and sixty years* churches continued to be built for gain. In fact, the wicked part of the people even began to build up again the secret oaths and combinations of the Gadianton. During this time the Nephites began to be proud like their brethren the Lamanites, owing to their exceeding riches. By *the year three hundred* both the Nephites and Lamanites were exceedingly wicked, the Gadiaton robbers spread across the face of the earth – there were none righteous except the disciples of Jesus (vv. 22-46).

The book of 4 Nephi concludes with words about the fate of the sacred records. Amos died after *three hundred and five years* had passed at which point his brother Ammaron kept the records in his stead. In *the three hundred twentieth year*, Ammaron was constrained by the

Holy Ghost and hid up the sacred records so that they might come again to the remnant of the house of Jacob according to the prophecies and promises of the Lord (vv. 47-49).

15

MORMON

The readers' journey continues with the thirteenth book found within the Book of Mormon, a nine-chapter book called the Book of Mormon that covers twenty pages in the 1830 edition and contains some 10,600 words. For the first time since 'The Words of Mormon', which stands between Omni and Mosiah, Mormon does more than offer editorial comments to the reader. The Book of Mormon picks up the narrative from the point at which Ammaron had hidden the sacred plates. Though not moving at the pace of 4 Nephi, the Book of Mormon does cover a lot of chronological ground, beginning with the year *three hundred and twenty-six* and concluding with the year *four hundred*, with three years covered per page on average.

The Book of Mormon can be divided into four parts, mirroring the chapter divisions in the 1830 edition of the Book of Mormon. Each part contains reference to the wars between the Nephites and Lamanites, mention of sacred plates/records, and words directed to the readers both ancient and future. The divisions are as follows:

Part One – Mormon Receives the Records, War Is Recounted, Mormon Makes a full Account on the Records, War Is Recounted, and Mormon Addresses his Readers (1.1-3.22)

Part Two – War is Recounted and Mormon Addresses his Readers (4.1-5.24)

Part Three – War Is Recounted, Mormon Offers a Lament, and Mormon Addresses his future Readers (6.1-7.10)

Part Four – The End of the Nephites Is Recounted, the Coming
    forth of the Record Is Foretold, the Readers Are
    Addressed (8.1-9.37).

Significantly, whilst Mormon is responsible for the first three parts,
owing to his death it is necessary for Mormon's son Moroni to provide the final part, completing the work of his father.

Part One of the Book of Mormon (1.1-3.22) picks up where 4
Nephi leaves off, beginning with the words, 'And now I, Mormon',
describing how it is that he winds up with the sacred records hidden
by Ammaron. Here the readers learn, in Mormon's own words, that
when he was but a sober child of the age of ten years, Ammaron
had charged him that when he was twenty-four years old he was to
go to the land of Antum, to a hill called Shim, and take the Plates of
Nephi – leaving the other records – to engrave upon them the
things he observed of his people (1.1-4).

Again the words 'And I, Mormon' appear as Mormon gives his
pedigree as a descendant of Nephi and recalls that when he was
eleven years of age he remembered Ammaron's words, despite being taken away to the land of Zarahemla. At this time the Nephites
(and their allies) and the Lamanites (and their allies) went to war,
with the Nephite army of over 30,000 being victorious. But wickedness prevailed upon the earth – so much so that the Lord took away
his three beloved disciples – and miracles of healing ceased, as did
the gifts of the Holy Ghost. Being fifteen years of age and of a sober mind, Mormon attempted to preach to his people but was forbidden, owing to the hardness of their hearts. In fact, the Gadianton robbers infested the land so much that the inhabitants hid up
their treasures in the earth; but the treasures became 'slippery' so
that the people could not hold or retain them. Evil abounded, fulfilling the words of Abinadi and Samuel the Lamanite (1.5-19).

In *the three hundred twenty-sixth year* Mormon, despite being only
sixteen years old, was appointed to lead the Nephite armies owing
to the fact that he was large in stature. During the next four years –
through *the three hundred thirtieth year*, Mormon's Nephite army withstood various attacks by the Lamanites and their king Aaron, even
though the Lamanite army of forty-four thousand outnumbered
Mormon's army of forty-two thousand. Significantly, at this point
the Nephites began to repent of their iniquity as prophesied by
Samuel. When 'I, Mormon' saw their lamentation 'my heart did

begin to rejoice within me', but this rejoicing was in vain for 'their sorrowing was not unto repentance', but was rather 'the sorrowing of the damned', who cursed God and wished to die. As a result of their open rebellion they were hewn down, and were pursued by the Lamanites during *the three hundred forty-fifth year* (2.1-16).

Finding himself close to the place where Ammaron had hidden the records Mormon took possession of the Plates of Nephi, making a full account of Nephite wickedness and abominations but he only offers an abbreviated account here in this record (2.17-19).

By *the three hundred forty-sixth year*, Mormon had fortified Shem and urged his army to fight 'for their wives, and their children, and their houses, and their homes'. But Mormon's thirty thousand strong army proved no match for the Lamanite fifty thousand strong force, for the Spirit of the Lord did not abide in the Nephites. But despite this fate they managed to regain some of the land of their inheritance during *the three hundred forty-ninth year*, making a treaty with the Lamanites the very next year in which the Nephites took possession of the land northward and ceded to the Lamanites the land southward (2.20-29).

For the next ten years the Nephites were not attacked by the Lamanites. During this time Mormon was commanded by the Lord to preach repentance, baptism, and the building up of the church. But his preaching was in vain for his people had hardened their hearts against the Lord (3.1-3). Then from *the three hundred sixtieth year* through *the three hundred sixty-second year* Mormon led the Nephite army to repeated victories, prompting them to boast of their own strength and to swear by heaven that they would avenge themselves upon the Lamanites (3.4-10). Such arrogance led Mormon to refuse to lead them into battle anymore, despite his love for them. The strength of his feeling being conveyed by another occurrence of the words, 'I, Mormon', he utterly refused to go up against his enemy, being instead an 'idle witness' (3.11-16).

Part One closes with a direct address by Mormon to his readers. First addressing the Gentiles and the House of Israel, he points out that the twelve tribes of Israel will return from the ends of the earth and be judged by the twelve disciples Jesus chose in the land of Jerusalem. Conversely, the remnant of his people will be judged by the twelve Jesus chose in this land, who in turn will be judged by the twelve chosen in the land of Jerusalem. Noting that what he writes is owing to what the Spirit manifests to him, Mormon warns that all must stand before the judgment-seat of Christ and be judged according to one's works. He also reminds them that they should believe the gospel of Jesus Christ, with Mormon confessing, 'And I would that I could persuade all ye ends of the earth to repent and prepare to stand before the judgment-seat of Christ' (3.17-22).

Part Two of the Book of Mormon (4.1-5.24) begins with additional words with regard to the warring between the Nephites and the Lamanites. In *the three hundred sixty-third year* the Nephites did go up to do battle with the Lamanites, but owing to their arrogance the Nephites were smitten – the wicked being punished by the wicked (4.1-5). The next year (*the three hundred sixty-fourth year*), the Nephites were able to drive back the attacks of the Lamanites, leading them again to boasting of their strength – even though thousands were slain on both sides (4.6-9). As *the three hundred sixty-sixth year* came to an end the Lamanites came again to attack the Nephites resulting in such horrible carnage that Mormon could hardly bring himself to write about it. 'And there was never so great wickedness among all the children of Lehi ...' (4.10-12). As a result of the Lamanite victories in which they took Nephite women and children as prisoners and sacrificed them, in *the three hundred sixty-seventh year* the Nephites drove the Lamanites out of their Nephite lands (4.13-15). Eventually, in *the three hundred seventy-fifth year* the Lamanites brought the full strength of their power down upon the Nephites, and from that time the Nephites could gain no power over their opponents. Despite their bold resistance, the Nephites could not withstand the Lamanites' repeated attacks (4.16-22). Such events convinced Mormon that now was the time to go to the hill Shim and retrieve all the records that Ammoron had hidden upon to the Lord (4.23). It was also at this time that Mormon repented of his oath not to lead the Nephites any longer, being reinstated as their leader. But now he was without hope, knowing the judgments of the Lord that awaited them. Though their resistance was valiant, and they were able to save a few cities by *the three hundred eightieth year*, the odds against them were overwhelming and only those who could flee faster than the Lamanites could pursue were spared (5.1-7).

As had Part One, Part Two of the Book of Mormon also concludes with Mormon directly addressing his readers (5.8-24). Beginning with his characteristic 'I, Mormon', he speaks to the Gentiles who have care for the House of Israel and then to the remnant of the House of Jacob. Reiterating that the time of the restoration will occur when God sees fit, Mormon prophesies of the time when unbelieving Jews will receive the gospel from Gentiles believing that Jesus is the Christ, the Son of the living God – a belief that will restore the Jews to the land of their inheritance. The posterity of the Lamanites will 'become a dark, a filthy, and a loathsome people ... because of their unbelief and idolatry', but God will not forget his promises to Abraham nor the prayers of the righteous (5.8-24).

The first section of **Part Three** of the Book of Mormon recounts the preparations for and fighting of the last battle described in the book (6.1-15). The climactic nature of the battle is immediately indicated by Mormon's words, 'And now I finish my record concerning the destruction of my people' as well as his characteristic, 'I, Mormon' in describing an epistle to the Lamanite king requesting permission to gather his people at the hill Cumorah in order to give them battle. This occurred when *the three hundred eighty-fourth year* had passed. For the second time in the span of five verses, 'I, Mormon' appears, this time in the context of describing his keeping the records entrusted to him and his decision to keep them from falling into the hands of the Lamanites by hiding them in the hill Cumorah, save it were a few plates he gave to his son Moroni (6.1-6). And so they waited as the Lamanite armies came against them hewing down ten thousand upon ten thousand. Mormon was wounded and left with only 24 other survivors, which included his son Moroni. It appears that as many as 230,000 people were killed in this gruesome battle, with the bodies left to molder upon the land (6.7-15).

Witnessing such annihilation brought forth anguish of soul for Mormon, who cried out for his people who had been slain:

> O ye fair ones,
>> how could ye have departed from the ways of the Lord!
> O ye fair ones,
>> how could ye have rejected that Jesus,
>> who stood with open arms to receive you!
> Behold, if ye had not done this, ye would not have fallen.
>> But behold, ye are fallen, and I mourn your loss.
> O ye fair sons and daughters,
>> ye fathers and mothers,

> ye husbands and wives,
> ye fair ones,
>> how is it that ye could have fallen!
> But behold, ye are gone,
>> and my sorrows cannot bring your return.[1]

Mormon follows this heart-felt lament with warnings about standing before the judgment-seat of Christ and further lamenting over their losses (6.16-22).

The last section of Part Three (7.1-10), like Parts One and Two before it, consists of words of Mormon addressed directly to his readers, but on this occasion he speaks to his future Lamanite readers – as a remnant of the House of Israel. Specifically, he reminds them of their identity as the House of Israel, instructs them on the necessity of their repentance and the laying down of their weapons of war – which they shall not pick back up except by the command of God – and putting off their delighting in the shedding of blood (7.1-4). Mormon goes on to make clear that they must come to a knowledge of the whole gospel, offering a summary of the salvific events involved in believing in Jesus Christ (7.5-7). As Mormon concludes his words in the Book of Mormon he returns to an emphasis on repentance and baptism in the name of Jesus and the gospel of Christ, which has been set forth in this record (the Book of Mormon[?]) and the record that will come to the Gentiles from the Jews (the Bible[?]), which record will be made known to you (the Lamanites) through the Gentiles by which knowledge of their fathers will be revealed (7.8-9). Such belief will result in their knowledge that they are a remnant of the seed of Jacob. In a parting blessing Mormon pronounces 'if it be so that ye believe in Christ, and are baptized, first with water, then with fire and with the Holy Ghost it shall be well with you in the day of judgment' (7.10).

Part Four of the Book of Mormon (8.1-9.37) recounts the end of the Nephites, the coming forth of the record in the latter days, and some final words addressed to the readers. The first section of Part Four (8.1-12) is rather clearly marked out by the words, 'Behold, I, Moroni', which stand at the section's beginning in v. 1 and the words, 'Behold, I am Moroni', which stand at the section's conclusion in v. 12. Here the readers learn that Moroni must finish the

---

[1] As set out in Hardy, *The Book of Mormon: A Reader's Edition*, pp. 566-67.

record of his father by writing a few things Mormon has commanded. Describing the aftermath of the final battle, Moroni reveals the
extermination of his people including that of his father, leaving Moroni alone to write about his people who are gone. A sense of resignation is detectable in his words,[2] 'And whether they slay me, I
know not'. Such despair continues when after underscoring his de-
termination to hide up the records in the earth he says, 'and whither
I go it mattereth not'. With regard to the record he says,

> I would write it also if I had room upon the plates, but I have
> not; and ore I have none, for I am alone. My father has been
> slain in battle, and all my kinfolk, and I have not friends nor
> whither to go; and how long the Lord will suffer that I may live I
> know not.

Four hundred years since the coming of Christ the Lamanites have hunted
down the Nephites and are now at war with one another and the
robbers. There are none but the wicked, save it be the disciples that
did tarry, whom the Lord has spared, and no one knows whether
they are still on the face of the land, though they have been seen by
Mormon and Moroni, to whom these disciples have ministered
(8.1-12).

Beginning with his pedigree Moroni says, 'I am the son of Mormon, and my father was a descendant of Nephi. And I am the same
who hideth up this record unto the Lord.' He notes that these
plates can only be brought forth out of the earth by the power of
God, by one whom the Lord blesses. While there might be faults in
the plates they are the faults of 'man' and should not detract from
the marvelous work God has done (8.13-22). At this point Moroni
shifts to a description of when the record shall come forth. The
saints who have gone before will, in accordance with the prophecies
of Isaiah, cry out from the dust unto the Lord who will remember
his covenant for he knows their faith, a faith that fuels a variety of
miraculous activities. Their prayers were also in behalf of the one
that the Lord shall suffer to bring these things forth. The record
will come from the earth in a day when miracles are thought to have
ceased, when the power of God is denied, when churches are de-
filed and lifted up with pride, when there are earthquakes, wars, ru-

---

[2] Cf. Hardy, *Understanding the Book of Mormon*, pp. 219-20.

mors of wars in foreign lands, great pollution upon the earth, and when churches are built up for gain. The Lord has revealed these things to Moroni who says to his future readers, 'Behold, I speak to you as if ye were present, and yet ye are not. But behold, Jesus Christ has shown you to me, and I know your doing.' Specifically, Moroni knows of their pride of heart, their fine apparel, and the adorning of their churches while they neglect the poor, needy, sick, and afflicted. Over such ones the sword of vengeance hangs (8.23-41).

Turning his attention to those who do not believe in Christ, Moroni warns of the impossibility of dwelling before the Lamb of God with a consciousness of one's guilt and filthiness and invites all such to turn to the Lord and cry to the Father to be cleansed by the blood of the Lamb (9.1-6). Moroni continues by addressing those who do not believe in the revelations of God: prophecies, gifts, healing, speaking in tongues, and interpretation of tongues (9.7-8). Such a position is impossible to reconcile with the truth:

> For do we not read that God is the same yesterday, today, and forever, and in him there is no variableness, neither shadow of changing. And now, if ye have imagined up unto yourselves a god who doth vary, and in whom there is shadow of changing, then have ye imagined up unto yourselves a god who is not a God of miracles (9.9-10).

Moroni then chronicles a variety of miracles divinely initiated within the pages of Scripture. These include the creation of Adam and the redemption of humankind brought by Jesus Christ, whose death brought to pass the resurrection. Going further to ask how all these things took place if God does not perform miracles, for Moroni the answer is self-evident. The miracles have not ceased owing to a changing God, but rather owing to the unbelief of 'the children of men'. Directing his words to those who believe, Moroni includes the same commands – almost *verbatim* – as one finds in Mk 16.15-18. He offers additional encouragement and advice for securing one's place in the kingdom of heaven (9.11-29).

Again using the imagery of speaking to his readers as though he speaks from the dead, Moroni offers some final observations about the record. He asks his readers not to condemn him, his father, nor other writers for their imperfections, but rather to give thanks to

God for the opportunity to be more wise than his people have been. Next, Moroni reveals that the record has been written in characters known as 'Reformed Egyptian', which they had inherited, making alterations according to 'our manner of speech'. If the records had been physically larger they could have been written in Hebrew, which would have resulted in no imperfection. The Lord knows the things written and has prepared means for their interpretation, for no other people knows their language. Moroni concludes by offering a few words on the purpose of the record – so that the Nephites might rid themselves of the blood of their brethren, restoring their brethren to the knowledge of Christ, and that God the Father might remember his covenant with the House of Israel. The book itself concludes with a final 'Amen' (9.30-37).

16

ETHER

The readers' journey continues with the fourteenth book found within the Book of Mormon, a fifteen-chapter book called the Book of Ether that covers thirty-four pages in the 1830 edition and contains some 18,595 words. The Book of Ether departs from the practice of picking up where the previous narrative leaves off, instead offering an abridgement of the twenty-four plates found by the people of Limhi that come from a far removed period of time. It appears that by including this book, Moroni is making good on Mormon's promise to the readers in Mosiah 28.17-19, and alluded to in Alma 37.21-32 as well as Helaman 6.28.[1] Thus, though the book is chronologically out of place, the readers would understand why it is included at this point in the Book of Mormon.

The structure of Ether is both simple and complicated at one and the same time. On the one hand, the book exhibits a rather straightforward movement that might be presented as falling into four parts:

Part One – Moroni Introduces the Book and Provides the
Genealogy of Ether (1.1-33)

Part Two – The Brother of Jared and the Relocation to the
Americas (1.34-6.18)

Part Three – The People Desire a King and the History of the
Regal Reigns (6.19-11.23)

---

[1] Hardy, *Understanding the Book of Mormon*, pp. 227-28.

Part Four – The Prophet Ether and the End of the Jaredites
(12.1-15.34).

On the other hand, this somewhat neat and tidy structure is complicated by the presence of numerous editorial comments by Moroni in every part of the book. Part One opens with a set of Moroni's comments (1.1-33), Part Two contains three such sets of comments (2.9-12; 3.17-20; 4.1-5.6), while Parts Three and Four contain one set of comments each (8.20-26 and 12.6-41, respectively). In some ways these remarks by Moroni might be thought to be intrusions into the flow of the document, but as will be seen, in each case Moroni offers relevant comment on the topic at hand. Thus, bearing in mind the simpler and more straightforward four-part structure, a more extensive structure – one that includes more detail as well as Moroni's editorial comments – would appear as follows:

Part One – Moroni Introduces the Book and Provides the
    Genealogy of Ether (1.1-33)
Part Two – The Brother of Jared and the Relocation to the
    Americas (1.34-6.18)
    Jared's Brother Appeals to God (1.34-43)
        The Journey Begins (2.1-8)
            [Moroni's Words of Warning (2.9-12)]
        The Sea Journey Preparations (2.13-3.5)
    Jared's Brother Sees the Lord (3.6-16)
            [Moroni's Comments on Jared's Brother Seeing the
            Lord (3.17-20)]
    Jared's Brother Receives a Commission to Write (3.21-28)
            [Moroni and the Emergence of the Record (4.1-5.6)]
    The Sea Journey (6.1-13)
    The People Prosper (6.14-18)
Part Three – The People Desire a King and the History of the
    Regal Reigns (6.19-11.23)
    The People Desire a King (6.19-26)
    A History of the Regal Reign (6.27-8.19)
            [Moroni's Words of Warning (8.20-26)]
    A History of the Regal Reign Continued (9.1-11.23)

In **Part One**, continuity between the Book of Mormon and the Book of Ether is provided by the opening words in the book, 'And now I, Moroni', indicating to the readers that the same voice that led them to the conclusion of the previous book will now lead them through the current one as well. In other words, the readers encounter a trusted narrator. But if they expected continuity with the narrative development witnessed in the Book of Mormon, they are quickly disabused of that expectation. Rather, they learn that Moroni intends to give an account from the 24 plates found by the people of Limhi called the Book of Ether. Thus, though there is a break in continuity with the book that immediately precedes at one level, at another level the readers would pick up on the continuity provided by this account to the overall sacred record, for previously Mormon had promised a recounting of this very book (Mosiah 28.17-19), alluding to it from time to time (Alma 37.21-32 and Helaman 6.28). Apparently, the story to be recounted begins with the days of Adam, but Moroni chooses to initiate his account beginning from the tower to the destruction of the people (1.1-6a).

Moroni next identifies the individual from whom this record comes: a character named Ether, a descendant of Coriantor. Providing an extensive genealogy, the record traces Coriantor back some 26 generations to Jared and his brother, who with their families and a few others were part of the generation present just before the Lord confounded the language of the people building the tower of Babel and scattered them upon all the face of the earth (1.6b-33).

Part Two of the Book of Ether (1.34-6.18), which chronicles the activities of Jared's brother from the Tower of Babel events to the establishment of a prosperous people in the Americas, is divided into several sections with three of the sections containing Moroni's words of warning and/or explanation. In the first section (1.34-43) it is revealed that owing to his size and might, Jared's brother was a man highly favored of the Lord. In fact, on three separate occasions in this section Jared asks that his brother, who is never named in the book (!), make three specific requests of the Lord, each of which Jared's brother does, with each request being answered. The requests are (1) that the language of Jared and his brother not be confounded when God confounded the language of the others; (2) that God not confound the language of their friends; and (3) that if the Lord drives them out of the land, perhaps they might be led to a land choice above all others. In responding to the last petition the Lord instructs the brother of Jared to gather all their people, flocks, seeds, etc. and meet the Lord in a particular valley that is northward from whence the Lord may indeed lead them to, 'a land which is choice above all the lands of the earth where he will make of them a great nation' (1.34-43).

Jared and his brother did as instructed, taking all the people and things specified, including 'deseret' (a 'honey bee'), into the valley of Nimrod. Here the Lord came down and talked with the brother of Jared in a cloud, but was hidden from him. The Lord went before them, in a cloud, to guide them. They traveled in the wilderness, building barges and crossing many waters, but the Lord would not allow them to stop short of the land of promise. The necessity of absolute obedience is stressed in a warning to the brother of Jared:

> And he had sworn in his wrath unto the brother of Jared, that whoso should possess this land of promise, from that time henceforth and forever, should serve him, the true and only God, or they should be swept off when the fullness of his wrath should come upon them.

Such stark words could not help but put the readers on notice that obedience or the lack thereof will play an important role in this story (2.1-8).

The importance of this warning is reiterated by the words of Moroni that immediately follow. Significantly, Moroni twice states the warning in near identical form, further underscoring the importance of this theme for the readers as the book unfolds. Moroni goes on to warn the Gentile readers specifically, calling for repentance from their iniquities to ensure that they do not call down the fullness of God's wrath upon them as they reside in this choice land in the future. He promises that those who possess the land shall be free from bondage, 'if they will but serve the God of the land' who Moroni explicitly identifies as Jesus Christ (2.9-12).

Picking up his narrative again, Moroni chronicles the people's journey to the great sea, where they dwelt in tents for four years. At this point, God reappears to the brother of Jared for the space of three hours, chastening him for not remembering to call upon the Lord! Repenting of this evil, the brother of Jared is forgiven with the stern warning, 'but thou shalt not sin anymore, for ye shall remember that my Spirit will not always strive with man'. With that warning given, God instructs the brother of Jared, 'Go to work and build, after the manner of barges which ye have hitherto built' (2.13-16a).

Building the barges to specification, the brother of Jared realizes that there are a few problems with the design of these small, airtight, light, dish-like vessels, the ends of which were peaked, and their length that of a tree. There was no means of steering, nor was there any means of taking in air, nor was there any light in the structures. As for steering, the Lord will propel them; as for air, they are to cut holes in the top and bottom of the structure, opening and closing the holes as needed (2.16b-25); as for a means of illumination, the brother of Jared fashioned 16 small, clear, transparent stones, bringing them to the Lord to touch which caused them to shine forth (3.1-5).

When the Lord touched each stone with his finger – perhaps a reference to the Spirit, the veil was taken off the eyes of the brother of Jared and he saw that the finger of the Lord was as a man's finger 'like unto flesh and blood'. Fearing that he would be smitten by the Lord, for he had not known that the Lord had a body of flesh and blood, the Lord reassured the brother of Jared that he would take up on himself flesh and blood and that his (Jared's brother's) faith was superior to any before him. In fact, Jared's brother's faith is so great that the pre-Incarnate Christ showed himself to the brother of Jared, redeeming him from the fall and bringing him back into the Lord's presence. Specifically, the Lord says,

> Behold, I am he who was prepared from the foundation of the world to redeem my people. Behold I am Jesus Christ. I am the Father and the Son ... Behold, this body, which ye now behold, is the body of my spirit; and man have I created after the body of my spirit; and even as I appear unto thee to be in the spirit will I appear unto my people in the flesh.

Clearly, this encounter with the Lord is one of the, if not the most, intimate of all accounts related in the Book of Mormon (3.6-16).

Again the words of Moroni appear in the story of the brother of Jared. On this occasion Moroni makes clear that the way in which Jesus had shown himself to the brother of Jared was 'in the likeness of the same body even as he showed himself unto the Nephites'. Significantly, this pre-Incarnate manifestation precedes Jesus' appearance to the Nephites by close to a couple of thousand years. After this experience the brother of Jared could not be kept from within the veil. He saw Jesus and was ministered to by him (3.17-20).

Picking the narrative back up, Moroni next narrates the Lord's instruction to the brother of Jared to treasure up these things in his heart, writing them, sealing them up, writing them in a language that no one can interpret – as it has been confounded by the Lord – but which can be understood by means of two stones. Showing the brother of Jared all the people of the world and the ends of the earth, the Lord withheld nothing from his sight. Again he instructs the brother of Jared to write the account and seal it up, and to seal up the two stones with it as the means for interpretation when the Lord will bring the writings about the brother of Jared forth in due time (3.21-28).

For a third time in Part Two the words of Moroni appear. Not only was the brother of Jared to seal up and not make known these words until Jesus was lifted up on the cross, but King Mosiah also kept them until Christ truly manifested himself. Owing to the fact that all have now dwindled in unbelief, Moroni has been commanded to hide these words again in the earth along with the interpreters. These words will come forth to the Gentiles in the day of their repentance says 'Jesus Christ, the Son of God, the Father of the heavens and of the earth'. Jesus continues to speak underscoring his authority and the connection between belief in his words and belief in his disciples. The one who believes the words Jesus has spoken will be visited with the manifestation of his Spirit confirming that these things are true, 'and he that will not believe me will not believe the Father who sent me. For behold, I am the Father, I am the light, and the life, and the truth of the world.' With this both Gentiles and the House of Israel are invited to call upon the Father in his name. At such a time the revelations written by John will be unfolded. Thus, when this record is received, the work of the Father will have commenced. Jesus' words conclude with words very similar to those repeated by Moroni in Mormon 9 and written in Mark 16, with an invitation to the readers to believe and a blessing pronounced on those who do (4.1-19). Moroni goes on to offer instruction to those (or the one) who shall find them, 'ye may be privileged that ye may show the plates unto those who shall assist to bring forth this work' for in the mouth of three witnesses shall these things be established (5.1-6).

When the narrative resumes the brother of Jared placed the sixteen stones in the vessels and brought all the people, animals, seeds, and food onto the vessels as well. Great storms propelled them across the waters, the vessels sometimes being buried in the deep, but no water could hurt them owing to the tightness of the vessels. And the voyagers sang daily praise unto God, having light continually. They were driven forth for 344 days. When they finally made landfall, they immediately bowed themselves down and shed tears of joy before the Lord for his tender mercies. Obviously, the brother of Jared did not need to be reminded of his earlier failure to call upon the Lord (6.1-13). Though they were but few when they landed, they began to be many. Being taught to walk humbly before the Lord, they multiplied and waxed strong in the land (6.14-18).

Part Three of the Book of Ether (6.19-11.23) recounts the people's desire for a king and the resulting history of the regal reigns. As the brother of Jared became old, he and Jared gathered the people together to number them and to know what the people desired of them before they went to the grave. The people made known that they desired a king to be appointed, a move that troubled the brother of Jared. But at Jared's insistence they finally appointed Jared's son Orihah as king – after several had refused to serve as king (6.19-27). In what follows, a brief historical sketch is offered that chronicles the reigns of the individuals listed in the genealogy with which the Book of Ether began. This history is full of stories of ascendency to the throne through peaceful transition, the intrigue of kings deposed by relatives desirous of the throne, the division of the kingdom into two, the re-enthronement of deposed monarchs living in captivity, and the utilization of secret combinations to take the kingdom from one person and give it to another (6.28-8.19). In the midst of this history the readers learn that prophets arose, sent by the Lord 'prophesying that the wickedness and idolatry of the people was bringing a curse upon the land, and they should be destroyed if they did not repent', a warning consistent with those previously given to the people. Though many mocked, the ministry of the prophets met with some success, with repentance not only staving off punishment but also causing the people to prosper (7.23-26).

In the midst of this historical recounting, the words of Moroni once again appear (8.20-26). This section is marked off in part by the fact that the words 'I, Moroni' stand at the beginning and the end of the passage (8.20, 26). On this occasion Moroni reflects upon the manner of the oaths and combinations employed in obtaining the kingdom (8.7-19), warning that such activity inevitably leads to destruction. The Gentiles in particular are warned about the dangerous nature of encountering such secret combinations for they overthrow the freedom of all lands and bring destruction of all people, being built up by the devil. Specifically, Moroni writes so that this evil and Satan may have no power over his Gentile readers in the latter-days.

At this point the survey of regal reigns continues in much the same way it had begun, though this section is even longer than the previous one (9.1-11.23). Murder and intrigue are the order of the day with certain righteous kings ruling from time to time, during which the Lord begins to take away the curse from the land and the people prosper (9.16). In point of fact, it is said of one king by the name of Coriantum that 'he even saw the Son of Righteousness, and did rejoice and glory in his day' (9.22), reminding the reader of the experience the brother of Jared had with the pre-Incarnate Jesus Christ. When iniquity again appeared shortly thereafter, prophets reappeared crying out about repentance and the curse of God (9.28). But on this occasion the people did not believe, resulting in a famine and the emergence of poisonous snakes, both of which eventually leading to repentance! A king by the name of Riplakish did not do right in the sight of the Lord having many wives and concubines (10.3), while Morianton was known for his many whoredoms (10.11). Conversely, under the reign of Lib it is written, 'And never could be a people more blessed than were they, and more prospered by the hand of the Lord' (10.28). Many prophets came in the reign of Com but they were rejected by the people (11.1-2) and were even put to death under Shiblom (11.5-6). Later, under the reign of Ethem, many prophets again prophesied that the Lord would destroy them if they did not repent. Sorrowful over the lack of repentance, the prophets withdrew from among the people (11.12-13). Even during the lifetime of Coriantor, who was born in captivity, the work of the prophets was met with rejection (11.20-22).

Part Four of the Book of Ether (12.1-15.34) finally introduces the book's namesake, the prophet Ether in earnest, chronicling his ministry activity, and recounting the end of the Jaredites. Contextualized in the reign of Coriantumr, Ether is introduced as a prophet of the Lord who could not be restrained from prophesying because the Spirit of the Lord was in him. Despite his crying from morning until the setting of the sun about great and marvelous things, the people did not believe because they saw them not (12.1-5).

After this brief introduction of the prophet Ether, the readers again encounter the words of Moroni in what will be his longest editorial comment in the entire book (12.6-13.12). The first part of his comment appears between the words 'I, Moroni' that stand at the beginning (12.6) and near the end (12.38). Specifically, Moroni responds to the lack of faith amongst Ether's hearers by arguing that 'faith is things which are hoped for and not seen'. He goes on to point to a number of exemplars of faith including Moses, Alma, Amulek, Nephi, Lehi, Ammon, the three disciples that did not taste death, and the brother of Jared whose faith is presented as a culminating example – 'the Lord could not withhold anything from his sight; wherefore he showed him all things, for he could no longer be kept without the veil' (12.10-21). Moroni goes on to point out that it is by faith that his fathers obtained the promise that the Nephite record should come to their (latter-day) brethren (the Lamanites) through the Gentiles. Fearing that the Gentiles will mock Moroni's efforts owing to his weakness in writing – an emphasis that literally surrounds his words about his inabilities to write well (12.23, 25) – Moroni calls out to the Lord who reassures him that no one will take advantage of his weakness, and the Lord's grace is sufficient to make weak ones become strong for those who have faith (12.26-28). These words comforted Moroni who recalled that mountains *can* be moved through faith even as Zerin experienced. Moroni also remembered that the Lord had prepared a house for the faithful in the mansion of the Father and that the Lord loved the world so much that he gave his life for the 'children of men'. Ultimately, Moroni prays for the Gentiles to be given grace. But such does not matter, says the Lord, for Moroni has been faithful and his garments are clean (12.29-37). Moroni concludes this portion of his remarks with a farewell to the Gentiles testifying that at the judgment seat they will know 'that I have seen this Jesus, and that he talked with me face to face, and that he told me in plain humility, even as a man telleth another in mine own language, concerning these things'. He goes on to commend them to seek this Jesus (12.38-41).

The attention of the second half of Moroni's remarks on this occasion shifts to the destruction of the people who rejected Ether's words (13.1-12). The content of Ether's prophesying commenced with the beginning of 'man', included the choice land from which the waters receded, and the identification that this was the place of the New Jerusalem which should come down out of heaven. Seeing the days of Christ, Ether prophesied of the New Jerusalem, the Jerusalem from which Lehi would come, and the remnant of Joseph that would come out of Jerusalem. It is this remnant that will be built upon this land. There shall be a new heaven and new earth for 'all things have become new', which will be accompanied by the great restoration.

Sadly, Ether's words met with rejection by his people so much so that he had to hide in a cave by day, going out to view what the Lord would do by night and in this way completing his record. At this time King Coriantumr began to be attacked and the Lord sent Ether to prophesy to him that if he and his family would repent they would be saved, but if not, every soul would be destroyed but Corinatumr. Yet he repented not (13.13-22). In the immediate aftermath, Coriantumr fought against Shared with five different outcomes described over the course of nine verses (13.23-31). As a result, a great curse came upon the land so that one's tools, swords, etc. had to be kept upon one's person lest they disappeared by morning (14.1-2). This was followed by a period of battles with the brother of Shared (Gilead), Lib, and Shiz, with the result being that no one was left to bury the dead, with bodies strewn upon the face of the earth, the stench of which became unbearable (14.3-30). After over 2,000,000 of his people had been slain Corinatumr 'began to sorrow in his heart'. Remembering the words of the prophets he appealed to Shiz to trade his kingdom for the lives of his people, but the people thirsted for battle and defeated the army of Shiz. After which the armies of Coriantumr pitched their tents by the hill Ramah where Mormon had hidden the plates. For the next four years both armies gathered for a final confrontation (15.1-14). As the story continues it recounts a society bent on total destruction, 'both men, women and children being armed with weapons of war'. Coriantumr again offers his kingdom if Shiz will spare the lives of his people. The story then focuses upon a continual dwindling of the forces on each side – 52 people of Coriantumr, 69 of Shiz; 27 of Coriantumr, 32 of Shiz – until only the two leaders survived, that is until Corinatumr cut off the head of Shiz, who interestingly enough though decapitated struggled for breath before dying (15.15-32). Thus standing near the beginning and the end of the Book of Mormon narrative are decapitations, forming an inclusio of sorts around the whole.[2] At which point, Ether went out to witness the results of his prophesying, completed his record, and hid it in a manner that the people of Limhi could find (15.33). The last words of Ether conclude the entire book: 'Whether the Lord will that I be translated, or that I shall suffer the will of the Lord in the flesh, it mattereth not, if it be that I am saved in the kingdom of God. Amen' (15.34).

---

[2] For this insight cf. Dan Vogel, *Joseph Smith: The Making of a Prophet* (Salt Lake City: Signature, 2004), p. 360.

17

MORONI

The last book that the readers encounter in their journey through the Book of Mormon is a ten-chapter book called the Book of Moroni that covers fifteen pages in the 1830 edition and contains some 7,037 words.

Although somewhat disparate in terms of content, the structure of the Book of Moroni appears to fall into four parts:

Part One – A Few More Things – Instructions with regard to the Holy Ghost, Ordinations, the Blessing of the Bread and Wine, Baptism, and Church Order (1.1-6.9)

Part Two – Mormon's Sermon on Faith, Hope, and Charity (7.1-48)

Part Three – Mormon's Epistle on Infant Baptism and his Epistle on the Wickedness of the Nephites and his Farewell to Moroni (8.1-9.26)

Part Four – Moroni's Farewell to the Lamanites and to All the Ends of the Earth (10.1-34).

As such, one can see a certain progression to the book.

As **Part One** of the Book of Moroni (1.1-6.9) opens the readers learn that there is continuity between the narrator of the previous book, which is explicitly mentioned, and the writer of this book. Thus, the voice that they have heard beginning with the last two chapters of the Book of Mormon continues to inform them. They also learn that Moroni had not intended to write more, but owing to the fact that he had not yet perished by the hand of the Lamanites, he has decided to write 'a few more things', a phrase mentioned twice in 1.4, that it might be of some worth to his (surviving) Lamanite brethren in some future day. On the one hand, Moroni's words might suggest to the readers a haphazardness in the way the contents of the book have been chosen, implying a certain randomness in selection. On the other hand, the realization that this book contains Moroni's last words just before his certain death might convey a sense of the contents' importance, for surely (so the readers might think) Moroni would not waste his time – at the point of death – on anything but the most important matters.

As the readers learn, the rest of Part One consists of an accounting of the way in which a variety of important aspects of church life was handled by Jesus and/or his disciples. The first such issue concerns the way in which the Holy Ghost was (and is to be) given. Jesus' instructions to the twelve, which were not heard by the multitude (3 Nephi 15.36-37), are:

> Ye shall call on the Father in my name, in mighty prayer; and after ye have done this ye shall have power that to him upon whom ye shall lay your hands, ye shall give the Holy Ghost; and in my name shall you give it, for thus do mine apostles.

On as many as they laid their hands, fell the Holy Ghost (2.1-3).

The second issue concerns the way in which the disciples, who were called elders, were to ordain priests and teachers. After prayer, hands are laid upon the candidate and the following words are recited:

> In the name of Jesus Christ I ordain you to be a priest … (or teacher) … to preach repentance and remission of sins through Jesus Christ, by the endurance of faith on his name to the end. Amen.

Such ordinations took place by the power of the Holy Ghost (3.1-4).

The third issue concerns the blessing upon the bread that was practiced by the elders and priests.

> O God, the Eternal Father, we ask thee in the name of thy Son, Jesus Christ, to bless and sanctify this bread to the souls of all those who partake of it; that they may eat in remembrance of the

body of thy Son, and witness unto thee, O God, the Eternal Father, that they are willing to take upon them the name of thy Son, and always remember him, and keep his commandments which he hath given them, that they may always have his Spirit to be with them. Amen. (4.1-3)

The fourth issue is the related one of the blessing upon the administering of the wine:

O God, the Eternal Father, we ask thee in the name of thy Son, Jesus Christ, to bless and sanctify this wine to the souls of all those who drink of it; that they may do it in remembrance of the blood of thy Son, which was shed for them; that they may witness unto thee, O God, the Eternal Father, that they do always remember him, and that they may have his Spirit to be with them. Amen. (5.1-2)

Though Jesus himself observed the breaking of bread and drinking of wine when he appeared amongst the Nephites, there were no recorded blessings on those occasions.

The fifth issue concerns baptism. Though baptism has been described often in the Book of Mormon and a formula has been prescribed for use during its practice (cf. 3 Nephi 11.25-26), the emphasis here is upon the qualifications for baptism and the events resulting from baptism. In order to qualify for baptism one must bring forth fruit worthy of baptism, have a broken heart and contrite spirit, and witness unto the church one's true repentance. After being baptized and cleansed by the power of the Holy Ghost, such ones are numbered among the people of the church, their names are recorded, and they are nurtured in the good word of God and prayer (6.1-4).

The sixth issue concerns the order of their lives together (6.5-9). The church is to meet together often to fast and pray and to partake of the bread and wine. Whoever committed iniquity was to be condemned by three witnesses of the church and if they did not repent their names were blotted out and they were not numbered among the people of Christ. But as often as they repented with real intent, they were forgiven. The nature of their meetings is described thus:

And their meetings were conducted by the church after the manner of the workings of the Spirit, and by the power of the

Holy Ghost; for as the power of the Holy Ghost led them whether to preach, or to exhort, or to pray, or to supplicate, or to sing, even so it was done.

With this, Part One concludes.

Part Two of the Book of Moroni (7.1-48) consists of a sermon by Moroni's father, Mormon, on faith, hope, and charity which he spoke in a synagogue built as a place of worship. The sermon itself constantly reminds of its Christian audience as the phrases 'my beloved brethren' or 'my brethren' appear throughout, sometimes indicating a change in the sermon's direction. Addressing the peaceable followers of Christ he describes how that men who are evil cannot do that which is good, for all good things come from God (7.1-14). Mormon next tells his readers, that it is given to them to judge, words that at first might strike the readers as standing in some tension with Jesus' earlier words with regard to judging in 3 Nephi 14. But as Mormon continues it becomes clear that the basis of their judgment is the Spirit of Christ which helps each person know good from evil, finally warning not to judge wrongfully lest one receive the same judgment oneself (7.15-19). The next section of the sermon focuses on the faith by which one can lay hold on every good thing. Specifically, God sent angels to minister with regard to the coming of Christ, as well as sending prophets to declare his coming so that even before Christ's Incarnation, people could be saved by faith in him. Following his coming, people continued to be saved by faith in his name. During this section Mormon asks rhetorically if miracles have ceased to occur or if angels have ceased to minister, answering strongly in the negative whilst underscoring the necessity of faith for both to continue (7.20-39). Moving on, Mormon asserts the interconnection between faith, hope, and charity, citing a few words similar to those found in 1 Corinthians 13 and 1 John 3-4. He concludes by equating charity with 'the pure love of Christ' and admonishes his readers to 'pray unto the Father with all the energy of heart, that ye may be filled with love' (Moroni 7.47-48).

Part Three of the Book of Moroni (8.1-9.26) is devoted to two epistles Mormon sent to his son Moroni; one devoted to a discussion of infant baptism and the destruction of Nephites, with the other devoted to the wickedness of the Nephites and his farewell to Moroni. Taken together with the preceding sermon, Mormon's voice, though physically extinguished, continues to speak to the readers, perhaps reminding them of the prominence played by Mormon and Moroni in the Book's title page content (and in the bulk of the book).

The first of the two epistles (8.1-30), which claims to have been written soon after Moroni's call to the ministry, displays a certain level of intimacy, as Moroni is called 'son' some nine times in these verses. The epistle itself is a focused attack upon the practice of infant baptism. Calling infant baptism 'a gross error', Mormon argues for its immediate cessation. For the Lord had revealed to Mormon that little children are whole, cannot sin, and the curse of Adam has no hold on them. In fact, the practice of infant baptism is a solemn mockery before God. Such children are 'alive in Christ' even from the foundation of the world. If not, 'God is a partial God ... a changeable God'. To suppose children need such baptism is 'the bitterest gall of hell'. This awful wickedness perverts the ways of God, for 'God is not a partial God, neither a changeable being; but he is unchangeable from all eternity to all eternity' (8.18). To claim that children need baptism denies the mercies of Christ, setting at naught the atonement (8.1-26). In the final lines of this epistle Mormon promises to write again if he does not go out soon to the Lamanites. The situation is grave. While Mormon requests the prayers of Moroni for the Nephites' repentance, he fears that the Spirit of the Lord has stopped striving with them and that they must soon perish (8.27-30).

In the second of Mormon's epistles (9.1-26) he again uses the phrase 'my son' often – some eight times. Primarily, Mormon informs Moroni of the great wickedness of the Nephites and the suffering of his people. The wives and children of slain men are made to eat the flesh of their loved ones, like unto wild beasts. This once 'civil and delightsome people' now delight in abomination! They are depraved and have strong perversion, delighting in everything but the good! Their wickedness exceeds that of the Lamanites! Mormon's prayer is that Moroni will survive to see either the repentance of the Nephites or their utter destruction, a fate like that of the Jaredites. With this observation the readers might now better understand the Book of Ether as a final parabolic tale of warning lest they too experience the same fate! Mormon hopes that he might see his son Moroni, to transfer the sacred records to him if nothing else.

Part Four of the Book of Moroni (10.1-34) consists of Moroni's farewell both to the Lamanites and to all the ends of the earth. The change from the words of Mormon to the words of Moroni is indicated to the readers by the reappearance of the words 'I, Moroni'. Perhaps somewhat surprisingly Moroni writes to his brethren, the Lamanites, reminding them that it has been *420 years since the sign of the coming of Christ* and informing them that he is now going to seal up the records. In this context some of the most famous words found in the entire Book of Mormon occur. Speaking to future readers he writes:

> And when ye shall receive these things, I would exhort you that ye would ask God, the Eternal Father, in the name of Christ, if these things are not true; and if ye shall ask with a sincere heart, with real intent, having faith in Christ, he will manifest the truth of it unto you, by the power of the Holy Ghost. And by the power of the Holy Ghost ye may know the truth of all things (10.4-5).

Standing where they do, these words function as a fitting conclusion to the sacred records with which the Book of Mormon has been so often concerned. But they also go some way toward closing the gap for the readers between the time of Moroni – and his certain death – and the time of the readers hundreds of years later. Following fast on the heels of this invitation, Moroni instructs his Lamanite readers not to deny the gifts of God, which are many. He then lists several of them including: the word of wisdom, the word of knowledge, exceeding great faith, gifts of healing, mighty miracles, prophesying, the beholding of angels and ministering spirits, tongues, interpretation of tongues, and divers kinds of tongues. He reminds the Lamanites that such gifts will never be done away with for Christ 'is the same yesterday, today, and forever' (10.8-19). Hearkening back to the themes of his father's sermon, Moroni closes this section by underscoring the importance of faith, hope, and charity (10.20-23).

Turning his attention to 'all the ends of the earth' Moroni exhorts them to remember his words for he does not lie and they will surely see him at the bar of God, at which point the Lord God will remind them of the many words he has spoken to them. 'His word shall hiss forth from generation to generation. And God shall show unto you, that that which I have written is true' (10.24-29). Moroni closes with an invitation for his readers to come unto Christ, utilizing words similar to a number of texts found in the Bible including Isaiah. Significantly, the name Christ appears six times in this short section (10.30-33). Moroni's final words conclude the book:

> And now I bid unto all, farewell. I soon go to rest in the paradise of God, until my spirit and body shall again reunite, and I am brought forth triumphant through the air, to meet you before the pleasing bar of the great Jehovah, the Eternal Judge of both quick and dead. Amen (10.34).

And with this, the readers come to the end of their journey through the Book of Mormon.

PART THREE

THE THEOLOGY OF THE BOOK OF MORMON

The survey of the contents of the Book of Mormon in Part Two lays the foundation for Part Three, the intent of which is to offer an overview of the major theological features, doctrines, and/or themes of the Book of Mormon. This task is complicated by the fact that, oddly enough, this aspect of the book has not received the kind of comprehensive treatment one would expect given its Scriptural status in the LDS family of churches.[1] Perhaps one of the reasons for this lacuna is the fact that for many restorationist churches, the Book of Mormon is not the final, or even most recent, of the documents that comprise restorationist Scripture, meaning that its theological teaching is not necessarily the final word on a given topic, but may sometimes be regarded as provisional at best.[2] Other contributing reasons for this situation may be that in the communities for which the Book of Mormon functions as Scripture, often 'theology' has been eschewed as not as meaningful for the tradition(s) as knowing the teachings of the group(s). But as the meaning of the word theology (study of God) reveals, everyone 'does' theology whether they claim to do so or not. This chapter does not intend to be comprehensive in its coverage but seeks to identify the major theological emphases in the book owing to the prominence of such themes in the book itself, or the effect certain teachings have had within the groups for whom the book functions as Scripture.

---

[1] Often the theology of the book is listed as themes in works devoted to the Book of Mormon, lacking the kind of detailed treatment one might expect of a book esteemed as Scripture. Though written for a popular audience and relatively brief, one of the more extensive treatments of the theology of the Book of Mormon is found in the recent study by Dale E. Luffman, *The Book of Mormon's Witness to Its First Readers* (Independence, MO: Community of Christ Seminary Press, 2013), especially pp. 126-79. Cf. also the relevant sections in Charles R. Harrell, *'This Is My Doctrine': The Development of Mormon Theology* (Salt Lake City: Greg Kofford Books, 2013), and Grant Underwood, 'The Book of Mormon Usage in Early LDS Theology', *Dialogue: A Journal of Mormon Thought* 17.3 (1984), pp. 35-74.

[2] This observation finds some resonance with comments on dogmatic theology by James E. Faulconer (*Faith, Philosophy, Scripture* [Provo, UT: Neal A. Maxwell Institute; Brigham Young University], p. 114), 'they (LDS) cannot have a dogmatic theology that is any more than provisional and heuristic, for a theology claiming to be more than that can always be trumped by new revelation'. With regard to the Book of Mormon, rather than dogmatic theology, such a risk of being 'trumped' by later revelation would not seem to be sufficient reason to avoid exploring the major theological emphases of this book held to be Scripture by so many in the LDS family of churches.

18

GOD

This chapter begins with the subject from which theology derives its name, God (θέος, 'theos'). Thus, it seeks to answer the question, what does the Book of Mormon teach about God. Though a complicated subject, there are a number of things one might gather about the God of the Book of Mormon.

The Existence of God

It almost goes without saying that the Book of Mormon advocates belief in the existence of God. While at first glance such a statement might appear to be a throwaway observation, in point of fact such a belief is no mere assumption, but is actually argued for in the text itself. The Book of Alma, in particular, provides evidence for the importance of this theme. First, this issue is raised in Amulek's words to Zeezrom (Alma 11.24), 'Believest thou that there is no God? I say unto you, Nay, thou knowest that there is a God, but thou lovest lucre more than him.' Later in the book (Alma 18.22-39), Ammon carefully leads King Lamoni to faith, beginning with the question, 'Believest thou that there is a God?' – to which King Lamoni responds, 'I do not know what that meaneth' – proceeding to the question, 'Believest thou that there is a Great Spirit?' to which King Lamoni responds, 'Yes'. At which point Ammon identifies the Spirit as God the creator of all things leading to King Lamoni's conversion. A similar conversation occurs between Aaron and the father of Lamoni culminating in his prayer, 'O God, Aaron hath told me that there is a God; and if there is a God, and if thou art God, wilt thou make thyself known unto me, and I will give away all my sins to thee, and that I may be raised from the dead, and be saved at the last day' (Alma 22.18). In these cases the existence of God is demonstrated in God's responses to believing hearts.

Perhaps the most important passage on this topic occurs later in Alma, when Korihor, the only individual identified in the Book of Mormon as 'Anti-Christ' (30.6), began to preach that there would be no Christ, no atonement, speaking against the prophecies, referring to God as 'some unknown being, who they say is God – a being who never has been seen or known, who never was nor ever will be' (30.28). In response to Alma's question, do you believe there is a God, Korihor answers, 'Nay', and goes on to ask Alma to show him a sign that he might be convinced that there is a God, that he has power, and that Alma's words are true (30.43). In responding to Korihor, Alma initially appeals to the testimony of all the brothers as sign enough, then to Scripture as evidence that there is indeed a God, and then to creation itself as a sign that there is a Supreme Creator. But Korihor persists in his demand for a sign, to which Alma responds indicating that Korihor's sign will be his being struck dumb. Korihor then responds, 'I do not deny the existence of a God, but I do not believe that there is a God; and I say also, that ye do not know that there is a God; and except ye show me a sign, I will not believe' (30.49).[1] Ironically, the sign Korihor is given, being struck unable to speak, adds yet another evidence of God's creation – his power, the very thing for which Korihor asked!

The Uniqueness of God

Not only is God's existence stressed in the Book of Mormon, but also his uniqueness. In the conversation between Amulek and Zeezrom cited earlier, in response to Amulek's claims about 'the true and living God', Zeezrom asks him directly, 'Is there more than one God?' to which Amulek responds, 'No' (Alma 11.28-29). It was precisely this aspect of Amulek's teaching that was picked up on by those who did not believe, witnessing against these prophets in particular that 'they testified that there was but one God' (Alma 14.5).

---

[1] Cf. esp. Luffman, *The Book of Mormon's Witness to Its First Readers*, pp. 127-30.

The understanding that there is but one God, not several gods, is underscored in a variety of other texts in the Book of Mormon, where the nature of God is being discussed (2 Nephi 31.21; Mosiah 15.4-5; Mormon 7.7). Thus, one could conclude that the Book of Mormon is rather clearly monotheistic in orientation.[2]

The Nature of God

Related to the aspect of God's uniqueness as the only God is the issue of his nature. The Book of Mormon is quite consistent in its testimony that God's nature and person are unchangeable. As early as 2 Nephi 27.23 the readers learn, 'For behold, I am God; and I am a God of miracles; and I will show unto the world that I am the same yesterday, today, and forever'. Significantly, miracles are specifically tied to God's unchangeable nature.[3] This unchangeable nature implies that he encompasses all; everything begins and ends with him, as Amulek says in Alma 11.39, 'Yea, he is the very eternal Father of heaven and earth, and all things which in them are; he is the beginning and the end, the first and the last'. Near the conclusion of the Book of Mormon (9.9-10), Moroni, writing in his father's stead, goes even further, with the words,

> For do we not read that God is the same yesterday, today, and forever, and in him there is no variableness, neither shadow of turning. And now, if ye have imagined up to yourselves a god who doth vary, and in whom there is shadow of changing, then have ye imagined up to yourselves a god who is not a God of miracles. But behold, I will show unto you a God of miracles, even the God of Abraham, and the God of Isaac, and the God of Jacob; and it is that same God who created the heavens and the earth, and all things that in them are.

Moroni goes even further still in 9.19, again speaking of the miraculous, 'And if miracles were wrought then, why has God ceased to be a God of miracles and yet be an unchangeable Being? And behold, I say unto you he changeth not; if so he would cease to be God; and he ceaseth not to be God, and is a God of miracles.' Thus, here if

---

[2] Cf. Harrell, 'This Is My Doctrine': The Development of Mormon Theology, p. 118.
[3] Cf. Luffman, The Book of Mormon's Witness to Its First Readers, pp. 131-32.

196 A Pentecostal Reads the Book of Mormon

God changes he ceases to be God. In his epistle on Infant Baptism, twice more will Mormon, via the Book of Moroni, speak to God's unchangeable nature. He argues,

> But little children are alive in Christ, even from the foundation of the world; if not so God is a partial God, and also a changeable God ... For I know that God is not a partial God, neither a changeable being; but he is unchangeable from all eternity to all eternity (Moroni 8.12, 18).

One of the theological challenges presented by the Book of Mormon involves precisely how God's nature is understood, for sometimes the book speaks of God in ways consistent with Trinitarian thought, while on other occasions God is spoken of in ways that do not seem to preserve the distinction between the Father and Jesus.[4] Often the book speaks of God in ways hard to distinguish from other Trinitarians. One of the classic examples of such an orientation is found in 2 Nephi 31.21, 'And now, behold, this is the doctrine of Christ, and the only and true doctrine of the Father, and of the Son, and of the Holy Ghost, which is one God, without end'. In a somewhat less clear passage the emphasis upon the fact that God is one appears again,

> And because he dwelleth in flesh he shall be called the Son of God, and having subjected the flesh to the will of the Father, being the Father and the Son – The Father, because he was conceived by the power of God; and the Son, because of the flesh; this becoming the Father and Son – And they are one God, yea, the very Eternal Father of heaven and earth. And thus the flesh becoming subject to the Spirit, or the Son to the Father, being one God, suffereth temptation, and yieldeth not to temptation, but suffereth himself to be mocked, and scourged, and cast out, and disowned by his people (Mosiah 15.2-5).

Perhaps more explicit still are the words of a famous text which speaks of a baptismal formula, 'for behold, verily I say unto you, that the Father, and the Son, and the Holy Ghost are one; and I am in the Father, and the Father in me, and the Father and I are one' (3 Nephi 11.27). Such words are reminiscent of the words of Jesus in

---

[4] Cf. the helpful discussion in Luffman, *The Book of Mormon's Witness to Its First Readers*, pp. 132-37.

John 17 where he describes the mutual indwelling of the Father and the Son. Embedded in a passage that describes the praise on the lips of one found guiltless on the day of judgment it is said that such a one will 'sing ceaseless praises with the choirs above, unto the Father, and unto the Son, and unto the Holy Ghost, which are one God, in a state of happiness which hath no end' (Mormon 7.7). To these overt statements might be added the testimony of the Three Witnesses that appears in the 1830 edition of the Book of Mormon, which concludes with the words, 'And the honor be to the Father, and to the Son, and to the Holy Ghost, which is one God'.

To these passages that convey an explicit sense of a Trinitarian understanding of God may be added whole categories of texts that would contribute to such a broad understanding of God. These include passages that have reference to the ascension of Jesus and/or to Jesus' sitting at the right hand of the Father in heaven (3 Nephi 7.27; 15.1; 17.4; Moroni 9.26); texts in which the risen Lord prays to or acts as an intercessor/advocate with the Father (Mosiah 15.8; Alma 33.11; 3 Nephi 19.19-20); places where the Lord subjects his will to that of the Father (Mosiah 15.7; 3 Nephi 15.14; 16.16); passages where prayer is offered to the Father in Jesus' name (3 Nephi 18.19; 20.31); texts where two or more members of the Godhead manifest themselves at the same time (1 Nephi 1.8-10; 3 Nephi 11.4-11); and texts that differentiate between different members of the Godhead (Mosiah 18.14; 3 Nephi 15.24; 20.26; 21.9).[5] Such texts serve as corroborating evidence of the Book of Mormon's Trinitarian understanding of God.

However, this general orientation is complicated by the fact that alongside these texts that suggest a Trinitarian view of God, the Book of Mormon contains several passages that are in keeping with more of a modalistic understanding of God.[6] For example, in Mosiah 3.17; 5.15; and 16.15 Christ is given the title 'the Lord Omnipotent', a title that is normally attributed to God the Father, perhaps

---

[5] For these categories and texts cf. Ari D. Bruening and David L. Paulsen, 'The Development of the Mormon Understanding of God: Early Mormon Modalism and Other Myths', *FARMS Review of Books* 13.2 (2001), pp. 109-69, cf. esp. pp. 124-28.

[6] Modalistic views of God generally hold that God is one, but that he may appear in difference modes – as Father, Son, or Spirit – but not in all three modes at the same time.

suggesting some confusion with regard to the identities of the Father and the Son. More significantly, in Mosiah 7.26-28 the readers learn that Christ is identified as the Father of all things, 'And because he said unto them that Christ was God, the Father of all things, and said that he should take upon himself the image of man … that man was created after the image of God'. There even seems to be some identity confusion, as it appears that both Father and Son are identified as 'the very Eternal Father of heaven and earth' (Mosiah 15.3; cf. also 3.8; 7.27; Helaman 14.12). In response to Zeezrom's question, 'Is the Son of God the very Eternal Father', Amulek says, 'Yes, he is the very Eternal Father of heaven and of earth, and all things which in them are; he is the beginning and the end, the first and the last' (Alma 11.39). A similar statement occurs in Ether 4.7. Later, Ether (4.12d) will record these words of Jesus Christ, 'For behold, I am the Father, I am the light, and the life, and the truth of the world'. Clearly, such texts call into question an understanding of the God of the Book of Mormon in a consistently Trinitarian fashion. Conversely, the preponderance of texts that seem to favor a Trinitarian framework cannot simply be set aside to argue for a consistently modalistic view of God in the book.[7] What is one to make of such divergent evidence? Based on the view(s) of God present in the Book of Mormon, perhaps on this point it would be best to say that the view of God in the Book of Mormon is basically Trinitarian with some modalistic fuzziness around the edges.

Unfortunately, limitations of space prohibit a more detailed discussion of the view of God in the Book of Mormon, though numerous other related topics certainly merit attention.

---

[7] Note Terryl Givens' sage-like observation on this tension, 'It is true that the Book of Mormon can raise more theological difficulties than it resolves in this regard'. Cf. Terryl Givens, *By the Hand of Mormon: The American Scripture that Launched a New World Religion* (Oxford: Oxford University Press, 2002), p. 201.

19

CHRIST

Certainly the most interesting and distinctive theological aspect of the Book of Mormon is its Christology – its treatment of the person and work of Christ. While too large a topic to be covered adequately in this short chapter, the following observations are offered to acquaint the reader with the major contours of Book of Mormon Christology.

A reading of the Book of Mormon reveals that the role of Christ is quite prominent. In point of fact, it has been noted that some form of a name or title for Jesus occurs on average every 1.7 verses or every two sentences in the Book of Mormon[1] and that only six of its 239 chapters do not contain some direct reference to 'the Saviour'.[2]

Pre-Christian Knowledge and Activities of Christ

One of the most radical aspects of the Book of Mormon is the fact that throughout the narrative, reference is made to details indicating that Book of Mormon peoples had access to considerable pre-

---

[1] Susan Ward Easton, 'Names of Christ in the Book of Mormon', *Ensign* (July 1978), pp. 60-61 and Susan Easton Black, *Finding Christ through the Book of Mormon* (Salt Lake City: Deseret Book, 1987), p. 15.

[2] Monte S. Nyman is cited as the source of this statistic by Robert J. Matthews, 'What the Book of Mormon Tells Us about Jesus Christ', in Paul R. Cheesman (ed.), *The Book of Mormon: The Keystone Scripture* (Provo, UT: Religious Studies Center, Brigham Young University, 1988), pp. 21-43.

Christian knowledge of Christ.[3] Examples of such knowledge appear as early as the first ten verses of the volume where Nephi, describing a vision experienced by his father Lehi, makes an allusion to Jesus and his twelve disciples:

> And being thus overcome with the Spirit, he was carried away in a vision, even that he saw the heavens open, and he thought he saw God sitting upon his throne, surrounded with numberless concourses of angels in the attitude of singing and praising their God. And it came to pass that he saw one descending out of the midst of heaven, and he beheld that his luster was above that of the sun at noon-day. And he also saw twelve others following him, and their brightness did exceed that of the stars in the firmament (1 Nephi 1.8-10).

With this, the readers are put on notice that in this book, detailed and accurate knowledge of Christ is not confined to the time after the incarnation, but will be given to those who live before his birth as well. A few chapters later, about a third of the way through 1 Nephi, even more is revealed about Christ:

> Yea, even six hundred years from the time that my father left Jerusalem, a Prophet would the Lord God raise up among the Jews; yea, even a Messiah; or, in other words, a Saviour of the world. And he also spake concerning the prophets: How great a number had testified of these things, concerning the Messiah, of which he had spoken, or this Redeemer of the world. Wherefore, all mankind was in a lost and in a fallen state; and ever would be, save they should rely on this Redeemer (1 Nephi 10.4-6).

After these words, Nephi goes on to make reference to the prophet who would come before the Messiah, preparing his way, crying in the wilderness, even baptizing the Messiah with water. This very Messiah would come, 'and after he had been slain, he should rise from the dead, and should make himself manifest, by the Holy Ghost, unto the Gentiles' (1 Nephi 10.7-14). Lehi, the readers are told, spoke these things 'by the power of the Holy Ghost; which

---

[3] Givens, *By the Hand of Mormon*, p. 199. Cf. also Melodie Moench Charles, 'Book of Mormon Christology', in Brent Lee Metcalfe (ed.), *New Approaches to the Book of Mormon: Explorations in Critical Methodology* (Salt Lake City: Signature Books, 1993), pp. 81-114.

power, he received by faith on the Son of God. And the Son of God was the Messiah, which should come' (1 Nephi 10.17).

The readers do not have to wait long to receive even more information about this Christ, for they next discover details about the Messiah's mother, knowledge given to Nephi who was caught away in the spirit of the Lord:

> And it came to pass that I looked and beheld the great city Jerusalem, and also other great cities. And I beheld the city of Nazareth; and in the city I beheld a virgin, and she was exceeding fair and white ... and an angel ... saith unto me, Nephi, what beholdest thou? And I saith unto him, a virgin, most beautiful and fair above all other virgins ... And he said unto me, Behold, the virgin which thou seest, is the mother of God, after the manner of the flesh (1 Nephi 11.13-18).

This Messiah is the Lamb of God, the Son of the Eternal Father, who is worshipped by many, is baptized in water as the Holy Ghost descends upon him, who healed all the sick and cast out many devils and unclean spirits, who after he was slain for the sins of the world, saw the twelve apostles of the Lamb confronted by the world (1 Nephi 11.24-36). This same Lamb of God would appear in the new world anointing twelve disciples of the Lamb to minister (1 Nephi 12.1-12).

The first mention of the name Jesus Christ – in the 1830 edition – is found in 1 Nephi 12.18 (in current LDS versification). Later, 2 Nephi 10.3 informs the readers that Christ should be his name, whereas 2 Nephi 25.19 notes, 'his name shall be Jesus Christ'. Mosiah 3.8 adds, 'And he shall be called Jesus Christ, the Son of God, the Father of heaven and earth, the creator of all things from the beginning; and his mother shall be called Mary'. Later, very specific and extraordinary signs about Jesus' birth (Helaman 14.3-7) and his death (Helaman 14.14-28) are prophesied.

2 Nephi 10.7 introduces the idea of believing in Christ when quoting the words of the Lord, 'When the day cometh when they shall believe in me, that I am Christ ... they shall be gathered in from their long dispersion'. In 2 Nephi 31.12-13, the Son's instructions concerning baptism are given which include being baptized 'in the name of Christ', with instructions to pray 'in the name of Christ' given in the very next chapter by Nephi (2 Nephi 32.9), with refer-

ences to the practice of baptism unto repentance and the establishment of the church before the coming of Christ being too numerous to mention. According to Jacob 4.5, individuals 'believed in Christ and worshipped the Father in his name'.[4]

Closely related to this phenomenon is the fact that on at least one occasion the Book of Mormon makes reference to a pre-Christian appearance of Jesus on earth. In the Book of Ether 3.6-20, the brother of Jared sees the finger of the Lord touching 16 stones one by one, and his finger 'was as the finger of a man, like unto flesh and blood'. Assuming that he would be struck dead for having seen the finger of God, the brother of Jared fell down. In this encounter the Lord says,

> Behold, I am he who was prepared from the foundation of the world to redeem my people. Behold, I am Jesus Christ. I am the Father and the Son ... And never have I showed myself unto man whom I had created, for never has man believed in me as thou hast. Seest thou that ye are created after mine own image? ... Behold, this body, which ye now behold, is the body of my spirit; and man have I created after the body of my spirit; and even as I appear unto thee to be in the spirit will I appear unto my people in the flesh.

Moroni notes that Jesus showed himself in the same 'manner and in the likeness of the same body even as he showed himself unto the Nephites'. Thus, despite the fact that the brother of Jared is said to have lived near the time of the events associated with the Tower of Babel, which predate the coming of Christ by millennia, Jesus appeared to him in the likeness of the form he appeared to the Nephites after the resurrection! Owing to the perfect knowledge of the brother of Jared, 'he could not be kept from within the veil; therefore he saw Jesus; and he did minister to him'.

It is one thing to have such unique events as these – with regard to the pre-Christian knowledge of Jesus – narrated, it is quite another to make sense of them theologically. While such phenomenon might be dismissed out of hand as not being capable of a theological explanation, the Book of Mormon itself offers something of a

---

[4] Givens, *By the Hand of Mormon*, p. 199.

way forward in Alma's words of instruction to his son Corianton
(Alma 39.17-19):

> Behold, you marvel why these things should be known so long
> beforehand. Behold, I say unto you, is not a soul at this time as
> precious to God as a soul will be at the time of his coming? Is it
> not as necessary that the plan of redemption should be made
> known unto this people as well as unto their children? Is it not
> easy at this time for the Lord to send his angel to declare glad
> tidings unto us as unto our children, or as after the time of his
> coming?

Clearly, the implication is that it is fundamentally unfair for one
generation to have access to the details of Jesus and his salvific mission while another does not. This theological explanation suggests
that it would be very surprising if such details were not available
across the generations, for God is certainly capable of accomplish-
ing this task in short order and to do otherwise would be extraordinarily unfair. As such, these words not only offer an explanation for
this distinctive aspect of the Book of Mormon, but also might be a
subtle critique of the comparatively limited revelation of such details in the Old Testament, indicating something of the Book of
Mormon's view of its own unique value.

If this is the theological rationale for the appearance of such pre-
Christian details, how might these details be thought of in constructing a Christology of the Book of Mormon? Recently, this theological challenge has been addressed by the proposal that this entire phenomenon might be helpfully described in theological terminology as 'Realized Messialogy'.[5] Drawing on the way in which
scholars of the Johannine literature in the New Testament have often spoken of the book's eschatological teaching as 'realized eschatology' – that the effects of the end are already felt in the present,
exemplified in phrases like 'already you are judged' or 'already you
have eternal life' – Nicholas Frederick has proposed a similar understanding of the Pre-Christian messianism found in the Book of
Mormon. Specifically, this move suggests that Christ's presence and
mission is so powerful, even before his coming to earth, that it

---

[5] For this suggestion cf. Frederick, 'Line Within Line: An Intertextual Analysis
of Mormon Scripture and the Prologue of the Gospel of John', p. 34.

breaks into the pre-Christian era, resulting in a messianism the power of which is felt and known equally before, during, and after the Messiah's appearance to the Nephites after his resurrection.[6]

Resurrection Appearances of Jesus to the Nephites in the Americas

In some ways even more astonishing than the pre-Christian knowledge described in the Book of Mormon is the book's claim that over a three-day period Jesus makes appearances to the faithful in the Americas after his resurrection. In and of itself the Christological significance of this claim is very difficult to overestimate, for in addition to the phenomenon itself, such appearances have extraordinary significance for a variety of Book of Mormon claims as well as for its Christology. Three of these implications will be highlighted here by way of example. First, clearly these appearances offer internal vindication for the numerous prophecies within the book about the coming of Christ. As such, these appearances offer a degree of continuity between the activities of the pre-Christian Christ and the resurrected Christ who now appears. Second, these appearances also give the basic Book of Mormon story line about Lehi's lineage in the new world a heightened significance owing to the fact that their history is deemed important enough for Jesus himself not only to make an appearance but also to spend an extended period of time with them, teaching and ministering to disciples and multitudes alike. Third, these appearances might also be thought to have implications for Christology in its own right, for if Jesus Christ dies for the sins of the whole world, then in these American resurrection appearances, concrete examples of his global influence and significance are offered that extend well beyond Jerusalem and the surrounding environs.

---

[6] John Turner notes, 'human beings in every age and place find salvation in the same way. The Book of Mormon's Jesus Christ is the Lord for all people in all places through all time, and people can read of him in many books.' John Turner, *Mormon Jesus: A Biography* (Cambridge, MA: Belknap Press, 2016), p. 33.

Jesus' Titles and Identities

As for Christ's identity, several other details should be mentioned. The Book of Mormon gives evidence of the virginal conception of Jesus (1 Nephi 11.13-20; 2 Nephi 17.14), a conception accomplished by the power of the Holy Ghost (Alma 7.10).[7] Jesus is known as the Son of God in the Book of Mormon, a term that appears to be tightly connected to Christ's becoming flesh – taking on human nature (Mosiah 7.27; 15.3, 5; 3 Nephi 1.14).[8] The title Only Begotten appears primarily in relationship to Jesus' pre-Incarnate existence. As such he will manifest himself in flesh (2 Nephi 25.12), will come being full of grace, mercy, and truth to take away the sins of the world (Alma 5.48), and will come in his glory (Alma 9.26) – the glory of the only begotten who is 'without beginning of days or end of years' (Alma 13.9).[9] The related title, Only Begotten of the Father, while retaining something of the pre-Incarnate meaning of its related term appears closely associated with the forgiveness of sin (Alma 12.33-34) and the atonement of Jesus (Jacob 4.11), an atonement established from the foundation of the world (Alma 13.5).[10]

Significantly, Jesus is referred to as Father on several occasions in the Book of Mormon. The words of the prophet Abinadi introduce this idea in a significant passage in Mosiah 15.1-4:

> I would that ye should understand that God himself shall come down among the children of men, and shall redeem his people. And because he dwelleth in flesh he shall be called the Son of God, and having subjected the flesh to the will of the Father, being the Father and the Son – The Father, because he was conceived by the power of God; and the Son, because of the flesh; thus becoming the Father and Son – And they are one God, yea, the very Eternal Father of heaven and earth.

---

[7] Cf. Harrell, 'This Is My Doctrine': The Development of Mormon Theology, p. 167.

[8] Kurt Widmer (Mormonism and the Nature of God: A Theological Evolution, 1830-1915 [Jefferson, NC: McFarland, 2000], p. 36) notes, 'In the 1830 Book of Mormon, "the Son" is used only to refer to the incarnate Jesus'.

[9] Harrell, 'This Is My Doctrine': The Development of Mormon Theology, p. 164.

[10] Frederick, 'Line Within Line: An Intertextual Analysis of Mormon Scripture and the Prologue of the Gospel of John', p. 86.

In this passage Jesus is identified as God coming down in the flesh and as such is called the Son of God. Twice in this passage he is called the Father and the Son. While obedience results in this initial identification, the meaning of these titles is revealed in the words that stand between their two occurrences. His title of Father is the result of his conception by the power of God, while his title Son is the result of his becoming flesh. At the same time, the final verse in this passage reveals that Jesus has not replaced the Father but these two are one God, the very Eternal Father. The passage appears to use the title Father as a way of referring to Jesus' divine nature and reserves the title Son as a reference to his human nature.[11] Part of the complexity of the passage is resolved if the title Father is taken as having reference to God. In a latter passage devoted to the re-demption of humanity the identification of Jesus as Father and Son functions in a similar fashion (Mormon 9.12), as it does in Jesus' words in Ether 3.14, 'Behold, I am Jesus Christ. I am the Father and the Son.'

Jesus is also identified as the Father of heaven and earth in a few passages (2 Nephi 25.12; Helaman 16.18), often with reference to his work and identity as the creator of heaven and earth as in Mosi-ah 3.8, 'And he shall be called Jesus Christ, the Son of God, the Fa-ther of heaven and earth, the creator of all things from the begin-ning' (cf. also Mosiah 7.27; Alma 11.38-39; Helaman 14.11-12; Ether 4.7).

Jesus might also be inferred to be Father, in some sense, in other passages in the Book of Mormon where he is not technically called Father. This evidence is in the form of texts that speak of the Chil-dren of Christ. In Mosiah 5.7-8, King Benjamin makes the follow-ing remarks:

> And now, because of the covenant which ye have made, ye shall be called the children of Christ, his sons, and his daughters; for behold, this day he hath spiritually begotten you; for ye say that your hearts are changed through faith on his name; therefore, ye are born of him and have become his sons and his daughters ... therefore, I would that ye should take upon you the name of Christ.

[11] Harrell, 'This Is My Doctrine': The Development of Mormon Theology, p. 176.

Rather clearly this passage introduces the idea that those who enter into the righteous covenant are children of Christ, begotten of him spiritually. As such, this text infers that in some sense Christ functions as 'Father' of those who have faith in and take upon themselves his name.[12] In a description of the near idyllic conditions that followed Jesus' visit to the Nephites it is said of the believers that 'they were in one, the children of Christ, and heirs to the kingdom of God' (4 Nephi 17). In Mormon 9.26, Moroni asks rhetorically, 'Who will despise the children of Christ', while Ether 3.14 notes, 'In me shall all mankind have light, and that eternally, even they who shall believe on my name; and they shall become my sons and my daughters'.

Jesus and the Atonement

Before concluding this short chapter on the Christology of the Book of Mormon a final word should be offered with regard to Jesus and the atonement. It almost goes without saying that Jesus' atoning death is foundational and integral to the Book of Mormon teaching about the atonement. Though the atonement can be spoken of almost exclusively in terms of the work of God (Alma 42.1-28), one of the most significant Book of Mormon atonement texts (Alma 34.8-16) focuses on the absolute necessity of the atonement lest all humankind unavoidably perish. The great and last sacrifice that is necessary must be an infinite and eternal one! This extraordinary sacrifice is to be given by the Son of God.[13] The Atonement will be discussed later in the section devoted to the fall, salvation, and the atonement.

---

[12] K.C. Kern ('Willing to Bear My Name: Nominal Appropriation, Atonement, and Salvation in Latter-day Saint Theology', a paper presented to the Tenth Annual Meeting of the Society for Mormon Philosophy and Theology at Utah Valley University, 2013) makes the intriguing observation that it is the one who 'takes upon' himself the transgressions of his people whose 'name must be taken up' by those who believe in him.

[13] On the atonement of Jesus in the Book of Mormon cf. Luffman, *The Book of Mormon's Witness to Its First Readers*, pp. 152-63.

20

THE HOLY GHOST*

Despite the fact that the Book of Mormon contains numerous mentions of the Spirit by a variety of names and titles, little attention has been devoted to the pneumatology of the Book of Mormon.[1] This chapter seeks to identify the broad contours of Book of Mormon pneumatology.

The Divinity, Nature, and Form of the Holy Ghost

As one reads the Book of Mormon it does not take long to learn that the Holy Ghost is spoken of, at times, in Trinitarian type language.[2] On several occasions the oneness of God is underscored with the Holy Ghost receiving explicit inclusion in this description

---

* A slightly different version of this chapter appears as J.C. Thomas, 'Book of Mormon Pneumatology', *Journal of Book of Mormon Studies* 24 (2015), pp. 217-30.

[1] The most extensive, and apparently only, study to date is Lynne Savage Hilton Wilson, 'Joseph Smith's Doctrine of the Holy Spirit Contrasted with Cartwright, Campbell, Hodge, and Finney' (PhD dissertation, Marquette University, 2010). As its title implies the focus of Wilson's study is the pneumatology of Joseph Smith more generally. However, it does offer a helpful starting point for a study of Book of Mormon pneumatology. Its primary contribution in this regard is found in a brief overview of the Holy Spirit in the Book of Mormon (pp. 260-62), an overview of Smith's doctrinal emphases in the Book of Mormon and Doctrine and Covenants (pp. 272-76), and several helpful appendices, especially the first portion of Appendix Four (pp. 381-411) that lists all the passages in which one of the terms for the Spirit occurs in the Book of Mormon.

[2] Vern G. Swanson, 'The Development of the Concept of a Holy Ghost in Mormon Theology', in G.J. Bergera (ed.), *Line upon Line Essays on Mormon Doctrine* (Salt Lake City: Signature Books, 1989), p. 89.

as is seen in the words of 2 Nephi 31.21, 'And now, behold, this is the doctrine of Christ, and the only and true doctrine of the Father, and of the Son, and of the Holy Ghost, which is one God, without end' (cf. also Alma 11.44; 3 Nephi 11.27-28, 36; Mormon 7.7). In some of these texts a note about the eternality of God is included, which in turn includes the eternality of the Holy Ghost (2 Nephi 31.21; Alma 11.44). Related to this aspect is the belief that, as is said of God and Jesus, 'the Spirit is the same, yesterday, today, and forever' (2 Nephi 2.4b). As for the physical form of the Holy Ghost, based upon 1 Nephi 11.11 it is sometimes suggested that the Spirit is in physical appearance as a man, where Nephi says of his revelatory experience, 'For I spake unto him as a man speaketh; for I beheld that he was in the form of a man; yet nevertheless, I knew that it was the Spirit of the Lord; and he spake unto me as a man speaketh with another'. However, this interpretation is complicated by the fact that a few verses later in a prophecy of the baptism of the Lamb of God, Nephi says, 'and after he was baptized, I beheld the heavens open, and the Holy Ghost come down out of heaven and abide upon him in the form of a dove' (1 Nephi 11.27), suggesting that at the very least the Spirit is not limited to one physical form.[3] Such a conclusion is reinforced by the fact that later the Holy Ghost is again described as descending upon Jesus in the form of a dove (2 Nephi 31.8). The Book of Mormon also records the words of the Zoramites that God was a Spirit, is a Spirit, and will be a Spirit forever (Alma 31.15), which might be understood as an apostate Zoramite doctrine.

The Holy Ghost and Prophecy

In the Book of Mormon there is a tight connection between the Spirit and prophecy, with the phrase 'the Spirit of prophecy' occurring on a number of occasions. This connection and phrase is made prominent as early as the book's title page, where the book's contents are said to have been written 'by the Spirit of prophecy and revelation'. As the narrative proper begins Lehi is filled with the Spirit and begins to prophesy (1 Nephi 5.17). The connection between the Spirit and prophecy is found in 2 Nephi 25.4 as well,

---

[3] Cf. Harrell, *'This Is My Doctrine': The Development of Mormon Theology*, p. 187.

where, the Spirit of prophesy is also said to make understandable the words of Isaiah, apparently indicating that the Spirit aids in the interpretation of Scripture. Another example of the relationship between the Spirit and prophesying is found in Jacob 4.15, 'I, Jacob, am led on by the Spirit unto prophesying; for I perceive by the workings of the Spirit which is in me, that by the stumbling of the Jews they will reject the stone upon which they might have build and have safe foundation' (cf. also Jacob 1.6; 4.6, 13). Abinadi also makes clear the connection between the Spirit of prophecy and true understanding when he responds to his accusers, 'Are you priests, and pretend to teach this people, and to understand the Spirit of prophesying, and yet desire to know of me what these things mean?' (Mosiah 12.25.) The relationship between the Spirit of prophecy and the (prophetic) preaching of the Gospel is made clear in Alma 8.24a where Alma proclaims to Amulek, 'And behold, I have been called to preach the word of God among all this people, according to the spirit of revelation and prophecy' – the fulfillment of his intended activity being described in 8.32. The revelatory work of the Spirit of prophecy is also underscored in many places in Alma (3.27; 4.13, 20; 5.47; 6.8; 10.12; 12.7; 13.26; 16.5; 25.16; 37.15; 45.10). The Spirit of prophecy and revelation also enable the sons of Mosiah to teach with power and the authority of God (Alma 17.3; cf. also 23.6 and 43.2). Thus, not surprisingly, one of the major aspects of the work of the Spirit in the Book of Mormon is its intimate relationship to prophetic work.

The Holy Ghost and Power

Another major dimension of the work of the Holy Ghost as described in the Book of Mormon is its close association with power. On numerous occasions a variety of things are said to have happened as a result of the power of the Holy Ghost.[4] As early as 1 Nephi 3.20 reference is made to the way in which the contents of the sacred records came about, 'the words which have been spoken by the mouth of all the holy prophets, which have been delivered to

---

[4] Wilson ('Joseph Smith's Doctrine of the Holy Spirit Contrasted with Cartwright, Campbell, Hodge, and Finney', pp. 273-74) notes that God's Spirit and power are linked together some 57 times in the Book of Mormon.

them by the Spirit and power of God'. In like manner, Nephi testifies that the things his father Lehi spoke were 'by the power of the Holy Ghost, which power he received by faith on the Son of God' and that he (Nephi) was desirous that he 'might see, and hear, and know of these things, by the power of the Holy Ghost' (1 Nephi 10.17) for 'the mysteries of God shall be unfolded ... by the power of the Holy Ghost' (1 Nephi 10.19). The power of the Spirit of God can also protect God's spokesperson from physical harm as when Nephi's brothers could not lay a hand upon him owing to the powerfulness of the Spirit of God (1 Nephi 17.52). The resurrection of the Messiah will be accomplished by the power of the Spirit (2 Nephi 2.8); in fact, the future Messiah will himself be manifested in the latter days in the power of the Spirit (2 Nephi 3.5). Further, it is said that Jesus will manifest himself to all who believe in him by the power of the Holy Ghost, working miracles, signs, and wonders (2 Nephi 26.13). The power of the Holy Ghost is especially connected to true precepts (2 Nephi 28.31), so much so that the power of the Holy Ghost enables angels to speak the words of Christ (2 Nephi 32.2). Not only this, but when one speaks 'by the power of the Holy Ghost the power of the Holy Ghost' carries the message to the hearts of humankind (2 Nephi 33.1). The power of the Holy Ghost also manifests knowledge (Jacob 7.12) and causes one to teach with power and authority (Mosiah 18.26). It is by means of the Power of the Holy Ghost that the virgin shall be overshadowed and conceive (Alma 7.10). Alma and Amulek 'went forth and began to preach and prophesy unto the people, according to the Spirit and power which God had given them' (Alma 8.32), while the power and Spirit of God leads to the conversion of many (3 Nephi 7.21). The power of the Spirit will be given unto believers by the Father to enable the spread of the word of restoration of the remnant of the house of Jacob (3 Nephi 21.2). In keeping with the fact that the power of the Holy Ghost is the way by which God works (3 Nephi 29.6), ordinations took place by the power of the Holy Ghost (Moroni 3.4), those baptized were cleansed by the power of the Holy Ghost (Moroni 6.4), the power of the Holy Ghost led the worshippers 'whether to preach, or to exhort, or to pray, or to supplicate, or to sing' (Moroni 6.9). It is the power of the Holy Ghost that enables one to confess that Jesus is the Christ (Moroni 7.44). This same power of the Holy Ghost led Mormon to the discovery of the reason why

Infant Baptism is mockery before God (Moroni 8.7, 23). Finally, the truth of the words written in the Book of Mormon will be manifested by the power of the Holy Ghost to those who ask with a sincere heart and real intent (Moroni 10.4-7). Thus, this aspect of Book of Mormon pneumatology underscores the dynamic nature of the Spirit's role.

The Holy Ghost's Activity Upon Individuals

Another major aspect of Book of Mormon pneumatology concerns the way in which the Spirit is spoken of as filling, being poured out upon, coming upon, or falling upon a variety of individuals. To a certain extent these expressions convey similar realities and might be thought of as functioning synonymously. On over a dozen occasions some form of the phrase 'filled with' or being 'full of' the Spirit appears.[5] When individuals are filled with the Spirit various phenomena occur. Lehi rejoiced as a result of being filled with the Spirit (1 Nephi 1.12). When he spoke to his sons after being filled with the Spirit, his sons did shake before him (1 Nephi 2.14). On another occasion when Lehi was filled with the Spirit he began to prophesy (1 Nephi 5.17). Significantly, the result of Nephi's claim to be full of the Spirit of God was 'that my frame has no strength' (1 Nephi 17.47). Being filled with the Spirit of prophecy enables one to understand the words of Scripture, specifically Isaiah (2 Nephi 25.4). Being filled with the Spirit is also closely associated with declaring the word of God (Alma 8.30; Helaman 5.45-46). As a result of being filled with the Spirit Ammon could perceive the thoughts of the king (Alma 18.16). Being filled with the Spirit is closely associated with the Sacrament of the Lord's Supper – where those involved cried and gave glory to Jesus (3 Nephi 20.9), with Water Baptism (Mosiah 18.10-14; 3 Nephi 30.2; Mormon 7.10), and with being born of God (Alma 36.24). On at least one occasion people were filled with the Spirit when Alma clapped his hands upon them (Alma 31.36).

---

[5] Specifically, cf. 1 Nephi 1.12; 2.14; 5.17; 17.47 ('full of the Spirit of God'); 2 Nephi 25.4; Mosiah 18.10-14; Alma 8.30; 18.16; 31.36; 36.24; Helaman 5.45-46; 3 Nephi 12.6; 20.9; 30.2; and Mormon 7.10. Wilson ('Joseph Smith's Doctrine of the Holy Spirit Contrasted with Cartwright, Campbell, Hodge, and Finney', p. 275) identifies seven such texts.

The Book of Mormon also contains nine references to the Spirit being 'poured out' upon various individuals.[6] As a result of the Spirit being poured into his soul, Jacob did confound his adversary, Sherem (Jacob 7.8). As with Spirit filling, when the Spirit is poured out it results in joy so great that Spirit recipients could not speak (Mosiah 4.20). Likewise, when Ammon saw that the Spirit had been poured out on the Lamanites, he was overpowered with joy (Alma 19.14). The pouring out of the Spirit revealed that there is no inequality amongst different peoples (Alma 16.16), for God extends his arm to all (Alma 19.36), because this pouring out of the Spirit includes the Lamanites (Helaman 6.36) and will include the Gentiles (3 Nephi 20.27). On at least two other occasions the Spirit is described as having fallen upon several individuals, including the twelve (1 Nephi 12.7) and as many as the disciples laid hands upon (Moroni 2.3).[7]

A related set of texts speaks of the Spirit being 'in' this or that individual. As with other pneumatological expressions in the Book of Mormon, there is a close connection between the presence of the Spirit of the Lord in an individual and the act of prophesying, specifically as it relates to Lehi (2 Nephi 4.12), Nephi (2 Nephi 25.4, 11), and Ether (Ether 12.2) – of whom it is said,

> And Ether was a prophet of the Lord; wherefore Ether came forth in the days of Coriantumr, and began to prophesy unto the people, for he could not be restrained because of the Spirit of the Lord which was in him.

The presence of the Spirit in an individual also leads to joy (Alma 7.5), knowledge and power (Alma 18.35; 38.6), discernment about when to speak (Alma 11.22), guidance for the journey (Alma 17.9), and softening of the heart (Alma 24.8).

A final set of passages connected to those surveyed to this point testifies to the ability of the Spirit to overcome or even carry an individual away. Specifically, when Lehi was overcome with the Spirit he was carried away in a vision (1 Nephi 1.7-8), as was Nephi who was caught away in the Spirit and taken to an exceedingly high

---

[6] Cf. Jacob 7.8; Mosiah 4.20; 18.10-14; 25.24; Alma 16.16; 19.14, 36; Helaman 6.36; and 3 Nephi 20.27.

[7] Cf. 1 Nephi 12.7; Moroni 2.3.

mountain (1 Nephi 11.1). This means of expression is used to describe Nephi's experience on other occasions as well (1 Nephi 14.30; 15.1; 2 Nephi 4.25). A similar phenomenon occurs when Nephi describes his vision of the virgin mother of God who is herself carried away in the Spirit (1 Nephi 11.19). Alma describes the sinking down of King Lamoni's queen owing to being overpowered by the Spirit (Alma 19.13). At the end of Alma's life a saying went abroad in the church purporting that Alma had been taken up by the Spirit or buried by the hand of the Lord even as Moses had been (Alma 45.19). Finally, Helaman notes that Nephi was taken away from his opponents by the Spirit (Helaman 10.16).

The Holy Ghost and Speaking in Tongues

A reading of the Book of Mormon reveals that a close connection exists between the Holy Ghost and speaking in tongues.

Specifically, an explicit connection is made between the experience of the baptism of fire and the Holy Ghost and speaking with tongues, coming initially in 2 Nephi 31.13, where the words of Jesus are prophetically quoted by Nephi with regard to salvation. The final portion of this verse reads:

> Yea, by following your Lord and your Savior down into the water, according to his word, behold, then shall ye receive the Holy Ghost; yea, then cometh the baptism of fire and of the Holy Ghost; and then can ye speak with tongues of angels, and shout praises unto the Holy One of Israel.

While other important salvific activity is found within this verse – following the Son, repentance of sins, taking upon oneself the name of Christ, and water baptism – it is the baptism of fire and of the Holy Ghost which enables one to speak with the tongues of angels. On the face of it, these words seem to imply that tongues speech functions as a proof or witness of reception of the baptism of fire and of the Holy Ghost. These words may even suggest that the baptism of fire and of the Holy Ghost prepares one for missionary activity.

Lest the connection between the baptism of fire and the Holy Ghost and speaking with tongues be missed, in the very next verse (2 Nephi 31.14), which contains a description of the way of salvation – a *via salutis* – by the voice of the Son, the connection is made again with a bit of additional information provided with regard to tongues speech.

> After ye have repented of your sins, and witnessed unto the Father that ye are willing to keep my commandments, by the baptism of water, and have received the baptism of fire and of the Holy Ghost, and can speak with a new tongue, yea, even with the tongues of angels, and after this should deny me, it would have been better for you that ye had not known me.

As before, there is a tight connection made between the reception of the baptism of fire and of the Holy Ghost and tongues speech with the same implications as the previous statement: it is only by means of the baptism of fire and of the Holy Ghost that one is now able to speak in tongues. On this occasion, the glossolalia is initially described as speaking with a 'new tongue',[8] before being identified as the same phenomenon as 'the tongues of angels', suggesting that these descriptions are to be understood as synonyms in the Book of Mormon.

This important connection is again reiterated in the next chapter of 2 Nephi (32.2-3a).

> Do you not remember that I said unto you that after ye had received the Holy Ghost ye could speak with the tongue of angels? And now, how could ye speak with the tongue of angels save it were by the Holy Ghost? Angels speak by the power of the Holy Ghost; wherefore, they speak the words of Christ.

Several things are conveyed in this short verse. First, it becomes clear that in this verse receiving the Holy Ghost is understood to be synonymous with the baptism of fire and of the Holy Ghost described earlier. Second, it almost goes without saying that this verse further underscores the tight connection between tongues speech and the baptism of fire and of the Holy Ghost. Third, in this verse the relationship between the Holy Ghost and tongues speech is mentioned three separate times. Fourth, the tongue of angels is identified as also tightly connected with the words of Christ, per-

---

[8] In Mk 16.17, the phrase 'they will speak with new tongues' occurs.

haps again pointing to a possible relationship between the phenomenon of tongues speech and missionary activity.

In the Book of Mormon tongues speech also comes to stand with and represent a whole matrix of spiritual activity that demonstrates the continuation of God's activity in the world, i.e. that the activity of God's Spirit has not ceased amongst believers. This function of tongues first appears in Omni 25 where Amaleki, in transferring the plates to King Benjamin, says,

> Wherefore, I shall deliver up these plates unto him, exhorting all men to come unto God, the Holy One of Israel, and believe in prophesying, and in revelations, and in the ministering of angels, and in the gift of speaking with tongues, and in the gift of interpreting languages, and in all things good.

The gift of speaking with tongues can also be listed as an example, along with others, of the way in which the Nephites have been highly favored of the Lord. Alma (9.20-21), notes

> Yea, after having been such a highly favored people of the Lord; yea, after having been favored above every other nation, kindred, tongue, or people; after having had all things made known unto them, according to their desires, and their faith and prayers, of that which has been, and which is, and which is to come; having been visited by the Spirit of God; having conversed with angels, and having been spoken unto by the voice of the Lord; and having the spirit of prophecy, and the spirit of revelation, and also many gifts, the gift of speaking with tongues, and the gift of preaching, and the gift of the Holy Ghost, and the gift of translation ...

Tongues speech as a sign of the continuous activity of the Spirit is so significant that Mormon (3 Nephi 29.6) warns that the denial of tongues, along with other items, is cause for judgment by Christ when he returns.

> Yea, wo unto him that shall deny the revelations of the Lord, and that shall say the Lord no longer worketh by revelation, or by prophecy, or by gifts, or by tongues, or by healings, or by the power of the Holy Ghost!

Clearly, in these words tongues function as the negative counterpoint to their earlier significance in Omni 1.25. Mormon (9.7-9) continues with a similar warning to those who do not believe in the miraculous.

> And again, I speak unto you who deny the revelations of God, and say that they are done away, that there are no revelations, nor prophecies, nor gifts, nor healing, nor speaking with tongues, and the interpretation of tongues. Behold, I say unto you, he that denieth these things knowest not the gospel of Christ; yea, he has not read the scriptures; if so, he does not understand them. For do we not read that God is the same yesterday, today, and forever, and in him there is no variableness, neither shadow of changing?

The rejection of God's continuous activity in the present, in this case with regard to tongues speech and the interpretation of tongues among other things, indicates one's enmity to the gospel of Christ.

Conversely, such warnings give way to earnest expectations that tongues speech will accompany those who preach the gospel, as indicated in Mormon 9.24-25.

> And these signs shall follow them that believe – in my name shall they cast out devils; they shall speak with new tongues; they shall take up serpents; and if they drink any deadly thing it shall not hurt them; they shall lay hands on the sick and they shall recover. And whosoever shall believe in my name, doubting nothing, unto him will I confirm all my words, even until the end of the earth.

The missionary context of these words make clear that tongues speech is an expected part of the divine signs that Christ will work in the confirmation of his word that is preached. The words 'until the ends of the earth' imply that such activity is to be an ongoing and normal part of the church's proclamation. Similarly, Mormon includes 'all kinds of tongues ... the interpretation of languages and divers kinds of tongues' as amongst those manifestations given by the Spirit of God to the church for its profit and expected to be present in its ministry (Moroni 10.15-16).

Before leaving this topic perhaps three additional passages should be examined that may have some relevance for the role of tongues in the Book of Mormon. Specifically, while there are no explicit examples of any individuals speaking in tongues in the Book of Mormon, Alma 19.29-30 tells of the actions of King Lamoni's queen, who, when she had arisen and stood on her feet and praised 'the blessed Jesus' for saving her 'from an awful hell',

> ... clapped her hands, being filled with joy, speaking many words which were not understood; and when she had done this, she took the king, Lamoni, by the hand, and behold he arose and stood upon his feet.

While certainty on the topic is perhaps beyond the reach of the interpreter, it should be observed that the reader of the Book of Mormon would not likely be taken aback by such a turn of events given the place of tongues speech in the book to this point and might possibly think of tongues speech as the logical explanation for the reason this queen's words were not understood.[9] Whilst her baptism of fire and the Holy Ghost is not recounted, her conversion is clearly conveyed and leads, through Lamoni, to the belief, conversion, baptism, and establishing of a church amongst his people.

Similarly, it is possible that tongues speech might be inferred in Helaman 5.45, where in response to the intercession by Aminadab on behalf of Nephi and Lehi, about three hundred souls experienced the following: 'And behold, the Holy Spirit of God did come down from heaven, and did enter into their hearts, and they were filled as if with fire, and they could speak forth marvelous words'. Clearly, these individuals are described as experiencing being filled with the Holy Spirit, an event that affected their speech patterns. While glossolalia is not explicitly mentioned its inference would be quite at home in this passage.[10]

Finally, one wonders if the marvelous words which Jesus prays to the Father in 3 Nephi 19.31-34, words so marvelous that tongue cannot speak nor can hand write down, is not a further reference to

---

[9] For this suggestion cf. Luffman, *The Book of Mormon's Witness to Its First Readers*, p. 191.

[10] I am indebted to Heather Hardy for this suggestion.

tongues speech, this time with Jesus as the speaker. On this occasion, the disciples, 'who were white, even as Jesus' – a clear reference to their spiritual development at this point in the book – understand in their hearts the words which he prayed. If so, Jesus continues to function as the exemplar for the spirituality of the disciples, as well as testify of a partial fulfillment of some of the internal promises made to the disciples in the book. That is, perhaps on this occasion the gift of the interpretation of tongues is in evidence.

In any case, perhaps enough certain examples of the role of tongues speech in the Book of Mormon have been offered to give evidence of its significance in the volume and, in turn, its role in the theology of the book.

The Holy Ghost Communicates

Amongst the other activities of the Spirit described in the Book of Mormon are those that indicate the way in which the Spirit communicates with individuals. In these passages the Spirit is described as speaking, manifesting, or delivering words and/or messages to someone. There are over 30 such references in the Book of Mormon beginning with 1 Nephi 2.17, where Nephi makes known to his brother Sam the things the Lord had manifested to him by his Holy Spirit. Ironically, the first words directly attributed to the Spirit in the book come in a series of commands the Spirit gives Nephi to kill Laban with Laban's own sword (1 Nephi 4.11, 12, 18). In this context, the Voice of the Spirit is identified as the source of these commands. Elsewhere, the activity of the Spirit is often closely connected to the revelation of prophetic words and/or messages (1 Nephi 10.22; 22.2; Mosiah 5.3; Alma 5.46-52; Mormon 3.16, 20; Moroni 8.9).

My Spirit Will not always Strive with 'Man'

Another important theme in Book of Mormon pneumatology is that on several occasions the Spirit is said to cease (or will cease) striving with 'man'. Such a fate can be the result of the rejection of the prophets (1 Nephi 7.14), procrastination of the day of repentance until the day of death (Alma 34.35), because the Spirit of the Lord does not dwell in unholy temples (Helaman 4.24), the hardness of hearts (Helaman 13.8; Ether 15.19), the presence of wickedness and unbelief (Mormon 1.14), persistence in sin (Ether 2.15), and denial of the Holy Ghost (Moroni 8.28; 9.4). When such an eventuality occurs, destruction follows speedily (2 Nephi 26.11). All of these words serve as warnings to the readers that one must be careful lest one fall into this situation. In like manner, the Book of Mormon contains numerous accounts of individuals who have or are in danger of denying (2 Nephi 28.4, 6; Jacob 6.8; Alma 39.5-6 – the most abominable sin; Helaman 4.12, 23; 3 Nephi 29.6; and Moroni 8.28), quenching (Jacob 6.8), hardening their hearts against (2 Nephi 33.2), rejecting (Alma 13.4), putting off (Alma 30.2), resisting (Alma 30.46; 32.28), or contending against (Alma 34.38) the Holy Ghost. Such activities would seem to come extraordinarily close to cause for the Spirit no longer to strive with humanity.

Other Dimensions of the Holy Ghost

A few other noteworthy aspects of Book of Mormon pneumatology are here surveyed. The Holy Ghost bears witness to the Father and the Son (1 Nephi 12.18; 2 Nephi 31.18; 3 Nephi 11.32, 36; 16.6; 28.11), is closely associated with water baptism (2 Nephi 31.12; 3 Nephi 19.13; 26.17; 28.18) and the baptism of fire (2 Nephi 31.13, 14; 3 Nephi 9.20; 11.35; 12.1, 2; 19.13; Ether 12.14), is related to the remission of sins (2 Nephi 31.17; Mosiah 4.3), teaches believers to pray (2 Nephi 32.8), entices individuals to believe in the Lord (Mosiah 3.19), results in individuals being born of the Spirit (Mosiah 27.24), results in believers being sanctified (Alma 5.54; 13.12; 3 Nephi 27.20), and knows all things (Alma 7.13). Numerous admonitions are given to receive the Holy Ghost and/or descriptions of those who did receive (2 Nephi 31.13, 18; 32.2, 5; 4 Nephi 1) and special emphasis is placed upon the reality and presence of the gifts of the Spirit (2 Nephi 32.2; Moroni 10.9-18).

While scores of other references to the Spirit have not been mentioned in this survey, perhaps enough has been offered to give some indication of the robust nature and major contours of Book of Mormon pneumatology.

21

The Fall, the Atonement, and Salvation

The Fall

The story of the Fall of humanity in the Book of Mormon is a complicated one, with the tensions of two somewhat antithetical ideas present that some might deem to be too difficult to reconcile. When commenting on the story, interpreters will sometimes represent one end of the polarity or the other as the primary emphasis, whilst minimizing or ignoring the other end of the spectrum owing to the uncomfortable interpretive tensions created. In this section, the discussion of the fall will, for the most part, follow its narrative development, without attempting to prejudice the presentation of the data in one direction or the other.

The first passage to contain a significant discussion of the fall in the Book of Mormon is 2 Nephi 2.14-28. Here, several things are revealed about the nature of the fall. After the creation of all things – including 'our first parents' – it was necessary for there to be an opposition, even as the forbidden fruit was in opposition to the tree of life. By this means God gave 'man' the opportunity to act for himself. At this point an angel, fallen from heaven – the devil, the father of all lies – said to Eve, 'Partake of the forbidden fruit, and ye shall not die, but ye shall be as God, knowing good and evil' (2 Nephi 2.18). When Adam and Eve had partaken of the forbidden fruit they were driven out of the garden of Eden. Their time was prolonged so that their state became a state of probation, for God gave a commandment that all should repent, for all were lost owing to the transgression of their parents. Of Adam's transgression it is said:

> And now, behold, if Adam had not transgressed he would not have fallen, but he would have remained in the garden of Eden. And all things which were created must have remained in the same state in which they were after they were created; and they must have remained forever, and had no end. And they would have had no children; wherefore they would have remained in a state of innocence, having no joy, for they knew no misery: doing no good, for they knew no sin. But behold, all things have been done in the wisdom of him who knoweth all things. Adam fell that men might be; and men are, that they might have joy. And the Messiah cometh in the fullness of time, that he may redeem the children of men from the fall. And because they are redeemed from the fall they have become free forever, knowing good from evil; to act for themselves ... Wherefore, men are free ... to choose liberty and eternal life ... or to choose captivity and death.

From this passage it is clear that the fall is the result of Adam's transgression that results in the expulsion from the garden. At the same time, this text suggests that the fall serves a redemptive purpose. Through this transgression, humankind moves from a state of innocence, where no joy or misery is known, to a state in which they can know joy, apparently through the gift of freedom of choice.[1] In some sense, Adam's transgression is connected to the very existence of 'men',[2] who though they need redemption, are now open to the possibility of experiencing joy.

But despite this redemptive aspect of the fall, later, the serious negative effects of the fall are still acknowledged, 'and the fall came by reason of transgression; and because man became fallen they were cut off from the presence of the Lord' (2 Nephi 9.6; cf. also

---

[1] This understanding of the fall is sometimes referred to as the fortunate fall (Harrell, 'This Is My Doctrine': The Development of Mormon Theology, p. 255; Givens, The Book of Mormon: A Very Short Introduction, p. 75) or beneficial fall (Luffman, The Book of Mormon's Witness to Its First Readers, p. 147).

[2] As Luffman (The Book of Mormon's Witness to Its First Readers, p. 147) observes, 'It is clear in this passage that all humanity traces its existence back to Adam's sin'.

Helaman 14.16). Such a predicament makes clear the need for an infinite atonement in order to avoid a certain death upon all men. Similarly, stern language is used in assessing the effects of the fall in Mosiah 3.19, 'For the natural man is an enemy to God, and has been from the fall of Adam, and will be, forever and ever, unless he yields to the enticings of the Holy Spirit …' and in Mosiah 16.3,

> yea, even that old serpent that did beguile our first parents, which was the cause of their fall; which was the cause of all mankind becoming carnal, sensual, devilish, knowing evil from good, subjecting themselves to the devil.

Not only are the affective implications identified, but also is Adam's alliance with the devil in committing this act.

Not withstanding such acknowledgements, the necessity of the fall continues to receive attention, as in Alma 12.26:

> And now behold, if it were possible that our first parents could have gone forth and partaken of the tree of life, they would have been forever miserable, having no preparatory state; and thus the plan of redemption would have been frustrated, and the word of God would have been void, taking none effect.

Though Alma (12.36) will remind that God punished humankind owing to the 'first provocation' – the fall – he goes on to explain the necessity of the fall, despite its negative ramifications, in even greater detail (42.5-10),

> For behold, if Adam had put forth his hand immediately, and partaken of the tree of life, he would have lived forever, accord-ing to the word of God, having no space for repentance; yea and also the word of God would have been void, and the great plan of salvation would have been frustrated … And now, ye see by this that our first parents were cut off both temporally and spir-itually from the presence of the Lord; and thus we see they be-came subject to follow after their own will … Therefore … it was expedient that mankind should be reclaimed from this spir-itual death. Therefore, as they had become carnal, sensual, and devilish by nature, this probationary state became a state for them to prepare; it became a preparatory state …

Thus, in the Book of Mormon the negative and positive implications of the fall sit side by side without final resolution. Suffice it to say that the book testifies both to the sinister provocations that result in the fall, along with its many extraordinarily evil implications, and the way in which the fall becomes the vehicle for human existence and spiritual reclamation.

The Atonement

As seen in the previous section, the atonement is closely connected to the fall in the Book of Mormon. Something of the importance of the atonement can be gauged by the fact that explicit atonement language appears about three dozen times in the Book of Mormon.[3] In addition to the numbers of times atonement terminology occurs in the book, certain passages appear to be primarily devoted to the topic.

The importance of the atonement in the Book of Mormon is conveyed, in part, by the fact that the atonement was not an afterthought in redemptive history, but was prepared from the foundation of the world, an observation made on two occasions in rapid-fire succession (Mosiah 4.6, 7)! Thus, when the antichrist Korihor argues 'that there could be no atonement made for the sins of men' (Alma 30.17) he anticipates his own condemnation and reveals just how far from the truth he is – that he has no understanding of this incredible reality. In point of fact, according to Jacob it has been revealed to him that the atonement is absolutely necessary, 'I know that if no atonement is made, all mankind must be lost' (Jacob 7.12), for no one is able to satisfy the demands of justice on their own (Alma 22.14; 34.11). For this reason, atonement must be offered by God himself (Mosiah 13.28, 34; Alma 42.15), for no one can satisfy the demands of justice but God (2 Nephi 9.25, 26; Mosiah 13.28; Alma 22.14; 34.11). Owing to the fact that the consequences of the fall are so great and the immensity of its effects so vast, only an infinite and eternal atonement will prove efficacious. Specifically, unless there is an infinite atonement it is impossible for corruption to put on incorruption, for humanity has fallen out of God's presence and only this extraordinary act can bring restoration

---

[3] Givens, *The Book of Mormon: A Very Short Introduction*, p. 78.

via a resurrection (2 Nephi 9.7). It is necessary because only an infinite atonement is infinite for all humankind, it atones for all the world (2 Nephi 25.16). Owing to the extent of the effects of the fall and the power of sin, there must be a great and last sacrifice to atone for what humanity cannot atone. Nothing short of this can atone for the sins of the world.[4] It is infinite in this sense and eternal in that its needs not be repeated (Alma 34.9, 12).

Such an infinite and eternal atonement is an atonement of his blood. It is not the law of Moses that is efficacious, nor the blood of a human, but the blood of the Messiah (Mosiah 3.15-17; Alma 21.9; Helaman 5.9). For the blood of the Christ atones for the forgiveness of sins making such forgiveness possible (Mosiah 3.11; 4.2; Alma 24.13; Moroni 8.20). This atonement atones for sins (Alma 33.22; 34.8; 36.17), even the sins of the world (Alma 42.23).[5] For this atonement to be effective it must be met with belief (2 Nephi 25.16).[6] The atonement is the key to redemption as Alma (42.17) notes:

> But God ceases not to be God, and mercy claimeth the penitent. And mercy cometh because of the atonement; and the atonement bringeth to pass the resurrection of the dead; and the resurrection of the dead bringeth back men into his presence.

The atonement also brings about reconciliation and is intimately connected to the resurrection of the dead (2 Nephi 10.23-25; Jacob 4.11, 12; Alma 42.23; Moroni 7.41). Significantly, the ordination of priests has its origins and preparation from the foundation of the world in the atonement of the Only Begotten Son (Alma 13.5). Rather clearly, in the Book of Mormon the effects of the atonement

---

[4] Givens (*The Book of Mormon: A Very Short Introduction*, p. 81) observes, 'So Christ, in a gesture of infinite mercy, offers himself a ransom to the demands of law, as the only being capable of paying a cumulative penalty as "eternal as the life of the soul" (Alma 42.16)'.

[5] Cf. Luffman, *The Book of Mormon's Witness to Its First Readers*, pp. 158-59.

[6] Luffman (*The Book of Mormon's Witness to Its First Readers*, p. 160), notes,

Simply put, the Book of Mormon commends to its readers that there is unlimited atonement, but limited grace. That is, atonement applies to all, but it depends on the willingness of the individual to receive its effect. In the Book of Mormon, the effect of grace is, therefore, limited by human decision and action.

were available to those who precede the coming of Jesus to the earth.[7]

Salvation/Redemption

In many ways this vast and expansive Book of Mormon topic may be summarized in two Book of Mormon passages: 2 Nephi 31.14-16 and 3 Nephi 11.31-40. The former reads:

> After ye have repented of your sins, and witnessed unto the Father that ye are willing to keep my commandments, by the baptism of water, and have received the baptism of fire and of the Holy Ghost, and can speak with a new tongue, yea, even with the tongue of angels, and after this should deny me, it would have been better for you that ye had not known me. And I heard a voice from the father, saying, Yea, the words of my Beloved are true and faithful. He that endureth to the end, the same shall be saved. And now, my beloved brethren, I know by this that unless a man shall endure to the end, in the following the example of the Son of the living God, he cannot be saved.

The latter, an exposition of the doctrine of Christ, underscores the importance of repentance and belief in the way of salvation.

> And I bear record that the Father commandeth all men, everywhere, to repent and believe in me. And whoso believeth in me, and is baptized, the same shall be saved; and they are they who shall inherit the kingdom of God ... And again I say unto you, ye must repent, and become as a little child, and be baptized in my name ... And again I say unto you, ye must repent, and be baptized in my name ...

From these two texts,[8] as well as a variety of others, one finds the following essential elements of redemption: belief, repentance and forgiveness of sins, the keeping of commandments (and enduring to the end), water baptism, and the baptism of fire and the Holy

---

[7] Cf. Harrell, 'This Is My Doctrine': The Development of Mormon Theology, pp. 286-87.

[8] Harrell ('This Is My Doctrine': The Development of Mormon Theology, p. 305) goes so far as to propose that 3 Nephi 11.31-40 describes the 'fulness of the gospel' in the Book of Mormon.

Ghost with the concomitant speaking with a new tongue.[9] The following discussion will briefly highlight the role of each of these
components in order to ascertain their role in salvation and redemption in the Book of Mormon.

Belief

The theme of belief in Christ is found in a variety of places in the
Book of Mormon. Beginning with prophetic foretellings of those
who will believe in Christ (2 Nephi 25.14, 16, 23; 30.7; Mosiah 3.12-
13), the book includes numerous encouragements for readers
and/or hearers to believe in Christ (2 Nephi 25.28-29; 33.10; Jacob
1.8; 4.5; Helaman 5.41; Mormon 10.7; Moroni 7.16, 32). It also describes those who have active belief or faith in Christ, both before
and after his coming (2 Nephi 25.24, 25; 33.7; Jacob 7.3; Enos 8;
Mosiah 4.2; Alma 25.16; 44.3; 46.14-15; Helaman 3.28; 15.9; 3
Nephi 19.22; 4 Nephi 36-37; Moroni 7.25, 39). Faith in Christ is
also related to discerning the truth of the Book of Mormon itself
(Moroni 10.4), which in turn is related to belief in Christ that leads
to salvation.[10] The Book of Mormon also contains scores of additional passages in which belief and/or faith is found, indicating
something of the significance of belief and/or faith in the book's
view of salvation and redemption, cf. especially Alma 32-34.

Repentance and the Forgiveness/Remission of Sins

The Book of Mormon says much about repentance with scores and
scores of references to this topic within its pages. As noted earlier,
repentance is closely associated with belief, with the former actually
being a result of the latter. Repentance, in turn, leads to remission
or forgiveness of sins as illustrated in 2 Nephi 25.24-26:

> And notwithstanding we believe in Christ ... And we talk of
> Christ, we rejoice in Christ, we preach of Christ, we prophesy of
> Christ, and we write according to our prophecies that our chil-
> dren may know to what source they may look for a remission of
> their sins.

---

[9] Givens (*The Book of Mormon: A Very Short Introduction*, p. 70) identifies the key
components as faith, repentance, baptism for remission of sins, and the gift of
the Holy Spirit as the core doctrines of Joseph Smith.

[10] Luffman, *The Book of Mormon's Witness to Its First Readers*, pp. 176-77.

The relationship between repentance and remission of sin is further underscored in 2 Nephi 31.17.

> For the gate by which ye should enter is repentance and baptism by water; then cometh a remission of your sins by fire and by the Holy Ghost.

The relationship between belief in Jesus and remission of sin is illustrated in Mosiah 3.13.

> Whosoever should believe that Christ should come, the same might receive remission of their sins.

The way in which this phenomenon occurs is illustrated in Mosiah 4.3, where King Benjamin's audience is overcome with conviction and cry out with one voice:

> O have mercy, and apply the atoning blood of Christ that we may receive forgiveness of our sins and our hearts may be purified ... And it came to pass that after they had spoken these words, the Spirit of the Lord came upon them, and they were filled with joy, having received a remission of sins ...[11]

The prophet Samuel, in speaking of the coming of Jesus Christ, also testifies to the relationship between belief, repentance, and the remission of sins.

> And if ye believe on his name ye will repent of all your sins, that thereby ye may have a remission of them through his merits (Helaman 14.13).[12]

Before leaving this aspect of redemption and/or salvation in the Book of Mormon it should perhaps be observed that often the conversion process described is (or is to be) accompanied by outward manifestations that include things like falling down as though dead, clapping of hands, and shouting.[13] Evidence of such phenomenon comes in the conversion stories of the multitude that hears the preaching of King Benjamin (Mosiah 27.11-30), Zeezrom (Alma

---

[11] Cf. also Alma 12.34; 13.16; 38.8.

[12] Cf. also 3 Nephi 7.25.

[13] Harrell, 'This Is My Doctrine': The Development of Mormon Theology, p. 305.

12.1-15.12), King Lamoni (Alma 18.38-19.33), and Alma (Alma 36.7-21), to cite a few examples.[14]

Baptism

Another important component in the Book of Mormon understanding of redemption/salvation is water baptism. Though not always accompanied by water baptism,[15] conversion stories often include or expect baptism as part of this process. Interestingly, the first references to water baptism come in the context of Lehi's prophecies with regard to the activity of a prophet who would prepare the way for and even baptize the Messiah, the Lamb of God (1 Nephi 10.9, 10; cf. also 11.27).[16] Such antecedents, however, quickly give way to specific instructions with regard to baptism and its absolutely significant role in salvation seen as early as Jacob's comments in 2 Nephi 9.23-24.

> And he commanded all men that they must repent, and be baptized in his name, having perfect faith in the Holy One of Israel, or they cannot be saved in the kingdom of God. And if they will not repent and believe in his name, and be baptized in his name, and endure to the end, they must be damned; for the Lord God, the Holy One of Israel has spoken it.

These two emphases – the baptism of the Messiah and the need for baptism on the part of believers – are tied together in 2 Nephi 31.4-13 where Jesus' example is held up by Nephi as instructive for would-be believers with Jesus' own words cited:

> And also, the voice of the Son came unto me, saying, He that is baptized in my name, to him will the Father give the Holy Ghost, like unto me; wherefore, follow me, and do the things which ye have seen me do.

---

[14] Cf. Luffman, *The Book of Mormon's Witness to Its First Readers*, pp. 164-74.

[15] Harrell, *'This Is My Doctrine': The Development of Mormon Theology*, p. 306.

[16] Something of the growing significance that baptism will play in the Book of Mormon is revealed in the 1840 version of the book's account of 1 Nephi 20.1 where the phrase 'waters of baptism' have been added to an extended quotation of Isaiah, 48.1 in particular. On this cf. Harrell, *'This Is My Doctrine': The Development of Mormon Theology*, p. 306. Givens (*The Book of Mormon: A Very Short Introduction*, p. 73) appeals to this precise phrase as evidence of the significance of water baptism in the Book of Mormon without noting the phrase's later (1840) insertion into the text.

From this point on in the narrative a number of people are described as being baptized, beginning with Alma's self baptism and baptism of Helam in the waters of Mormon followed by the baptism of an additional 204 souls (Mosiah 18.7-16). The formula used to baptize Helam is as follows:

Helam, I baptize thee, having authority from the almighty God, as a testimony that ye have entered into a covenant to serve him until you are dead as to the mortal body; and may the Spirit of the Lord be poured out upon you; and may he grant unto you eternal life, through the redemption of Christ, whom he has prepared from the foundation of the world.

The narrative implies that this formula was used by Alma with the others as well for the text says,

and again, Alma took another, and went forth a second time into the water, and baptized him according to the first, only he did not bury himself again in the water. And after this manner he did baptize every one that went forth to the place of Mormon (Mosiah 18.15-16a).

The desires of King Limhi and his people to be baptized were fulfilled at the hand of Alma 'after the manner he did his brethren in the waters of Mormon' (Mosiah 25.17-18), all of whom 'did belong to the church of God'. Later, when baptism was rejected by certain young believers (Mosiah 26.1-4), Alma's previous activity at the waters of Mormon is praised by the voice of the Lord (Mosiah 26.15), making even clearer the crucial role of baptism in salvation and in the establishment of the church.

For behold, this is my church; whosoever is baptized shall be baptized unto repentance, And whomsoever ye receive shall believe in my name; and him will I freely forgive (Mosiah 26.22).

Following these divine words of affirmation Alma baptizes many others (Mosiah 26.37).

Such baptismal activity continues to be recounted through much of the rest of the book. As many as 3,500 individuals are said to have been baptized in the waters of Sidon (Alma 4.4-5), while others are baptized in Zarahemla (Alma 6.2) and in Melek (Alma 8.5). Zeezrom is baptized (Alma 15.12), as are many from the region round about Sidon (Alma 15.14), many of King Lamoni's people (Alma 19.35), and thousands – even tens of thousands – under the judgeship of Helaman (Helaman 3.24, 26 respectively). Returning Nephites are baptized (Helaman 5.17), as are eight thousand Lamanites (Helaman 5.19), many of Samuel's converts at the hand of Nephi (Helaman 16.1, 3-5), as well as Nephi's converts (3 Nephi 1.23). Many others are baptized at the hands of those ordained by Nephi (3 Nephi 7.24-26), many at the hands of the three transfigured Nephites (3 Nephi 28.18), many others at the hands of the disciples who formed the church (4 Nephi 1), as well as many elders, priests, and teachers (Moroni 6.1-4). Such frequent mention and in some cases spectacular numbers indicate something of the significant salvific role water baptism plays in the Book of Mormon.

But water baptism's significance in the Book of Mormon is not simply communicated by the number of times baptisms are described. Its significance is also underscored by Jesus' repeated teaching about the practice as well as his numerous commands to continue in the observance of this necessary practice. Not only does he give instruction with regard to the formula that is to be utilized – replacing the earlier formula used by Alma it would appear – but he also gives instruction with regard to its mode.

> And now, behold, these are the words, which ye shall say, calling them by name, saying, Having authority given me of Jesus Christ, I baptize you in the name of the Father, and of the Son, and of the Holy Ghost. Amen. And then shall ye immerse them in the water, and come forth again out of the water (3 Nephi 11.23b-26).

On numerous occasions Jesus includes commands to practice water baptism in explicating his doctrine (3 Nephi 11.33-34, 37-38; 21.6; 23.5; 27.16, 20), adding his voice to the numerous other voices previously advocating the practice. He also gives authority to the disciples to baptize believers in water (3 Nephi 12.1-2). He makes clear how certain church practices and discipline affect only those who are baptized (3 Nephi 18.11, 16, 30). In addition to Jesus' admonitions with regard to the practice, others are also described as being commissioned to preach the necessity of baptism, some of whom go so far as to advocate in writing its practice (Mormon 3.2; 7.8, 10; 9.23; Moroni 7.34; 8.10, 25).

Holy Spirit

Owing to the previous section devoted to the Holy Ghost and the citation of numerous baptism texts that lift up the relationship of the Holy Ghost to baptism, it hardly seems necessary to repeat those materials here. Suffice it to say that the gift of the Holy Ghost is an expected and necessary component of the way of salvation found in the Book of Mormon, the evidence of which appears to be demonstrable and concrete – speaking with the tongue of angels or a new tongue.

Keeping the Commandments

Though sometimes overlooked in summaries or surveys of the Book of Mormon understanding of salvation and redemption, keeping the commandments is not only a prominent aspect of the way of salvation described therein but also plays a prominent role in the broader narrative itself. In the summary of redemption cited above found in 3 Nephi 11.31-40, it appears that a witness to the Father that one is willing to keep 'my' commandments is shown primarily by reception of baptism of water. But for the readers of the Book of Mormon such a witness could hardly help but remind them of the fact that scattered throughout the book are frequent admonitions and warnings that 'if one keeps the Lord's commandments' one shall prosper in the land. Mosiah 18.10 makes such a connection clear.

> Now I say unto you, if this be the desire of your hearts, what have you against being baptized in the name of the Lord, as a witness before him that ye have entered into a covenant with him, that ye will serve him and keep his commandments, that he may pour out his Spirit more abundantly upon you?

This theme of keeping the commandments is introduced as early as 1 Nephi 2.20 and 22 in the words of the Lord to Nephi.

> And inasmuch as ye shall keep my commandments, ye shall prosper, and shall be led to a land of promise; yea, even a land which I have prepared for you; yea, a land which is choice above all other lands … And inasmuch as thou shalt keep my commandments, thou shalt be a ruler and a teacher over thy brethren.

A couple of chapters later Nephi recalls these words, 'Inasmuch as thy seed shall keep my commandments, they shall prosper in the land of promise' (1 Nephi 4.14). Similar words to these are found in a variety of other places (2 Nephi 1.9, 20, 31, 32; 4.4; Jarom 1.9; Omni 1.6; Mosiah 1.7; 2.22, 31, 36; 12.15; 25.24; Alma 9.13, 28; 36.1, 30; 37.13, 43; 38.1; 46.23; 48.15, 25; 49.30; 50.20; 62.51; Helaman 3.20; 4.15; 12.1; 3 Nephi 5.22; 6.5; Ether 2.8-10; 7.26; 14.1-2; 15.3). An emphasis on 'keeping the commandments' is also abundantly referenced (for example, cf. 1 Nephi 15.25; 17.13; 2 Nephi 31.7, 14; Jacob 2.29; Enos 10; Mosiah 4.6; 6.6; 13.14; 18.10; 21.31, 32; 23.14; Alma 7.15; 25.14; 38.2; 45.6; Helaman 5.6; 10.4; 15.5; 3 Nephi 12.20; 15.10; 18.14; Moroni 4.3). Thus, salvation in the Book of Mormon is no mere passive event but must be met at every step with obedience evidenced in keeping the divinely given commandments.

A Dark and Loathsome People

A final aspect of the view of salvation and redemption found in the Book of Mormon should perhaps be mentioned before moving to the next major section of the book's theology. Texts in various places in the book argue that skin color is a sign of one's spirituality.[17] Specifically, the book teaches that the Lamanites have dark skin owing to their disobedience to God and that if and when they repent their skin will actually become white. This understanding makes its first appearance in 1 Nephi 12.22-23 in a description of an angel's words to Nephi about his contentious brothers (later called the Lamanites).

> And the angel said unto me, Behold these shall dwindle in unbelief. And it came to pass that I beheld, after they had dwindled in unbelief they became dark, and loathsome, and a filthy people, full of idleness and all manner of abominations.

In this text those who turn from the faith – 'dwindle in unbelief' – take on both physical and spiritual characteristics intended to convey their spiritually deplorable condition. While the word dark could theoretically be understood as a spiritual – not physical – description, other Book of Mormon texts make clear that the word dark has reference to skin color.

---

[17] Harrell, *'This Is My Doctrine': The Development of Mormon Theology*, pp. 409-10.

In 2 Nephi 5.21-23, in words describing that the Lamanites were cut off from the presence of the Lord, the text states:

> And he had caused the cursing to come upon them, yea, even a sore cursing, because of their iniquity. For behold, they had hardened their hearts against him, that they had become like unto flint; wherefore, as they were white, and exceedingly fair and delightsome, that they might not be enticing unto my people, the Lord God did cause a skin of blackness to come upon them, and thus saith the Lord God, I will cause that they shall be loathsome unto thy people, save they shall repent of their iniquities. And cursed shall be the seed of him that mixeth with their seed; for they shall be cursed even with the same cursing. And the Lord spake it, and it was done.

Several things may be deduced from this passage. First, rather clearly in this text the darkness, in this case blackness, has reference to the skin color of the Lamanites, clarifying the words of 1 Nephi 12.23 in this manner. Second, it is clear that their skin color is tied to their spiritual condition as before they hardened their collective hearts they were 'white, and exceedingly fair and delightsome', but now possess 'a skin of blackness'. Third, in this passage it is self-evident which skin color is preferable; white over black. Fourth, the black color of Lamanite skin is owing to a curse that comes from the hand of God himself. Fifth, the purpose of this curse of black skin is not only punitive, but is also deemed to be a deterrent to keep the Nephites from mixing with the Lamanites and thereby becoming contaminated spiritually and physically. Those who do so 'mix' stand in danger of falling under the same curse. Sixth, the only remedy for this loathsome condition is repentance on the part of those so cursed.

This very remedy is envisioned for the remnant later in the book (2 Nephi 30.6) where it is prophesied:

> And then shall they rejoice; for they shall know that it is a blessing unto them from the hand of God; and the scales of darkness shall begin to fall from their eyes; and many generations shall not pass away among them, save they shall be a white and delightsome people.

When the seed of Lehi are brought to faith by the Gentiles not only will their spiritual blindness come to an end but so also will the effects of the curse of blackness, for over time such ones will become 'a white and delightsome people'. From this passage it appears that the curse is not immediately removed upon repentance but occurs only over the span of several generations.

This theme is picked up in the very next book where Jacob warns his Nephite readers that they are in danger of becoming even more sinful than the Lamanites and subject to the curse upon their skin.

> Behold, the Lamanites your brethren, whom ye hate because of their filthiness and the cursing which hath come upon their skins, are more righteous than you; for they have not forgotten the commandment of the Lord, which was given unto our fathers – that they should have save it were one wife, and concubines they should have none, and there should not be whoredom committed among them ... O my brethren, I fear that unless ye shall repent of your sins, that their skins will be whiter than yours, when ye shall be brought with them before the throne of God. Wherefore, a commandment I give unto you, which is the word of God, that ye revile no more against them because of the darkness of their skins ... (Jacob 3.5, 8-9a)

The faithfulness of the Lamanites in keeping the commandment with regard to monogamous purity is lifted up in this passage to the shame of the disobedience of the Nephites. Whether or not this obedience has caused the Lamanites' skin to turn whiter or the Nephite disobedience has resulted in darker skin the text does not say. It is clear, however, that such transformations are the text's eschatological expectations. Interestingly, this passage instructs the Nephites no longer to revile the darkness of the Lamanite skin but to use it as a reminder of their own filthiness (v. 9b).

However, this reminder does not seem to have been remembered by the time of Alma 3.6-10, the next passage in which this theme is found.

> And the skins of the Lamanites were dark, according to the mark which was set upon their fathers, which was a curse upon them because of their transgression and their rebellion against their brethren ... And their brethren sought to destroy them, there-

fore they were cursed; and the Lord God set a mark upon them
... And this was done that their seed might be distinguished
from the seed of their brethren, that thereby the Lord God
might preserve his people, that they might not mix and believe in
incorrect traditions which would prove their destruction. And it
came to pass that whosoever did mingle his seed with that of the
Lamanites did bring the same curse upon his seed. Therefore,
whosoever suffered himself to be led away by the Lamanites was
called under that head, and there was a mark set upon him.

In some ways this passage serves as a comprehensive summary of
all that has come before on this topic, save the idea that their dark
skin is to serve as a reminder of Nephite iniquities. Lamanite physical darkness of skin, the fact that such skin color is a curse from
God, and the way in which this color is designed to be a deterrent
to the Nephites are all acknowledged here.

In 3 Nephi 2.14-16 the phenomenon of dark Lamanite skin turning white is described.

And it came to pass that those Lamanites who had united with
the Nephites were numbered among the Nephites; and their
curse was taken from them, and their skin became white like unto the Nephites; and their young men and their daughters became exceedingly fair, and they were numbered among the Nephites, and were called Nephites.

For the first time in the Book of Mormon the actual transformation
from dark skin to white skin is described. Clearly, this transformation is the result of the complete conversion of those Lamanites
who believed and were assimilated into the Nephites. In this case
their spiritual purity is matched by the whiteness of their skin.

Such preoccupation with skin color as an indicator of spirituality
is further explained by a text that occurs in 3 Nephi 19.25-30 where
Jesus is depicted as praying with and for his disciples.

And it came to pass that Jesus blessed them as they did pray unto him; and his countenance did smile upon them, and the light
of his countenance did shine upon them, and behold, they were
as white as the countenance and also the garments of Jesus; and
behold, the whiteness thereof did exceed all the whiteness, yea,
even there could be nothing upon earth so white as the white-

ness thereof … [Jesus prays for their purity] … And when Jesus
had spoken these words he came again unto his disciples; and
behold, they did pray steadfastly, without ceasing, unto him; and
he did smile upon them again; and behold, they were white, even
as Jesus.

Although this passage contains nothing about the curse of dark
skin, read as part of the narrative whole that precedes, it in some
ways explains why white skin is so desired in the Book of Mormon,
for Jesus not only possesses a white countenance and garments, but
he is the whitest of all. The transformation described in these verses
reveals that the goal for the disciples is to be spiritually white – to
be as white as Jesus himself. In the light of this reality, the darkness
of Lamanite skin is all the more loathsome.

This theme of transformation continues in 4 Nephi 10.

And now, behold, it came to pass that the people of Nephi did
wax strong, and did multiply exceedingly fast, and became an exceedingly fair and delightsome people.

Following on the logic of the previous narrative accounts there can
be little mistaking the implication of these words. The Nephites'
becoming 'an exceedingly fair and delightsome people' entails the
idea that their spiritual progress is reflected in their physical appearance, the color of their skin.

Despite the book's positive turn with regard to the possibility of
such transformation, and perhaps lest the readers forget all that is at
stake, Mormon (5.15) warns what will become of the Lamanites.

For this people shall be scattered, and shall become a dark, a
filthy, and a loathsome people, beyond the description of that
which ever hath been amongst us, yea, even that which hath
been among the Lamanites, and this because of their unbelief
and idolatry.

Thus, near the end of the book,[18] the relationship between spirituality and skin color remains in play.[19]

---

[18] It is possible that the statement about the change wrought upon the Lamanites in Ether 12.14 has reference to the removal of their curse, but such is un-
clear.

[19] Such a consistent emphasis in the book – the theme appears in nearly half
of the books in the Book of Mormon – has caused more than one Book of

Mormon interpreter unease and has led at least one to call upon the church 'to confess and repent of such attitudes and practices' resulting from 'The Lamanite Legacy'. Cf. Luffman, *The Book of Mormon's Witness to Its First Readers*, pp. 182-87.

22

ECCLESIOLOGIES

It does not take long to discover that the topic of ecclesiology in the
Book of Mormon is quite a complicated one. While the book itself
will state that there are 'save two churches only',[1] this statement
contrasts with the 'many churches' (2 Nephi 26.20) and other
churches described elsewhere in the text. This section will outline
the teaching from the Book of Mormon about these churches, their
characteristics, and nature.

The Great and Abominable Church

Aside from an ambiguous phrase, 'the brethren of the church' that
appears in 1 Nephi 4.26, the first mention of the church occurs in 1
Nephi 13.1-9 in a vision given to Nephi.

> And it came to pass that I saw among the nations of the Gentiles
> the foundation of a great church. And the angel said unto me,
> Behold the foundation of a church that is most abominable
> above all other churches, which slayeth the saints of God, yea,
> and tortureth them and bindeth them down, and yoketh them
> with a yoke of iron, and bringeth them down into captivity. And
> it came to pass that I beheld this great and abominable church;
> and I saw the devil that he was the foundation of it. And I saw
> gold, and silver, and silks, and scarlets, and fine-twined linen, and

---

[1] On this bifurcation cf. Harrell, *'This Is My Doctrine': The Development of Mormon
Theology*, pp. 85-87.

all manner of precious clothing; and I saw many harlots. And the angel spake unto me, saying, Behold the gold, and the silver, and the silks, and scarlets, and fine-twined linen, and the precious clothing, and the harlots are the desires of this great and abominable church. And also for the praise of the world do they destroy the saints of God, and bring them down into captivity.

In this first mention of the church it is clear that this great and abominable church, whose founder is the devil, is a murderous, oppressive, and proud institution that loves riches and sexual excess. It is equally clear that despite the fact that the true church has not yet been described, the great church is not God's church but is rather the complete opposite. A few verses later it is revealed that this great and abominable church is responsible for the removal of many plain and precious truths from the book of the Lamb of God (1 Nephi 13.28). Similarly, this church is guilty of digging a great pit by which to lead away the souls of men to hell (1 Nephi 14.3-4).

It is at this point that the readers learn of the existence of another church (1 Nephi 14.9):

Behold there are save two churches only; the one is the church of the Lamb of God, and the other is the church of the devil; wherefore, whoso belongeth not to the church of the Lamb of God belongeth to that great church, which is the mother of abominations; and she is the whore of all the earth.

This great and abominable church fights against the Lamb of God and his church (1 Nephi 14.8-17). But this church is destined to turn upon itself, spilling its own blood and tumbling to the ground (1 Nephi 22.13-14). It is just this kind of church that needs to fear the judgment (1 Nephi 22.23; cf. also 2 Nephi 28.18).

Corrupt Churches

A number of subsequent Book of Mormon texts speak of certain corrupt churches. As early as 2 Nephi 26.20-33 such churches are singled out. In this passage their characteristics are said to include: pride, denial of the power and miracles of God, exaltation of their own wisdom and learning, oppression of the poor, secret combinations, priestcrafts – those who preach for gain, envyings, strifes, and malice. Later (2 Nephi 28.1-23), such churches are described as each claiming to be the Lord's church but are not of the Lord, they and their priests shall contend with one another, relying on their learning and denying the Holy Ghost, denying miracles, advocating a life of leisure with an accommodating attitude toward sin, teaching vain and foolish doctrines. These churches have become corrupt because of pride, false teachers, false doctrine, robbing the poor, wearing fine clothing, wickedness, abominations, and whoredoms.

It appears that these same churches are described again in Mormon 8.32, 36, 38.

> Yea, it shall come in a day where there shall be churches built up that shall say, Come unto me, and for your money you shall be forgiven of your sins ... And I know that you do walk in the pride of your hearts; and there are none save a few only who do not lift themselves up in the pride of their hearts, unto the wearing of very fine apparel, unto envying, and strifes, and malice, and persecutions, and all manner of iniquities; and your churches, yea, even every one, have become polluted because of the pride of your hearts ... O ye pollutions, ye hypocrites, ye teachers, who sell yourselves for that which will canker, why have ye polluted the holy Church of God? Why are ye ashamed to take upon you the name of Christ? Why do ye not think that greater is the value of an endless happiness than that misery which never dies – because of the praise of the world?

Priestcraft

One of the issues that arises in relation to corrupt churches is what is called priestcraft in the Book of Mormon. The term – priestcrafts – is introduced, though not defined, in 2 Nephi 10.5 in a description of those who would eventually crucify the Christ, indicating that the word will have a sinister association as the book unfolds. Later in 2 Nephi 26.29-30a a definition of sorts is offered.

> He commandeth that there shall be no priestcrafts; for behold, priestcrafts are that men preach and set themselves up for a light unto the world, that they may get gain and praise of the world, but they seek not the welfare of Zion. Behold, the Lord hath forbidden this thing.

In this definition priestcraft seems to include paid clergy that work for their own benefit, not for the good of the church.

Such a definition takes on fuller shape in Alma 1.3-12, 16-18 where a certain Nehor advocated 'that every priest and teacher ought to become popular; and they ought not to labor with their hands, but they ought to be supported by the people'. Nehor's preaching met with such success that he established a church that put his words into practice, whereby he was supported with money and exhibited pride of heart and wore costly apparel, even killing Gideon who attempted to withstand him. These actions prompted Alma to say:

> Behold, this is the first time that priestcraft has been introduced among this people. And behold, thou art not only guilty of priestcraft, but hast endeavored to enforce it by the sword; and were priestcraft to be enforced among this people it would prove their entire destruction (Alma 1.12).

Apparently the earlier appearances of this theme were not nearly as significant as its occurrence here suggests. But despite Alma's words,

> ... this did not put an end to the spreading of priestcraft through the land; for there were many who loved the vain things of the world, and they went forth preaching false doctrines; and this they did for the sake of riches and honor (Alma 1.16).

The practice, though not the word, is inferred in Alma 2.1, where a certain Amlici is described as 'being after the order of the man that slew Gideon by the sword', drawing many people unto himself (other such references to Nehor include Alma 2.20; 6.7; 21.4; 24.28-29).

Priestcrafts are also mentioned by Jesus as one of several examples of the future sinful condition of the nations (3 Nephi 16.10). He also prophesies the destruction of priestcrafts at some point in the future (3 Nephi 21.19) in the midst of a citation of Mic. 5.8-15. In a final plea, Mormon cites words of Jesus as Mormon pleads with his readers to turn from 'your priestcrafts' and 'come unto me' (Jesus) (3 Nephi 30.2). To all of this might be added the preaching of Korihor, who was called Anti-Christ, and embodied many of the characteristics of corrupt churches and priestcrafts (Alma 30.6-60).

Zoramite Worship

Before leaving this topic, the worship in synagogues where the Zoramites worshipped should perhaps receive some attention (Alma 31.12-29). They gathered on one day of the week and built a place for standing at the center of the synagogue from which each individual worshipper uttered the identical prayer.

> Holy, holy God we believe that thou art God, and we believe that thou art holy, and that thou wast a spirit, and that thou art a spirit, and that thou wilt be a spirit forever. Holy God, we believe that thou hast separated us from our brethren; and we do not believe in the tradition of our brethren, which was handed down to them by the childishness of their fathers; but we believe that thou hast elected us to be thy holy children; and also that thou hast made it known to us that there shall be no Christ. But thou art the same yesterday, today, and forever; and thou hast elected us that we shall be saved, whilst all around us are elected to be cast by thy wrath down to hell; for the which holiness, O God, we thank thee; and we also thank thee that thou has elected us, that we may not be led away after the foolish traditions of our brethren, which doth bind them down to a belief of Christ, which doth leave their hearts to wander far from thee, our God. And again we thank thee, O God, that we are a chosen and a holy people. Amen.

After this they returned to their homes never speaking of God again until they reassembled the next week. In addition to their denial of Christ, election is also underscored. In the following verses, Alma will condemn this wicked and perverse people whose hearts are set on gold, silver, and all manner of fine goods, with hearts filled with pride and great boasting.

The Church of the Lamb of God

Standing in contrast to these illegitimate churches or places of worship is the Church of the Lamb. As noted earlier the church of the Lamb is introduced in 1 Nephi 14.10 alongside the Great and Abominable Church. Here it is revealed that if one does not belong to this church one belongs to that great church. Here the church of

the Lamb of God is small but they are saints. Armed with righteousness and the power of God this church was seen to withstand
the attacks of the much larger and wicked Great and Abominable
Church (1 Nephi 14.11-15). Later, 2 Nephi 9.2 states that the House
of Israel will be restored to the true church and fold of God, indicating something of the way in which Israel will be enfolded into
this church. These visions of the church give way to the reality of its
creation in the Book of Mosiah (18.17) where those baptized by
Alma 'were called the church of God, or the church of Christ, from
that time forward'. Among other things priests were ordained, one
for every fifty of their number, being instructed to teach those
things that he and the holy prophets had spoken. Their message
was to be nothing but 'repentance and faith', 'no contention', with
'one faith and one baptism' (Mosiah 18.18-22). The priests of this
church were to work 'with their own hands for their support' and
were not to depend upon the people for their support, though
needy priests could receive the charity of the people as well as other
needy folk (Mosiah 18.23-29). In Zarahemla the church, under the
leadership of ordained priests and teachers, grew into seven different bodies, but all were one church, joining the church of God
(Mosiah 25.19). When the king put an end to the persecution of the
church, he reiterated that 'all their priests and teachers should labor
with their own hands for their support' (Mosiah 27.5). Ironically,
this persecution of the church of God would lead to the conversion
of Alma (Mosiah 27.8-17).

The theme of self-supporting priests continues in Alma 1.25-28
with the establishment of the church in various locales and continues in the Book of Alma (6.1; 8.1). In Alma 13.1-20 a detailed explanation is given of the ordination of ancient high priests, like Melchizedek, who were called from the foundation of the world
through the atonement of the Only Begotten Son to be high priests
forever. Something of the content of the preaching of the church's
priests is revealed in Alma 16.13-21, where those priests:

> Did preach against all lyings, and deceivings, and envyings, and
> strifes, and malice, and revilings, and stealing, robbing, plunder-
> ing, murdering, committing adultery, and all manner of lascivi-
> ousness, crying that these things ought not so to be – holding
> forth things which must shortly come; yea, holding forth the

coming of the Son of God, his sufferings and death, and also the resurrection of the dead.

The theme of self-supporting priests also reappears in Alma 30.30-35, indicating something of the significance of this concept for the book.

Despite its foundation, this church would periodically battle with pride in its ranks (Helaman 3.1, 33), with some dissensions actually leading to bloodshed (Helaman 4.1). Iniquity would result in the church's dwindling (Helaman 4.23), with the church eventually being broken up owing to financial inequality – among other inequalities – in the land (3 Nephi 6.10-16). Jesus instructs the church to pray in 'my' church even as he has prayed (3 Nephi 18.16). He also promises to establish his church amongst the Gentiles provided they 'repent and hearken unto my words, and harden not their hearts' (3 Nephi 21.22).

Eventually, the true church of Christ would be despised and persecuted, even being cast into prison owing to their belief in the miraculous.

They did cast them into furnaces of fire, and they came forth receiving no harm. And they also cast them into dens of wild beasts, and they did play with the wild beasts even as a child with the lamb; and they did come forth among them, receiving no harm. And they did smite upon the people of Jesus; but the people of Jesus did not smite again (4 Nephi 31-34).

Moroni contains several chapters of relevance in establishing this aspect of Book of Mormon ecclesiology. In chapter 3 the ordination of priests and teachers by the laying on of hands by the power of the Holy Ghost is described with these words of commission:

In the name of Jesus Christ I ordain you to be a priest (or if he be a teacher, I ordain you to be a teacher), to preach repentance and remission of sins through Jesus Christ, by the endurance of faith on his name to the end. Amen (Moroni 3.3).

In Moroni 4 the manner of administering the flesh and blood of Jesus is described with the following prayer:

O God, the Eternal Father, we ask thee in the name of thy Son, Jesus Christ, to bless and sanctify the bread to the souls of all those who partake of it; that they may eat in remembrance of the body of thy Son, and witness unto thee, O God, the Eternal Father, that they are willing to take upon them the name of thy Son, and always remember him, and keep his commandments which he hath given them, that they may always have his Spirit to be with them. Amen (Moroni 4.3).

Likewise the blessing on the wine is described in very similar terms in chapter 5.

O God, the Eternal Father, we ask thee in the name of thy Son, Jesus Christ, to bless and sanctify this wine to the souls of all those who drink of it; that they may do it in remembrance of the blood of thy Son, which was shed for them, that they may witness unto thee, O God, the Eternal Father, that they do always remember him, that they may have his Spirit to be with them. Amen (Moroni 5.2).

According to 3 Nephi 18.11, only those baptized are eligible to sit at the Lord's table.

The order of the church's worship in their meetings is described in Moroni 6.5-9:

And the church did meet together oft, to fast and to pray, and to speak one with another concerning the welfare of their souls. And they did meet together oft to partake of bread and wine, in remembrance of the Lord Jesus. And they were strict to observe that there should be no iniquity among them; and whoso was found to commit iniquity, and three witnesses of the church did condemn them before the elders, and if they repented not, and confessed not, their names were blotted out, and they were not numbered among the people of Christ. But as often as they repented and sought forgiveness, with real intent, they were forgiven. And their meetings were conducted by the church after the manner of the workings of the Spirit, and by the power of the Holy Ghost; for as the power of the Holy Ghost led them whether to preach, or to exhort, or to pray, or to supplicate, or to sing, even so it was done.

These words are followed in chapter 8 by a scathing denunciation of infant baptism, a practice the church is to reject for a variety of theological reasons.

23

ANGELS

At first glance it might not appear that the role of angels in a given book merits a place in a section devoted to theology, but the role of angels in the Book of Mormon is so prevalent and their influence so extensive that some attention to Book of Mormon angelology seems not only appropriate but also necessary.[1]

The topic of angelic beings occurs for the first time very early in the Book of Mormon when Lehi,

> overcome with the Spirit and the things which he had seen ... was carried away in a vision, even that he saw the heavens open, and he thought he saw God sitting upon his throne, surrounded with numberless concourses of angels in the attitude of singing and praising their God (1 Nephi 1.8).

Such an introduction of the theme prepares the readers for the way in which such angelic beings are not only closely associated with God in the Book of Mormon, but will also become spokespersons for God at various points throughout the book. It might not be going too far to suggest that their 'attitude of singing and praising God' will inform all they do in the volume.

One of the first ways an angel actually functions in the book is an intervention by the angel of the Lord on behalf of Nephi and

---

[1] Graham St. John Stott, 'Talking to Angels; Talking of Angels: Constructing the Angelology of the Book of Mormon', *Theology and Religion* 19 (2012), pp. 92-109.

Sam when their brothers Laman and Lemuel were speaking harsh words to them, even smiting them with a rod. The text reads:

> And it came to pass as they smote us with a rod, behold, an angel of the Lord came and stood before them, and he spake unto them, saying, Why do you smite your younger brother with a rod? Know ye not that the Lord hath chosen him to be a ruler over you, and this because of your iniquities? (1 Nephi 3.29-30).

The intervention by the angel of the Lord on behalf of one of the Lord's chosen would not be the last such intervention in the book. The word of the angel would prove so significant that on at least two occasions appeal will be made to it as encouragement for Laman and Lemuel to do God's will (1 Nephi 4.3; 7.10).

This initial encounter with an angel of the Lord gives way to what will become one of the most significant, if not the most significant, functions of angels in the Book of Mormon. Beginning in 1 Nephi 11.14, an angel appears to Nephi functioning as his interpretive guide as Nephi is shown prophetic visions of the coming of Jesus in the old world (11.19-36), the coming of Jesus in the new world (12.1-12), unbelief and war amongst Lehi's descendants (12.13-23), the great and abominable church (13.1-9), the arrival of the Gentiles in the new world (13.10-19), the Gentiles with the record of the Jews (13.20-29), the restoration of the gospel (13.30-37), other sacred records coming forth (13.38-41), the repentance of the Gentiles (13.42-14.7), the wrath of God being poured out (14.8-17), the appearance of John the apostle (14.18-30), as well a vision of that awful hell (15.29). Such revelatory work on the part of the angel leads to the inevitable conclusion that Nephi's angels have ministered to him, a verdict Laman comes close to drawing, though in hostility to Nephi (1 Nephi 16.38). In this verse the idea of angels ministering to an individual appears to have reference, in part, to the revelation conveyed by the angel, in this case to Nephi. According to Nephi, angels have appeared and spoken from time to time, even to his brothers (17.45), perhaps a reference back to the events described in 1 Nephi 3.29-30.

The idea of angels ministering to various individuals is an important one in the Book of Mormon including a variety of texts documenting this activity (1 Nephi 16.38; 2 Nephi 4.24; Jacob 7.5, 17; Helaman 5.48; 3 Nephi 7.18; 17.24; 19.14, 15). Often it is observed that angels prophesied (Mosiah 3.2), delivered (Mosiah 4.1; Alma 8.18), spoke (Mosiah 5.5; 27.11, 14, 17; Helaman 5.11; 13.7; 14.9, 26; 16.14), appeared (Mosiah 27.32; Alma 8.14a; 10.7), and conversed with men (Helaman 5.39). Such revelations can be quite detailed at times. In 2 Nephi 6.11 an angel adds commentary on a text in Isaiah, while in 2 Nephi 10.3 an angel reveals to Jacob that the name of the righteous branch under discussion is to be Christ. In 2 Nephi 25.19 an angel of God reveals that his name is to be Jesus Christ the Son of God. In Alma an angel can give specific instructions on a particular man to be found as well as the holy character of that man (Alma 8.20; 10.8, 9).[2]

There are other aspects of Book of Mormon angelology worthy of mention. As seen earlier, to speak in tongues can be referred to as speaking with the tongue of angels (2 Nephi 31.13-14; 32.2-3). The faces of Nephi and Lehi are said to have shone as the faces of angels (Helaman 5.36), while Jesus is mistaken for an angel when he descended (3 Nephi 11.8). God is said to declare in the presence of angels in a fashion that suggests that they function in some way as witnesses of his words (Helaman 10.6). It is said that all the angels rejoice over the faithfulness of the generation to which Jesus appears, for this generation will not be lost (3 Nephi 27.20). Interestingly, the three transformed Nephite disciples are likened to angels who can show themselves to anyone they please if they ask the Father in the name of Jesus (3 Nephi 28.30). Belief in ministering angels comes to represent the whole matrix of belief in the continuing activity of God in the world. The first of these tests of fellowship appears in Omni 25.[3] Significantly, the ability to behold angels and ministering spirits is listed among spiritual gifts, perhaps implying that not all are able to do such (Moroni 10.14).

Before concluding this chapter on angels a few words should perhaps be devoted to what the Book of Mormon says about the

---

[2] This aspect of angelic ministry is so extensive in the Book of Mormon that Graham St. John Stott claims that in the book, as well as the thought of Joseph Smith, all religious experience is associated with the ministry of angels, not denying the precedence of one channel of revelation over another, seeing the ministry of angels and the spirit as equivalents. This last observation appears to be based, in part, on an overly restrictive Book of Mormon pneumatology. Cf. G. St. John Stott, 'Talking to Angels; Talking of Angels: Constructing the Angelology of the Book of Mormon', pp. 92-109.

[3] Cf. also Moroni 7.22-37.

devil and angels. According to Lehi, and based upon all that he claims to have read, he 'must needs suppose that an angel of God … had "fallen from heaven"; wherefore he became a devil, having sought that which was evil before God' (2 Nephi 2.17). Because of this, he sought the misery of all humankind, thus lying to Eve and Adam. The devil is later identified in this manner with the warning that the spirit of believers can become like him; devils, even angels of the devil, shut out from the presence of God beguiled by him who transformed himself into an angel of light (2 Nephi 9.8-9). Such a fate is to be avoided at all costs, for those who are filthy are the devil and his angels, who shall go into everlasting fire prepared for them (2 Nephi 9.16; cf. also Jacob 3.11 and Mosiah 26.27). Later, Korihor confesses that the devil deceived him by taking the form of an angel and commissioning his message pleasing to carnal minds (Alma 30.53). In a prophecy of a time too late for repentance, it will be as though the unrepentant will be surrounded by demons, which in reality are 'the angels of him who sought to destroy our souls' (Helaman 13.37). Similarly, 3 Nephi notes that unless repentance occurs the devil will laugh and his angels rejoice at their calamity (3 Nephi 9.2). In a final word about the devil's angels, Mormon informs his readers that they may be assured that neither the devil nor his angels persuade people to do good (Moroni 7.17). Thus, while not nearly as extensive as the book's teaching about the angels of God, the testimony of the Book of Mormon about the devil and his angels identifies them as the opposite of God's angels in terms of origins, activities, nature, and destiny.

24

WAR AND PEACE

As anyone with even a cursory knowledge of the Book of Mormon is aware, an exceedingly large amount of space is devoted to the causes, descriptions, and aftermath of a variety of wars. It might not be going too far to say that the theme of war is part of the book's very fabric, with some extended sections of the book devoted wholly to war. In point of fact, there is so much space describing war that even a sympathetic reader of the Book of Mormon might find him/herself dreading another encounter with and question the need for the mind-numbing monotone of yet more battles.

Whatever is to be made of this theme theologically, it is difficult to dispute the fact that the book – which begins with a divinely ordered murder of Laban by Nephi (1 Nephi 4.10-19) and a vision guided by an angel in which the descendants of one brother come close to annihilation at the hands of their kin (1 Nephi 12.13-23) – marches unrelentingly on to the extermination of a whole people (Mormon 6.7-15; 8.1-10). The exact nature of this eventuality is prophesied on more than one occasion (Mosiah 12.8; Alma 45.1-14; Helaman 13.5-16) and not even an appearance of Jesus himself alters its ultimate course! In the end, all the Nephites die, survived only by their sacred records; slaughtered at the hands of their brothers, the Lamanites. But the violence does not stop with the description of this tragic end. For the reader of the Book of Mormon encounters another book (the Book of Ether), chronologically misplaced though it is, that recounts the wars and destruction of two other entire peoples![1]

While this topic figures too prominently within the pages of the Book of Mormon to be treated in any sort of detail in this short chapter, a few illustrative comments might here be appropriate. First, war seems to be described at almost every turn (for example cf. Enos 24; Jarom 6-7, 13; Omni 3, 7, 10, 17, 24; Mosiah 9.11-10.21; Alma 46.1-62.41). Second, the Lamanites are often presented as being the cause for war owing to their character – they are said to have 'delighted in wars and bloodshed' (Jacob 7.25) and to love murder and would drink the blood of beasts (Jarom 6). On the great preponderance of occasions they are often portrayed as the instigators of conflict.[2] Third, the Nephite rationale or justification for war is given on various occasions with one of the most significant coming in Mormon's praise of Captain Moroni in Alma 48.11-20. Of Captain Moroni it is said that he was a strong and mighty man with perfect understanding who did not delight in bloodshed (cf. also Alma 48.16; 55.19), was firm in the faith of Christ, who had 'sworn with an oath to defend his people, his rights, and his country, and his religion, even to the loss of his blood' (Alma 48.13). Following the lead of Moroni, the Nephites were taught to defend themselves even to the shedding of blood if necessary. They were taught never to give offense, never raising a sword except to preserve their lives. It is even said that if all were like Moroni, 'the very powers of hell would have been shaken forever' (Alma 48.17).[3] Fourth, the humane treatment of prisoners of war by the Nephites is emphasized on more than one occasion (Alma 55.22-27; 62.8-9, 29), perhaps

---

[1] On Ether's location and function Andrew Bolton observes,

Completely misplaced chronologically, it appears that Moroni added the Jaredite story as an appendix to reinforce the theme of destructive violence by an unrepentant, disbelieving people. Despite prophetic warnings, the Jaredite civilization ended with even greater tragedy – the destruction of both sides (Ether 5-6; LDS 12-15).

See Andrew Bolton, 'Anabaptism, the Book of Mormon, and the Peace Church Option', *Dialogue: A Journal of Mormon Thought* 37.1 (2004), pp. 87-88.

[2] Ironically, as Joshua Madson points out, much of even that violence is instigated by individuals who have their origin amongst the Nephites. Joshua Madson, 'A Non-Violent Reading of the Book of Mormon', in P.Q. Mason, J.D. Pulsipher, and R.L. Bushman (eds.), *War and Peace in Our Time: Mormon Perspectives* (Salt Lake City: George Kofford Books, 2012), pp. 20-22.

[3] On the rationale for war see also Alma 43.45-46.

suggesting that the Nephites held the moral high ground over their enemies who did not reciprocate. Fifth, it is often stated, or implied, that God was with or on the side of this or that group in battle, the example of the 2,000 striplings who respond to Helaman's call being an extraordinary case in point (Alma 53.8-22; 56.1-19, 54-57; 57.6-27). For despite their many battles, in which thousands of others perish, not one soul among the 2,000 was lost in any battle (58.39)! Sixth, rather than war bringing liberation, protection, and safety, it seems to have resulted in the eventual degradation of all involved. As Mormon observes:

> And it is impossible for tongue to describe, or for man to write a perfect description of the horrible scene of the blood and carnage which was among the people, both of the Nephites and of the Lamanites; and every heart was hardened, so that they delighted in the shedding of blood continually. And there never had been so great wickedness among all the children of Lehi, nor even among all the House of Israel, according to the words of the Lord, as was among this people (Mormon 4.11-12).

Such mixed narrative signals are enough to give the reader pause as to the appropriateness of resorting to war and violence – even in the defense of one's own life – as he or she looks back over the Book of Mormon narrative from the vantage point of the book's conclusion.[4]

But the readers are not left simply to reflect upon the enigmatic nature of the way in which wars have not seemed to accomplish their hoped for ends. For running alongside the mixed signals about war and violence are several texts that appear to subvert – or at least complicate – what appears to be the book's tacit endorsement of the use of violence. Specifically, five sets of texts convey the idea that violence is to be renounced completely or embraced only when divinely commanded.

---

[4] For the idea that a proper understanding of this issue in the Book of Mormon must be based upon a narrative reading of the whole book, not upon proof-texts or individual case-studies, cf. Madson, 'A Non-Violent Reading of the Book of Mormon', pp. 14-16.

First, standing at the very physical, if not structural and theological, center of the Book of Mormon[5] is one if its most memorable and remarkable stories; the story of the conversion and activity of Lamanite converts who become known as the Anti-Nephi-Lehies. The story has already been recounted in Part Two of this study. The missionary activity of the sons of Mosiah leads not only to the conversion of King Lamoni but also in turn many of his people. One of the results of the people's conversion is that they voluntarily laid down their weapons, not fighting against God or their brethren anymore (Alma 23.7). These converts were hated by those who did not convert, a hatred that would result in the taking up of arms against the converted Lamanites. In the face of impending attack, King Anti-Nephi-Lehi addressed his people, underscoring that in the light of the fact that God had been gracious to forgive them their many sins and murders committed, 'let us stain our swords no more with the blood of our brethren', for if these swords are taken back up and stained again, perhaps they can no longer be washed bright (Alma 24.7-14). Thus, these converts buried their weaponry, resolving to bear arms no more. Their conversion was firm, preferring death to sin. Going out to meet their enemies they bore no arms and as over one thousand of these converts were slain, their unconverted Lamanite brothers threw down their own weapons, with more than a thousand brought to the knowledge of the truth. Eventually, the Anti-Nephi-Lehies flee to the Nephites, their spiritual brethren, who take them in and give them the land of Jershon. They were regarded as 'perfectly honest and upright in all things' and could never take up arms against their brethren again (Alma 27.27-30). After the passage of many years their resolve would be tested when they were moved with compassion, seeing the sacrifices of their Nephite brethren for the safety of the Anti-Nephi-Lehies, and were desirous to take up arms once again in defense of their country. Significantly, Helaman and his brethren 'overpowered'

---

[5] By various estimates there are a total of 283,443 words in the Book of Mormon. The word count by the end of Alma 27 is about 141,721 words, indicating that the story of the remarkable Lamanite conversion and its exceptional aftermath stands at, and encompasses, the physical center of the book. While such a detail might simply be thought a happy or random coincidence, narratively such a location takes on special significance and meaning, as it structurally highlights the contents of this section of the book. I am indebted to John Hilton III for assistance in acquiring word count data on the Book of Mormon.

them and would not allow it, fearing the Anti-Nephi-Lehies might lose their souls if they did again bear arms (Alma 53.13-15). It was this dilemma that lead to the decision of the Anti-Nephi-Lehi sons, the 2,000 striplings, to follow Helaman into battle, where it appears they were divinely protected. Though the renunciation of arms appeared to last for only one generation,[6] its strategic presence in the book's structure, the impact of this action upon Helaman and his brethren – who refuse their help militarily owing to the converts' oath, and the esteem in which the Anti-Nephi-Lehies continued to be held – by Jesus himself (3 Nephi 9.20) – all converge to impress upon the reader that violence is not the only Book of Mormon option even when one's life is endangered.

Second, in keeping with the actions of the Anti-Nephi-Lehies are various words spoken by Jesus. In 3 Nephi 12.21-22, Jesus says:

Ye have heard that it has been said by them of old time, and it is also written before you, that thou shalt not kill, and whosoever shall kill shall be in danger of the judgment of God. But I say unto you, that whosoever is angry with his brother shall be in danger of his judgment ...

Jesus' words rule out the killing of another human being, words which to this point in the Book of Mormon have only been lived out by the Anti-Nephi-Lehies. Jesus will go on to advocate the reconciliation of brothers between whom an aught has come (3 Nephi 12.23).

Related to this prohibition spoken against killing are the words of Jesus found in 3 Nephi 12.39.

And behold, it is written, an eye for an eye, and a tooth for a tooth. But I say unto you, that ye shall not resist evil, but whosoever shall smite thee on thy right cheek, turn to him the other also.

---

[6] Givens (*The Book of Mormon: A Very Short Introduction*, pp. 48-51) focuses less on the theological implications of this set of stories for a Book of Mormon theology of war and peace, proposing that the thing that ties together these two different attitudes toward war is the fact that the actions of both are based on a covenant taken by each group. He writes, 'The moral of this story, where righteous pacifism and righteous warfare find comfortable co-existence, would seem to be that faithfulness to covenants righteously entered into trumps both' (p. 51).

Clearly, such words go well beyond the prohibition about killing to include a prohibition against any actions of retaliation for evil one may experience. Thus, rather than striking back the one who strikes a believer, one is to offer the other cheek to be struck as well. Similarly, Jesus advocates responding to lawsuits for one's property by a generous gift to the one who brings such a suit.

The words of 3 Nephi 12.43-45 are also of relevance to this topic.

> And behold it is written also, that thou shalt love thy neighbor and hate thine enemy. But behold, I say unto you, love your enemies, bless them that curse you, do good to them that hate you, and pray for them who despitefully use you and persecute you; that you may be children of your Father who is in heaven; for he maketh his sun to rise on the evil and on the good.

Not only is it wrong to kill, Jesus demands love of enemy. He goes beyond the passive response of not taking life, to the active response of actually loving, blessing, doing good to, and praying for one's enemies. The implications of these and other words of Jesus on the topic of war are not difficult to imagine.

Third, the power of Jesus' words is illustrated in the Book of Mormon in a couple of ways. On the one hand, the most extensive period of peace described in the Book of Mormon is the two hundred years from the time Jesus appeared to the Nephites in which there is no contention owing to the love of God (4 Nephi 15). The contrast between this 'golden age' brought about by the keeping of Jesus' words and the short periods of peace won by military means in the book could not be starker.[7] On the other hand, at the end of this period when priests and false prophets 'did smite upon the people of Jesus … the people of Jesus did not smite again' (4 Nephi 34). Rather clearly, there were, at the end of this two hundred year period, still some followers of Jesus living out his commands about non-retaliation.[8] These texts continue to challenge the place that military might occupies in the Book of Mormon.

---

[7] Joshua Madson, 'With God on Our Side', unpublished paper, p. 13.

[8] Andrew Bolton, 'Is the Book of Mormon an Asset or Liability for Becoming a Peace Church?', *John Whitmer Historical Association Journal* 19 (1999), p. 35, and Bolton, 'Anabaptism, the Book of Mormon, and the Peace Church Option', p. 87.

Fourth, very near the conclusion of the book that bears his name, Mormon appears to offer a rather clear critique of war and violence.

> Know ye that ye must lay down your weapons of war, and delight no more in the shedding of blood, and take them not again, save it be that God shall command you (Mormon 7.4).

Several things are significant about these words. It is striking how closely the different components of this verse mirror the words spoken earlier about the Anti-Nephi-Lehies. They lay down their weapons; they delight no more in the shedding of blood; they take up their weapons no more. Rather clearly, these words direct the reader back to the example of the Anti-Nephi-Lehies and their renunciation of weaponry and shedding blood. Would the reader take this as Mormon's way of indicating that his readers should follow their example rather than the path of war? At the same time, the words 'save it be that God shall command you', point the reader back to 1 Nephi 4.10-19 where the Spirit three times commands Nephi to kill Laban. Such an indicator suggests that 1 Nephi 4.10-19 and Mormon 7.4 serve as an inclusio of sorts around the bulk of the book.[9] Significantly, the story that stands at the book's center, around which the inclusio is formed, is that of the Anti-Nephi-Lehies! How would the reader take the proviso 'save it be that God shall command you'? Does it suggest that the reader would reconsider whether or not Nephi actually heard from the Spirit about killing Laban, when Nephi kills him, takes the sword of Laban, 'puts on' Laban's armor, and even speaks with Laban's voice (1 Nephi 4.19-20)?[10] Or would it serve as an extraordinary warning that, ow-

---

[9] Cf. the similar, though not identical, observation by Madson, 'A Non-Violent Reading of the Book of Mormon', p. 27.

[10] Madson ('With God on Our Side', pp. 6-9) proposes that the appearance of the words of Jn 11.50 in 1 Nephi 4 that identify Laban's death with that of Jesus, and Nephi's hesitancy to kill Laban, among other things, reveal that this text is at odds with the voice of the Spirit of Truth and begs for a reassessment of its meaning as well as the meaning of Mormon 7.4-5. For the way in which these texts are traditionally understood 'are inconsistent with a Christo-centric reading' which places the Paraclete at the center of the interpretive process. Madson argues:

> A Christo-centric reading suggests that Nephi was not following the God revealed through Jesus but the spirit and voice of his culture ... The spirit that speaks to Nephi is not the Paraclete or the defender of the accused ... It is

ing to the example of the Anti-Nephi-Lehies and the futility of war as depicted within the Book of Mormon, one must be absolutely certain that God is commanding such action and that the shedding of blood must not be considered short of divine directive? In any case, Mormon's less than enthusiastic advocacy for war near the book's conclusion would temper the reader's overall theological assessment of the role of war and peace in the Book of Mormon.[11]

Fifth, among the final words preserved by his son Moroni (7.3-4), Mormon emphasizes the peaceable nature of true believers.

> Wherefore, I would speak unto you that are of the church, that are the peaceable followers of Christ ... And now, my brethren, I judge these things of you because of your peaceable walk with the children of men.

The occurrence of the world 'peaceably' in Mosiah 4.13 helps define the meaning of 'peaceable' here. There, in King Benjamin's words, the term appears in the context of non-violence, 'And ye will not have a mind to injure one another, but to live peaceably, and render to every man according to that which is his due'. Thus, near the end of the Book of Mormon, the war-worn Mormon reinforces the attitude that the people of God are to exhibit: they are to be peaceable, even with regard to 'the children of men' – not having a mind to injure anyone. In these words, the words of Jesus would ring in the ears of the reader.

It would seem that the theology of war and peace contained in the Book of Mormon must be worked out from the dialectic of a number of positive depictions of war and its necessity, on the one

---

the voice of Caiaphas. It is the voice of Satan, the accuser. Nephi, against his initial feeling, repeats what had happened throughout the ancient world and continues even today: *killing in the name of* security and unity.

For Madson, the Book of Mormon itself undermines violence as a legitimate means of response.

[11] To this Bolton ('Is the Book of Mormon an Asset or Liability for Becoming a Peace Church?', pp. 35-36) would add,

The fact of later apostasy and two accounts of peoples being destroyed by war – genocide in Mormon 1:1-4:2 [RLDS; 1.1-8.41 LDS] and complete mutual destruction in Ether 6:1-106 [RLDS; 13.1-15.34 LDS] – apocalyptically highlights rather than undermines the teachings of Jesus. The grim realism of both accounts, in contrast to the almost romanticizing of the just war ethic in Alma, takes seriously the corrupting nature of human sin and sends a clear prophetic warning to our own day.

hand, and the devastating critique of war and the apparent praise of a renunciation of bearing arms that appears in the book's conclusion, on the other hand.

25

THE THEOLOGY OF THE PLATES AND
TESTIMONY ABOUT THE BOOK OF MORMON

It almost goes without saying that the plates from which the Book of Mormon claims to come are theologically significant as is the testimony the book bears to their emergence and significance. This chapter seeks to identify the theological significance of the plates as well as the book's testimony about itself.

The importance of the records upon which the Book of Mormon claims to be based is revealed in part by the fact that the book begins with the testimony of Nephi:

> Yea, having had a great knowledge of the goodness and mysteries of God, therefore I make a record of my proceedings in my days. Yea, I make a record in the language of my father, which consists of the learning of the Jews and the language of the Egyptians. And I know my record is true; and I make it with my own hands; and I make it according to my knowledge (1 Nephi 1.1c-3).

When seeking to obtain the plates from Laban, Nephi offers the first of several reasons why it is important for these (and other) plates to be preserved:

> And behold, it is the wisdom in God that we should obtain these records, that we may preserve unto our children the language of our fathers; and also that we may preserve unto them the words which have been spoken by the mouth of all the holy prophets, which have been delivered unto them by the Spirit and power of

God, since the world began, even down unto this present time (1 Nephi 3.19-20).

Several aspects of this verse are significant. First, the process is itself described as the wisdom of God. Second, the preservation of the plates, it seems, will ensure the preservation of the language of their fathers (Egyptian?). Third, the plates must be preserved so that the words spoken by holy prophets, delivered by the Spirit and power of God from the beginning of time until the present, will be preserved.

According to 1 Nephi 5.10-21 it will be by means of the plates' preservation that they shall go forth to all nations and never perish, for they are of 'great worth' and must be preserved for 'our children'. Later in 1 Nephi (19.1-7) it is said that Nephi should write upon them about his father Lehi, their time in the wilderness, and the more plain and precious parts of their prophecies. Specifically, they are to be kept for the instruction and knowledge of 'my people', being passed from one generation to another with the purpose of giving knowledge to their children and in order that his brethren would know 'the doings of the Lord in other lands' (1 Nephi 19.21-22).[1]

According to Jacob (4.2-3) one purpose of writing and preserving the plates is so that 'our children' will have 'a small degree of knowledge concerning us, or concerning our fathers ... their first parents'. Enos 13-18 adds another explanation with regard to the plates' preservation: it is so that record might be brought forth to the Lamanites so that they might be brought to salvation. In response to his prayer, God promised Enos to save the records and bring them forth as desired. For Jarom (1-2), the plates are for the benefit of 'our brothers the Lamanites' for they tell about prophesying and revelation. To this, Mormon (in Words of Mormon 7) adds that they are preserved for a purpose that he does not know but is content that God knows (cf. also Alma 37.1). For Mosiah (1.3), the

---

[1] According to Axelgard ('1 and 2 Nephi: An Inspiring Whole', pp. 60-62), 1 and 2 Nephite might be read 'as a nonstop commentary on the importance of records'. This importance is revealed by the obtaining of the plates from Laban, the fact that Nephi's education seems to have come from Lehi and his plates, that great spiritual experiences accompany their reading, and Nephi's unwavering work in keeping these sacred records, even when his work results in a duplicate account.

plates keep the people from suffering in ignorance, for the records are true. Part of Mosiah's purpose (28.10-20) is so that he should discover (reveal) to every creature who should possess the land, the iniquities and abominations of his people.

In 3 Nephi it is reiterated that the records are just and true (5.18; 8.1). Significantly, still later in 3 Nephi 23.6-7 Jesus has the records brought to him and corrects them with regard to the resurrection of many dead at the time of his own resurrection. This addition was, along with the other records, to be taught by them. Later in 3 Nephi (26.8-10) Mormon gives an additional reason for writing:

> And these things have I written, which are a lesser part of the things which he taught the people; and I have written them to the intent that they may be brought again unto this people; from the Gentiles, according to the words which Jesus hath spoken. And when they shall have received this, which is expedient that they should have first, to try their faith; and if it so be that they shall believe these things, then shall the greater things be made manifest unto them.

Rather clearly, Mormon anticipates that the plates will be revealed and lead his people through the Gentiles to faith (cf. also 4 Nephi 47-49). In addition to belief, these books, which are written and preserved, will become the basis for future judgment (3 Nephi 27.23-27). Related to this is the idea found in the Book of Mormon 9.35 that 'these things are written that we may rid our garments of the blood of our brethren, who have dwindled in unbelief'. Finally a discouraged Moroni (1.1-4) hopes that perhaps his words 'may be of worth unto my brethren, the Lamanites in some future day'.

Closely related to the theological purposes of the plates is the testimony found about the Book of Mormon itself. There are at least six passages that offer such testimony, four of which occur in 2 Nephi. The first is found in 2 Nephi 3.3-25, where Lehi reveals to his last-born son Joseph, that they are descendants of Joseph, the son of Jacob. He then goes on to cite the prophetic words of the former Joseph with regard to the appearance of a righteous branch, a seer, the fruit of Joseph's loins. He will write bringing knowledge of their fathers in the latter days. 'His name shall be called after me, and ... after the name of his father'. He will bring Joseph's people salvation forever.

I will make for him a spokesman ... And the words which he shall write shall be the words which are expedient in my wisdom should go forth unto the fruit of thy loins. And it shall be as if the fruit of thy loins had cried unto them from the dust.

These and other words indicate that a seer named Joseph will arise, who will bring salvation.[2]

The second text occurs in 2 Nephi 27.6-23, following Isaiah 29, where it is prophesied that

the Lord God shall bring forth unto you the words of a book, and they shall be the words of them which have slumbered ... But the book shall be delivered unto a man ... and he shall deliver these words unto another ... the book shall be hid from the eyes of the world ... save it be that three witnesses shall behold it by the power of God, beside him to whom the book shall be delivered; and they shall testify to the truth of the book and the things therein ... the Lord God shall say to him ... Take these words which are not sealed and deliver them to another, that he may show them unto the learned, saying, Read this, I pray thee. And the learned shall say, Bring hither the book, and I will read them ... And the man shall say, I cannot bring the book, for it is sealed. Then shall the learned say, I cannot read it.

The emergence of the book is prophesied, as is the fact that there would be three witnesses, and that the words of the book would be examined by a learned scholar who would request the sealed book as well.

The third text, 2 Nephi 29.1-14, promises that the words of the seed of Nephi will hiss forth from the mouth of God to the ends of the earth as 'a standard unto my people'. This revelation will be met with skepticism on the part of those who claim that the Bible is all sufficient Scripture. But just as the Bible came from the Jews, there are more nations than one, and God has more to say than what he says to just one nation.

For I command all men, both in the east and in the west, and in the north and in the south, and in the islands of the sea, that they shall write the words which I speak unto them; for out of

[2] On this identification cf. Hardy, *Understanding the Book of Mormon*, pp. 76-78 and Harrell, *'This Is My Doctrine': The Development of Mormon Theology*, p. 57.

the books that shall be written I will judge the world, every man according to their works, according to that which is written. For behold, I shall speak unto the Jews and they shall write it; and I shall also speak unto the Nephites and they shall write it; and I shall also speak unto the other tribes of the House of Israel, which I have led away, and they shall write it; and I shall also speak unto all nations of the earth and they shall write it (2 Nephi 29.11-12).

The text goes on to say that all will have access to the book(s) of the other and at a certain point 'my word also shall be gathered in one' (2 Nephi 29.14). Thus, not only is testimony given about the emergence of the Book of Mormon but also a variety of other Scriptures from around the world.

In the fourth text, 2 Nephi 33.10-12, Nephi issues a challenge to believe the words that he has written and to believe in Jesus:

And now, my beloved brethren, and also Jew, and all the ends of the earth – hearken unto these words and believe in Christ; and if ye believe not in these words, believe in Christ, and if ye shall believe in Christ ye will believe in these words, for they are the words of Christ, and he has given them unto me; and they teach all men that they shall do good. And if they are not the words of Christ, judge ye – for Christ will show unto you, with power and great glory, that they are his words, at the last day; and you and I shall stand face-to-face before his bar; and ye shall know that I have been commanded of him to write these things, notwith-standing my weakness.

Whilst these words may have reference only to the words that Nephi writes, at another level they seem to envision both the Book of Mormon as a whole and its contemporary (latter day/present day) readers.[3]

The fifth text, 3 Nephi 21.1-10, appears to prophesy the making known of Nephite history to the (future) Gentiles, who in turn will make this known to the House of Israel. This will be the marvelous work and a wonder described by Isaiah (29.14, see also Isa. 52.14 and 3 Nephi 20.44). Of the one who will bring it forth it is said:

---

[3] On the latter, cf. esp. Hardy, *Understanding the book of Mormon*, p. 9.

And behold, the life of my servant shall be in my hand; therefore they shall not hurt him, although he shall be marred because of them. Yet I will heal him, for I will show unto them that my wisdom is greater than the cunning of the devil.

The final text mentioned here is perhaps the most famous or well-known passage in the entire Book of Mormon, Moroni 10.4-5, which issues the challenge for the reader of the book to pray and ask God whether its contents are true or not.

And when ye shall receive these things, I would exhort you that ye would ask God, the Eternal Father, in the name of Christ, if these things are not true; and if ye shall ask with a sincere heart, with real intent, having faith in Christ, he will manifest the truth of it unto you, by the power of the Holy Ghost. And by the power of the Holy Ghost ye shall know the truth of all things.

In many ways these words are a fitting conclusion to a book, the legitimacy for which appears to be a matter of faith. In fact, it appears that Moroni realizes that nothing short of the reader exercising faith will convince him or her of the truth of his account.[4]

---

[4] Cf. esp. Hardy, *Understanding the Book of Mormon*, p. 224. Joseph M. Spencer points out that the text's assumption is that these things are true, thus the words 'if these things are *not* true'. Cf. J.M. Spencer, *An Other Testament: On Typology* (Salt Lake City: Salt Press, 2012), p. 31 n. 21. Gardner (*Second Witness: Fourth Nephi-Moroni*, p. 408) observes, 'He doesn't ask that we pray to see if they are true but rather to ask if they are *not* true. Why this unusual request? Moroni is testifying to something that he knows is true. The truth is so obvious that the only reason for asking is if his future reader does not yet know it was true.'

26

ESCHATOLOGY – THE RETURN OF JESUS, RESURRECTION, AND THE GATHERING OF ISRAEL AND THE ESTABLISHMENT OF THE NEW JERUSALEM

Book of Mormon eschatology is distinctive in several ways. This short survey will focus on three aspects: the return of Jesus, the resurrection, and the restoration.

The Return of Jesus

The Book of Mormon speaks often of the coming of Jesus. However, the vast preponderance of these texts have reference to what might be called Jesus' first coming to earth, in the old world and the new (Jacob 4.4; Mosiah 3.15, Alma 13.24, 25, 26; 16.16; 25.15; 39.16, 17, 19; Helaman 8.17-18; 14.2, 3). Surprisingly, it appears that there are only two or three passages in the Book of Mormon that mention the second coming of Jesus, with two of these texts being restatements of 'Old Testament prophecies concerning the final judgment day of the Lord'.[1] The first passage appears in 3 Nephi 24.2, where Jesus quotes Mal. 3.2 and raises the question, 'But who may abide the day of his coming, and who shall stand when he appeareth?' Two chapters later (3 Nephi 26.3-5), Jesus provides an explanation to the question he posed by way of Malachi.

---

[1] Harrell, '*This Is My Doctrine': The Development of Mormon Theology*, pp. 445-46.

> And he did expound all things, even from the beginning until the time that he should come in his glory – yea, even all things which should come upon the face of the earth, even until the elements should melt with fervent heat, and the earth should be wrapt together as a scroll, and the heavens and the earth should pass away; and even unto the great and last day, when all people, and all kindreds, and all nations and tongues shall stand before God, to be judged of their works, whether they be good or whether they be evil – If they be good, to the resurrection of everlasting life; and if they be evil, to the resurrection of damnation; being on a parallel, the one on the one hand and the other on the other hand, according to the mercy, and the justice, and the holiness which is in Christ, who was before the world began.

Of significance in this passage is the phrase 'until the time that he should come in his glory', clearly a reference to the return of Jesus to the earth. The rest of the passage's content reveals that the time of his return appears to be at the time of the final judgment, 'the great and last day', when all people will be resurrected to receive everlasting life or damnation. It appears that Jesus' coming coincides with the time of the earth's end.[2]

About a chapter later, the second Book of Mormon text that mentions the coming of Jesus appears (3 Nephi 27.16-17).

> And it shall come to pass, that whoso repenteth and is baptized in my name shall be filled; and if he endureth to the end, behold, him will I hold guiltless before my father at that day when I shall stand to judge the world. And he that endureth not unto the end, the same is he that is also hewn down and cast into the fire, from whence they can no more return, because of the justice of the Father.

This passage also places Jesus in the context of judgment that he will deliver at the end owing to the justice of the Father.

The coming of Jesus is mentioned a final time in 3 Nephi 29.2:

> And ye may know that the words of the Lord, which have been spoken by the holy prophets, shall all be fulfilled; And ye need

---

[2] Cf. Harrell, 'This Is My Doctrine': The Development of Mormon Theology, p. 446.

not say that the Lord delays his coming unto the children of Israel.

Though the mention of the Lord's coming in this passage is almost pedestrian, its location on the lips of Mormon as one of his final admonitions in 3 Nephi underscores its certainty and the need for vigilance in watching for all the things spoken by the holy prophets to be fulfilled.

From these few texts one discovers the essence of Book of Mormon eschatology. It falls into a broad outline consisting of four phases. 1) Jesus will come in his glory at the time of the end (3 Nephi 26.3); 2) the heavens and the earth will pass away (3 Nephi 26.3); 3) all will be resurrected to stand before the Lord to be judged according to their works (3 Nephi 26.4); 4) Those who have done good works will enter into 'endless life and happiness' whilst those whose works are evil will be handed over to the devil and damnation (Mosiah 16.10-11).[3]

The Resurrection

One of the major eschatological events described in the Book of Mormon is the resurrection[4] of the dead at the time of the return of Jesus and the final judgment, as noted in the previous section. However, it should be observed that the resurrection expected at the end of time is anticipated by the resurrection that accompanies Jesus' own resurrection before his appearance to the believers in the old world and the Nephites in the new world.[5] Mosiah 15.21-25 describes this resurrection:

> And there cometh a resurrection, even a first resurrection: yea, even a resurrection of those that have been, and who are, and who shall be, even until the resurrection of Christ (for so shall he be called). And now, the resurrection of all the prophets, and all

---

[3] Here I draw heavily from Harrell, *'This Is My Doctrine': The Development of Mormon Theology*, p. 447.

[4] For an analysis of the way in which different Book of Mormon characters use the term resurrection cf. John Hilton III and Jana Johnson, 'Who Uses the Word Resurrection in the Book of Mormon and How Is It Used?' *Journal of the Book of Mormon and Other Restoration Scripture* 21.2 (2012), pp. 30-39.

[5] Harrell, *'This Is My Doctrine': The Development of Mormon Theology*, p. 461.

those that have believed in their words, or all those that have kept the commandments of God, shall come forth in the first resurrection; therefore, they are the first resurrection. They are raised to dwell with God who has redeemed them; thus they have eternal life through Christ, who has broken the bands of death. And these are those who have part in the first resurrection; and these are they that have died before Christ came, in their ignorance, not having salvation declared unto them. And thus the Lord bringeth about the restoration of these; and they have a part in the first resurrection, or have eternal life, being redeemed by the Lord. (And the little children also have eternal life.)

Those who do not believe have no part in this first resurrection (Mosiah 15.26). The hope of having part in the first resurrection is encouraged by Alma (Mosiah 18.9), while Helaman (14.25) describes this hoped for event as, 'And many graves shall be opened, and shall yield up many of their dead; and many saints shall appear unto many'. According to Alma, this first resurrection should not be confused with the raising of the spirit or the soul after death, but is 'the reuniting of the soul with the body, of those from the days of Adam down to the resurrection of Christ' ... 'in other words, their resurrection cometh to pass before the resurrection of those who die after the resurrection of Christ' (Alma 40.18-19).

Alma (40.9) makes clear that there is a space of time that must pass between death and the resurrection, whether the first resurrection or the final resurrection that occurs at the end of time. During this time the spirits of the righteous are taken home to God, 'received into a state of happiness', which is called paradise, while the spirits of the wicked are cast into outer darkness. They remain in this state until the time of the resurrection (Alma 40.11-14).

As for the final resurrection, several things can be observed. First, as noted earlier, the final resurrection is closely associated with the second coming of Jesus (3 Nephi 26.3-5; 27.16-17). Second, the final resurrection includes all humankind, both good and evil (2 Nephi 9.12, 22). Third, the final resurrection is consistently presented as preceding the final judgment at the last day (2 Nephi

9.22; Jacob 6.9; Mosiah 16.10-11; Alma 33.22).[6] This understanding is exemplified in the words of 2 Nephi 9.15,

> And it shall come to pass that when all men shall have passed from this first death until life, insomuch as they have become immortal, they must appear before the judgment-seat of the holy one of Israel; and then cometh the judgment, and then shall they be judged according to the holy judgment of God.

At the final judgment, they are:

> to be judged of their works, whether they be good or whether they be evil – If they be good, to the resurrection of everlasting life; and if they be evil, to the resurrection of damnation; being on a parallel, the one on the one hand and the other on the other hand, according to the mercy, and the justice, and the holiness which is in Christ, who was before the world began (3 Nephi 26.4b-5).

Fourth, this resurrection is closely connected to the restoration of those things spoken by the prophets. Specifically,

> Yea, this bringeth about the restoration of those things of which has been spoken by the mouths of the prophets. The soul shall be restored to the body, and the body to the soul; yea, and every limb and joint shall be restored to its body; yea, even a hair of the head shall not be lost; but all things shall be restored to their proper and perfect frame. And now, my son, this is the restoration of which has been spoken by the mouths of the prophets (Alma 40.22-24; cf. also Alma 11.43-44).

In contrast, an awful death shall come upon the wicked. Fifth, the final resurrection leads to the world to come and eternal life for the righteous. As Moroni 7.41 states:

> And what is it that ye shall have hope for? Behold, I say unto you that ye shall have hope through the atonement of Christ and the power of his resurrection, to be raised unto eternal life, and this because of your faith in him according to the promise.

---

[6] Harrell (*'This Is My Doctrine': The Development of Mormon Theology*, p. 447) notes that the phrase the 'last day' occurs over 50 times in the Book of Mormon and all the occurrences appear to have reference to the last day of the earth.

The Gathering of Israel and the Establishment of the New Jerusalem

Another Book of Mormon eschatological theme that deserves mention in this survey is the gathering of Israel and the related topic of the establishment of the New Jerusalem upon the earth. Various Book of Mormon passages state that Israel, currently dispersed around the world, will begin to believe in the Gospel owing to the efforts of believing Gentiles and will begin to gather 'home to the lands of their inheritance' (2 Nephi 9.2). Apparently, this temporal gathering – which appears to include modern Jews (2 Nephi 25.15-16) – is predicated upon their spiritual conversion to the Gospel preached amongst them.[7] As 2 Nephi 6.11 states, '[N]evertheless, the Lord will be merciful unto them, that when they shall come to the knowledge of their Redeemer, they shall be gathered together again to the lands of their inheritance'. Similarly in 2 Nephi 10.7, 'When the day cometh, that they shall believe in me, that I am Christ, then have I covenanted with their fathers that they should be restored in the flesh, upon the earth, unto the lands of their inheritance' (cf. also 2 Nephi 9.1-2).

Closely related to the theme of gathering is the idea of the New Jerusalem. Speaking of the theme of gathering 3 Nephi 20.22 notes,

> and behold, this people will I establish in this land, unto the fulfilling of the covenant which I made with your father Jacob; and it shall be a New Jerusalem. And the powers of heaven shall be in the midst of this people; yea, even I will be in the midst of you.

Rather clearly, the New Jerusalem is established as a result of the conversion and gathering of Israel (cf. also 3 Nephi 21.23-24). At the same time, the Book of Mormon appears to suggest that there is some discontinuity between this understanding of New Jerusalem and its description in Ether. For, according to Ether 13.2-3, this choice land is where God desires that all 'men' should serve him – 'the place of the New Jerusalem, which should come down out of heaven, the holy sanctuary of the Lord'. This location should be-

---

[7] Cf. Harrell, 'This Is My Doctrine': The Development of Mormon Theology, pp. 402-10.

come 'a holy city of the Lord ... built unto the house of Israel' (Ether 13.5). Further,

> And there shall be a new heaven and a new earth; and they shall be like unto the old save the old have passed away, and all things have become new. And then cometh the New Jerusalem; and blessed are they who dwell therein, for it is they whose garments are white through the blood of the Lamb; and they are they who are numbered among the remnant of the seed of Joseph, who were of the house of Israel (Ether 13.9-10).

Thus, it appears that in the Book of Mormon the idea of the gathering of Israel and the New Jerusalem are tightly connected and encompass the dwelling of gathered Israel in both pre-resurrection and post-resurrection manifestations of the New Jerusalem, which itself appears to be an elastic term in the book.

27

A FEW OTHER MATTERS

Before concluding this Part devoted to the theology of the Book of Mormon, a few additional theological issues merit brief mention, each for differing reasons.

Murmuring

An additional interesting theological aspect of the Book of Mormon is the role and meaning that murmuring plays in the book. The theme is especially prominent in 1 Nephi, with references occurring in 2 Nephi, Mosiah, Alma, and 3 Nephi as well.

Murmuring appears for the first time in the Book of Mormon in 1 Nephi 2.11 and alerts the reader to its meaning and function within the book. Here Laman and Lemuel murmur against their father Lehi for several reasons. First, they consider Lehi to be a visionary man, perhaps indicating that murmuring will function as an inappropriate response to the prophetic. This understanding is confirmed in 1 Nephi 2.12 where it is noted that the brothers did not know the 'dealings of God'. Second, the brothers murmur because Lehi led them out of their home in Jerusalem. Third, they murmur because Lehi caused them to abandon their financial resources in Jerusalem. Finally, they murmur owing to the fact that they assumed they would eventually die in the wilderness. Later (1 Nephi 3.5), the brothers will also murmur against Nephi for requiring a hard thing of them, the retrieving of the plates from Laban, whilst Nephi is favored because he did not murmur (1 Nephi 3.6). The sinister nature of murmuring is underscored by the fact that the next time the

brothers murmur it follows a visitation by an angel and focuses upon the impossibility of being able to accomplish what the angel
commands; they do not believe that Laban will be delivered into
their hands (1 Nephi 3.31). Perhaps here one might take murmuring
to be a vocalization of disbelief.[1] Once again Nephi admonishes his
brothers, who murmur, but ultimately follow him (1 Nephi 4.4).
Later, Nephi reveals that Laman and Lemuel would not murmur if
they were righteous (1 Nephi 16.3).

Sufferings and afflictions also become the occasion for murmuring, which might be understood as an indicator of the spirituality of
the individuals in question. Such suffering would not only cause
Laman and Lemuel, along with the sons of Ishmael, to murmur, but
even Lehi himself (1 Nephi 16.20), who is quickly chastened by the
Lord (1 Nephi 16.25). Reminiscent of the actions of the brothers
described earlier in the book, when Ishmael dies his daughters
murmur against Lehi for bringing them out from the land of Jerusalem. But by way of contrast, the Nephite women bore children in
the wilderness and became strong like men, bearing their journeyings without murmuring (1 Nephi 17.3).

The theme of murmuring against the prophetic again occurs
when Laman and Lemuel murmur against Nephi for proposing to
build a ship, thinking him to be a fool, accusing him of being a
dreamer, even disputing his prophetic insight that Jerusalem has
been destroyed (1 Nephi 17.17-22). Nephi commands his brothers
to murmur against their father no longer, instructing them instead
to aid in his own work (1 Nephi 17.49). Despite his many afflictions, Nephi refuses to murmur (1 Nephi 18.16). Lehi later instructs
his sons that they have murmured against Nephi owing to his plain
speech to them (2 Nephi 1.26), while Nephi will recall the many
ways in which his brothers have murmured against him (2 Nephi
5.3-4).

> Yea, they did murmur against me, saying, Our younger brother
> thinks to rule over us; and we have had much trial because of
> him; wherefore, now let us slay him, that we may not be afflicted
> more because of his words. For behold, we will not have him to
> be our ruler; for it belongs to us, who are the elder brethren, to
> rule over this people. Now I do not write upon these plates all

---

[1] I am indebted to my friend Derrick Harmon for this observation.

the words which they murmured against me. But it suffereth me to say, that they did seek to take away my life (2 Nephi 5.3-4).

Not only is resentment expressed over the fact that the law of primogenitor has been violated, by their younger brother ruling over the elder brothers, but also the murmuring against his prophetic role is hardly concealed. That such attitudes are a sign of not properly discerning the work of God is later revealed in a quotation of Isaiah 29 where Nephi's words, 'and they that murmured shall learn doctrine' (2 Nephi 27.35), suggest something of the remedy for murmuring (cf. also 1 Nephi 2.12). A final reference in 2 Nephi (29.8) indicates something of the relationship between murmuring and opposition to the work of God. Here, God addresses those who speak against the additional Scriptural revelation that comes forth in the Book of Mormon asking, 'Wherefore murmur ye, because that ye shall receive more of my word?'

For the most part in the rest of the Book of Mormon the theme of murmuring is closely connected to suffering (Mosiah 21.6; Alma 58.35; 60.4), the persecution of the church (Mosiah 27.1), and fear of punishment (Alma 17.28). Murmuring as opposition to the work of God appears a couple more times (Alma 19.19; 22.24). The final occurrence of the term appears on the lips of Jesus and may hint that murmuring in some ways opposes the work of God when he asks why the people murmur over the name of the church, which must take upon itself his name (3 Nephi 27.4).

Thus, murmuring functions in the Book of Mormon primarily as an expression of ignorance of and/or opposition to the prophetic work of God. Those who murmur are clearly those who are not deemed to be spiritually mature, at the least, while those who refuse to murmur are praised. In fact, on only one occasion does murmuring appear to have a positive function. In Mosiah 27.1 the church murmurs to King Mosiah owing to the persecution it is experiencing, resulting in a royal decree of protection for the church from such hostilities.

Polygamy

Owing to the fact that several groups for whom the Book of Mormon functions as Scripture have at one point or another adopted or advocated the practice of polygamy, it seems fitting that some attention be devoted to this theme within the book.

It may come as a bit of a shock to first-time readers of the Book of Mormon to find that polygamy is explicitly and consistently condemned within the book. The most scathing condemnations occur in the Book of Jacob:

> And now it came to pass that the people of Nephi, under the reign of the second king, began to grow hard in their hearts, and indulge themselves somewhat in wicked practices, such as like unto David of old desiring many wives and concubines, and also Solomon, his son (Jacob 1.15).

This condemnation continues in Jacob 2.23-4.14 in remarkably clear and explicit language, where Jacob discusses the 'grosser crimes' of the people including:

> excusing themselves in committing whoredoms, because of the things which were written concerning David, and Solomon his son. Behold, David and Solomon truly had many wives and concubines, which thing was abominable before me, saith the Lord ... Wherefore, I, the Lord God, will not suffer that this people shall do like unto them of old. Wherefore, my brethren, hear me, and hearken to the word of the Lord, for there shall not any man among you have save it be one wife; and concubines he shall have none. For I, the Lord God, delight in the chastity of women, and whoredoms are an abomination before me (Jacob 2.23-28).

Chief among the reasons for such a condemnation is the effect such sexual relationships have upon the 'daughters of my people'.

> For behold, I, the Lord, have seen the sorrow, and I heard the mourning of the daughters of my people in the land of Jerusalem, yea, and in all the lands of my people, because of the wickedness and abominations of their husbands. And I will not suffer, saith the Lord of hosts, that the cries of the fair daughters of this people, which I have led out of the land of Jerusalem, shall come unto me against the men of my people, says the Lord of hosts. For they shall not lead away captive the daughters of my people because of their tenderness, save I shall visit them with a sore curse, even unto destruction; for they shall not commit

whoredoms, like unto them of old, saith the Lord of hosts (Jacob 2.31-33).

With such forbidden behavior the Nephites have outdone their Lamanite brethren.

Behold, you have done greater iniquities than the Lamanites our brethren. Ye have broken the hearts of your tender wives, and lost the confidence of your children, because of your bad examples before them; and the sobbings of their hearts ascend up to God against you (Jacob 2.34-35).

Behold, the Lamanites your brethren, whom ye hate because of their filthiness and the cursing which hath come upon their skins, are more righteous than you; for they have not forgotten the commandment of the Lord, which was given to our fathers – that they should have save it were one wife, and concubines they shall have none, and there should not be whoredoms committed among them (Jacob 3.5).

Behold, their husbands love their wives, and their wives love their husbands; and their husbands and their wives love their children; and their unbelief and their hatred towards you is because of the iniquity of their fathers; wherefore, how much better are you than they, in the sight of your great creator?

Wherefore, ye shall remember your children, how that ye have grieved their hearts because of the example that ye have set before them; and also, remember that ye may, because of your filthiness, bring your children unto destruction, and their sins be heaped upon your heads at the last day (Jacob 3.7-10).

A plainer condemnation of the practice of polygamy is difficult to imagine.

Later in the Book of Mormon, condemnation of the behavior of wicked King Noah includes the support he takes for himself and his priests and their wives and their concubines (Mosiah 11.4), for he spent his time 'in riotous living with his wives and his concubines' (Mosiah 11.14). Narratively, reference to polygamy may also be inferred in Mosiah 12.29, where whoredoms are again condemned. Significantly, despite the huge number of widows and fatherless children owing to war, polygamy is not recommended as a solution to this crisis.

> Now there was a great number of women, more than there was of men; therefore King Limhi commanded that every man should impart to the support of the widows and their children, that they might not perish with hunger; and this they did because of the greatness of their number that had been slain (Mosiah 21.17).

The testimony of the Book of Mormon is consistent in its opposition to polygamy.

The Role of Women

Another issue worthy of some attention is the role of women in the Book of Mormon. Despite the overall length of the book there is surprisingly little attention given to women with only three women actually named![2] To be sure, there are several passages that suggest women are to be thought of as on an equal footing with men. These include the following words of Nephi, Mosiah, and Alma:

> And he cometh into the world that he may save all men, if they will hearken unto his voice: for behold, he suffereth the pains of all men; yea, the pains of every living creature, both men women, and children, who belong to the family of Adam (2 Nephi 9.21).

> He invited them all to come unto him and partake of his goodness; and he denieth none that come unto him, black-and-white, bond and free, male and female ... and all are alike unto God, both Jew and Gentile (2 Nephi 26.33).

---

[2] More than one interpreter demonstrates the embarrassment of this omission as can be gauged in part by the apologies and/or explanations offered in its defense. Cf. Camille S. Williams, 'Women in the Book of Mormon: Inclusion, Exclusion, and Interpretation', *Journal of Book of Mormon Studies* 11.1 (2002), pp. 66-79, 111-14, and Camille Fronk, 'Desert Epiphany: Sariah and the Women in 1 Nephi', *Journal of Book of Mormon Studies* 9.2 (2000), pp. 5–15. Luffman (*The Book of Mormon's Witness to Its First Readers*, pp. 187-95) offers a helpful survey and analysis of gender representation in the Book of Mormon. He concludes, 'The significant absence of women's voices in the dictated text of the Book of Mormon is best addressed when it is acknowledged that unquestioned patriarchy is prevalent in the narrative text, and it is confessed that this representation is not an adequate representation of the gospel of God' (pp. 194-95).

And now, because of the covenant which ye have made ye shall be called the children of Christ, his sons, and his daughters ... ye say that your hearts are changed through faith on his name; therefore, ye are born of him and have become his sons and daughters (Mosiah 5.7).

Now this restoration shall come to all, both old and young, both bond and free, both male and female, both the wicked and the righteous; and even there shall not so much as a hair of their heads be lost; but all these thing shall be restored to its perfect frame, as it is now, or in the body, and shall be brought and be arraigned before the bar of Christ the Son, and God the Father, and the Holy Spirit, which is one Eternal God, to be judged according to their works, whether they be good or whether they be evil (Alma 11.44).

He imparteth his word by angels unto men, yea, not only unto men but women also (Alma 32.23).[3]

To these one might even add the remarkable words of 1 Nephi 11.18 where in the 1830 edition of the Book of Mormon the mother of the Messiah is called 'the mother of God'. However, despite these passages, for the most part, women seem to function as props in the book, serving as wives, mothers, daughters, sisters, slaves, and harlots.[4] In point of fact, there is hardly a heroine to be found within the book's pages. One text even seems to suggest that the phenomenon of the Nephite women who bore children in the wilderness and *became strong like men* – bearing their journeyings without

---

[3] The following somewhat 'negative' testimony might also be noted:

wherefore, he that fighteth against Zion, both Jew and Gentile, both bond and free, both male and female, shall perish: for they are they which are the whore of all the earth; for they which are not for me, are against me, saith our God (2 Nephi 10.16).

[4] As Francine R. Bennion observes,

Women were primarily accessories to men, dependent upon them not only for survival but also for identity, which is presented as a matter of relationship to a man, usefulness to a man, or use by men. Whatever their strengths or virtues, women were subsidiary to men, shown making decisions only when their men were absent or helpless.

'Women and the Book of Mormon: Tradition and Revelation', in Marie Cornwall and Susan Howe (eds.), *Women of Wisdom and Knowledge* (Salt Lake City: Deseret, 1990), p. 171.

murmuring – is to be seen as a good thing (1 Nephi 17.2). This section will focus on the three named women, as well as a couple of incidents dealing with one or more female characters, and then offer a few concluding observations.

Sariah

The first woman to appear in the book is the first woman named; Sariah the wife of Lehi. Not only is she named, but Sariah also actually speaks in the text. Unfortunately, her words are not altogether praiseworthy. For when Nephi and his brothers return from the wilderness it is revealed that she had feared her sons had perished and that she had complained against Lehi as being a 'visionary man', complaining that he had led the family out of the land of their inheritance and that her sons are now no more (1 Nephi 5.2, 3). But Lehi comforted Sariah with words of explanation and encouragement and when the sons returned Sariah says:

> Now I know of a surety that the Lord hath commanded my husband to flee into the wilderness; yea, and I also know of a surety that the Lord hath protected my sons, and delivered them out of the hands of Laban, and given them power whereby they could accomplish the thing which the Lord hath commanded them (1 Nephi 5.8).

Through the encouraging work of Lehi and the appearance of her sons before her eyes, Sariah's complaining is turned to confessions both of her husband as a prophetic figure and the Lord's activity on her family's behalf. Significantly, despite her role early in the book, her death is not recounted.[5]

The Stolen Daughters of the Lamanites

Mosiah 20.1-26 recounts the story of the abduction of twenty-four Lamanite daughters by the priests of King Noah. The news of their abduction resulted in a Lamanite attack upon King Limhi and his people, as the Lamanites assumed the people of Limhi had orchestrated and carried out the abductions. However, when the king of the Lamanites was left for dead and then brought before King Limhi, he revealed the reason for breaking their peace. At this point Gideon, the king's captain, discerned that the priests of King Noah

---

[5] Luffman, *The Book of Mormon's Witness to Its First Readers*, p. 189.

had perpetrated this kidnapping, communicated this to the Lamanite king through King Limhi, and a peace was arranged between the peoples. Eventually, the Lamanite daughters would be discovered with their captors, but the young women would plead for the lives of their 'husbands' (Mosiah 23.25-39). The story of the kidnapping of these Lamanite daughters illustrates the way in which women, even as part of an intriguing story seem to be little more than props in this Book of Mormon narrative.

King Lamoni's Wife and her Servant Abish
On the occasion of the conversion of King Lamoni via the ministry of Ammon, a son of Mosiah, the Book of Mormon tells of the actions of two women; King Lamoni's wife – who is unnamed – and Abish her servant girl (Alma 18.40-19.36). As a result of his conversion, King Lamoni falls down to the earth as though dead, at which point his wife and his sons mourn him. However, the queen called Ammon, suspecting that her husband was not dead, a suspicion that Ammon confirms. In response to the queen's belief in his word Ammon observes, 'Blessed art thou because of thy exceeding faith; I say to thee woman, there has not been such great faith among all the people of the Nephites' (Alma 19.10). On the next day the king arose with a startling testimony of his conversion after which he and his wife sunk down, being overjoyed. Ammon also fell down owing to his own joy at what God had done. When the servants of the king saw this they too prayed unto the Lord, resulting in all of them falling down, save one servant girl named Abish, who had converted to the Lord many years beforehand – though secretly – as a result of a remarkable vision given to her father. Recognizing these events as being the result of the hand of God, Abish ran from house to house, making known these happenings to the people. But rather than resulting in belief on the part of the crowds, the sight of King Lamoni, his wife, servants, and the Nephite prophet resulted in contentions and murmurings amongst the people. In point of fact, when one of their number decided to kill Ammon, he himself was struck dead, with the result that fear came upon all those assembled. Eventually, Abish – sorrowful for these events – takes the hand of the queen, who arose and testified of her own conversion. She then 'clapped her hands',[6] filled with joy, and spoke many

---

[6] The wording of the 1830 edition.

words no one understood. When the queen took the hand of her husband, he arose, offered words of testimony – words believed by many who heard them, leading to their conversion and baptism.

In some ways this narrative illustrates the role of women in the Book of Mormon. Although the queen exhibits faith for which she is highly praised and is instrumental in the king's rising from the earth, and although the servant girl Abish has good intentions in making known the activity of God amongst the people, her evangelistic efforts fall short. It is only King Lamoni's words that lead to the conversion of many of his people. The women appear to function in a subordinate role.[7]

The Harlot Isabel

The third and final named woman contained in the Book of Mormon is found in Alma's words of rebuke to his son Corianton for not giving heed to Alma's words.

> And this is not all, my son. Thou didst do that which was grievous unto me; for thou didst forsake the ministry, and did go over into the land of Siron, among the borders of the Lamanites, after the harlot Isabel. Yea, she did steal away the hearts of many; but this was no excuse for thee, my son. Thou shouldest have tended to the ministry wherewith thou wast entrusted (Alma 39.3-4).

Clearly, the real focus of these verses is Corianton's misbehavior. In some ways Isabel functions as an archetype of the dangers of harlotry, for not only does she apparently entice Corianton to go after her in foreign lands, but she is also presented as a harlot who has committed sexual immorality with many lovers. As such, she serves as an example of the kind of woman to be avoided.

The Abused Handmaiden of Morianton

Another female case study found in the Book of Mormon concerns a certain maidservant who belonged to Morianton who planned to take land in the north for his people. His plans would have been carried out except for the fact that

> Morianton being a man of much passion, therefore he was angry with one of his maid servants, and he fell upon her and beat her much. And it came to pass that she fled, and came over to the

---

[7] Cf. Luffman, *The Book of Mormon's Witness to Its First Readers*, pp. 190-92.

camp of Moroni, and told Moroni all things concerning the matter, and also concerning their intentions to flee to the land northward (Alma 50.30-31).

This maid servant is a sympathetic figure in a couple of ways. First, she is abused by a passionate man. Second, she becomes the instrument by means of which Moroni and his army are preserved. Yet the reader is left wanting to know more about her for when she serves her purpose she disappears from the narrative, receiving neither further mention nor praise for her role.

The Daughter of Jared

The final woman mentioned in the Book of Mormon is, in many respects, perhaps the most interesting and literarily fully developed female character in the book. She is first mentioned in Ether 8.8, in the midst of a story devoted to the intrigue surrounding a certain Jared, who had rebelled against his father to gain half the kingdom, who captured his father, and then lost a military engagement with his brothers who were angry with him over the treatment of his father, and ultimately, sparing his life but taking his kingdom. Jared's daughter, who was 'exceeding fair' and 'exceeding expert', devised a plan to enable her father to recapture his throne. She proposes to dance for Akish, a powerful figure, to please him to the point that he would want her as his wife. She says,

> I will please him that he shall desire me to wife; wherefore if he shall desire of thee that ye shall give me to him to wife, then shall ye say, I will give her if ye will bring to me the head of my father the king (Ether 8.10).

The plan was carried out so that Akish did ask Jared for his daughter to which Jared consented, providing Akish would bring Jared the head of his father. Entering into secret combinations, eventually Jared was restored to his throne, but Akish would kill Jared in the end and rule in his place. Clearly, the daughter of Jared is presented as a capable person who has a voice but is culpable in designing and executing this murderous plot that involves the reintroduction of secret combinations, an abominable thing in God's sight.[8] And with this ignominious story the role of women comes to an end.

---

[8] Luffman, *The Book of Mormon's Witness to Its First Readers*, p. 193.

Concluding Observations on Women in the Book of Mormon

What theological sense might be made of such meager evidence with regard to women in the Book of Mormon? An examination of the structural locations of the stories about the women here surveyed may offer a starting point as the narratives appear to be connected in an almost mirrored kind of fashion.

First, it may well be significant that the stories of Book of Mormon women are framed by the narratives involving Sariah, on the one hand, and the daughter of Jared, on the other hand. Both women are given voice and more space is allotted to them than normally devoted to women. However, the potential optimism which Sariah's appearance brings, despite her need for Lehi's intervention to help her understand spiritual realties, gives way to a disheartening, conspiratorial figure in the actions of Jared's daughter, who aside from some sympathy shown for her father, is a wholly culpable person. The fact that she is the last woman mentioned in the book may suggest that a negative view of women wins out by the book's end. Significantly, whilst Sariah has Lehi to function as a spiritual guide, the daughter of Jared does not have such a guide, perhaps suggesting that women are to be viewed as in need of a man's moral oversight.

Second, there may also be an implied contrast between the stolen daughters of the Lamanites and the abused handmaiden of Morianton. Whereas the stolen daughters seem resigned to their fate, and will even defend their captor husbands when they are discovered, the abused handmaiden demonstrates a strength, not only to break free from her oppressive lord, but also to save the Nephite forces through information shared with them upon her escape. At the least, the abused handmaiden exhibits an active rather than passive disposition, coming closer to a heroine than most of the other women in the book.

Third, it appears that in some ways King Lamoni's wife and the servant girl Abish stand in contrast to the harlot Isabel. While both the former individuals may be viewed positively, despite the mixed signals sent to the reader as to their overall function, the harlot Isabel is viewed in wholly negative terms. The actions of Lamoni's wife and Abish again suggest that women may very well need supervision by a male to insure that they accomplish God's will in their lives, while Isabel may represent the opposite.

Obviously there are a number of other mentions of women in the book that merit some consideration and reflection but perhaps those given here can contribute something to the theology of women in the Book of Mormon.

Hell

Though not often mentioned in discussions about Book of Mormon content and theology, the book actually has a lot to say about hell. In point of fact, eight of the books found within the Book of Mormon contain one or more reference(s) to hell. Not only do these frequent references indicate that a belief in hell is part of the fabric of the book, but also on occasion the Book of Mormon will make explicit statements making this belief clear. For example in 2 Nephi 28.21-22, it is said of the devil's work,

> And others will he pacify, and lull them away into carnal security, that they will say, All is well in Zion; yea, Zion prospereth, all is well – and thus the devil cheateth their souls, and leadeth them away carefully down to hell. And behold, others he flattereth away, and telleth them there is no hell; and saith unto them, I am no devil, for there is none …

The clear implication of these words is that the existence of hell is real and anyone who would deny its existence is doing the work of the devil. This truth is later played out in Sherem's words of confession, 'And he spake plainly unto them, that he had been deceived by the power of the devil. And he spake of hell, and of eternity, and of eternal punishment' (Jacob 7.18). This theme is also found in Ammoron's words of reply to Moroni in Alma 54.22: 'And if it be so that there is a devil and a hell, behold will he not send you there to dwell with my brother whom you have murdered, whom ye have hinted that he hath gone into such a place?'

In the Book of Mormon hell is known as an awful place (1 Nephi 15.29, 35; Alma 19.29; 54.7) from which the souls of people need redemption and deliverance (2 Nephi 1.15; 33.6; Alma 5.6). It is everlasting in nature (1 Nephi 14.3; Helaman 6.28; Moroni 8.13), an ongoing reality, whose gates stand open to receive (3 Nephi 11.40; 18.13), often enlarging itself (2 Nephi 15.14). The constant nature of the threat hell poses is revealed in 2 Nephi 4.32 when

Nephi prays, 'May the gates of hell be shut continually before me, because that my heart is broken and my spirit is contrite' (2 Nephi 4.32). The depths of hell (1 Nephi 12.16) is identified as 'beneath' (2 Nephi 24.9) and is something into which one can go down (1 Nephi 14.3 [2x]; 2 Nephi 2.29; 24.15; 26.10; 28.10; Alma 30.60; 31.17; Moroni 8.14) or into which one is thrust or cast (2 Nephi 28.15; 3 Nephi 12.30)

The danger of hell (3 Nephi 12.22) or hell fire (Mormon 8.17) is its close relationship to death (2 Nephi 9.10-36; 28.23; Moroni 8.21) and the pains (Jacob 3.11; Alma 14.6; 26.13; 36.13; 37.16) and chains (Alma 5.7, 9; 12.11; 13.30; 26.14) that torment and capture those whom the devil drags there. As Alma 12.11 notes:

> And they that will harden their hearts, to them is given the lesser portion of the word until they know nothing concerning his mysteries; and then they are taken captive by the devil, and led by his will down to destruction. Now this is what is meant by the chains of hell.

On two occasions in the Book of Mormon individuals are called a 'child of hell'; Zeezrom by Amulek (Alma 11.23) and Ammoron by Moroni (Alma 54.11). Perhaps such a title suggests that these are among those who will dwell with the damned souls in hell (Mormon 9.4). On one occasion Book of Mormon readers are reassured by Jesus that whoever builds upon the foundation of his doctrine, 'the gates of hell shall not prevail against them' (3 Nephi 11.39), while the gates of hell will stand open to receive those who build upon a sandy foundation (3 Nephi 11.40).

The Book of Mormon makes clear the identity of those who go to or belong to hell. The devil's kingdom (2 Nephi 2.29) specifically awaits the wicked (1 Nephi 14.3), the liar (2 Nephi 9.34), those who commit whoredoms (2 Nephi 9.36), those who have no salvific knowledge (2 Nephi 15.14), those who commit works of darkness (2 Nephi 26.10), those who preach or teach false doctrine (2 Nephi 28.15; Alma 30.60), a 'child of hell' (Alma 11.23; 54.11), the hard hearted (Alma 12.11), those who build on a sandy foundation (3 Nephi 11.40; 18.13), the one who calls a brother 'Raca' (3 Nephi 12.22), the one who would condemn the record that comes forth as the Book or Mormon (Mormon 8.17), and those who advocate that children need infant baptism thereby implying that an infant otherwise is confined to hell (Moroni 8.14, 21). Such a list reveals the seriousness with which hell is taken in the Book of Mormon and the importance of its readers not falling into any of these categories whose activities, or lack thereof, result in the eternal, never-ending torment of hell.

PART FOUR

RECEPTION HISTORY OF
THE BOOK OF MORMON

It almost goes without saying that the Book of Mormon has had a rather remarkable influence in its relative short history, yet this aspect of its study has only recently begun to receive the kind of interest it deserves.[1] Reception history as a discipline, unlike the history of interpretation, does not focus so much on whether this or that individual or group has correctly interpreted a given text, in this case the Book of Mormon, but rather is concerned to trace the impact of that text throughout history without judgment. New Testament scholar Ulrich Luz likens the method to identifying the paths that a mountain stream takes down the contours of a mountain rather than seeking to focus on the water's source.[2] Part Four is devoted to sampling a variety of ways in which the Book of Mormon's impact upon its readers may be gauged. While a comprehensive study of this topic is beyond the scope of a work of this size, this Part will offer various categories of influence with two or more examples of each category.

---

[1] On this cf. Givens, *The Book of Mormon: A Very Short Introduction*, pp. 103-25 and Gutjahr, *The Book of Mormon: A Biography*, pp. 111-95.

[2] Ulrich Luz, *Matthew in History* (Minneapolis, MN: Fortress, 1994), p. 24.

28

GROUPS FOR WHOM THE BOOK OF MORMON
FUNCTIONS AS SCRIPTURE

Perhaps it would be most appropriate to begin this Part with a survey of those groups for whom the Book of Mormon has or does function as Scripture, for without such groups it is likely that the book would have generated little by way of reception history.

Church of Christ

It hardly comes as a surprise that the first church for whom the Book of Mormon functioned as scripture was established by those instrumental in the production of the Book of Mormon in the first place. After an epiphany in which Joseph Smith and Oliver Cowdery testify that they received the priesthood and baptized one another, the Church of Christ appears to have been organized on 6 April 1830 in either Fayette or Manchester, New York with six members: Joseph Smith, Jr, Oliver Cowdery, Hyrum Smith, Peter Whitmer, Jr, Samuel H. Smith, and David Whitmer.[1] Within a month there would be forty members.[2] Something of the significance of the Book of Mormon for this new church is found in the *Book of Commandments* 24.7-11 which describes 'The Articles and

---

[1] Richard Lyman Bushman, *Joseph Smith: Rough Stone Rolling* (New York: Vintage Books, 2005), p. 109.

[2] Fawn M. Brodie, *No Man Knows My History: The Life of Joseph Smith* (New York: Vintage, 1995), p. 87.

Covenants of the church of Christ. Given in Fayette, New York. June, 1830':

> 7 ... [God] gave him power, by the means which were before prepared, that he should translate a book;
>
> 8 Which book contained a record of a fallen people, and also the fullness of the gospel of Jesus Christ to the Gentiles;
>
> 9 And also to the Jews, proving unto them, that the holy scriptures are true;
>
> 10 And also, that God doth inspire men and call them to his holy work, in these last days as well as in days of old, that he might be the same God forever. Amen.
>
> 11 Which book was given by inspiration, and is called the book of Mormon, and is confirmed to others by the ministering of angels, and declared unto the world by them.[3]

In addition to the numerous converts that were being attracted to the young church by means of the Book of Mormon, another tangible effect of the text was seen at the 26 September conference, when Oliver Cowdery and Peter Whitmer, Jr were commissioned as the first missionaries to the Lamanites,[4] a people group whose only evidence for existence was contained in the Book of Mormon. On 3 May 1834, the Church of Christ would change its name to the Church of Latter Day Saints at a conference in Kirtland, Ohio and in 1838 to the Church of Jesus Christ of Latter Day Saints.[5]

During this period, several editions of the Book of Mormon would appear. Following the original 1830 edition, a second edition was published in Kirtland in 1837, a third edition appeared in 1840 published in Nauvoo (printed in Cincinnati), the first British edition was published in 1841 in Liverpool, and a new impression of the 1840 edition was published in Nauvoo in 1842. In all, somewhere

---

[3] *A Book of Commandments for the Government of the Church of Christ Organized according to Law, on the 6th of April 1830* (Zion: W.W. Phelps & Co., 1833), pp. 37-38.

[4] Mark A. Scherer, *The Journey of a People: The Era of Restoration, 1820 to 1844* (Independence, MO: Church of Christ Seminary Press, 2013), p. 129.

[5] Scherer, *The Journey of a People: The Era of Restoration, 1820 to 1844*, pp. 288-89.

between sixteen and eighteen thousand copies of the book appeared during this twelve-year span.[6]

Church of Jesus Christ of Latter Day Saints

After the deaths of Joseph and Hyrum Smith in Carthage, Missouri on 24 June 1844, the Church of Jesus Christ of Latter Day Saints entered into a period of crisis caused in major part by the lack of a clearly chosen, legitimate leader, with several claimants vying for leadership. Eventually, Brigham Young would make the argument that the church should be led at this point by the Quorum of the Twelve, of which he was lead, until such time as the church could decide upon a leader.[7] Young would wind up leading tens of thousands of the Mormon following west to Utah, where the LDS faithful would be free to form a society of their own, relatively safe from interference and persecution.

The Place of the Book of Mormon in the Utah LDS Church

For this largest segment of the LDS constituency, the Book of Mormon was an important part of the church's works of Scripture. Within a few years the second (1849) and third (1852) editions of the British versions would appear, as would a private edition published in New York by James O. Wright. A major LDS edition would appear in 1879, published simultaneously in Salt Lake City and Liverpool, under the direction of Orson Pratt, who introduced additional chapter divisions and for the first time versification and footnotes to the book. The next major LDS edition appeared in 1920 in Salt Lake City where the text was placed into double columns for the first time in a LDS version of the book. This was followed by the next major LDS edition in 1981, which included corrections, new introductory materials, new chapter summaries, and new footnotes. A multi-volume text-critical edition of the Book of Mormon was published over the course of several years from 1988-2007 by Royal Skousen with FARMS support. In 2004, Grant Hardy edited and produced, with the University of Illinois Press, a version that is based on the 1920 edition, but has been reformatted to read more like its original presentation with helps of various kinds

---

[6] Gutjahr, *The Book of Mormon: A Biography*, p. 201.
[7] Turner, *Brigham Young*, pp. 110-18.

for the reader.[8] By 2006, the Book of Mormon would be translated into well over 100 languages of the world.[9]

Perhaps the best-known influence of the book throughout much of LDS history is its role in the conversion experience of proselytes. LDS literature is filled with accounts of individual testimonies of how the Book of Mormon led to the conversion of the individual in question. Often these testimonies include the way in which the book stood in harmony with the Bible. Over the years, these conversion accounts would include a testimony based on the teaching of Moroni 10.4-5:

> And when ye shall receive these things, I would exhort you to ask God, the Eternal Father, in the name of Christ, if these things are not true; and if you shall ask with a sincere heart, with real intent, having faith in Christ, and he will manifest the truth of it to you, by the power of the Holy Ghost; and by the power of the Holy Ghost, ye may know the truth of all things.

Lack of Impact on the Utah LDS Church

Ironically, despite the significance of the Book of Mormon for the LDS Church, demonstrated in part by continued publication of a variety of editions of the Book of Mormon over the years, for much of that time the Book of Mormon did not attract a great deal of attention from the Mormon faithful. According to Terryl L. Givens, only two years after the book's appearance, Joseph Smith himself delivered a stinging rebuke of the faithful for their neglect of the book.[10] Even Brigham Young seemed at times to show a decided preference for the Bible over the Book of Mormon:

> In all my teachings, I have taught the gospel from the Old and New Testaments. I found therein every doctrine and the proof of every doctrine the Latter-day Saints believe in, as far as I know, therefore I do not refer to the Book of Mormon as often as I otherwise should. There may be some doctrines about which little is said in the Bible, but they are all couched therein, and I

[8] Gutjahr, *The Book of Mormon*, pp. 201-203.

[9] Gutjahr, *The Book of Mormon*, pp. 205-208.

[10] Givens, *The Book of Mormon: A Very Short Introduction*, p. 108.

believe the doctrines because they are true, and I have taught them because they are calculated to save the children of men.[11]

On an earlier occasion he would note, 'With us the Bible is the first book, the Book of Mormon comes next, then the revelations in the book of Doctrines and Covenants, then the teaching of the living oracles'.[12] Nor did the book influence the church's worship as much as one might have expected. Givens notes that out of more than four hundred songs in the current LDS hymnal only six employ Book of Mormon themes or language.[13]

A final surprising area with regard to the Book of Mormon's lack of influence has to do with the development of later doctrinal teaching within the LDS church. At any number of places, from the nature of God to polygamy, the teaching of the book was not influential enough to withstand changes in doctrine that resulted from the continuing revelation that was part of this family of the LDS tradition. Perhaps the continual adoption of doctrinal practices and beliefs that on various occasions stood in opposition or tension with earlier Mormon teaching as represented in the Book of Mormon was a contributing factor to this lack of influence. At any rate, the Book of Mormon has a rather mixed effective history within the history of the LDS church.

The Intentional Appropriation of the Book of Mormon

Such neglect would begin to reverse with Ezra Taft Benson's inaugural sermon as church president in 1986, calling the church to a systematic incorporation of the Book of Mormon into their lives, devotion, worship, study, and educational pursuits.[14] As a result, the book has become much more prominent within the LDS church in nearly every corner of Mormon life and faith from Sunday Schools to seminaries, from universities to general conferences, from scholarly conferences to sermons, from church worship to home study.[15]

It almost goes without saying that in terms of sheer numbers the reception history of the Book of Mormon in the Church of Jesus

---

[11] Brigham Young, *Journal of Discourses* 16 (May 25, 1873), p. 71.

[12] Brigham Young, *Journal of Discourses* 9 (May 25, 1862), p. 297.

[13] Givens, *The Book of Mormon: A Very Short Introduction*, p. 108.

[14] Givens, *The Book of Mormon: A Very Short Introduction*, pp. 109-11.

[15] Cf. Givens, *By the Hand of Mormon*, p. 242.

Christ of Latter Day Saints, a church with a claimed membership that is now in excess of 16,000,000, dominates the landscape of those groups for whom the Book of Mormon functions as Scripture.

James Strang

Though the majority of the LDS community would follow Young's lead and carve out a Mormon home in Utah and its environs, perhaps as many as ten to twenty thousand either refused to make the trek or returned from the west. Many of these Mormons were scattered across the mid-west either following one of the other claimants or awaiting the time when the church would be led by the 'seed of Joseph'. One of the most significant early groups for which the Book of Mormon functioned as Scripture was the church for which James Jesse Strang served as prophet.[16] A convert of only five months' standing at the time of the death of Joseph Smith, Jr, Strang would almost come out of nowhere to lead one of the most successful early branches of the LDS family of churches.

In a number of ways Strang was a logical successor to Joseph Smith, Jr, for many of those caught in the post-assassination era of the LDS church, for he not only produced 'direct' evidence from Smith that he was to be the successor to the prophet and seer, but he also reproduced or recapitulated in his life a number of events from Smith's life.[17]

Perhaps his most famous and effective claim to succession was the production of a letter, which was said to come from Joseph Smith (Smith's signature appears on the letter), appointing Strang as successor if anything were to happen to the prophet and seer. The relevant parts of the letter indicate that Smith had a prophetic insight into the fact that he would soon face martyrdom with the following said of Strang:

---

[16] For the fascinating story of James Jesse Strang cf. Roger Van Noord, *King of Beaver Island: The Life and Assassination of James Jesse Strang* (Urbana and Chicago: University of Illinois Press, 1988).

[17] Cf. Robin S. Jensen, 'Gleaning the Harvest: Strangite Missionary Work, 1846-1850' (MA thesis, Brigham Young University, 2005).

and to him shall the gathering of the people be, for he shall plant a stake of Zion in Wisconsin ... and behold, my servants James and Aaron shall plant it, for I have given them wisdom ... Behold, my servant James shall lengthen the cords and strengthen the stakes of Zion; and my servant Aaron shall be his counsellor, for he hath wisdom in the gospel and understandeth the doctrines and erreth not therein.

Not only would 'the city of Voree ... be a strong hold of safety to my people, and they that are faithful and obey me I will there give them great prosperity', but the letter also included the command,

And now I command my servants, the Apostles and Priests and Elders of the Church of the Saints, that they communicate and proclaim this my word to all the saints of God in all the world, that they may be gathered unto and round about the city of Voree and be saved from their enemies, for I will have a people to serve me.

In addition to the 'letter of appointment', as it became known, Strang told that at the very time of Smith's murder he was anointed with oil in Burlington, Wisconsin by an angel to lead the church in Smith's stead,[18] indicating a direct point of continuity with Smith's own angelic appeals as well as a point of contact with the standard story about Book of Mormon origins.

But the parallels with Smith's life and work, as well as the Book of Mormon, would become even more similar when the words of a January 1845 vision revealed to Strang's followers [by means of Strang himself], 'Serve and obey me and I will give unto [Strang] the plates of ancient records ... and he shall translate them'.[19] On 1 September 1845, Strang claims another angelic encounter whereby he received the Urim and Thummim and saw plates buried under an oak tree, which four men at his direction uncovered; plates which Strang was happy for all to see, unlike Smith's plates. These three brass plates had writing and figures on both sides. Strang completed the translation on 18 September 1845 saying that they were the record of Rajah Manchou or Vorito, an ancient resident of the Voree area. And like the 'prophetic' mention of Joseph Smith in

---

[18] Van Noord, *King of Beaver Island*, pp. 4, 6, 9, and 60.
[19] Van Noord, *King of Beaver Island*, p. 33.

the Book of Mormon, so these plates foretold the coming of both Joseph and Strang, 'The forerunner men shall kill, but a mighty prophet shall dwell. I will be his strength and he shall bring forth thy [Rajah Manchou's] record. Record my words and bury them in the hill of promise.'[20]

Strang would eventually translate another set of plates, the Plates of Laban mentioned in the Book of Mormon, as *the Book of the Law of the Lord*, which would serve as a foundational document for his communal version of the Church of Jesus Christ of Latter Day Saints. Like Smith, who oversaw the construction of the Kirtland Temple, Strang's followers would lay claim to ownership and oversight of this significant site in Kirtland. Like Smith, who shortly before his death underwent a secret coronation in Nauvoo by the Council of Fifty as 'King, Priest, and Ruler over Israel on Earth',[21] so Strang's Coronation would see him installed as King James the First over his version of Nauvoo on Beaver Island, Michigan.[22] Like Smith, who began as a fierce opponent of polygamy but ultimately become a practitioner, so Strang would oppose then embrace polygamy, eventually marrying five different women, his first plural wife initially travelling with him disguised as his male secretary.[23] Like Smith, who expressed his political aspirations by announcing his candidacy for the Presidency of the United States in 1844, Strang was actually twice elected to the Michigan State Legislature, where he served with distinction.[24] Like Smith, who was assassinated in 1844 owing in large part to disgruntled ex-followers, so Strang was assassinated in 1856 by two of his disgruntled followers.[25]

While Strang was rejected by those who identified with Brigham Young as leader of the LDS church, he was never far from the minds of this larger group.[26] The pages of their respective publica-

---

[20] Van Noord, *King of Beaver Island*, p. 35.
[21] Scherer, *The Journey of a People: The Era of Restoration, 1820 to 1844*, p. 428. Cf. also Bushman, *Rough Stone Rolling*, p. 523.
[22] Van Noord, *King of Beaver Island*, pp. 93-110.
[23] Van Noord, *King of Beaver Island*, pp. 79-92.
[24] Van Noord, *King of Beaver Island*, pp. 178-94.
[25] Van Noord, *King of Beaver Island*, pp. 233-66.
[26] For a very helpful analysis of this period cf. Robin Scott Jensen, 'Mormons Seeking Mormonism: Strangite Success and the Conceptualization of Mormon Ideology, 1844-50', in Newell G. Bringhurst and John C. Hamer (eds.), *Scattering*

tions were filled with accusations with regard to the legitimacy of the claims to leadership by their rivals. Strang would gather perhaps as many as 2,600 followers to Voree, Wisconsin and then to Beaver Island, Michigan, many of whom would eventually leave his group, with a surprising number ending up as part of the Reorganization.[27] The Strangite movement began to whither with Strang's death. Today, there are only two small active congregations of the Church of Jesus Christ (Strangite) meeting in Burlington (Voree, Wisconsin)[28] and in Artesia, New Mexico, with a few unorganized congregations in Arizona. In all these congregations the Book of Mormon continues to be regarded as Scripture.

The Church of Jesus Christ (Headquartered in Monongahela, Pennsylvania)

Another group that holds the Book of Mormon to be scripture also traces its origins to the Church of Christ founded in 1830, claiming that its leader was the legitimate heir to Joseph Smith, Jr. The claimant in question was Sidney Rigdon – Smith's first counselor and only remaining member of the First Presidency at the time of Smith's murder. Rigdon had moved to Pittsburgh, Pennsylvania in order to qualify as Smith's Vice-Presidential Nominee, as the US Constitution requires that the President and Vice-President be from different states. Rigdon claimed that as a result of his position he should act as guardian for the church until such time as a rightful successor could be chosen. However, his offer of leadership was shunned in favor of the case made by Brigham Young.

As a result, Rigdon, who opposed polygamy, was excommunicated. He moved back to Pittsburgh and on 6 April 1845 formally organized the 'Church of Christ', which sought to distinguish between the true and false doctrines of the church, holding to the Book of Mormon as one of their books of scripture. Though

---

of the Saints: Schism within Mormonism (Independence, MO: John Whitmer Books, 2007), pp. 115-40.

[27] Vickie Cleverly Speek, 'From Strangites to Reorganized Latter Day Saints: Transformations in Midwestern Mormonism, 1856-79', in Newell G. Bringhurst and John C. Hamer (eds.), *Scattering of the Saints: Schism within Mormonism* (Independence, MO: John Whitmer Books, 2007), pp. 141-60.

[28] Speek, 'From Strangites to Reorganized Latter Day Saints', p. 153.

Rigdon's organization would soon disintegrate, in 1862 his convert William Bickerton would reestablish and lead the church thereafter.[29]

Today the 'Church of Jesus Christ' has about 19,000 members worldwide, making it the fourth largest group to trace its origins to the restoration tied to Joseph Smith, Jr. The church, headquartered in Monongahela, Pennsylvania, continues its emphatic belief in the Book of Mormon and publishes its own version. The volume closely follows LDS versification and contains an introduction, an extensive index, and cross references – the latter two prepared by Eugene Perri. The church is committed to racial inclusivity, the charismatic activity of the Spirit, the practices of water baptism, the Lord's Supper, footwashing, Joseph Smith's first vision, and an unpaid ministry among other things.[30]

Community of Christ (formerly the Reorganized Church of Jesus Christ of Latter Day Saints)

The years following the death of Joseph Smith, Jr were frustrating for a number of members of the Church of Jesus Christ of Latter Day Saints. Several thousand choose not to follow Brigham Young for reasons ranging from polygamy to a lack of confidence in Young as the divinely appointed successor. A number of these would identify with James Strang for a while, but many of these would be disaffected and after his assassination this group would begin to disintegrate. Others would form a loose association of churches in search of a reorganized LDS church. As Mark Scherer would note, 'on 6 April 1860, at Amboy, Lee County, Illinois, a prophetic movement in search of a prophet met a prophet in search

---

[29] C. Ashton, A.B. Cadman, and W.H. Cadman (compliers), *A Brief History of the Church of Jesus Christ* (Monongahela, PA: The Church of Jesus Christ Headquarters, 2005).

[30] Cf. the discussion by Larry Watson, 'The Church of Jesus Christ (Headquartered in Monongahela, Pennsylvania), Its History and Doctrine', in Newell G. Bringhurst and John C. Hamer (eds.), *Scattering of the Saints: Schism within Mormonism* (Independence, MO: John Whitmer Books, 2007), pp. 190-205. Cf. also W. Cadman, J.L. Ambrust, and W.D. Wright (compliers), *Faith and Doctrine of the Church of Jesus Christ* (Greensburg, PA: The Church of Jesus Christ – Print House, 1983).

of a prophetic movement'.[31] For at this meeting Joseph Smith III, the son of Joseph Smith, Jr offered himself as leader of this emerging organization.

From the beginning the new leader identified 'the Bible as the scriptural foundation for the church' and the Book of Mormon as an important scriptural witness, though auxiliary to the Bible.[32] The RLDS would identify with the Book of Mormon as Scripture and over the years would do much to propagate the book and its message. By 1874 the Reorganized Church of Jesus Christ of Latter Day Saints, as this new organization would be known, would publish the first RLDS version in Plano, Illinois and by 1892 the second RLDS edition would be published at Lamoni, Iowa. It would be the first Book of Mormon edition to use double columns. A third RLDS edition would follow in 1908 also published in Lamoni. In 1953 yet another RLDS edition would be appear, this time published in Independence, Missouri, to be followed by the New Authorized Version in 1966, which modernized the book's language,[33] an edition rejected by the RLDS church at the 1966 World Conference.[34]

The reception history of the Book of Mormon in this group would be felt, for example, in the establishment of 'stakes' (3 Nephi 10.10) and in the naming of its headquarters town, Lamoni – which was the name of a pacifist king in Alma 24.[35] As early as 1899 the Book of Mormon would be translated into Hawaiian[36] and by 1906 into German.[37] Something of the significance of the Book of Mormon for the RLDS is revealed in its acquisition in 1903 of the Printer's Manuscript of the Book of Mormon.[38] As time went on the Community of Christ (the name recently adopted by the RLDS

---

[31] Mark A. Scherer, *The Journey of a People: The Era of Reorganization, 1844 to 1946* (Independence, MO: Community of Christ Seminary Press, 2013), p. 90.

[32] Scherer, *The Journey of a People: The Era of Reorganization, 1844 to 1946*, p. 97.

[33] Gutjahr, *The Book of Mormon*, p. 202.

[34] On the history of the various RLDS editions cf. Richard P. Howard, *Restoration Scriptures: A Study of their Textual Development* (Independence, MO: Herald Publishing House, 1969), pp. 53-63.

[35] Scherer, *The Journey of a People: The Era of Reorganization, 1844 to 1946*, p. 187 n. 10.

[36] Scherer, *The Journey of a People: The Era of Reorganization, 1844 to 1946*, p. 362.

[37] Scherer, *The Journey of a People: The Era of Reorganization, 1844 to 1946*, p. 372.

[38] Scherer, *The Journey of a People: The Era of Reorganization, 1844 to 1946*, pp. 393-97.

church) would eventually engage the Book of Mormon in ways that few others within the LDS stream of families would do. Specifically, Community of Christ scholars would be at the cutting edge of interpreting the Book of Mormon in its nineteenth-century environment, seeking to place Joseph Smith within his historical context to determine his own contributions to the book.[39] This new approach to the Book of Mormon appears to have the approval of the church and its leadership. The current statement on Scripture reads,

> We affirm the Bible as the foundational scripture for the church. In addition, Community of Christ uses the Book of Mormon and the Doctrine and Covenants – not to replace the witness of the Bible or improve on it, but because they confirm its message that Jesus Christ is the Living Word of God.

The Community of Christ is the second largest group, next to the Utah LDS Church, to trace its origins to the restoration begun by Joseph Smith, Jr for whom the Book of Mormon functions as Scripture.

Church of Christ (Temple Lot)

With roots deep in the restoration movement, the Church of Christ (Temple Lot), with headquarters on the site of the Temple Lot in Independence, Missouri, is another restoration church for which the Book of Mormon functions as Scripture.[40] The church traces its origins to Joseph Smith, is heavily dependent on the teaching of John Whitmer and was influenced by its early leaders, Granville Hendrick in particular. The organization's primary claim to fame is that it owns the property on which it is believed Joseph Smith, Jr prophesied a temple would be built in the New Jerusalem. Thus, its real estate is of eschatological significance. The Church of Christ (Temple Lot) holds that the Book of Mormon, as 'The Stick of Joseph',[41] is an additional witness to Jesus Christ and that together

---

[39] Cf. especially Luffman, *The Book of Mormon's Witness to Its First Readers*.

[40] For a historical overview of the Church of Christ (Temple Lot) cf. Apostle B.C. Flint, *An Outline History of the Church of Christ (Temple Lot)* (Independence, MO: Board of Publications The Church of Christ [Temple Lot], 1953 [3rd ed. 1979]).

[41] Flint, *An Outline History of the Church of Christ (Temple Lot)*, p. 29.

with the Bible constitutes 'the fullness of the Gospel'. One of the clear impacts of the Book of Mormon upon the Church of Christ (Temple Lot) is the calling of missionaries to the Lamanites (Native Americans) at various points in its history.[42] The church publishes its own edition of the Book of Mormon, which draws heavily on the Printer's Manuscript and is identical in chapter divisions and versification to the edition published by the Community of Christ. The church has a membership of ca. 2,400.[43]

Remnant Church of Jesus Christ of Latter Day Saints

Formed in 2000 as a result of changes in the RLDS church, the Remnant Church of Jesus Christ of Latter Day Saints is another church for which the Book of Mormon functions as Scripture. The church has a membership of between 1,500 and 2,000. It is head-quartered across the street from the Community of Christ Temple and near the Temple Lot in Independence, Missouri. Generally speaking the Remnant Church's *raison d'etre* is to call the Community of Christ back to its originally more conservative theological positions on a variety of matters. With regard to the Book of Mormon, the Remnant Church has reacted to the move by some in the RLDS/Community of Christ church to view the book within its nineteenth-century environment, not as a book of history that is to be taken literally. The church has recently announced plans to build a temple within the next few years in Jackson County, Missouri.[44]

---

[42] Flint, *An Outline History of the Church of Christ (Temple Lot)*, pp. 149-51.

[43] On the Church of Christ (Temple Lot) cf. R. Jean Addams, 'The Church of Christ (Temple Lot), Its Emergence, Struggles and Early Schisms', in Newell G. Bringhurst and John C. Hamer (eds.), *Scattering of the Saints: Schism within Mormonism* (Independence, MO: John Whitmer Books, 2007), pp. 206-23. Cf. also Jason R. Smith, 'Scattering of the Hedrickites', in Newell G. Bringhurst and John C. Hamer (eds.), *Scattering of the Saints: Schism within Mormonism* (Independence, MO: John Whitmer Books, 2007), pp. 224-46.

[44] Cf. William D. Russell, 'The Remnant Church: An RLDS Schismatic Group Finds A Prophet of Joseph's Seed', *Dialogue: A Journal of Mormon Thought* 38.3 (Fall, 2005), pp. 75-106.

Mormon Fundamentalism (FLDS)

Today there are an estimated 37,000 individuals who refer to themselves as Mormon Fundamentalists, by which they mean that they have never left the fundamentals of the faith, most notably polygamy, that have been abandoned by the Utah LDS Church. The Book of Mormon functions as Scripture for all of these individuals and the groups to which they belong.[45] Broadly speaking, these fundamentalist groups may be categorized as follows: a variety of independent groups; the Fundamentalist Church of Jesus Christ of Latter Day Saints (FLDS) – for which Warren Jeffs served as prophet with a membership of ca. 8,000; Centennial Park – an offshoot of the FLDS; the Nielson-Naylor Group – an offshoot of the Centennial Park group; the Bountiful (Creston, Canada) Groups – also an offshoot of the FLDS; and the Allred Group(s) (Apostolic United Brethren) – the second largest fundamentalist Mormon organization at 7,500 members.

Splinter Groups

There are many splinter groups within the wider LDS family of churches for whom the Book of Mormon functions as Scripture. These groups are too numerous to obtain accurate numbers, with many of them actually existing 'under the radar' so to speak. For example, it is estimated that some 200 splinter groups emerged from the fallout over the redefinition of the RLDS Church alone.[46]

---

[45] This section draws heavily from Anne Wilde, 'Fundamentalist Mormonism: Its History, Diversity and Stereotypes, 1886-Present', in Newell G. Bringhurst and John C. Hamer (eds.), *Scattering of the Saints: Schism within Mormonism* (Independence, MO: John Whitmer Books, 2007), pp. 258-89.

[46] Russell, 'The Remnant Church', p. 80.

29

EARLY 'GENTILE' RESPONSES TO THE BOOK OF MORMON

Some of the book's earliest impact may be gauged by the comments of outsiders who did not find in the Book of Mormon a second book of Scripture. The following examples are intended to serve as representative responses the Book of Mormon generated amongst those who did not believe its claims.

Rochester Daily Advertiser and Telegraph

The first evidence here cited comes from just after the publication of the Book of Mormon in the form of a notice about its appearance in the April 2, 1830 edition of the *Rochester Daily Advertiser and Telegraph* (Volume 4 No. 1057), a newspaper published some 15-20 miles from Palmyra, New York.

BLASPHEMY – 'BOOK OF MORMON,'
alias THE GOLDEN BIBLE.

The 'Book of Mormon' has been placed in our hands. A viler imposition was never practised. It is an evidence of fraud, blasphemy and credulity, shocking to the Christian and moralist. The 'author and proprietor' is one 'Joseph Smith, jr.' – a fellow who, by some hocus pocus, acquired such an influence over a farmer of Wayne county, that the latter mortgaged his farm for $3,000, which he paid for printing and binding 5000 copies of this blasphemous work. The volume consists of about 600 pages, and is divided into the books of Nephi, of Jacob, of Mosiah, of Alma, of Mormon, of Ether, and of Helaman. – 'Copy-right secured!' The style of the work may be conjectured from the 'preface' and 'testimonials' which we subjoin.[1]

Though other earlier newspaper articles make various mentions of the 'The Golden Bible', this account appears to be the first to follow the actual publication of the Book of Mormon. The piece reveals several things about its writer and, no doubt, some of his readers. First, it is clear that the writer is quite unimpressed with the book and its claims. Using the language of 'viler imposition', 'fraud', 'blasphemy', 'credulity', and its 'shocking' nature, the impact of the book upon the writer is in no way positive. In point of fact, the impression left is that the book is wholly without merit. Second, the writer appears to be somewhat familiar with some of the claims about the book's origin and means of publication. The words 'The Golden Bible' may indicate some familiarity on the writer's part with the story of the golden plates from which the book is said to originate. His use of the language 'hocus pocus' may even suggest that Smith's previous work as a seer and treasure hunter was not unknown to him. His anonymous, and somewhat sympathetic, description of Smith's benefactor, a clear reference to Martin Harris, indicates that he was aware of Harris' role in the publication of the book. Third, the writer has rather clearly paid some attention to the actual contents of the book for he specifically mentions Smith's role as 'author and proprietor', the approximate length of the book, correctly identifies the names of several of the books contained within the Book of Mormon – a knowledge not shared by several of the earlier newspaper writers who get certain basic details wrong,[2] and includes the book's 'Preface' as well as the testimonies of the various witnesses who claim to have seen and/or handled the plates from which the book is claimed to have come.

---

[1] *Rochester Daily Advertiser and Telegraph* Volume 4 No. 1057 (April 2, 1830).

[2] Cf. Donald Q. Cannon, 'In the Press: Early Newspaper Reports on the Initial Publication of the Book of Mormon', *Journal of Book of Mormon Studies* 16.2 (2007), pp. 4-15, 92-93.

Alexander Campbell

The second representative response comes in the form of a very detailed article from the pen of Restorationist minister Alexander Campbell. The piece is found in the February 7th 1831 edition of the *Millennial Harbinger*, a paper published by Campbell in Bethany, Virginia. This extensive essay, which is too long to reproduce here in its entirety, is amazingly comprehensive in its range, especially given the fact that the Book of Mormon had been in print for perhaps less than a year. From the title, 'An analysis of the book of Mormon with an examination of its internal and external evidences, and a refutation of its pretenses to divine authority', the purposes of the essay are immediately made clear to its readers, with the size of the piece indicating something of its heft; it is around 9,000 words in length. Noting that, 'EVERY age of the world has produced imposters and delusions', Campbell begins an extended survey (about 1,000 words) of individuals and groups he deems to fit into this category before proceeding 'to notice the most recent and the most impudent delusion which has appeared in our time', the Book of Mormon. From here Campbell offers a rather detailed (3,400 word) introduction to the book beginning with the names of the books contained therein, their individual page lengths, and the fact that the Book of Mormon itself stands at 588 pages. He then proceeds to offer an extensive overview of the contents of the books, identifying the story line of the whole, with very little by way of evaluative comment in this section.

Turning to what he calls 'Internal Evidences', Campbell offers a scathing critique of the book focusing on ten specific, but interlocking points. First, he argues that Joseph Smith is the true author of the book, whom he says is 'as ignorant and impudent a knave as ever wrote a book', for, according to Campbell, Smith misunderstands that God's carefully stipulated laws with regard to the priesthood of Aaron are approbated by the Book of Mormon making priests of the linage of Joseph. Second, for Lehi and Nephi to forsake Jerusalem and its temple for another promised land

> … is so monstrous an error, that language fails to afford a name for it. It is to make God violate his own covenants, and set at nought his own promises, and to convert his own curses into blessings. Excision from the commonwealth of Israel, and ban-

ishment from Jerusalem and the temple, were the greatest curses the law of Moses knew.

Third, Smith has more Jews living in the new world than anywhere else on earth! Fourth, unlike the Babylonian exiles, who hung their harps in the willows owing to their separation from the temple, Nephi and his descendants shed not a tear. Fifth, though Malachi insists that the Law of Moses be kept until the Messiah comes, 'Nephi and Smith's prophets institute ordinances and observances for the Jews, subversive of Moses, 500 years before the Great Prophet came'. Sixth, 'The twelve Apostles of the Lamb, are said by Paul, to have developed certain secrets, which were hid for ages and generations ... but Smith makes Nephi say the same things 600 years before Paul was converted!' Seventh, in perhaps Campbell's most famous statement he charges:

> This prophet Smith, through his stone spectacles, wrote on the plates of Nephi, in his book of Mormon, every error and almost every truth discussed in N. York for the last ten years. He decides all the great controversies – infant baptism, ordination, the trinity, regeneration, repentance, justification, the fall of man, the atonement, transubstantiation, fasting, penance, church government, religious experience, the call to the ministry, the general resurrection, eternal punishment, who may baptize, and even the question of freemasonry, republican government, and the rights of man.

Eighth, Smith 'is better skilled in the controversies of New York than in the geography or history of Judea', citing several errors made in the book. Ninth, he has the Israelites practicing a distinctively Christian institution (the Church) before Jesus is ever born. Tenth, the book is clearly written by one man, not the several described in the Book of Mormon – a critique for which Campbell offers numerous 'Smithisms' taken from the book. Of this '... translation made through stone spectacles, in a dark room, and in the hat of the prophet Smith from the REFORMED EGYPTIAN' Campbell says,

> I would as soon compare a bat to the American eagle, a mouse to a mammoth, or the deformities of a spectre to the beauties of Him whom John saw in Patmos, as to contrast it with a single

chapter in all the writings of the Jewish or Christian prophets. It is as certainly Smith's fabrication as Satan is the father of lies, or darkness the offspring of night.

Campbell concludes his sharp critique by challenging the external witnesses to the book and the witness of the book itself to self-examination citing an extensive quotation from Isaiah 44, a stinging move given the place of Isaiah in the Book of Mormon.

Mark Twain

A final example of 'Gentile' reception comes from the pen of a well-known literary giant, Mark Twain. In his 1872 book, *Roughing It*, Twain devotes an entire chapter (16) to his thoughts on the Book of Mormon, a copy of which he had acquired on a recent trip to Salt Lake City, reading it to pass the time on his return trip back east.[3] While too lengthy to include in its entirety, the chapter is typical Twain.

Twain begins by observing that not many have seen the Mormon Bible, except the 'elect' or taken the trouble to read it. But wasting little time Twain cuts to the chase observing, 'The book is a curiosity to me, it is such a pretentious affair, and yet so "slow," so sleepy; such an insipid mess of inspiration. It is chloroform in print.[4] If Joseph Smith composed this book, the act was a miracle – keeping awake while he did it was, at any rate.' (p. 617) As for its prose and style he remarks,

> The book seems to be merely a prosy detail of imaginary history, with the Old Testament for a model; followed by a tedious plagiarism of the New Testament. The author labored to give his words and phrases the quaint, old-fashioned sound and structure of our King James's translation of the Scriptures; and the result

---

[3] Cf. Mark Twain, *The Innocents Abroad and Roughing It* (The American Library; New York, NY: Penguin Putnam, 1984).

[4] The way in which this charge in particular proved to be sensitive to more than one 'Mormon' reader appears to be evidenced by the official 'Pronouncing Vocabulary' contained in 1920-1981 inexpensive copies of the Book of Mormon designed primarily for investigators, insisting that Ether begin with a short *e*. When compared with suggestions for other names beginning with an E, the instruction with regard to Ether proves to be an anomaly. Cf. Hardy, *Understanding the Book of Mormon: A Reader's Guide*, p. 327 n. 11.

is a mongrel – half modern glibness, and half ancient simplicity and gravity … Whenever he found his speech growing too modern – which was about every sentence or two – he ladled in a few such Scriptural phrases as 'exceeding sore,' 'and it came to pass,' etc., and made things satisfactory again. 'And it came to pass' was his pet. If he had left that out, his Bible would have been only a pamphlet.[5]

After offering random comment on the title page, which he quotes in full, Twain quotes the testimony of the three witnesses followed by that of the eight, saying of the latter,

And when I am far on the road to conviction, and eight men, be they grammatical or otherwise, come forward and tell me that they have seen the plates too; and not only seen those plates but 'hefted' them, I *am* convinced. I could not feel more satisfied and at rest if the entire Whitmer family had testified.[6]

From here Twain lists the names of the individual books, offering an overview of the whole, providing periodical observations along the way. He describes 1 Nephi as 'a plagiarism of the Old Testament', states that the phrase, 'for the space of many days' is 'more Scriptural than definite',[7] notes that polygamy, which was added 'by Brigham Young after Joseph Smith's death', is said to be an abomination in Jacob 2, though Young 'suffers' it, and cites the greater grandeur and picturesqueness of Jesus and his American apostles.[8] Of the Book of Ether Twain says, it 'is an incomprehensible medley of if "history," much of it relating to battles and sieges among peoples whom the reader has possibly never heard of; and who inhabited a country which is not set down in the geography'. He marvels at the remarkableness of the names, especially king Coriantumr, and that only after losses of possibly five to six million of his people, is it said of the king, 'and he began to sorrow in his heart', which prompts Twain to observe, 'Unquestionably it was time'.[9]

---

[5] Twain, *The Innocents Abroad and Roughing It*, p. 617.
[6] Twain, *The Innocents Abroad and Roughing It*, p. 619.
[7] Twain, *The Innocents Abroad and Roughing It*, p. 620.
[8] Twain, *The Innocents Abroad and Roughing It*, p. 621.
[9] Twain, *The Innocents Abroad and Roughing It*, p. 622.

Moving toward the end, Twain focuses upon the four year preparation for war, ' – after which ensued a battle, which, I take it, is the most remarkable set forth in history, – except, perhaps, that of the Kilkenny cats, which it resembles in some respects'.[10] Quoting at length the description of the battle and the fact that Ether has only written a hundredth part of the story, Twain quips, 'It seems a pity he did not finish, for after all his dreary former chapters of commonplace, he stopped just as he was in danger of becoming interesting'.[11] His concluding words are pure Twain, 'The Mormon Bible is rather stupid and tiresome to read, but there is nothing vicious in its teachings. Its code of morals is unobjectionable – it is "smouched" from the New Testament and no credit given.'[12]

Taken together these three responses provide examples of the way a whole swath of 'Gentile' readers responded to the book during the nineteenth century.

---

[10] Twain, *The Innocents Abroad and Roughing It*, p. 623.
There once were two cats of Kilkenny
Each thought there was one cat too many
So they fought and they fit and they scratched and they bit
Til (excepting their nails and the tops of their tails)
Instead of two cats there weren't any! – Traditional
[11] Twain, *The Innocents Abroad and Roughing It*, p. 624.
[12] Twain, *The Innocents Abroad and Roughing It*, p. 624.

30

MUSIC AND THE BOOK OF MORMON

Early Hymns

The impact of the Book of Mormon upon music can already be seen shortly after the book's publication. This evidence comes in the form of the appearance in 1835 of *A Collection of Sacred Hymns for the Church of the Latter Day Saints* in Kirtland, Ohio.[1] Complied by Emma Smith, with the assistance of William W. Phelps,[2] the hymnal consists of a short preface, the words of 90 hymns arranged into the categories of Sacred Hymns (1-36), Morning Hymns (37-42), Evening Hymns (43-48), Farewell Hymns (49-52), On Baptism (53-56), On Sacrament (57-61), On Marriage (62), and Miscellaneous (63-90). Owing to the fact that the hymnal contained lyrics, but no musical scores, symbols designating the appropriate metric pattern or tune to which the songs were to be sung accompanied each hymn. A five-page index, arranged in alphabetical order of the hymns' opening line, concludes the volume. Though only five years removed from the publication of the Book of Mormon, at least seven hymns (16, 23, 26, 63, 70, 72, 90) show some influence of the Book of Mormon, with several revealing significant influence. This section will focus on three hymns as exemplars.

---

[1] Emma Smith (Selector), *A Collection of Sacred Hymns for the Church of the Latter Day Saints* (Kirtland, OH: F.G. Williams & Co., 1835).
[2] Cf. Linda King Newell and Valeen Tippetts Avery, *Mormon Enigma: Emma Hale Smith* (Urbana and Chicago: University of Illinois Press, 2nd edn, 1994), pp. 57-58.

Hymn 63   P.M.

1 O stop and tell me, Red Man,
Who are ye? why you roam?
And how you get your living?
Have you no God; – no home?

2 With stature straight and portly,
And deck'd in native pride,
With feathers, paints and broaches,
He willingly replied: –

3 'I once was pleasant Ephraim,
'When Jacob for me pray'd;
'But oh! how blessings vanish,
'When man from God has stray'd!

4 'Before your nation knew us,
'Some thousand moons ago,
'Our fathers fell in darkness,
'And wander'd to and fro,

5 'And long they've liv'd by hunting,
'Instead of work and arts,
'And so our race has dwindled
'To idle Indian hearts.

6 'Yet hope within us lingers,
'As if the Spirit spoke: –
'He'll come for your redemption,
'And break your Gentile yoke:

7 'And all your captive brothers,
'From every clime shall come,
'And quit their savage customs,
'To live with God at home.

8 'Then joy will fill our bosoms,
'And blessings crown our days,
'To live in pure religion,
'And sing our maker's praise.'[3]

---

[3] *Sacred Hymns*, pp. 83-84.

It should come as no surprise that the teaching of the Book of Mormon with regard to Native Americans would turn up in the hymnody of the movement. The entirely of Hymn 63 is devoted to just this topic.

The song begins with an enquiry on the part of the worshipper as to the origins and identity of the 'Red Man' (1.1-4), which offers the opportunity for the Native American not only to answer this seemingly straightforward question, but to offer unwitting testimony to the Book of Mormon, and the views found therein, with regard to the origins of the Native Americans.

In most every verse of each stanza the influence of the Book of Mormon can be detected. Specifically, the description of this symbolic figure's stately comportment in the second stanza reflects the general attitude of the Book of Mormon about the potential of the Nephites and Lamanites for righteous and noble lives. The hymn shifts its focus to the man's response.

Three major emphases are revealed in the Native American's response. First, his words confirm what the Book of Mormon has reported about the origins and history of North American Native Peoples, that he is descended from Jacob the patriarch, from Ephraim's linage (3.1-4). Second, as described in the Book of Mormon, the speaker confirms the fall of this godly race of people into the darkness of sin and rebellion from God (4.1-4), echoing the book's view that the hunter-forager lifestyle is the equivalent of idleness and the opposite of work and the arts, which leads to the dwindling of the race (5.1-4). Third, the hope found in the Book of Mormon for the conversion of the Lamanites is heard in the last three stanzas, which focus on the Spirit's speaking to the lost tribe about redemption (6.1-4), an eschatological return of the tribes from every climate where salvation will be experienced (7.1-4), and the resulting experience of joy, blessings, and pure religion (8.1-4).

It is difficult to imagine a hymn that bears more of the distinctive influence of the Book of Mormon than this one found in the 1835 edition of the *Sacred Hymns*.

Hymn 16   P.M.

1 An angel came down from the mansions of glory,
And told that a record was hid in Cumorah,
Containing the fulness of Jesus's gospel;

And also the cov'nant to gather his people.
O Israel! O Israel!
In all your abidings,
Prepare for your Lord
When you hear these glad tidings.

2 A heavenly treasure; a book full of merit:
It speaks from the dust by the pow'r of the Spirit;
A voice from the Savior that saints can rely on,
To watch for the day when he brings again Zion.
O Israel! O Israel!
In all your abidings,
Prepare for your Lord
When you hear these glad tidings.

3 Listen O isles, and give ear ev'ry nation,
For great things await you in this generation:
The kingdom of Jesus, In Zion shall flourish;
The righteous will gather; the wicked must perish.
O Israel! O Israel!
In all your abidings,
Prepare for your Lord
When you hear these glad tidings.[4]

In this hymn the influence of the Book of Mormon is unmistakable. The song bears its imprint in three ways. First, there is emphasis placed upon the fact of the Book of Mormon and its supernatural origins, with reference made to the revealing angel (1.1), Cumorah (1.2), the heavenly treasure (2.1), and the fact that it speaks from the dust (2.2). Second, the content of the Book of Mormon impacts the hymn in its reference to it 'containing the fullness of Jesus's gospel' (1.3). The words, 'A voice from the Savior that saints can rely on' in 2.3, may reveal a double meaning. On the one hand, in that the Book of Mormon is, as stated in 1.3, 'the fullness of Jesus's gospel' and, consequently, the Book itself is conterminous with Jesus' voice. On the other hand, owing to the large swaths of space devoted to the words of Jesus in the Americas as found in 3 Nephi, this lyrical verse may also show signs of another dimension of direct influence. Third, the hymn also reflects the eschatological outlook

---

[4] *Sacred Hymns*, pp. 22-23.

of the Book of Mormon. Specifically, this influence can be found in the words, 'the covenant to gather your people' (1.4), 'to watch for the day when he brings again Zion' (2.4), and the refrain included in the chorus, 'Prepare for your Lord' (1.7; 2.7; 3.7). As such the impact of the book upon this hymn is clear.

Psalm 73   L.M.

> 5 He prophesied of this our day,
> That God would unto Israel say,
> The gospel light you now shall see,
> And from your bondage be set free.
>
> 6 He said God would raise up a seer,
> The hearts of Jacob's sons to cheer,
> And gather them again in bands,
> In latter days upon their lands.
>
> 7 He likewise did foretell the name,
> That should be given to the same,
> His and his father's should agree,
> And both like his should Joseph be.
>
> 8 This seer like Moses should obtain,
> The word of God for man again;
> A spokesman God would him prepare,
> His word when written to declare.
>
> 9 According to his holy plan,
> The Lord has now rais'd up the man,
> His latter day work to begin,
> To gather scatter'd Israel in.[5]

In Hymn 73, of which only stanzas 5-9 of the song's 14 stanzas are provided here, the focus of the hymn is easy to see as is the impact of the Book of Mormon upon it. There appear to be two primary emphases in the presented stanzas of this hymn. First, the prophetic role of Joseph Smith is celebrated as being foretold from of old and as active in the present. Specifically, there is an emphasis upon his day being prophesied (5.1), his being raised up (6.1, 9.2), his likeness to Moses in obtaining, speaking, and writing the word of God (8.1-

---

[5] *Sacred Hymns*, pp. 95-96.

4) and even his name being foretold, like that of his father (7.1-4)! Second, the eschatological gathering of the lost tribe(s) is celebrated (6.2-3; 9.4).

The Book of Mormon – The Musical

While most readers outside of the LDS families may not know much about the hymns compiled by Emma Smith, nor much about the contents of most of the individual songs, many are aware of a Broadway musical called *The Book of Mormon*. The award winning musical by Trey Parker, Matt Stone, and Robert Lopez is the satirical story of two ill matched Mormon missionaries who are sent from Provo, Utah to Uganda on their initial mission, a place where no converts have ever been baptized. When they arrive in this war-torn country they discover that no one is remotely interested in their Book of Mormon story. After the more promising of the two leaves, for a variety of reasons, the less promising Elder Cunningham, who knows very little about the Book of Mormon, succeeds in making converts after telling an amalgam of Mormon like stories illustrated with examples taken from the world of science-fiction. The moral of the musical seems to be that religion can be a good thing if it is not taken too literally.[6]

Whilst the phenomenon of the Book of Mormon, and its resulting Mormonism, makes a powerful impact upon the musical at a variety of places, with notable exceptions the lyrics reveal that Book of Mormon content actually has a very limited impact. One of the primary exceptions are found in 'Joseph Smith American Moses' where reference is made to 'Golden Plates' and the song 'I Believe' which is a parody based upon the instruction found in Moroni 10.3-5, that if one who reads the Book of Mormon and asks with a sincere heart as to its truthfulness the Holy Ghost 'will manifest the truth of it to you'. The major exception is found in 'All American Prophet', which with minor editing will be cited in full.

All American Prophet

Elder Price
You all know the Bible is made of testaments old and new

[6] Gutjahr, *The Book of Mormon*, pp. 192-95.

You've been told it's just those two parts, or only one if you're a
   Jew
But what if I were to tell you – there's a fresh third part out
   there
Which was found by a hip new prophet who had a little ...
   Donny Osmond flair?

Have you heard of the All-American prophet?
The blond-haired, blue-eyed voice of God!
He didn't come from the Middle East like those other holy men
No, God's favorite prophet was All-American!

*I'm gonna take you back to Biblical times, 1823. An American man
named Joe livin' on a farm in the holy land of Rochester, New York!*

Elder Cunningham
You mean the Mormon prophet Joseph Smith?

Elder Price
That's right! That young man spoke to God!

Elder Cunningham
He spoke to God?

Elder Price
And God said 'Joe, people really need to know
That the Bible isn't two parts, there's a part three to The Bible,
   Joe!
And I, God, have anointed you to dig up this part three
That's buried by a tree on a hill in your backyard!'

Elder Cunningham
*Wow! God says go to your backyard and start digging, that makes perfect
sense!*

Elder Price
Joseph Smith went up on that hill and dug where he was told!
And deep in the ground Joseph found shining plates of gold!

Joseph Smith
What are these golden plates?
Who buried them here and why?

Elder Price
Then appeared an angel: his name was Moroni!
(Ahhhhh …)

Moroni
I am Moroni …
The All-American angel! (All-American!)
My people lived here long, long ago! (So long ago!)
This is a history of my race, please read the words within
We were Jews who met with Christ, but we were All-American!

But don't let anybody see these plates except for you …
They are only for you to see …
Even if people ask you to show the plates to them, don't
Just copy them onto normal paper
Even though this might make them question if the plates are real
    or not …
This is sort of what God is going for …

Elder Price
Joseph took the plates home and wrote down what he found inside
He turned those plates into a book then he rushed into town and cried:

Joseph Smith
Hey! God spoke to me and gave me this blessed ancient tome
He commanded me to publish it and stick it in ev'ry home

Elder Cunningham
Wow! So the Bible is actually a trilogy and the Book of Mormon is Return of the Jedi?! I'm interested!

Elder Price
Now many people didn't BELIEVE the prophet Joseph Smith
They thought he made up this part three that was buried by a tree on the hill in his backyard (Liar!)
But Joe said –

Joseph Smith
This is no lie, I speak to God all the time
And he told me to head west!
So I'll take my part three from the hill with the tree

Feel free if you'd like to come along with me
To the promised land! (*The promised land?*)
Paradise, on the west coast!
Nothing but fruit and fields as far as the eye can see!

All
Have you heard of the All-American prophet?
He found a brand-new book about Jesus Christ!
We're following him to paradise, we call ourselves Mormon
And our new religion is All-American!

Elder Cunningham
Wow, how much does it cost?

Elder Price
The Mormons kept on searching for that place to settle down
But every time they thought they found it they got kicked out of
    town
And even though people wanted to see the golden plates
Joseph never showed 'em!

...

Now comes the part of our story that gets a little bit sad
On the way to the promised land, Mormons made people mad
Joseph was shot by an angry mob and knew he'd soon be done:

Joseph Smith
You must lead the people now, my good friend Brigham Young
Oh God, why are you letting me die without having me show
people the plates?
They'll have no proof I was telling the truth or not
They'll have to believe it just ... 'cause
Oh ... I guess that's kinda what you were going for
Blargggh ...

Elder Price

*The prophet Joseph Smith died for what he believed in. But his followers,
they kept heading west. And Brigham Young led them to paradise. A
sparkling land in Utah they called Salt Lake City. And there the Mormons multiplied! And made big Mormon families!! Generation to generation*

until finally ... they made ME!!! And now it's my job to lead you where those early settlers were led long ago!!!

ALL (Elder Cunningham)
Have you heard of the All-American prophet? (*Kevin Price!*)
The next in line to be the voice of God?! (*My best friend!*)
He's gonna do something incredible and be Joseph Smith again!
'Cause Kevin Price the prophet is all, all, all ...
All-American!
(*If you order now, we'll also throw in a set of steak knives!*)
All-American![7]

Students of the Book of Mormon can easily detect the major aspects of the book's story and the story about the book that have here been satirized.

---

[7] Trey Parker, Robert Lopez, and Matt Stone, *The Book of Mormon Script Book: The Complete Book and Lyrics of the Broadway Musical* (New York: HarperCollins, 2011), pp. 35-42.

31

ART AND THE BOOK OF MORMON

It should come as no surprise that the Book of Mormon has influenced a variety of visual artists who have sought to bring to life some of the memorable scenes depicted in the Book of Mormon.

David Hyrum Smith and Lehi's Dream

One of the first extant paintings of a Book of Mormon scene comes from the brush of the son with whom Emma was pregnant when Joseph was murdered in the Carthage Jail in Carthage, Illinois, some thirty miles from Nauvoo. David Hyrum Smith would become known for his missionary activity, his poetry, songs, and paintings within the Reorganized Church of Jesus Christ of Latter Day Saints and beyond. A sensitive, artistic young man, David produced several famous paintings of scenes from in and around Nauvoo, where he spent much of his early life.[1]

What is not always appreciated about David Hyrum as an artist is the fact that amongst his numerous paintings and sketches is found perhaps the earliest extant painting of a scene depicted in the Book of Mormon. Though the date of composition is uncertain, it was clearly created sometime before 1877, at which time David was institutionalized in the Northern Illinois Hospital and Asylum for

---

[1] For a very helpful biography of David Hyrum's life cf. Valeen Tippetts Avery, *From Mission to Madness: Last Son of the Mormon Prophet* (Urbana and Chicago: University of Illinois Press, 1998). Cf. also the informative chapter that discusses David's life and times in detail in Scherer, *The Journey of a People: The Era of Reorganization, 1844 to 1946*, pp. 264-307.

*'Courtesy Community of Christ and the Lynn Smith Family'

332 A Pentecostal Reads the Book of Mormon

the Insane in Elgin, Illinois, shortly after his thirty-second birthday. As the canvas twice has the word Plano on the back of the painting, it appears that the work was composed sometime between the fall of 1873 and the spring of 1874. Entitled 'Lehi's Dream of the Tree of Life' the painting is based upon a scene described in 1 Nephi 8.2-35.

This 24 1/8" x 19 15/16" oil on canvas color painting depicts Lehi, led by a man dressed in white standing by the tree that bore white fruit. Lehi is depicted as looking back over his left shoulder at his wife Sariah and his sons Sam and Nephi, motioning to them with his right hand, in which he holds some of the white fruit, whilst with his left hand, holding on to an iron rope (Book of Mormon 'rod of iron') wrapped around the tree and apparently stretching back along the river. In the distant background, the tiny figures at whom he looks are barely visible. Across the river, in which individuals are pictured in the act of drowning, is a 'spacious' building almost suspended in mid-air, in which can be seen individuals in fine attire pointing at Lehi in derision for eating of the tree's fruit. As in the story from 1 Nephi, Lehi is clearly the dominate figure in the painting. Three things underscore Lehi's prominence in the scene. First is his location in the foreground, being almost literally the center of the scene. Second, his large size emphasizes his importance in the painting. Whilst the man in white, perhaps an angelic guide, is slightly larger than Lehi, likely indicating his own spiritual significance, Lehi dwarfs all other figures in the scene. Third, his location near and his physical contact with the tree, by means of the iron rod and the fruit he holds in his right hand, indicate that whilst others are destroyed and even mock him, Lehi is successful in his salvific pursuit. Interestingly, all of the figures appear to be Caucasians, suggesting something about the way in which David's context influenced how he experienced and internalized the story.

Clearly the power of the Lehi story, which generated this beautiful painting, is a great example of the reception history of the Book of Mormon. The painting is now on public display in the Community of Christ Visitors Center in Nauvoo.

Reuben Kirkham and the Book of Mormon Panorama

During the early 1880's the Book of Mormon would have an impact on a distinctive contemporary art form. From Spring 1883 to January 1884, Utah LDS artist Reuben Kirkham would design and complete a series of 23 scenes from the Book of Mormon to be displayed in Panoramic fashion, interspersed with songs, musical instrumental pieces, as well as various character sketches for which Kirkham was widely known.[2]

The scenes chosen for depiction included the following: (1) Ancient Nephites; (2) Lehi Leaves Jerusalem; (3) Hill of Cumorah; (4) Lehi's Prayer; (5) The First Camp by the Red Sea; (6) The Angel Appears to Lehi and the Brethren; (7) Nephi Breaks his Bow; (8) The Building of the Ship; (9) The Storm on the Ocean; (10) Morning in the Promised Land; (11) Evening in the Promised Land; (12) Lehi's Last Address to his Sons and Daughters; (13) The Workshop in which Nephi Makes Swords to Protect his People; (14) The Death of Sherem the False Teacher; (15) Ammon and his Brethren and the City of Nephi; (16) Finding the Records of the Jaredites; (17) The Surprise in the Field; (18) The Martyrdom of Abinadi the Prophet; (19) The Daughters of the Nephites Stand Forth to Plead with the Lamanites; (20) Alma Baptizing in the Waters of Mormon; (21) The Daughters of the Lamanites Surprised by Priests of Noah; (22) Last Battle of King Limhi; and (23) The Last Battles of the People of Limhi.[3]

The presentation was witnessed and approved by the leaders of the LDS church on 5 March 1884 at a special performance just for them. According to the Friday, 25 May 1883 edition of the *Ogden Daily Herald*, the individual panels were 7' x 9'. The panorama played scores of times throughout Utah. Despite what appears to have been a successful run, sadly, none of the original panels are extant, though a photo of 'Alma Baptizing in the Waters of Mormon' does exist in private hands. This panel depicts the Book of Mormon scene as occurring in a grove with Alma and a male candidate standing in the midst of a small pool of water, surrounded by a variety of on-lookers, both male and female. There is one small

---

[2] On this whole topic cf. Donna L. Poulton, *Reuben Kirkham: Pioneer Artist* (Springville, UT: Cedar Fort, Inc., 2011), pp. 121-31.

[3] Poulton, *Reuben Kirkham*, pp. 121-24.

Photograph of a panel from Reuben Kirkham's Book of Mormon Panorama
ca. 1884
Collection of Connie Edwards Webb and Elaine Edwards Wood

child present as well. All the onlookers have the appearance of being Caucasians, attired in clothing normally associated with 'biblical'
times. The photo shows something of the intricacy of detail and
artistry of Kirkham's paintings, work that made the Book of Mormon story available to hundreds, perhaps even thousands in this
form.[4]

Minerva Teichert and the Book of Mormon Murals

Among the numerous other artists to depict the Book of Mormon
visually, this section concludes with Minerva Teichert and her extensive contributions in mural form.[5] Born in Ogden, Utah on 28
August, 1888, she grew up on a ranch in Pocatello, Idaho. She studied at the Art Institute of Chicago and the Art Students League in
New York before returning to Idaho and then Wyoming. Known
for her western scenes, Teichert turned her full attention to the
Book of Mormon, depicting more than forty scenes from the book
in mural fashion. In this project she combined her two great pas-
sions, the Book of Mormon and mural painting, producing a set of
Book of Mormon murals that would enable large audiences, both
believers and unbelievers, to be exposed to the story of the book.
She applied Hab. 2.2, 'that he who runs may read', to this project.

Her productivity was enormous, and though working without a
patron, she undertook this daunting task as a labor of love. Much of
her art would wind up at Brigham Young University with which she
bartered her art for tuition credit for her children and other worthy
young students. She donated her Book of Mormon murals to the
university. Teichert often sketched out her intended scene in oil on
ca. 11" x 17" paper before producing the 36" x 48" murals. Her
work is colorful, epic, and sweeping, being near comprehensive in
coverage of the book, perhaps qualifying her as the most significant
LDS artist in terms of the Book of Mormon reception history in art.

Among her many claims to fame is her careful inclusion of
women in her art. Not only was Teichert intentional about includ-

---

[4] For the image cf. also Poulton, *Reuben Kirkham*, pp. 122-23.

[5] Much of what follows draws heavily on John W. Welch and Doris R. Dant,
The Book of Mormon Paintings of Minerva Teichert (Provo and Salt Lake City, Utah:
BYU Studies and Bookcraft, 1997) and Marian Eastwood Wardle, *Minerva Teichert:
Pageants in Paint* (Provo, Utah: BYU Press, 2007).

ing the few scenes from the Book of Mormon in which women were a part, but she also created a number of murals in which minor details and/or the implications of minor details legitimately called for the depiction of women in the scene. One such mural was generated by 1 Nephi 7.5 and 16.7-8, which describes Nephi and his brothers taking wives from the daughters of Ishmael. The resulting mural, entitled *Love Story* – which appears on the cover of this volume – depicts five females clad in festive and colorful garments in the scene's center celebrating the betrothal weddings with dancing and the playing of tambourines, while horns and cymbals in the hands of the males accompany their rejoicing. The mural is classic Teichert, where a detail in the Book of Mormon is teased out making the inclusion of women quite overt, whereas the text is considerably more reticent about their inclusion.

Unlike the other artists considered in this section on the reception history of the Book of Mormon in art, Teichert does not present her subjects exclusively as Caucasians, but shows the influence of a knowledge of their Book of Mormon heritage (middle-eastern) and the debates of her day about the subjects' possible context(s) in the Americas (likely Mexican or Central American).

Minerva Teichert died on 3 May, 1976.

32

Disastrous Interpretations of the Book of Mormon

As with its predecessor, the Bible,[1] part of the reception history of the Book of Mormon includes disastrous interpretations, which here defined, resulted in the loss of life. Two tragic examples, taking place within five years of one another on opposite ends of the country involving excommunicated members of two different LDS family of churches, sadly illustrate this point.

American Fort, Utah – 24 July 1984

On 24 July 1984, in American Fort, Utah, LDS wife and mother, Brenda Lafferty, and her fifteen-month-old daughter, Erica, were brutally murdered by two of her husband's brothers. The resulting, unspeakable carnage left the small community in deep shock from which it has still not completely recovered. In the weeks to follow, it became clear that the killings themselves and the manner in which they were carried out were, unbelievably, inspired and influenced in part by the Book of Mormon and a specific account within it.[2]

---

[1] For a brief overview of some disastrous interpretations of the Apocalypse cf. John Christopher Thomas, *The Apocalypse: A Literary and Theological Commentary* (Cleveland, TN: CPT Press, 2012), pp. 51-55.

[2] Cf. Jon Krakauer, *Under the Banner of Heaven: A Story of Violent Faith* (New York: Anchor Books, 2004), upon which this section is heavily dependent, for a fuller account of these tragic events.

The murders were committed by self-styled prophet, Ron Lafferty, and his brother, Dan Lafferty. A former LDS member who had been excommunicated for seeking to live out a polygamous lifestyle with his 14-year-old step-daughter as his second wife, Ron had moved from the confines of the Church of Jesus Christ of Latter Day Saints into the more shadowy world of Mormon Fundamentalism, which hearkened back to a previous era in LDS history, before it had 'strayed' from the teachings of founder Joseph Smith, Jr. Ron would go so far as to invoke a prophetic calling and status for himself and receive new revelations for himself and his small handful of followers. During the months leading up to the murders, Ron had been active in a 'School of the Prophets' he helped to organize in which some 20 revelations had been given to him and processed by the small group. In late March, a fateful revelation came to him, which read:

> Thus sayeth the Lord unto My servants the Prophets. It is My will and commandment that ye remove the following individuals in order that my work might go forward. For they have truly become obstacles in My path and I will not allow My work to be stopped. First thy brother's wife Brenda and her baby, then Chole Law [a former LDS Relief Society President who had supported Ron's ex-wife in her divorce from him], then Richard Stowe [the LDS leader who excommunicated Ron]. And it is My will that they be removed in rapid succession and that an example be made of them in order that others might see the fate of those who fight against the true Saints of God. And it is My will that this matter be taken care of as soon as possible and I will prepare a way for My instrument to be delivered and instructions be given to my servant Todd [a drifter who was at that time living and working with Watson Lafferty, one of the other Lafferty brothers]. And it is My will that he show great care in his duties for which I raised him up and prepared him for this important work and is he not like unto my servant Porter Rockwell [who served as a body guard to both Joseph Smith and Brigham Young]? And great blessing awaits him if he will do My Will, for

I am the Lord thy God and have control over all things. Be still and know that I am with thee. Even so Amen.[3]

In a later revelation Ron was identified as 'the mouth of God' and Dan as 'the arm of God', suggesting to the brothers that Dan was to do the actual killings.

The brothers also received direction from a passage standing near the beginning of the Book of Mormon, 1 Nephi 3.1-4.29. In this passage Nephi seeks to secure from Laban, plates upon which sacred and family history were written. Eventually finding him drunk, Nephi describes his encounter with the Spirit and his resultant actions.

> And it came to pass that I was constrained by the spirit that I should kill Laban; but I said in my heart, never at any time have I shed the blood of man, and I shrunk and would that I might not slay him.
>
> And the spirit saith unto me again, behold the Lord hath delivered him into thy hands; yea, and I also knew that he had sought to take away my own life; yea, and he would not hearken unto the commandments of the Lord; and he also had taken away our property.
>
> And it came to pass that the spirit said unto me again, slay him, for the Lord hath delivered him into thy hands. Behold the Lord slayeth the wicked to bring forth his righteous purpose: It is better that one man should perish, than that a nation should dwindle and perish in unbelief.
>
> And now, when I, Nephi, had heard these words, I remembered the words of the Lord ... And again – I knew that the Lord had delivered Laban into my hands, for this cause: that I might obtain the records according to his commandment. Therefore I did obey the voice of the spirit, and took Laban by the hair of the head, and I smote off his head with his own sword (1 Nephi 4.10-18).

This text converged with another revelation given to Ron in which Dan was likened 'unto Nephi of old for never since the beginning

---

of time have I had a more obedient son'.[4] Armed with this understanding, Dan was willing to do anything for the Lord and carried
out these gruesome and cold-blooded murders without remorse,
understanding himself to be doing God's will, in a way he claimed
that was like they did in the Scriptures.[5] Mercifully, Chole Law was
not at home when the brothers came to kill her and they missed the
turn to Richard Stowe's house, thus, the additional 'removals' never
took place. Ron and Dan Lafferty are on Utah's Death Row awaiting execution, still convinced of their individual 'innocence' and
faithfulness to God.

Kirtland, Ohio – 17 April 1989

On 17 April 1989, on a farm outside Kirtland, Ohio, self-appointed
prophet Jeffery Lundgren, with the assistance of a small community
of disciples (who numbered as high of 29 at one point), shot and
killed five of his followers.[6] Each member of the Avery family,
Dennis, his wife Cheryl, and daughters Trina (age 15), Rebecca (age
13), and Karen (age 6), were individually brought out to a barn
where they were bound, gaged, and then shot by Lundgren.

Lundgren was raised in the Reorganized Church of Jesus Christ
of Latter Day Saints near Independence, Missouri. He began dating
fellow RLDS member Alice Keeler during college, marrying her
when she became pregnant. While serving in the US Navy during
the Vietnam War, Lundgren became an avid student of Scripture,
especially the Book of Mormon. Drifting from job to job, usually
losing each one for one reason or another, Lundgren became convinced that the RLDS church was losing its way theologically, exemplified in the move in the 1984 World Conference to open the
priesthood to female members, a decision reaffirmed at the 1986
World Conference.

Lundgren felt that he was to move his family to Kirtland, Ohio
to work, in exchange for housing, as a volunteer guide at the

---

[4] Krakauer, *Under the Banner of Heaven*, p. 167.

[5] Jesse Hyde, '1984 Lafferty Case Still Haunts: 2 Brothers Show no Remorse
for Brutal Killings', *Deseret News* (Tuesday July 27, 2004).

[6] Cf. Pete Earley, *Prophet of Death; The Mormon Blood-Atonement Killings* (New
York: William Morrow and Co., 1991), upon which much of the following is
based, for a fuller account.

Kirtland Temple, the first temple constructed in the LDS move-ment. Here his fundamentalism hardened as he became convinced that the current RLDS prophet was a false prophet; that Lundgren was being called to take the place of Joseph Smith, Jr as prophet and seer – for only he really knew the chiastic pattern in Scripture; that God would reveal golden plates to him just as he had to Smith; and that the Kirtland Temple, not Independence, Missouri was the location of Jesus Christ's return to earth.

Specifically, Lundgred believed that on 1 May he was to take over the Kirtland Temple, kill all those who lived within a one mile radius of the Temple, kill Dale Luffman's (the RLDS stake presi-dent who had confronted Lundgren about his growingly bizarre teachings) family before his eyes as a blood atonement to cleanse the Temple, decapitate Luffman, and then chant a specific prayer that would cause an earthquake killing everyone in Kirtland, usher-ing in the return of Jesus on 3 May (Lundgren's birthday) and the millennium.[7] The method of murder to be used on Rev Luffman in particular was chosen owing to the way in which Nephi was in-structed to kill Laban in 1 Nephi 4.10-18, decapitation.

As time passed, 1988 turned out not to be the year for the 1 May take over, Lundgren explained that the delay was the result of his followers being sinful and needing to be cleansed by a blood sacri-fice. In order for Lundgren to become 'endowed with power' he must kill the 'wicked', offering them as a blood-atonement sacrifice to God. Some of his followers must die.[8] Around this time, Rev Luffman had prepared papers of excommunication for Lundgren, who was formally excommunicated from the RLDS Church shortly afterwards.

Lundgren had decided that the Avery family members were to be sacrificed based in part on the Book of Alma [9.17],

And he that will harden his heart, to him is given the lesser por-tion of the word, until they know nothing concerning his myster-ies; and then they are taken captive by the Devil, and led by his will down to destruction.

---

[7] Earley, *Prophet of Death*, pp. 225-26.
[8] Earley, *Prophet of Death*, pp. 257-58.

Because the Averys, who lived some distance from the communal farm, did not attend Lundgren's nightly classes they were deemed to have hardened their hearts. In fact, Lundgren said that God had provided the family as a sacrifice for the group.[9]

The effect of 1 Nephi 4 provided resolve for his followers before the murders[10] and served as a guiding text to interpret the heartless murders after they had been committed, which Lundgren read to the group after the gruesome acts. Lundgren then observed, 'This is just the beginning. The scriptures say we will have to kill many, many more.'[11]

Jeffrey Lundgren was sentenced to death for his murderous activity and died on 24 October 2006 by lethal injection in Lucasville, Ohio. Several of his accomplices, including his wife, Alice, and son, Damon, are serving long prison sentences for their parts in these heinous crimes.

---

[9] Earley, *Prophet of Death*, pp. 268-69.

[10] Follower Greg Winship is quoted as saying, 'If God can tell Nephi to slay Laban, then he can tell me to kill whomever', Earley, *Prophet of Death*, p. 274.

[11] Earley, *Prophet of Death*, p. 295.

Conclusion to Part Four

Clearly, the Book of Mormon has had an incredible history of reception, ranging from intended to unintended effects. Whether the book's effects upon its readers are deemed as positive or negative, they all testify to the book's powerful influence. This survey offers a small slice of such a reception history. The topic itself is worthy of a more comprehensive examination than exists to date.

PART FIVE

PENTECOSTALISM AND THE BOOK OF MORMON

Part Five of this study consists of a comparison of Pentecostalism and the Book of Mormon. Specifically, the following chapters will identify historical and theological connections between Book of Mormon themes and some Pentecostal forerunners and/or early leaders, examine early Pentecostal responses to and critiques of the Book of Mormon and the religion(s) it spawned, and compare Pentecostal theology with the theology of the Book of Mormon.

33

HISTORICAL AND THEOLOGICAL CONNECTIONS BETWEEN BOOK OF MORMON THEMES AND SOME PENTECOSTAL FORERUNNERS AND EARLY LEADERS

Perhaps surprising to some, there are a number of individuals who either anticipated the modern Pentecostal movement or served as early leaders whose beliefs were similar to certain of those found within the Book of Mormon. A few of these individuals or their followers actually had contact with one or more of the groups for whom the book functions as Scripture. This chapter offers a brief survey of some of the more notable figures for illustrative purposes.

Edward Irving (1792-1834)

Educated at the University of Edinburgh, where he graduated at age seventeen, in 1822 Edward Irving accepted the pastorate of a small Church of Scotland congregation in London. Within just a few years the church grew to the point that a new building had to be constructed in Regent Square, with massive crowds attending. Discerning his role as a prophetic figure, Irving became convinced that the five-fold ministry gifts of apostles, prophets, evangelists, pastors, and teachers (Eph. 4.11) had been lost or abandoned by the modern church and, consequently, the ministry of the Holy Spirit was no longer manifest within the church. Eventually, the manifestation of the charismata (including glossolalia, prophecy, and healing) occurred in his parish as well as in churches where he had preached. Being censured for advocating and presiding over such activities, Irving led some eight hundred members from the Regent Street Church to form the Catholic Apostolic Church. The church would eventually have twelve apostles, give a prominent place to prophecy, healing, and glossolalia, and exhibit a strong eschatological orientation.[1]

Significantly for this study, a Rev. John Hewett from a church in Barnsley, England, that was part of the Catholic Apostolic Church, made contact with Joseph Smith in June 1835 seeking to explore the possibility of affiliation with the Mormons owing to their being 'kindred spirits'. Alerted to the Mormons and their thought by means of a church owned newspaper, Hewett's contact by post was followed by a personal visit. Hewett's letter of introduction promised numbers of his people would join the ranks, despite any persecution that might come. They called themselves 'saints' with Hewett writing, 'O, may our faith increase that He may have Evangelists, Apostles, and Prophets, filled with the power of the Spirit, and performing His will in destroying the works of darkness'.[2] After the Kirtland visit, Hewett's expected return did not materialize as he apparently settled in nearby Painesville, Ohio instead, securing an appointment as Preceptor of Painesville Academy.[3]

Something of the vulnerability felt by Joseph Smith, owing to the similarities between the LDS and the Irvingites, can be detected by an editorial apparently written by Smith several years later that appeared in the *Times and Seasons*. In this five-page essay entitled, 'Try the Spirits', Smith devotes about half the space to the Irvingites, explaining their origins, beliefs, and practices as well as offering reasons why he rejects their claims to authentic manifestations of the

---

[1] Cf. D.D. Bundy, 'Irving, Edward', in S.M. Burgess, G.B. McGee, and P.H. Alexander (eds.), *Dictionary of Pentecostal and Charismatic Movements* (Grand Rapids: Zondervan, 1988), pp. 470-71. For an extensive treatment cf. G. Strachan, *The Pentecostal Theology of Edward Irving* (Peabody, MA: Hendrickson, 1988).

[2] Bushman, *Rough Stone Rolling*, p. 271. Significantly, as Grant Underwood points out, 'The first [Irvingite] apostle was called by prophecy in 1832, and by 1835, the same year the LDS Quorum of the Twelve was reconvened in Kirtland, the full number of twelve Irvingite apostles had been commissioned'. Cf. Grant Underwood, *The Millenarian World of Early Mormonism* (Urbana and Chicago: University of Illinois Press, 1993), p. 134.

[3] Underwood, *The Millenarian World of Early Mormonism*, p. 135.

Spirit in the last days.[4] Despite the fact that the Irvingites 'have counterfeited the truth perhaps the nearest of any of our modern sectarians', Smith offers four enumerated reasons why he found the Irvingites lacking.

> 1st. The church was organized by women and 'God placed in the church first apostles, secondarily prophets:' and not first women; but Mr. Irving placed in his church women; secondarily apostles; and the church was founded and organized by them. A woman has no right to found or organize a church; God never sent them to do it.

> 2nd. Those women would speak in the midst of a meeting and rebuke Mr. Irving, or any of the church; now the scripture positively says, 'thou shalt not rebuke an elder, but entreat him as a father;' not only this but they frequently accused the brethren, thus placing themselves in the seat of satan who is emphatically called 'the accuser of the brethren.'

> 3rd. Mr. Baxter [an early Irvingite leader] received the spirit on asking for it without attending to the ordinances, and began to prophesy, whereas the scriptural way of attaining the gift of the Holy Ghost is by baptism, and by laying on hands.

> 4th. As we have stated in regard to others the spirit of the prophets, are subject to the prophets; but those prophets were subject to the spirits; the spirit controlling their bodies at pleasure.[5]

Several aspects of this editorial are deserving of note. First, the fact that this response came several years after the Mormons' first encounter with the Irvingites suggests that the latter's growth and similarities in teaching were seen in some ways as creating a rival for Smith and his church.[6] Second, Smith's primary criticism, that the Irvingite church was created by women, appears on the one hand to be consistent with the depiction of the role of women in the Book of Mormon, while on the other hand illustrates one of the differ-

---

[4] 'Try the Spirits', *Times and Seasons* (April, 1842), pp. 743-47, cf. esp. pp. 746-47.

[5] 'Try the Spirits', pp. 746-47.

[6] On the more extensive relationship between Irvingite thought and early Mormonism cf. the helpful discussion in Underwood, *The Millenarian World of Early Mormonism*, pp. 134-38.

ences between the Book of Mormon/early Mormonism and these forerunners of the modern Pentecostal movement, where women have and do play prominent roles in gospel proclamation and church planting. Third, it would be interesting to ask whether Smith's words about Spirit reception and the laying on of hands would have been offered with the same emphasis earlier, owing to the fact that there are no instances in the Book of Mormon where individuals are actually described as receiving the Spirit in this fashion – the words of Jesus notwithstanding (Moroni 2.1-3).[7]

John Alexander Dowie (1847-1907)

Born in Edinburgh, Scotland, John Alexander Dowie emigrated to Australia as a young man, where he decided to go into Christian ministry. Returning to Edinburgh for his theological training, he subsequently returned to Australia, where he eventually served in a very successful pastorate before abruptly resigning. Becoming convinced of the importance of divine healing, Dowie, his wife, and their two children migrated to the USA in 1888. Travelling and ministering throughout the western portion of the country, Dowie would eventually establish a headquarters near Chicago for his rapidly growing following. Establishing the Christian Catholic Apostolic Church in a city he built and called Zion City – where more than six thousand of his followers would gather – Dowie went on to benefit from a masterful public relations move, where he held meetings across from the entrance to the 1893 Chicago World's Fair. Dowie believed in healing, prophecy, and apostolic Christianity. He would eventually identify himself as a prophet, as Elijah the Restorer, and then the First Apostle of an end-time Apostolate.[8]

Significantly, Dowie himself made a visit to Salt Lake City on his way across America. This encounter appears to have occurred sometime during 1890 when he first makes known his intentions.[9]

---

[7] Harrell, *This Is My Doctrine*, p. 306.

[8] Cf. E.L. Blumhofer, 'Dowie, John Alexander', in S.M. Burgess, G.B. McGee, and P.H. Alexander (eds.), *Dictionary of Pentecostal and Charismatic Movements* (Grand Rapids: Zondervan, 1988), pp. 248-49 and David William Faupel, 'Theological Influences on the Teachings and Practices of John Alexander Dowie', *Pneuma* 29.2 (2007), pp. 226-53.

[9] 'Travel Plans', *Leaves of Healing* 1.5, 6, 7 (1890), p. 1.

In a sermon preached several years later, Dowie would reflect back on his considerable time spent in Salt Lake City. Claiming to have studied the LDS church closely and having been given access to the internal workings of the church, Dowie says that he was treated as a prince of the church, finding that the LDS church was 'the best organized and most clearly scripturally organized of all churches' keeping close to the Apostolic model.[10] Apparently, Dowie came to explore the possibility of joining the LDS church, as well as the possibility of being brought into the church as an Apostle. When this did not occur he left Utah 'to establish his own organization'.[11] Dowie would go on to have a global significance and eventually influence numbers of Pentecostal leaders – especially in the Finished Work stream of the tradition.

What has not been widely known or fully appreciated until more recently is the extent to which Dowie's teachings would overlap with that of the LDS movements. This includes the significant role of Isaiah, the headquarters cities of Zion, the similarity in organization between Zion and Nauvoo, the similarities with regard to the prophetic and apostolic nature of leadership, the belief in continuous revelation, the expectation of the recovery of ancient texts that would be on a par with the Old and New Testaments as Scripture, and the belief that God was once a man and that humanity could become gods.[12]

Stung from his rejection by the LDS church, Dowie planned to bring 3,000-5,000 crusaders to Utah to convert the Mormons in 1904,[13] a challenge to which the LDS church leadership responded with the promise that he would make few inroads with the membership, charging that

> Much of what is good in Dowieism is clearly borrowed from the doctrines of the Church. It is clearly plagiarism. The distinctive Dowie features are almost repulsive. Such a system can make no

---

[10] 'Opening of Zion's Hall of Seventies', *Leaves of Healing* 5.14 (January 28, 1899), p. 255.

[11] Faupel, 'Theological Influences on the Teachings and Practices of John Alexander Dowie', p. 243.

[12] Faupel, 'Theological Influences on the Teachings and Practices of John Alexander Dowie', p. 244.

[13] 'Dowieites Are Coming', *Salt Lake City Herald* (February 11, 1904), p. 2.

lasting impression upon a people that lives in the light of the truth.[14]

But things were not quite what they seemed in such public communications. On the one hand, a survey of Salt Lake City newspapers of the era reveals over 136 references to Dowie[15] indicating that the LDS church and its members monitored his work closely, perhaps suggesting that owing to the numerous similarities between the groups they viewed Dowie as more of a threat than their public words indicated. On the other hand, it now appears that it was part of Dowie's plan, in his attempt to convert the Mormons, to reveal the reinstitution of plural marriage as part of God's eschatological plan and to invite his new converts to join him in Mexico to initiate the practice,[16] something about which there is some evidence of speculation in the press.[17] The effect of such a strategy so soon after the LDS Church's renunciation of the practice in the Manifesto is difficult to calculate but easily imagined. Dowie died before being able to actualize his plans.

Charles Fox Parham (1873-1929)

A final example to be offered in this chapter on the historical and theological connections between Book of Mormon themes and some Pentecostal forerunners and early leaders is Charles Fox Parham, widely considered to be one of the fathers of the modern Pentecostal movement. Parham, a former Methodist minister who with his wife Sarah opened a healing home in Topeka, Kansas in 1898, had visited a number of early holiness sites, including Frank Sandford's school in Shiloh, Maine, and Dowie's Zion City, Illinois. Convinced that tongues was the bible evidence of Spirit Baptism in the Book of Acts, at a watch night service on 31 December, 1900/1 January 1901, one of Parham's students, Agnes Ozman, was baptized in the Spirit and spoke in tongues. In the next few days over

---

[14] 'Dowie is Coming', *The Chicago Record-Herald* (September 2, 1903), p. 2.

[15] Faupel, 'Theological Influences on the Teachings and Practices of John Alexander Dowie', p. 251.

[16] Faupel, 'Theological Influences on the Teachings and Practices of John Alexander Dowie', p. 246.

[17] Cf. esp. 'Did Dowie Preach Polygamy in Zion?' *Salt Lake City Telegram* (April 2, 1906).

half of the student body of thirty-four would also experience this Spirit Baptism and speak in tongues. Parham's best known future student would turn out to be an African-American minister, William Seymour, who, owing to the segregation laws in force in much of the South, had to sit outside Parham's Houston, Texas classroom with the door ajar to hear Parham's teaching. Seymour eventually moved to Los Angeles, California where he would lead the great 1906-1908 Azusa Street revival, a revival movement that helped transform the religious landscape of the twentieth century and beyond.[18]

What is not as well known is the fact that Parham held rather tenaciously throughout his life to a form of British-Israelism. Emerging in the nineteenth century as a rough contemporary to the Book of Mormon, British-Israelism taught that Anglo-Saxons as a race were the descendants of the Ten Lost Tribes of Israel. This view became tied to racist thinking of the time with the result that Anglo Saxon came to mean the white people of North America in contrast to any persons of color whether African Americans, Native Americans, or those of Mexican, Spanish, and Asian origins. In contrast to Book of Mormon teaching, Native Americans were not seen to be descendants of the tribes of Israel, but in keeping with the Book of Mormon British-Israelism gave a theological definition to race and color indicating one's propensity to being able to receive theological and spiritual truths – thus indicating something of one's spiritual destiny.[19] Though there are major differences between the Book of Mormon understanding of the origins of the inhabitants of North America and Parham's understanding, it may not be insignificant that both views espouse non-traditional explanations for the inhabitants of the continent. It even appears that there were significant

---

[18] J.R. Goff, 'Parham, Charles Fox', in S.M. Burgess, G.B. McGee, and P.H. Alexander (eds.), *Dictionary of Pentecostal and Charismatic Movements* (Grand Rapids: Zondervan, 1988), pp. 660-61. Cf. also J.R. Goff, *Fields White Unto Harvest: Charles F. Parham and the Missionary Origins of Pentecostalism* (Fayetteville, AR: The University Press of Arkansas, 1988).

[19] Cf. esp. Leslie Dawn Callahan, 'Fleshly Manifestations: Charles Fox Parham's Quest for the Sanctified Body' (PhD dissertation, Princeton University, 2002), pp. 103-14.

LDS leaders who espoused certain British-Israelism ideas around the same time as Parham.[20]

Conclusion

The extent of the contact between some of the forerunners and early leaders of Pentecostalism with one of the religious movements spawned by the Book of Mormon is more extensive than has often been acknowledged. Some of the theological resemblances are remarkable and suggest that the traditions likely viewed one another as competing rivals owing to certain theological similarities. Something of the extent of this relationship is seen in the next chapter that examines early Pentecostal responses to and critiques of the Book of Mormon and the religion(s) it spawned.

---

[20] According to Bruce A. Van Orden, George Reynolds, an important LDS leader (1842-1909) and rough contemporary of Parham, made use of the work of Anglo-Israelism advocates in his books, *Are We of Israel?* (Salt Lake City: Geo. Q. Cannon & Sons, 2nd edn, 1895) and *The Book of Abraham: Its Authenticity Established As a Divine and Ancient Record* (Salt Lake City: Deseret News Printing and Publishing Establishment, 1879), as did his assistant James M. Anderson in his own later works, *The Present Time and Prophecy* (Salt Lake City: Deseret News Press, 1933) and *God's Covenant Race* (Salt Lake City: Deseret News Press, 1937). While this view was never sanctioned as *the* official view of the church, it did have prominent spokespersons – including an oft cited Brigham Young quote from 1863 – in and around the time of Parham, indicating at least some theological overlap between individuals within the respective Pentecostal and LDS traditions. Cf. esp. Bruce A. Van Orden, *The Life of George Reynolds: Prisoner for Conscience' Sake* (Salt Lake City: Deseret Book Company, 1992), pp. 137-45. Cf. also Bruce A. Van Orden, 'Anglo-Israelism and Its Impact on Mormon Theology', a paper presented to the 1984 Meeting of the Mormon History Association, located in the Special Collections and Archives, Marriott Library, University of Utah. A very similar paper was presented earlier on 28 August 1982 to the 1982 Meeting of the Sunstone Theological Symposium in Salt Lake City, Utah. For the idea that British-Israelism influenced certain aspects of Mormon thought cf. Underwood, *The Millenarian World of Early Mormonism*, p. 133 and p. 158 n. 25.

34

EARLY PENTECOSTAL RESPONSES TO AND CRITIQUES OF THE BOOK OF MORMON AND THE RELIGION(S) IT SPAWNED

Significantly, one finds several references to the Book of Mormon and the religion(s) it spawned in the early periodical literature generated by the Pentecostal movement. As a precursor to this survey it should be observed that the first reference to Mormonism by an early Pentecostal leader may very well come from R.G. Spurling, one of the founders of the Church of God (Cleveland, TN) in his little book, *The Lost Link*.[1] Though published in 1920, the composition itself has its origins in the last decade of the nineteenth century, in 1897 to be precise.[2] In a discussion of possible opposition to his argument that one must be led by the Spirit, Spurling writes,

> But some one will say, 'You said that every one should be led by the Spirit. Now suppose someone would claim that the Spirit led them to steal or curse or fight or have more wives than one as do the Mormons?' We answer the questions first by saying all these things are violations of the New Testament and cannot be upheld by the Church. Mormons will say Paul said, 'Bishops and deacons should be the husband of one wife,' and that implies that others might have more. But stop, you can't make that hold good. A widow cannot become a church charge unless she has

---

[1] Richard G. Spurling, *The Lost Link* (Turtletown, TN: self-published, 1920).

[2] Cf. J.G. Marshall, *A Biographical Sketch of Richard G. Spurling, Jr.* (Cleveland, TN: Pathway Press, 1974), p. 21

been the wife of one husband, having washed the saints' feet, also brought up children, and followed every good work. Paul said the wife of one husband. You have the same right to say that women had more husbands than one and of course women did not practice polygamy. While on this subject I want to say some adulterous hearted men who would walk after the flesh in its ungodly lust will say look at Abraham and Jacob and David who had more than one wife. Why did God suffer it? He suffered it because He had made such an extravagant promise to Abraham /to greatly multiply his seed as the sand of the sea – without number. This helped them to multiply but Paul says the law has changed since then. Heb. 7:12.[3]

It is not surprising that in this first reference to Mormonism, Spirit activity and polygamy would be referenced, owing to the prophetic nature of the movement and the recently announced manifesto rejecting the practice of polygamy by the LDS church.

It appears that the first mention of Mormonism in the periodical literature of Pentecostalism comes in a question and answer section in an early edition of *The Bridegroom's Messenger* 1.14 (May 15, 1908), p. 2. The question is posed

1. 'Why don't you write about the Mormons talking in tongues?'

The answer follows:

(1). I know of no well authenticated facts concerning the 'tongues' movement among that people. I am not willing to receive the statements of their leaders upon that or any other subject. My acquaintance with them in the Rocky Mountain states and territories back in the early seventies was not approving – so far as their conduct or their word was concerned. They also claim many faith cures, prophesying, etc. No one rejects faith healing, or spiritual discernment because Mormons claim the gifts. Why use their claims of 'tongues' against true disciples talking in 'tongues?'

(2). However false Mormon leadership may be, doubtless God may have a people even among them. The writer met with such a one in Utah in 1872, an elderly woman. She was once a zealous

[3] Spurling, *The Lost Link*, pp. 11-12.

Methodist and in her blind sincerity told me that to her 'the Mormons seemed like the old-fashioned Methodists.' She still seemed to be saintly, serious, a real child of God. 'In every nation he that feareth Him and worketh righteousness is accepted with Him,' and the Holy Spirit will take up His abode in such a heart, whatever be his or her religious associations.[4]

In this short note it is clear that Mormon leadership is not to be trusted, that healing and prophecy are found amongst the Mormons, and that the comparison of Pentecostal glossolalia to that of Mormonism is not appreciated, to say the least. Yet, amazingly, the response takes an unexpectedly generous turn when addressing the possibility of true believers being found amongst the Mormons. It appears that the case of the elderly woman mentioned in the quote is taken as an indication that God may have a people even among them.[5]

Another reference to Mormonism appears in 1911 in *The Bridegroom's Messenger* where it is noted:

The spread of Mormonism in the last decade has planted that ungodly system in many states in violation of the laws of the United States, and yet they are working unmolested. Some stubborn facts about Mormonism we will give in the next issue of the Messenger.[6]

As promised, the next issue of the *Bridegroom's Messenger* includes a synopsis of Mormon teaching. Based on an article by B.J. Hendrick in *McClure's Magazine*, the primary focus of this piece is the place of polygamy in Mormon practice and theology, exaltation and the plu-

---

[4] 'Questions Concerning Tongues', *The Bridegroom's Messenger* 1.14 (May 15, 1908), p. 2.

[5] The next reference to Mormonism comes in a note that 'two or three' Mormon missionaries had visited Cades Cove, Tennessee sometime in 1908 or 1909, but that their stay had not been viewed positively. *The Latter Rain Evangel* 2.9 (June, 1910), p. 17. However, other sources indicate that the efforts of these Mormon missionaries (or others who may have preceded them) resulted in a few converts – primarily the Harmon family – in the area, where a Methodist church appears to have made space available for them to worship. A.R. Shields, *The Cades Cove Story* (Gatlinburg, TN: Great Smokey Mountains Natural History Association, 1977), p. 38 and interview with Derrick Harmon, 29 August 2015, a descendant of the Harmon family.

[6] 'Importance of Doctrinal Teaching', *The Bridegroom's Messenger* 4.83 (April 1, 1911), p. 2.

rality of gods, and the relationship between the spirit of the human and God. The reason for this detailed article is described as follows:

> Some of God's dear children, and some who have received the Pentecostal experience, have become interested in Mormonism by listening to Mormon elders who come to their door, give out the literature, tell of wonderful things having been revealed to their leaders, and talk knowingly of deeply spiritual truths, such as divine healing, the baptism of the Spirit with speaking in tongues, etc. Like all other false teachers, they will keep the errors covered until the victim is sufficiently fascinated with their false system of religions.[7]

Clearly, owing to a number of similarities between the movements, Mormonism was perceived as a threat by this early Pentecostal writer.

The next reference to Mormonism comes in an article that announces the formation of a society designed to place the claims of Mormonism before the public, with special reference to polygamy, Mormon financial resources, the numbers of converts immigrating from Europe, and Mormon proselytizing techniques.[8]

The first clear reference to the Book of Mormon in early Pentecostal periodical literature comes in an edition of *Confidence*, published by A.A. Boddy in the UK.

> 'We take the Scriptures literally,' continued Mr. Boddy, 'we believe they are inspired of the Holy Ghost and written by those whom God chose as his channels; and we believe that the Christian Scriptures are the final revelation of God, and need not be expanded either by a Book of Mormon or by Mrs. Eddy's "Science and Health."'[9]

In these words, the rejection of the Book of Mormon, as well as 'Science and Health', is based in part on the belief that the Bible is the final, complete inscripturated revelation of God. Not only do they reveal early Pentecostalism's commitment to Scripture, but also

---

[7] 'False Doctrine', *The Bridegroom's Messenger* 4.84 (April 15, 1911), p. 1.

[8] 'The Growth of Mormonism', *The Bridegroom's Messenger* 6.121 (November 15, 1912), p. 4.

[9] A.A. Boddy, 'Christian Science', *Confidence* 4.7 (July, 1911), p. 165.

the fact that despite a belief in continuing revelation, additional inscripturated revelation was not an expectation of the movement.

A second reference to the Book of Mormon occurs in an article
entitled, 'God's Word versus Man's Word' in *The Latter Rain Evangel*.

> Those who have been less spiritual have been led into grievous
> error, as the Roman Catholic church in accepting the Apocry-
> pha, the Mohammedans in accepting the Koran and the Mor-
> mons in accepting the Book of Mormon as inspired of God ...
> Also the Mormon religion, which is a blot upon our twentieth
> century civilization and is a menace to the government of the
> United States today, need never have been had the followers of
> Joseph Smith stood firm against the false claims of the Book of
> Mormon as being inspired of God ... The friends of Joseph
> Smith must have thought that the Book of Mormon did their
> hearts good, else why should a poor ignorant, uncultured man of
> loose morals have had such a following? The series of books we
> are now discussing may well seem to 'do our hearts good' for
> they hold out to us the promise of that deliverance and power so
> many are feeling the need of today. The question is not, Do
> these books seem to do our hearts good, *but are they truth*? Can
> anything be really God's truth for us that is based on the false
> foundation of coming to us with the weight and authority of his
> word if that word shows such claims to be untrue? 'To the law
> and to the testimony: if they speak not according to this word
> surely there is no light in them.' Isa. 8:20. 'Learn not to go be-
> yond the things that are written.' 1 Cor. 4:6, R. V.[10]

In would appear likely that the writer here makes reference to Moroni's invitation to the reader to ask God with a sincere heart
whether the Book of Mormon is not true (Moroni 10.4-5). Significantly, the writer does not question whether any of the books under
discussion are capable of doing 'our hearts good', but rather refo-
cuses the discussion on whether the books are to be equated with
truth. It is clear that the writer does not share the view that the do-

---

[10] 'God's Word versus Man's Word', *The Latter Rain Evangel* (December,
1912), pp. 14-15.

ing good to one's heart is sufficient to determine if a book is indeed
a word from God.[11]

In an exposition of the 'Basis of Union for the Pentecostal Holi-
ness Church', G.F. Taylor, drawing heavily on *Nelson's Encyclopedia*,
describes Mormonism as falling into two camps: the LDS and
RLDS churches. He begins his article by saying 'We state that The
Pentecostal Holiness Church is utterly opposed to Mormons'.[12]
Taylor then comments on the Book of Mormon:

> He [Smith] claims that the volume was composed of gold plates
> eight inches by seven inches, fastened by three golden rings,
> written in 'reformed Egyptian,' interpreted by the aid of two
> crystals, (Urim and Thummim) set like spectacles in a silver bow,
> it gave a summary of American History from Babel to 420 A. D.
> Its authors were the prophet Mormon and his son Moroni.[13]

Taylor goes on to describe LDS history, doctrine, and practice –
with an occasional lapse in accuracy – for example stating that
Smith's eldest son Joseph became head of the church after his father's death – noting that they 'take as the basis of their doctrine,
the Bible, so far as it is correctly translated, they say; the Book of
Mormon, and Doctrines and Covenants'. Taylor concludes:

> Our Basis of Union makes it clear that we are opposed to the
> Mormons. We oppose them because of the claims of their
> founder, Joseph Smith. We oppose them because they discredit
> parts of the Bible and hold other books to be as much or more
> inspired than the Bible. We are opposed to anything that takes

---

[11] A later reference to Mormonism comes in a description of A.A. Boddy's
travel through Salt Lake City, with a mention of the tabernacle, temple, and a
presentation by a female guide of Mormonism as a system. A.A. Boddy, 'Towards
the Rockies', *Confidence* 5.12 (December, 1912), p. 282. A few years later the *Weekly Evangel* gave extensive coverage to the translation of the Book of Abraham and
the fact that Smith's translation was not borne out by the outside Egyptologists
who examined the characters. 'The Uncovering of the Mormon Fraud', *Weekly
Evangel* 106 (September 4, 1915), p. 100. When speaking on the rampant rise of
divorce and the rise of unconventional marriages, Andrew Fraser remarks, 'We
cannot countenance anything that savors of Mormon theory or of Mormon practice in the Pentecostal movement'. Andrew L. Fraser, 'Marriage and Divorce', *The
Latter Rain* 8.1 (October, 1915), p. 8.

[12] G.F. Taylor, 'Mormons', *The Pentecostal Holiness Advocate* 2.6 (June 6. 1918),
p. 4.

[13] Taylor, 'Mormons', p. 4.

honor from Jesus and gives it to another, and this is just what Mormonism does. We are opposed to setting aside of certain portions of Scripture in order to establish any doctrine, and Mormonism does this. We hold the Bible to be inspired in its entirety, and Mormonism denies this.

There are a number of doctrinal points in the Mormon faith that we can not endorse; but they are entirely wrong on the basis of their faith by following other books besides the Bible I do not think it necessary to carry the discussion further.[14]

Without question, Taylor rejects Mormon claims for and based on the Book of Mormon and he is especially troubled by any perceived Mormon rejection of the Bible and resentful of claims being made in favor of the Book of Mormon as Scripture.

In answer to the question 'What is Mormonism?', E.N. Bell writes,

It is a false system of religion invented by Joseph Smith ... It has a new and false Bible called the Book of Mormon ... It would take volumes to expose all the false things in the history of Mormonism ... None of our people should listen to a Mormon preacher for two minutes. They preach many nice and good things at the first, and the convert does not learn all its evils for years. Stay away from Mormonism.[15]

The last example to be offered in this chapter comes from the *Latter Rain Evangel* in an article entitled, 'Mormonism!: A Survey of Its Blasphemous Pretentions and Evil Practices'.[16] Of the Book of Mormon the writer says,

Their claims and statements for the Book of Mormon are fraudulent and blasphemous, but they trap the unwary by laying stress on the growing apostasy, and emphasizing some of the great truths of Scripture, such as the resurrection of the body, miracles, revelations, millennial rule of Christ, tithing and the gifts of

---

[14] Taylor, 'Mormons', p. 4.

[15] E.N. Bell, 'What is Mormonism?', *The Pentecostal Evangel* 330/331 (March 6, 1920), p. 5.

[16] 'Mormonism!: A Survey of Its Blasphemous Pretentions and Evil Practices', *The Latter Rain Evangel* 12.5 (February, 1920), pp. 20-22.

the Spirit, and keep in the background the dangerous and blasphemous claims in their book until they have the confidence of those who are not well-informed, and then the soul who is really seeking for God is caught in the meshes of his false net that is spread for his feet.[17]

While indicating that he regards the Book of Mormon as fraudulent and blasphemous, the writer does indicate that the book also affirms 'some of the great truths of Scripture'. Then quoting *The Christian Statesman*, the author goes on to say:

Joseph Smith, the so-called prophet, produced 'The Book of Mormon,' being a pretended record of ancient inhabitants of the American hemisphere, covering a period of several hundred years before and after the Christian era. This book was asserted to be a translation, under divine authority and inspiration to Joseph Smith, from certain plates of gold, delivered to him by an angel, upon which plates the narrative or scripture was engraved in character which Smith called 'Reformed Egyptian.' In plain words, the 'Book of Mormon,' is the Mormon Bible for the Western hemisphere as our Holy Scriptures are a record of God's dealings with people dwelling in the Eastern hemisphere. Joseph Smith left a copy of the 'Reformed Egyptian' characters … Riley in his great work on 'the Founder of Mormonism' demonstrates that this page of characters was written by Joseph Smith with his left hand, and there is clearly traceable in it, when shown in a mirror, the letters J O E. Further, no archaeologist has ever found in the ruins of ancient edifices in America any character corresponding with 'Reformed Egyptian': although LePlongeon and others have discovered characters like the ancient Egyptian. The gold plates for the Book of Mormon were assumedly engraved by a priest; and it is impossible to assume that the language he used in writing would not have been shown up on some of the edifices, ruins of which had been uncovered in both North and South America.[18]

---

[17] 'Mormonism!: A Survey of Its Blasphemous Pretentions and Evil Practices', p. 20.
[18] 'Mormonism!: A Survey of Its Blasphemous Pretentions and Evil Practices', p. 21.

The writer concludes with a final warning:

> Pastors and Christian workers should be on the alert to protect
> their flock against this subtle invasion, for when once caught in
> the meshes their organization is so complete and discipline over
> their people such that it is practically impossible to break away
> from it.[19]

Several things might be concluded from this evidence scattered
across the early Pentecostal periodical literature. First, it is clear that
early Pentecostalism had some familiarity with the Book of Mormon and the religion(s) it spawned. Specifically, these early journals
show knowledge of Mormon claims as to the book's origins, its
theological contents, its extra-canonical status, and its claims over
against the Bible – or claims made for the Book of Mormon over
against the Bible. Second, more than one of the quotes reveals a
concern about the potential danger Mormonism posed for
individual Pentecostals. For the most part it appears that the similarities between the two movements' teachings was thought to have
the potential to lead away some faithful and sincere Pentecostals
into theological error. Third, at least one enquiry was made about
the distinctive Pentecostal practice of speaking in tongues and the
fact that such had found a place, at least for a while, amongst Mormons. While this enquiry was treated with a certain degree of derision by the editor, its inclusion does suggest that such a practice was
known amongst the Mormons. Fourth, often Mormonism was
condemned in part owing to its (former) practice of polygamy, a
practice that was no longer sanctioned by the LDS Church after
1890. Several references in the early Pentecostal periodical literature
suggest that the practice continued unofficially at the time of the
writings here examined, from 1908-1920. Fifth, at least on one occasion a distinction was made between the LDS and RLDS churches, though there appears to be some confusion as to which of the
groups Joseph Smith III assumed leadership and the timing of his
taking up leadership. Sixth, there is a clear and consistent rejection
of Mormonism and its leadership across early Pentecostalism. The
rationale for much of this rejection centered on the distinctive

---

[19] 'Mormonism!: A Survey of Its Blasphemous Pretentions and Evil Practices', p. 22.

claims made by and about Joseph Smith and the Book of Mormon. Specifically, there was a rejection of the need for additional inscrip-turated revelation beyond the Bible and Mormon claims that ap-peared to exalt the Book of Mormon whilst deprecating the role and function of the Bible. Seventh, despite such clear and con-sistent rejection, at least on one occasion – in fact, in one of the ear-liest references to Mormonism – an attitude of generosity about salvation for individual Mormons and even for the possibility that a people of God could be raised up by God amongst them was seen as a distinct possibility. Eighth, on at least one occasion it appears that an early Pentecostal critique took the shape of a response to the invitation of Moroni 10.4-5, making a distinction between 'feel-ing' and 'truth' as sufficient means of verification for the Book of Mormon and its claims. Such a distinction reveals something about the acquaintance by the writer with the invitation of Moroni 10.4-5 and how seriously that invitation was taken.

35

A COMPARISON OF PENTECOSTAL THEOLOGY WITH THE BOOK OF MORMON

While sometimes viewed simply as a Spirit movement preoccupied with pneumatology, the theological heart of the Pentecostal movement is actually quite Christo-centric, revolving around the 'Full' or 'Five-fold Gospel' – that Jesus Is Our Savior, Sanctifier, Holy Ghost Baptizer, Healer, and Soon Coming King.[1] Thus, one of the ways in which Pentecostalism and the Book of Mormon might be compared and contrasted is to begin with a brief synopsis of Pentecostal belief on each element of the Five-fold Gospel and compare these themes with their appearance, or lack thereof, in the Book of Mormon. Therefore, this chapter will take the Pentecostal Five-fold Gospel as its starting point.[2] In what follows each of these elements will be briefly described, an accompanying sacramental sign appropriate for each of these emphases will be identified, and a compari-

---

[1] Some of the first interpreters to make this identification were D.W. Dayton, *The Theological Roots of Pentecostalism* (Peabody, MA: Hendrickson, 1991), and S.J. Land, *Pentecostal Spirituality: A Passion for the Kingdom* (JPTSup 1; Sheffield: Sheffield Academic Press, 1993) now *Pentecostal Spirituality: A Passion for the Kingdom* (Cleveland, TN: CPT Press, 2010). Subsequent research confirms that in the first generation of the Pentecostal tradition, this five-fold paradigm is found across the movement.

[2] Owing to the fact that the Pentecostal and Charismatic movements number in the neighborhood of 600,000,000 global adherents and are diverse in many respects, some shorthand and generalizations will of necessity be made in this chapter. Although other Pentecostals might construct this section differently, the five-fold paradigm has the advantage of actually being the paradigm that birthed the tradition.

son with and contrast from the teaching of the Book of Mormon highlighted.[3]

The Five-fold Gospel and the Book of Mormon

Unlike some confessional groups for whom an emphasis is placed upon an *ordo salutis* (order of salvation), for Pentecostals emphasis is placed upon what might be called a *via salutis* (a way of salvation) as salvation itself is conceived of as a journey having a distinctive narrative flow. In agreement with a Wesleyan understanding of grace, Pentecostals understand that one must respond to the grace offered him or her before moving to the next grace divinely made available. In this sense Pentecostals often speak of 'walking in the light as one has the light'.

Most, but not all, Pentecostals are Trinitarian.[4] Thus, despite its Christocentric orientation, Pentecostalism does not emphasize Jesus at the expense of the Father or Holy Spirit. Rather, the redemptive work made possible in the Son is understood as originating in the

---

[3] It should be underscored that the purpose of this chapter is to show similarities and dissimilarities between Pentecostalism and the Book of Mormon. It should not in any way be considered a comparison of Pentecostalism and Mormonism, for example, or any other belief system for which the Book of Mormon functions as Scripture. Whilst this comparison between a theological system of over one hundred years standing and a book that stands at the front end of a theological tradition it helped to spawn has certain limitations and might be thought a bit artificial as a result, it should make clearer the differences and similarities between Pentecostalism and what is actually contained in the Book of Mormon itself. Limited though it is, the results of this engagement might function as a standing point for more comprehensive analyses and comparisons of Pentecostalism with various groups within the restoration movement that trance their origins to Joseph Smith. For example, a comparison of Pentecostalism with the theology of the Church of Jesus Christ (Monongahela, Pennsylvania) – a group for which the Book of Mormon functions as Scripture but no other pieces of the Smith corpus function as such – reveals a remarkable number of similarities including the on-going practice of the spiritual gifts (including glossolalia) and the practice of footwashing. One might expect that comparisons with groups that accept additional documents of the Smith corpus as Scripture – such as the LDS church and the Community of Christ – would reveal fewer similarities and perhaps greater differences between the traditions, owing in part to the additional sacred texts employed. Thus, this initial exploration might have implications beyond its somewhat narrow focus.

[4] For a helpful piece on Oneness Pentecostalism cf. D.A. Reed, *'In Jesus' Name': the History and Beliefs of Oneness Pentecostals* (JPTSup 31; Blandford Forum: Deo, 2008).

will, desire, and action of the Father who loves the world so much that he gave his unique Son so that all who believe in him should not be destroyed but have eternal life (Jn 3.16). In turn, the Spirit is indispensible in the soteriological experiences of believers. This basic theological understanding is essential for a proper appreciation of the work of Jesus in the Five-fold Gospel.

Jesus Is Savior

Central to a Pentecostal understanding of salvation is the person of Jesus.[5] In fact, each element of the full Gospel is dependent upon him and in a very real way each element is salvific, conveying a distinct aspect of the full Gospel to the recipient.

Most Pentecostals believe that humankind stands under the condemnation of sin as a result of the fall of humanity through Adam and Eve. The extent of the effect of the fall is understood in various ways, but nearly all would agree that in the fall the image of God in humanity has been affected in some way. The restoration of the human being into the image of God and into full fellowship with God is at the heart of what salvation is all about. Divine salvation is made possible through the atoning life and death of Jesus Christ, who lived, suffered, and died for humanity as a sin offering, who, being sinless, destroyed the works of the devil, in particular, sin, death, and the grave. It is the life, death, and resurrection that make possible the transformation of men and women into righteous and holy believers. Jesus' work as Savior is complex with many facets.

Jesus' work as Savior in the life of an individual usually is thought of as beginning with an offer of prevenient grace, grace that goes before – before one is even conscious of one's sinful condition. The Spirit begins to draw or woo one into a space where he or she may have an opportunity to respond to the divine offer of forgiveness that is to come. During this time the Spirit begins to convict one of sin, creating within one a realization of the need for

---

[5] For discussions of the Five-fold Gospel cf. J.C. Thomas (ed.), *Toward a Pentecostal Ecclesiology: The Church and the Five-fold Gospel* (Cleveland, TN: CPT Press, 2010); K.J. Archer, *The Gospel Revisited: Towards a Pentecostal Theology of Worship and Witness* (Eugene, OR: Pickwick, 2011); and V.-M. Kärkkäinen, 'A Full Gospel Ecclesiology of *Koinonia*: Pentecostal Contributions to the Doctrine of the Church', in S.D. Moore and J.M. Henderson (eds.), *Renewal History & Theology: Essays in Honor of H. Vinson Synan* (Cleveland, TN: CPT Press, 2014), pp. 175-93.

forgiveness by God. Such conviction ultimately leads to such an opportunity at which point the individual must choose to respond to God's offer of forgiveness by accepting it or rejecting it. If one rejects this offer he or she may or may not have another opportunity in the future. If one accepts this offer a number of things happen almost simultaneously. The order in which these changes are discussed does not necessarily imply the order in which they occur in the life of the believer nor that these changes are unrelated to one another.

Among the changes that occur when the message of the Gospel is met with faith on the part of an individual are changes in one's legal status. When one asks for and experiences forgiveness of sin, the believer is justified by the Father on the basis of the Son's atoning work.[6] Legally, this change moves the individual from being declared guilty of violating the law of God to being declared 'not guilty' by God as judge. Such justification of the believer is, at one level, a judicial act where the new believer moves from the status of guilty before the law to the status of not guilty. Thus, despite the individual's guilt from sin, he or she receives a not guilty verdict on the basis of Jesus' atoning work. This change in status is accompanied by a transformative change as one is justified in the Spirit. Another legal change of status involves the move from being estranged from God to becoming adopted as a son or daughter of God; from being outside the family of God to becoming a legal heir with Christ Jesus.

However, such changes in status and identity are not confined to the realm of the judicial but are accompanied by dynamic changes experienced by the believer. When one comes to know Jesus as Savior, he or she experiences a change of character described as regeneration, new birth, or being born from above – i.e. being born again – (John 3). Such a salvific change is transformational in nature, where one's being experiences a change from one life and nature to another that comes from God himself. One is no longer a child of the devil but is born of God. The legal adoption as a son or daughter of God, combined with one's spiritual birth from above results in the believer becoming a part of an extended family of believers

---

[6] For a comprehensive Pentecostal view of Justification cf. F.D. Macchia, *Justified in the Spirit* (Grand Rapids: Eerdmans, 2010).

with God as Father and Jesus the Savior as elder Brother. From this point the Holy Spirit begins to dwell within the individual believer. Such dynamic changes result in an assurance of one's salvation owing to the intimate presence of the Spirit in the life of the believer. Simply put, one is a new creation.

The accompanying sacramental sign of this salvific experience is water baptism. Several things are signified in this spiritual act. These are enumerated for clarification purposes only. First, water baptism is a sign of the complete cleansing from sin one experiences in knowing Jesus as Savior. It is the once-for-all bath that signifies a new spiritual status with regard to sin. Second, water baptism signifies the believer's mystical identification with the death, burial, and resurrection of Jesus Christ. This sign points to the believer's full identification with his or her new Lord. Third, water baptism is a sign of the believer's incorporation into the body of Christ. One enters individually into the body where he or she is received into the communion of the saints by means of the ministry of the Holy Spirit. Thus, salvation is not understood simply as an individual experience, but as a communal one as well. Water Baptism is the sign of one's incorporation into the redeemed community. Fourth, the experience of water baptism is an enacted proclamation that Jesus is the Messiah, the Savior of the world, and is a sign of the believer's individual identification with this proclamation. Consequently, water baptism is normally a public event.

A final note should be made with regard to this sacramental sign. Most Pentecostals use the baptismal formula found in Mt. 28.19, 'baptizing them in the name of the Father, and of the Son, and of the Holy Spirit', though baptism 'in the Name of Jesus' is also found, especially amongst Oneness Pentecostals. Pentecostals are nearly uniform in practicing baptism by immersion.

When this understanding of Jesus as Savior is compared with the Book of Mormon – and the previous survey of Book of Mormon Theology – several things become immediately apparent. First, the idea of a 'fortunate fall' appears to be a foreign idea with regard to Pentecostal soteriology. Whilst there is a tension present in the Book of Mormon between an emphasis upon the devastating effects of the fall and a positive dimension of the fall, such an understanding does not find a place within Pentecostal soteriology. Second, 'born again' (Mosiah 27.25; Alma 5.49; 7.14), 'born of the

Spirit' (Mosiah 27.24), and 'born of God' (Mosiah 27.28; Alma 5.14; 22.15; 36.5, 23, 24, 26; 38.6) language is found with some frequency in Mosiah and Alma before almost disappearing from the book, though the idea of believers being children of God (Mosiah 18.22; Alma 6.6; 30.42; 31.16; 3 Nephi 12.9, 45; 4 Nephi 39) and/or children of Christ (Mosiah 5.7; 4 Nephi 17; Mormon 9.26; Moroni 7.19) may not be far from the same idea. Third, the language of justification hardly leaves a trace in the Book of Mormon. Though there is much on justice, judgment, and sin, there are only a few texts where 'justify' appears (1 Nephi 16.2; 2 Nephi 2.5; 7.8; 15.33; 28.8; Jacob 2.14; Mosiah 14.11) and none of these seem to describe positively the justification of the sinner. Fourth, interestingly enough in a book that often mentions God as Father, there are only a few references to believers as children of God (Mosiah 18.22; Alma 6.6; 30.42; 31.16; 3 Nephi 12.9, 45; 4 Nephi 39), with nearly as many references to believers as children of Christ (Mosiah 5.7; 4 Nephi 17; Mormon 9.26; Moroni 7.19), a concept that is wholly missing in Pentecostal theology.[7] Fifth, as has been noted in the Book of Mormon Theology section, water baptism plays a prominent role in the Book of Mormon narrative. There are many aspects of the practice of water baptism that overlap between Pentecostal practice and the Book of Mormon. Among these are that baptism is to be performed by immersion, eventually is to include the Trinitarian formula in its performance, is a sign of repentance, and in some way is connected to the baptism of Jesus. While there is not the same kind of theological reflection on other aspects of the rite's meaning as has been mentioned in Pentecostal theology, the Book of Mormon also mentions a significant number of other aspects of baptism such as: following the example of Christ, fulfilling all righteousness, humbling oneself and being obedient to the commandments of God, following Jesus, as a sign of entrance into the fold of God, as a sign of witness to entering the covenant (cf. esp. 2 Nephi 31; Mosiah 18.1-21). As seen above, there is a very tight connection between water baptism and speaking in tongues in some Book of Mormon texts, an idea that is not foreign to Pentecostal thought

---

[7] There are nearly as many references to a child of the devil (Alma 5.39, 41; 10.28), hell (Alma 11.23; 54.11), and or the kingdom of the devil (Alma 5.25).

but water baptism is not necessarily the expected moment for such glossolalic activity, except amongst certain Oneness Pentecostals.

Jesus Is Sanctifier

In keeping with the metaphor of salvation as *via salutis* (a way of salvation), the believer is next invited to know Jesus as Sanctifier. Salvation does not simply deal with one's past sins, but also makes provisions for the believer not to be dominated by continuing or future sin. As one writer notes, though 'sin may remain it does not reign'.[8] Sanctification results in whole-hearted devotion to God, a perfection of love for God and neighbor, and a deliverance from the bondage of sin in the form of breaking loose or being set free from addictions, life controlling habits, and life-styles that are destructive or counter-productive to a life of holiness. Such sanctification entails wholeness and healing in the life of the believer. In response to those who would argue that one is never more of a Christian than after conversion, holiness advocates would liken sanctification to a human passing through puberty – the person is technically the same person (and not more of a person), but the remarkable nature of change and maturation in the individual is difficult to deny. To know Jesus as Sanctifier leads to a transformation of one's affections, those deep-seated dispositions that are at the core of one's identity. This offer of salvific grace on the part of Jesus to the believer is based on his atoning life and death and made possible by the work of the *Holy* Spirit.

The accompanying sacramental sign of this soteriological experience is Footwashing (cf. esp. John 13.1-20 and 1 Timothy 5.10).[9] The practice of footwashing, or washing the saints' feet, as instituted by Jesus signifies the continual cleansing that is available to believers as they make their way along life's journey. According to the words of Jesus in the Gospel according to John, footwashing is connected to Peter's eternal destiny, supplements or extends the effects of the once-and-for-all bath of water baptism as a sign of continual cleansing from sin, and is to be regularly practiced by be-

---

[8] A paraphrase of John Wesley, 'Sermon 46: On Sin in the Believer', in *The Works of Wesley 2: Wesley's Standard Sermons* (ed. E.D. Sugden; Grand Rapids, MI: Francis Asbury Press, 1955), p. 364.

[9] Cf. J.C. Thomas, *Footwashing in John 13 and the Johannine Community* (Cleveland, TN: CPT Press, 2nd edn, 2014).

lievers. As such, when the believer receives the footwashing at the hand of a brother or sister, he or she experiences the visible sign of the continual cleansing available and previously (sometimes simultaneously) experienced in one's journey. When the believer performs this sign for another believer, he or she participates communally in the reconciliation and cleansing of a fellow believer in the on-going salvation made possible by Jesus. This sign makes plain one's place in the sanctified community.

When this understanding of Jesus as Sanctifier is compared with the Book of Mormon a couple of things become clear. First, sanctification language does not appear infrequently in the Book of Mormon. Several references are found within quotations from Isaiah that speak of the sanctification of God, the holy One (Isa. 5.16; 8.13; 29.23/2 Nephi 15.16; 18.13; 27.34), or have reference to God's sanctified/mighty ones (Isa. 13.3/2 Nephi 23.3). Sanctification language is also used with reference to the Law (Jacob 4.5); those who have been brought into the church and sanctified by the Holy Spirit (Alma 5.54); the ordination of priests who have been sanctified by the Holy Ghost (Alma 13.11-12); the purification and sanctification of humble believers suffering persecution (Helaman 3.35); those who respond to the invitation of Jesus to repent and be baptized who will be sanctified by the reception of the Holy Ghost (3 Nephi 27.20); the three Nephites who were 'sanctified in the flesh' (3 Nephi 28.39); the recipients of the ancient records who are sanctified in God even as was the brother of Jared (Ether 4.7); the bread and wine of the Lord's Supper (Moroni 4.3; 5.2); and those who are perfect in Christ having been sanctified by him through the shedding of his blood (Moroni 10.32, 33). As becomes evident, the focus of sanctification language in the Book of Mormon is upon God, sacred objects, and special individuals in God's economy. Others mentioned are described as having a sanctifying experience, but for the most part such experiences seem to be part of the initial salvation experience. One exception to this general idea might be found in Helaman 3.35, where the purification and sanctification of the heart is tied to one's becoming firmer and firmer in the faith of Christ – the yielding of one's heart unto God.

Second, whilst it is sometimes observed that there is no mention of the washing of feet in the Book of Mormon,[10] there does seem to be one – to this point undetected – example of a footwashing described in 3 Nephi 17.10. On this occasion many who had been healed and made whole by Jesus bowed at his feet and as many as could kissed his feet 'insomuch that they did bathe his feet with their tears'. However, footwashing as a distinctive act alongside water baptism is not found within the Book of Mormon. Thus, it does not function as a sign of sanctification in the book as it does in many strands of Pentecostalism.

Jesus Is Holy Spirit Baptizer

Perhaps the best-known element of the Five-fold Gospel to those outside of Pentecostalism is the belief that Jesus is the Holy Spirit Baptizer.[11] Following closely on the heels of salvation and sanctification is the Baptism of the Holy Spirit, which is believed to come upon the sanctified life. After all, it is the *Holy* Spirit who comes upon such a person. Spirit Baptism is seen as a distinct work of the Spirit that overlaps but is distinct from the work of the Spirit in salvation and sanctification. If in regeneration the Spirit indwells the believer, in the work of Spirit Baptism Jesus is understood to baptize, immerse, or saturate the believer with the Holy Spirit. Thus, Pentecostals hold that whilst all believers are indwelt by the Spirit, not all have been baptized in the Spirit. Not that it is a different Spirit who is operative here, but rather a distinct work of the same Spirit that is experienced. If in water baptism, water is the element into which one is immersed, in Spirit Baptism the Spirit is the element into which one is immersed. This gift is yet another grace offered to the believer on the way of salvation. Jesus himself (the one upon whom the Spirit descended [Jn 1.32-33] and the who was given the Spirit without measure [Jn 3.34]) is the one who baptizes with the Holy Spirit.

The purpose of Spirit Baptism is tightly connected to the related issues of harvest and witness. Rooted in the Jewish harvest feast of Pentecost, the Baptism of the Holy Spirit was experienced by 120

---

[10] So D.A. Wangsgard, 'Washing of Feet', in D.H. Ludlow (ed.), *Encyclopedia of Mormonism* (New York: Macmillan, 1992), IV, p. 1550.

[11] On this whole issue cf. F.D. Macchia, *Baptized in the Spirit: A Global Pentecostal Theology* (Grand Rapids: Zondervan, 2006).

believers on the Day of Pentecost as recorded in Acts 2. The resulting harvest of souls that day was numbered at 5,000 men (apparently not including women and children). This harvest, as well as the
harvest that would go to the ends of the earth, was accomplished by
witness of the 120 (and others) who were saturated by the Holy
Spirit that Jesus poured out upon them. The Acts narrative makes
clear that those who experienced Spirit Baptism became witnesses
to the life, ministry, death, and resurrection of Jesus, who would
bring forgiveness of sin to those who believe in his name. The
transformation of the 120 into fearless witnesses to the mighty acts
of God includes their being clothed with power from on high. That
is to say, Spirit Baptism is a means by which believers are empowered for witness in the face of a hostile world. At the same time,
Jesus' words 'ye shall *be* witnesses' also suggest that the experience
of Spirit Baptism is a soteriological experience in which believers
are personally transformed into witnesses when so baptized.[12] Pentecostals hold that every believer may be baptized in (or filled with)
the Holy Spirit in order to carry out the mission of Jesus.

The accompanying sacramental sign of this soteriological experience is Glossolalia or speaking in tongues as the Spirit gives the
speaker the utterance or the ability to speak (cf. Acts 2, 11, 19). In
point of fact, most Pentecostal denominations, and not a few outside such groups, affirm that speaking in tongues is the initial evidence that one has been so baptized. For Pentecostals, tongues
speech is the visible sign *par excellence* of the presence of God within
the community.[13] Tongues as initial evidence of Spirit Baptism has
been understood to include the following 'kinds' of glossolalia:
known languages unknown to the speaker, unknown languages,
heavenly languages, 'new' languages, tongues of angels, as well as a
phenomenon known as 'stammering lips'. Glossolalia is understood
as: eschatological, theophanic language; language of divine self-

[12] On Spirit Baptism as soteriological in nature cf. esp. K.E. Alexander,
'Boundless Love Divine: A Re-evaluation of Early Understandings of the Experience of Spirit Baptism', in S.J. Land, R.D. Moore, and J.C. Thomas (eds.), *Passover, Pentecost & Parousia: Studies in Celebration of the Life and Ministry of R. Hollis
Gause* (JPTSup 35; Blandford Forum: Deo, 2010), pp. 145-70.
[13] Cf. F.D. Macchia, 'Tongues as a Sign: Towards a Sacramental Understanding of Pentecostal Experience', *Pneuma: The Journal of the Society for Pentecostal Studies*
15.1 (Spring, 1993), pp. 61-76.

disclosure;[14] and/or as exilic, immigrant language.[15] Pentecostals hold that such glossolalia is divine in origin and will accompany the Spirit Baptism of each individual.

When this understanding of Jesus as Holy Spirit Baptizer is compared with the earlier treatment of Book of Mormon pneumatology numerous things become apparent almost immediately. First, and quite significantly, the traditions seem to share a view that Spirit Baptism is accompanied by tongues speech. Whilst not a surprise to find such a theological commitment within Pentecostalism, it is for some quite an unexpected discovery to find such a connection within the Book of Mormon. Second, both Pentecostalism and the Book of Mormon see a relationship between this experience and missionary activity. Third, as with Pentecostalism the Book of Mormon sees a connection between Spirit Baptism and prophesying. Fourth, despite their shared understandings, the traditions' understandings of Spirit Baptism diverge in a rather basic way. For most Pentecostals – with the exception of some Oneness Pentecostals, Spirit Baptism is a distinct work of the Spirit that is normally thought to be subsequent to the conversion experience – though many Pentecostals know individuals who were baptized in the Spirit at the same time they were converted. The Book of Mormon does not appear to see the experience as subsequent to conversion but as part of the conversion experience. On this view, the Book of Mormon appears closer to the position of certain non-Pentecostal Christian groups that question distinct works of the Spirit in terms of Spirit Baptism, though the book affirms charismatic works of the Spirit. Fifth, the function of tongues speech in the Book of Mormon seems primarily to be evidence that one has experienced the baptism of fire and the Holy Ghost, is used in missionary activity, and is a sign of God's continuing revelation and spiritual manifestations.

Jesus Is Healer

A fourth element of the Five-fold Gospel to receive attention here is the belief that Jesus is our healer.[16] Pentecostals not only believe

---

[14] F.D. Macchia, 'Sighs too Deep for Words: Toward a Theology of Glossolalia', *Journal of Pentecostal Theology* 1 (1992), pp. 47-73.

[15] Cf. D. Augustine, *Pentecost, Hospitality, and Transfiguration: Toward a Spirit-inspired Vision of Social Transformation* (Cleveland, TN: CPT Press, 2012).

[16] On this whole topic cf. K.E. Alexander, *Pentecostal Healing: Theology and Practice* (JPTSup 29; Blandford Forum: Deo, 2006).

that Jesus performed signs of healing during his earthly ministry but that he also continues to bring physical, as well as spiritual, healing to individuals. Such healing is not simply viewed as the alleviation of physical suffering, as significant as that may be, but is rooted and grounded in Jesus' atoning life, death, and resurrection. As such, healing has a soteriological function as it is provided for in the atonement of Jesus and functions as a foretaste of the eschatological health anticipated at the return of Jesus. Pentecostals believe that healing is an on-going reality currently available to believers. Healings are salvific encounters whereby individuals come face-to-face with the proclamation of the Gospel in deed. One may choose to respond to such an encounter in faith or fail to respond to the extension of such grace, but in both cases one has encountered the Gospel. Whilst not everyone who prays for physical healing experiences physical healing, there is within the Pentecostal tradition an expectancy that the prayer of faith will save the sick, that the Lord will raise them up, and that the appropriate response to illness in the first instance is always prayer. For those not healed, prayer is the gateway to additional discernment with regard to the purpose of a given infirmity, whether it is divine, demonic, or unattributed in origin.[17]

The accompanying sacramental sign of this soteriological experience is the practice of anointing the sick with oil. Oil was often considered a healing agent in antiquity. The Christian practice of anointing the sick with oil was set forth in Jas 5.14 and apparently commissioned by Jesus himself (Mk 6.13). For Pentecostals, the use of oil in prayer for the sick is a sign of the presence of the Holy Spirit to heal. The use of oil also signifies the eschatological presence of God who brings the effects of the future age into the present. As the community engages in this practice, elders and others participate in times of prayer for the sick. This sacramental sign is a visible reminder of God's presence to heal and, though not considered to function magically, in many cases anointing with oil accompanies individual acts of divine healing.

As with the other elements of the Five-fold Gospel examined to this point, there are similarities with and differences about the role

---

[17] Cf. J.C. Thomas, *The Devil, Disease, and Deliverance: Origins of Illness in New Testament Thought* (Cleveland, TN: CPT Press, 2010).

of healing in Pentecostalism and in the Book of Mormon. By far most references to healing in the Book of Mormon are in connection to Jesus. There are passages that directly attribute healings to Jesus (1 Nephi 11.31; 3 Nephi 17.9, 10; 26.15), texts that predict his healing activities (2 Nephi 25.13; 26.9; Mosiah 3.5; 14.5), as well as those that include his own offer of healing or his words about the topic (3 Nephi 9.13; 17.7, 8; 18.32; 21.10; 25.2). Moses is also mentioned as a healing agent, with the brazen serpent episode receiving special attention (1 Nephi 17.41; 2 Nephi 25.20; cf. also Alma 33.20, 21 for those who refused to make use of this means of healing). Others through whom acts of healing are attributed or implied include Alma and Amulek (Alma 15.5, 8, 10), Nephi (3 Nephi 7.22), the disciples of Jesus (4 Nephi 5), and those (unnamed individuals) who (will?) possess the spiritual gift of healing (Moroni 10.11). At the same time, reference can be made to places where healing is withheld (2 Nephi 13.17; 16.10), not offered (Jacob 2.9), not received (Alma 33.20, 21), or ceases because of iniquity (Mormon 1.13). There are also warnings given to those who might be tempted to conclude that God no longer heals (3 Nephi 29.6; Mormon 9.7). Finally, healing can be spoken of as having specific reference to the soul rather than physical healing (Jacob 2.8).

As for the differences and similarities the following are the most important. First, the Book of Mormon appears to share with Pentecostalism the view that physical healing is based upon the atoning death of Jesus (2 Nephi 25.13). Second, the Book of Mormon also shares the belief that healing is to be an on-going part of the ministry of the church. Third, the Book of Mormon indicates that the spiritual gift of healing is to be operative within the church (Moroni 10.11). Fourth, at the same time, little space is devoted to how the ministry of healing is to be continued – as set forth in James 5 for example, a text that has had an extraordinary impact on the practice and theology of Pentecostalism. Fifth, as such there is no mention of the practice of anointing with oil for healing. Sixth, neither does the Book of Mormon seem to imply that individual believers – outside Jesus, the prophets, the disciples, and those with the gift of healing – play a role in the ongoing healing ministry of the church as one finds within Pentecostalism. Thus, whilst healing plays a not insignificant role in the Book of Mormon, it does not seem to rise to the level of emphasis placed upon it at the heart of Pentecostal theology and practice.

Jesus Is Soon Coming King

The fifth element of the Pentecostal Five-fold Gospel is the belief that Jesus is our soon coming King. In many ways this element of the Five-fold Gospel is the engine that drives the train of Pentecostal theology and ministry for it motivates the concern for salvation, sanctified living, empowerment for service, prayer for the sick, as well as prayer for the effects of the eschatological age to be brought to bear already into the present. It is the same Jesus that one knows as Savior, Sanctifier, Spirit Baptizer, and Healer who is the soon returning king. Thus, the return of Jesus is understood to be the blessed hope of the church and is a longed for event. The expectation of the return of Jesus permeates Pentecostal life and practice, igniting the fire of missionary activity. Most Pentecostals envision a personal, bodily return of the resurrected Jesus at which time the dead in Christ will arise. After this resurrection, believers will join the Lord for a thousand year period on a restored earth, a time during which Satan is bound and is not able to tempt the inhabitants until the end of the thousand years. Following a final cataclysmic battle, the present heaven and earth flee from before the presence of God as a final judgment occurs. After this judgment, a new heaven and new earth are created. The resulting New Jerusalem is both a people and a place, where believers experience the unmediated presence of God and the Lamb and are transformed more and more into his likeness, experiencing the fullness of salvation.[18]

The accompanying sacramental sign of this soteriological experience is the observance of the Lord's Supper or the Eschatological Banquet.[19] In some ways, observance of the Lord's Supper is a moment where past, present, and future converge for the worshipping community. The act is connected to previous redemptive history by its overt ties to the Passover meal celebrated by Israel as a constant reminder of God's deliverance of his people from the

---

[18] Cf. L.R. McQueen, *Toward a Pentecostal Eschatology: Discerning the Way Forward* (JPTSup 39; Blandford Forum: Deo, 2012), and D.W. Faupel, *The Everlasting Gospel: The Significance of Eschatology in the Development of Pentecostal Thought* (JPTSup 10; Sheffield: Sheffield Academic Press, 1996).

[19] On this topic cf. C.E.W. Green, *Toward a Pentecostal Theology of the Lord's Supper: Foretasting the Kingdom* (Cleveland, TN: CPT Press, 2012).

hand of the mightiest military power of that day. It is also clearly connected to the last supper which Jesus shared with his disciples, itself the culmination of numerous daily meals shared by them to this point, a meal in which he institutes the observance of the Lord's Supper. This past event reminds believers of the way in which their salvation is rooted and grounded in the broken body and shed blood of Jesus. At the same time, the Lord's Supper has a present dimension in which all believers globally sit together at the Lord's table in fellowship and solidarity with their Lord. It is a sign of the church's participation with and in Jesus. Finally, this meal is eschatologically conditioned, as its very observance is a proclamation of the Gospel until Jesus comes again in his return. Such eschatological associations are not only found in Paul's comments on the proper observance and meaning of the meal (1 Corinthians 11), but are also deeply embedded in the meaning of the meal in the Gospel according to John, where Jesus' words about eating his flesh and drinking his blood are intimately connected to words about being raised at the last day (John 6). Thus, the Lord's Supper is also seen and experienced as an anticipation of the great eschatological banquet that awaits believers after the resurrection.

When compared with Book of Mormon, as noted in the section devoted to the theology of the Book of Mormon, several things become evident. First, overt texts that mention the return of Jesus in the Book of Mormon are scant with such references occurring only in 3 Nephi 24.2, 27.16-17, and 29.2, two of which are restatements of prophecies from the Old Testament. Second, despite such a paucity of references to the return of Jesus this does not mean that there is little or no eschatological teaching in the book. Third, both Pentecostalism and the Book of Mormon share a belief in the resurrection of the dead, the final judgment, and the establishment of the New Jerusalem. Fourth, the Lord's Supper does not appear to have the same eschatological associations in the Book of Mormon as in Pentecostal theology and practice. Thus, this comparison reveals how different the eschatological orientation of the Book of Mormon is from that of Pentecostalism, where the return of Jesus plays an extraordinarily significant role in its overall theological focus.

Other Theological Issues of Interest

At least three other topics should perhaps be briefly addressed in a comparison of Pentecostalism and the Book of Mormon – Prophecy, Continuing Revelation, and the Role of Women.

Prophecy

Pentecostals believe in the continuing presence and function of the gift of prophecy in the contemporary world. It might not be going too far to say that Pentecostals believe and practice the prophethood of all believers,[20] for in the experience of Spirit Baptism, Pentecostals understand that *all* believers are brought into prophetic activity. At the same time, Pentecostals believe that any member of the community may be called to function in a prophetic manner and that those regularly used to function in such a manner are considered to have been given the gift of prophecy for the community. Based on the teaching of Scripture, both men and women are included in this prophetic calling. The work of those moved upon by the Spirit to function is this role includes both foretelling (prediction) and forth-telling (proclamation), with such prophetic words and works always subject to the discernment of the body of Christ. Like the many other gifts of the Spirit, prophecy is not seen to work in isolation from, or in an authoritative manner over against, the rest of the body. Rather, all prophetic activity is subject to the discernment of the body as the believing community seeks to determine whether or not such words and actions are deemed to come from the Spirit of Truth or the spirit of deception (1 Jn 4.1-6). Such Spirit led discernment is a hallmark of Pentecostal worship and practice.

It almost goes without saying that prophecy is a defining characteristic of the Book of Mormon. However, there are significant differences between its view and that of Pentecostalism. First, in contrast to a somewhat democratized view of the prophetic found within Pentecostalism, the Book of Mormon appears for the most part to focus on individual prophets and their roles around which the faithful gather and against which the unfaithful rebel, i.e. oppos-

---

[20] For this understanding cf. Roger Stronstad, *The Prophethood of All Believers* (Cleveland, TN: CPT Press, 2010), and Robby C. Waddell, *The Spirit of the Book of Revelation* (JPTSup 30; Blandford Forum: Deo, 2006).

ing the prophets' words and directives. Outside the mention of the spiritual gift of prophecy, there are few indications that individual believers are envisioned to play a part in the prophetic ministry of the church. Second, it also appears that the role of the community in assessing and discerning prophetic words and proclamations is minimal at best. Thus, it would seem that rather than viewing prophetic activity as being subject to the discernment of the community, the Book of Mormon views the community as being subject to the prophet's own sense of calling and directives. Such differences have clear implications for the way in which the prophetic gift is envisioned to function.

Continuing Revelation

Owing to belief in the on-going activity and ministry of the Holy Spirit, Pentecostals believe in continuing revelation of the mind and will of God. Pentecostals understand that whilst there is more to be revealed by the Spirit than what is contained in Scripture, the Spirit always speaks in a manner consistent with the voice of the Spirit recorded in Scripture. Consequently, words and even writings can be understood as inspired in some sense for a specific task or moment of time, but are not understood to rise to the level of canonical Scripture for the movement. Evidence of this phenomenon can be seen in the various books mentioned in the Bible which are either no longer extant or have been deemed by the discernment of the Christian community not to rise to the level of canon (cf. Num. 21.14; Josh. 10.13; 1 Sam. 10.25; 2 Sam. 1.18; 1 Kgs 9.29; 11.41; 14.19, 29; 16.20; 1 Chron. 27.24; 29.29; 2 Chron. 12.15; 13.22; 20.34; 24.27; 32.32; 33.19). Examples of this phenomenon can also be seen within the history of Pentecostalism where among some groups messages in tongues and the interpretations thereof have been written down and preserved as an indication of the 'inspired' nature of the content,[21] but such 'messages' have not been deemed to rise to the level of canonical inspiration, rather they seem to have a 'local' or 'temporally conditioned' function or purpose.

This understanding stands in significant contrast to the understanding of the topic in the Book of Mormon, where continuing revelation not only underscores the reason of being for the Book of

---

[21] Melissa L. Archer, *'In the Spirit on the Lord's Day': A Pentecostal Engagement with Worship in the Apocalypse* (Cleveland, TN: CPT Press, 2015), pp. 103-107.

Mormon, but also for the appearance of other scriptural records.[22] As 2 Nephi 29 makes clear the Book of Mormon advocates a view that sacred Scripture will emerge from all the Jewish tribes as well as all the nations of the earth – such Scripture being a record of God's words to each. The contrast of Pentecostal thought and that of the book of Mormon is rather easily seen.

The Role of Women

A final observation should perhaps be offered with regard to the role of women within Pentecostalism. Despite the diversity of thought found across the breadth of the Pentecostal and charismatic traditions, from the very beginning of the movement women have been powerful ministry partners with men (and children) in the proclamation of the Full Gospel. Owing to the outpouring of the Holy Spirit upon all flesh and the teaching of Scripture with regard to the role of women in ministry, women have been deemed worthy to serve as pastors, evangelists, teachers, prophets, deacons, and co-laborers in apostolic ministry. The names of women ministers are spread across Pentecostal publications from the beginning of the movement to the present.[23]

A comparison of this understanding of the role of women in the ministry of the church with the role of women in the Book of

---

[22] This statement is not meant to imply that the Book of Mormon has no place for inspired words that do not become Scripture, but rather to underscore the fact that whilst Pentecostals believe in continuing revelation they do not believe in continuing revelation that expands the boundaries of the canon of Scripture.

[23] Cf. J.C. Thomas, 'Women, Pentecostals, and the Bible: An Experiment in Pentecostal Hermeneutics', in *The Spirit of the New Testament* (Blandford Forum: Deo, 2005), pp. 233-47, and J.C. Thomas, 'Biblical Reflections on Women in Ministry', in L.R. Martin, *Toward a Pentecostal Theology of Preaching* (Cleveland, TN: CPT Press, 2015), pp. 135-40. There are New Testament examples of women who served as **apostle** (Junia in Romans 16.7); **prophet** (Mary [Lk. 1.46-55], Elizabeth [Lk. 1.44-45], Anna [Lk. 2.36-38], the four daughters of Philip [Acts 21.9], women in Corinth [1 Cor. 11.2-16], and the negative example of the woman Jesus calls Jezebel, who is condemned not for her gender but her false teaching [Rev. 2.20]); **evangelist** [the Samaritan woman who has more converts than anyone else in the narrative with the possible exception of John, Jn 4.39]; **teacher** (Priscilla who taught Apollos [Acts 18.24-26]); **deacon** (Phoebe [Rom. 16.1]); **house church host** (Mary [Acts 12.12] and Nympha [Col. 4.15]); as well as **co-laborers** and **fellow-servants** with Paul (Prisca, Mary, Tryphaena, Persis, the mother of Rufus, Julia, the sister of Nerseus [Rom. 16.1-15], Euodia and Syntache [Phil. 4.2], and Claudia and Apphia [2 Tim. 4.21]).

Mormon reveals a significant contrast. As noted in the section on the theology of the Book of Mormon, the relatively meager role women play within the book – primarily as props as they relate to men – indicates that their role and function is quite restrictive when compared to Pentecostalism, both nearer the time of its origins as well as in many of its contemporary versions. Such different emphases with regard to the role and place of women are significant, revealing still another difference in the theology and ministry of Pentecostalism and the Book of Mormon.

Concluding Observations

As this chapter reveals there are points of surprising overlap and significant differences between Pentecostal thought and practice, on the one hand, and the theological emphases of the Book of Mormon, on the other hand. Hopefully, this chapter, along with the previous two, helps to underscore such similarities and dissimilarities, perhaps serving as a basis for future conversations between Pentecostalism and those for whom the Book of Mormon functions as Scripture.

PART SIX

BOOK OF MORMON ORIGINS

Without question, the most contested aspect of Book of Mormon studies has to do with the question of origins. An examination of the literature devoted to the Book of Mormon, both by those for whom the book functions as Scripture and those for whom it does not, reveals that the vast majority of such studies, regardless of their methodological orientation, is devoted to one aspect or another of the claims about the book's origins.[1] Thus, most of these studies consist of some form of evidentialism designed either to prove the truthfulness of the book as ancient records of a history of the Nephite and Lamanite peoples, or to disprove such claims. The scope of this literature is unbelievably voluminous as claims and counter-claims often pass one another like the proverbial ships passing in the night. However, as this work has sought to demonstrate, there are many other profitable avenues of Book of Mormon study worth examining, about which readers for whom the book functions as Scripture and those who do not hold it as such can discuss aside from the issue of origins, an issue that has sometimes been described as a non-starter. It may very well be that in the end the readers of Part Six will fall along such familiar lines. Yet, a book that seeks to serve as an introduction to the Book of Mormon is more or less obligated to include a section devoted to the question of origins to orient its readers to this much-contested aspect of the Book of Mormon story.

Rather than offering an overview of the whole, as John-Charles Duffy has helpfully provided,[2] Part Six will present the relevant information in a manner similar to how a New Testament scholar might approach the issue of the authorship of a contested New Testament set of documents like the Pastoral Epistles. Such a discussion would normally begin with an examination of the text itself for any claims with regard to authorship to the Pastorals – and any early external sources that speak to the issue. The discussion would then move to a consideration or listing of the complications to such

---

[1] As Givens (*The Book of Mormon: A Very Short Introduction*, p. 4) notes, 'What the Book of Mormon claims to be is so radical that the storms of controversy over its origins and authenticity have almost completely obscured the text itself'.

[2] Perhaps the best guide to this whole area of study is John-Charles Duffy's 'Mapping Book of Mormon Historicity Debates: A Guide for the Overwhelmed – Part I and Part II', *Sunstone Magazine* http://www.sunstonemagazine.com/cate gory/mapping-mormon-issues/.

a view of authorship stated in rather stark terms. For example, it would normally be noted that there are historical, theological, and linguistic problems that complicate the view that the Pastorals were written during the lifetime of Paul.[3] Following this section, attention would be turned to the way in which a variety of readers have sought to respond to such starkly stated complications focusing on their resulting reading strategies. These responses would include the following: despite any complications some readers continue to assign the Pastorals to the hand of Paul; others assign them to a Pauline amanuensis who was given more authority in drafting the letter(s) than usual; others assign the Pastorals to a disciple of Paul who wrote the letters after the apostle's death from Pauline fragments; while others do not believe the letters are connected to Paul in any tangible way.

The three chapters devoted to the issue of Book of Mormon origins will roughly follow such an approach. First, the standard or traditional story of the book's origins will be given in the words of those involved in the book's production; specifically, the words of Joseph Smith, Jr. The second of the following chapters presents complications, stated rather starkly, to the standard or traditional story that have arisen over the years. For those who know these issues there will be few surprises. Finally, the differing responses to these complications by various readers are described and some reflection offered. In this way, it is hoped that all readers will be able to find themselves at one point or another in what is presented and to appreciate the attempt that is here made to assess various dimensions of this contentious aspect of Book of Mormon studies.

---

[3] For example, cf. the discussion of such issues in W.D. Mounce, *Pastoral Epistles* (WBC 46; Nashville: Thomas Nelson, 2000), pp. lxxxiii-cxviii.

36

THE STANDARD OR TRADITIONAL STORY

Identifying the story of the origins of the Book of Mormon is complicated in at least a couple of ways. First, it appears that, surprisingly, Joseph Smith felt little urgency to talk about the book's origins with the first somewhat extended account not occurring until November 1832, some two years after the book's publication. Second, the quest for a standard or traditional story of the book's origins is further complicated by the fact that there is not one standard story of origins but several stories, each with unique features and not a few differences amongst them.

The first extant account of Book of Mormon origins comes in the form of what appears to be Joseph Smith's earliest attempt to write a history of his life, found on the first three sheets – six written pages – of a collection of documents known as Kirtland Letter Book A.[1] According to the record, this account was written sometime between the Summer of 1832 and November of the same year. Though quite extensive, owing to its significance it is included here in its entirety.[2]

History, circa Summer 1832

A History of the life of Joseph Smith Jr. an account of his marvilous experience and of all the mighty acts which he doeth in the

---

[1] Though this account 'has fewer details than later accounts', Scherer (*The Journey of a People: The Era of Restoration, 1820 to 1844*, p. 75 n. 1) believes it to be the more accurate account.

[2] Words within angled brackets < > designate additions to the text by scribal correctors, whilst words within square brackets [ ] designate editorial additions.

name of Jesus Ch[r]ist the son of the living God of whom he
beareth record and also an account of the rise of the church
of Christ in the eve of time according as the Lord brought forth
and established by his hand <firstly> he receiving the testamony
from on high seccondly the min istering of Angels thirdly the reception of the holy Priesthood by the ministring of – Aangels to
adminster the letter of the ~~Law~~ <Gospel—> < –the Law and
commandments as they were given unto him—> and ~~in~~ <the>
ordinencs, forthly a confirmation and reception of the high
Priesthood after the holy order of the son of the living God
pow er and ordinence from on high to preach the Gospel in the
administration and demonstration of the spirit the Kees of the
Kingdom of God confered upon him and the continuation of
the blessings of God to him &c——

I was born in the town of Charon [Sharon] in the <State> of
Vermont North America on the twenty third day of December
AD 1805 of goodly Parents who spared no pains to in-
struct<ing> me in <the> christian religion[.] at the age of about
ten years my Father Joseph Smith Seignior moved to Palmyra
Ontario County in the State of New York and being in indigent
circumstances were obliged to labour hard for the support of a
large Family having nine chilldren and as it require d ~~their~~ exer-
tions of all that were able to render any assistance for the support of the Family therefore we were deprived of the bennifit of
an education suffice it to say I was mearly instruct tid in reading
~~and~~ writing and the ground <rules> of Arithmatic which
const[it]uted my whole lite rary acquirements. At about the age
of twelve years my mind become seriously imprest [p. 1] with regard to the all importent concerns ~~of~~ for the well fare of my immortal Soul which led me to searching the scriptures believeing
as I was taught, that they contained the word of God thus apply-
ing myself to them and my intimate acquaintance with those of
differant denominations led me to marvel excedingly for I discovered that <they did not ~~adorn~~> ~~instead of~~ adorning their
profession by a holy walk and Godly conversation agreeable to
what I found contained in that sacred depository this was a grief
to my Soul thus from the age of twelve years to fifteen I pondered many things in my heart concerning the sittuation of the
world of mankind the contentions and divi[si]ons the

wicke[d]ness and abominations and the darkness which pervaded
the of the minds of mankind my mind become excedingly distressed for I become convicted of my sins and by searching the
scriptures I found that mand <mankind> did not come unto the
Lord but that they had apostatised from the true and liveing faith
and there was no society or denomination that built upon the
gospel of Jesus Christ as recorded in the new testament and I felt
to mourn for my own sins and for the sins of the world for I
learned in the scriptures that God was the same yesterday to day
and forever that he was no respecter to persons for he was God
for I looked upon the sun the glorious luminary of the earth and
also the moon rolling in their magesty through the heavens and
also the stars shining in their courses and the earth also upon
whic h I stood and the beast of the field and the fowls of heaven
and the fish of the waters and also man walking forth upon the
face of the earth in magesty and in the strength of beauty whose
power and intiligence in governing the things which are so ex-
ceding great and [p. 2] marvilous even in the likeness of him who
created him <them> and when I considered upon these things
my heart exclai med well hath the wise man said the <it is a>
fool <that> saith in his heart there is no God my heart exclaimed all all these bear testimony and bespeak an omnipotant
and omnipreasant power a being who makith Laws and de-
creeeth and bindeth all things in their bounds who filleth Eternity who was and is and will be from all Eternity to Eternity and
when <I> considered all these things and that <that> being
seeketh such to worshep him as wors hip him in spirit and in
truth therefore I cried unto the Lord for mercy for there was
none else to whom I could go and to obtain mercy and the Lord
heard my cry in the wilderne ss and while in <the> attitude of
calling upon the Lord <in the 16th year of my age> a piller of
fire light above the brightness of the sun at noon day come
down from above and rested upon me and I was filled with the
spirit of god and the <Lord> opened the heavens upon me and
I saw the Lord and he spake unto me saying Joseph <my son>
thy sins are forgiven thee. go thy <way> walk in my statutes and
keep my commandments behold I am the Lord of glory I was
crucifyed for the world that all those who believe on my name
may have Eternal life <behold> the world lieth in sin and at this

time and none doeth good no not one they have turned asside
from the gospel and keep not <my> commandments they draw
near to me with their lips while their hearts are far from me and
mine anger is kindling against the inhabitants of the earth to visit
them acording to thir ungodliness and to bring to pass that
which <hath> been spoken by the mouth of the prophe ts and
Ap[o]stles behold and lo I come quickly as it [is] wr itten of me
in the cloud <clothed> in the glory of my Father and my soul
was filled with love and for many days I could rejoice with great
Joy and the Lord was with me but could find none that would
believe the hevnly vision nevertheless I pondered these things in
my heart ~~about that~~ ~~time my mother~~ ~~and~~ but after many days [p.
3] I fell into transgressions and sinned in many things which
brought a wound upon my soul and there were many things
which transpired that cannot be writen and my Fathers family
have suffered many persicutions and afflictions and it came to
pass when I was seventeen years of age I called again upon the
Lord and he shewed unto me a heavenly vision for behold an
angel of the Lord came and stood before me and it was by night
and he called me by name and he said the Lord had forgiven me
my sins and he revealed unto me that in the Town of Manchester Ontario County N.Y. there was plates of gold upon which
there was engravings which was engraven by Maroni & his fathers the servants of the living God in ancient days and deposited by th[e] commandments of God and kept by the power
thereof and that I should go and get them and he revealed unto
me many things concerning the inhabitents of of the earth which
since have been revealed in commandments & revelations and it
was on the 22d day of Sept. AD ~~182~~ 1822 and thus he appeared
unto me three times in one night and once on the next day and
then I immediately went to the place and found where the plates
was deposited as the angel of the Lord had commanded me and
straightway made three attempts to get them and then being excedingly frightened I supposed it had been a dreem of Vision but
when I considred I knew that it was not therefore I cried unto
the Lord in the agony of my soul why can I not obtain them behold the angel appeared unto me again and said unto me you
have not kept the commandments of the Lord which I gave unto you therefore you cannot now obtain them for the time is not

yet fulfilled therefore thou wast left unto temptation that thou mightest be made accquainted ~~of~~ with the power of the advisary therefore repent and call on the Lord thou shalt be forgiven and in his own due time thou shalt obtain them [p. 4] for now I had been tempted of the advisary and saught the Plates to obtain riches and kept not the commandme[n]t that I should have an eye single to the Glory of God therefore I was chastened and saught diligently to obtain the plates and obtained them not untill I was twenty one years of age and in this year I was married to Emma Hale Daughtr of Isaach [Isaac] Hale who lived in Harmony Susquehan[n]a County Pensylvania on the 18th January AD, 1827, on the 22d day of Sept of this same year I obtained the plat[e]s—and ~~the~~ in December following we mooved to Susquehana by the assistence of a man by the name of Martin Har[r]is who became convinced of th[e] vision and gave me fifty Dollars to bare my expences and because of his faith and this rightheous deed the Lord appeared unto him in a vision and shewed unto him his marvilous work which he was about to do and <h[e]> imediately came to Suquehannah and said the Lord had shown him that he must go to new York City <with> some of the characters so we proceeded to coppy some of them and he took his Journy to the Eastern Cittys and to the Learned <saying> read this I pray thee and the learned said I cannot but if he w ould bring the blates [plates] they would read it but the Lord had forbid it and he returned to me and gave them to <me> <to> translate and I said ~~I said~~ cannot for I am not learned but the Lord had prepared ~~speettieke~~ spectacles for to read the Book therefore I commenced translating the characters and thus the Propicy [prophecy] of Isiaah was fulfilled which is writen in the 29 chaptr concerning the book and it came to pass that after we had translated 116 pages that he desired to carry them to read to his friends that peradventur he might convince them of the truth therefore I inquired of the Lord and the Lord said unto me that he must not take them and I spake unto him (Martin) the word of the Lord [p. 5] and he said inquire again and I inquired again and also the third time and the Lord said unto me let him go with them only he shall covenant with me that he will not shew them to only but four persons and he covenented withe Lord that he would do according to the word

of the Lord therefore he took them and took his journey unto
his friends to Palmire [Palmyra] Wayne County & State of N
York and he brake the covenent which he made before the Lord
and the Lord suffered the writings to fall into the hands of wicked men and Martin was Chastened for his transgression and I also was chastened ~~also~~ for my transgression for asking the Lord
the third time wherefore the Plates was taken from me by the
power of God and I was not able to obtain them for a season
and it came to pass afte[r] much humility and affliction of Soul I
obtained them again when Lord appeared unto a young man by
the name of Oliver Cowd[e]ry and shewed unto him the plates in
a vision and also the truth of the work and what the Lord was
about to do through me his unworthy Servant therefore he was
desiorous to come and write for me ~~and~~ to translate now my
wife had writen some for me to translate and also my Brothr
Samuel H Smith but we had become reduced in property and my
wives father was about to turn me out of doores ~~I~~ & I had not
where to go and I cried unto the Lord that he would provide for
me to accom plish the work whereunto he had commanded me
[*4 lines blank*] [p. [6]][3]

Several aspects of this earliest account are significant for the
purposes of this study.

First, according to this report, from the age of twelve to the age
of fifteen, Smith was distressed by the dissensions and divisions of a
Christianity that had apostatized from the faith of the New Testament. Being convicted of his own sinfulness and his need for
mourning he did not know where to turn.

Second, sometime during his sixteenth year he cried out to the
Lord for mercy, as there was no one else to whom he could turn.

Third, it was during this time of prayer that the Lord heard his
cry in the wilderness.

Fourth, at this point a pillar of light, brighter than the noon day
sun came down from heaven upon him and he was filled with the
spirit of god.

---

[3] Karen Lynn Davidson, David J. Whittaker, Mark Ashurst-McGee, and
Richard L. Jensen (eds.), *Joseph Smith Histories, 1832-1844.* (Vol. 1 of the Histories
series of The Joseph Smith Papers I; Dean C. Jessee, Ronald K. Esplin, and Richard Lyman Bushman [eds.]; Salt Lake City: Church Historian's Press, 2012), pp.
2-22.

Fifth, the heavens opened and Joseph saw the Lord who pronounced that Joseph's sins had been forgiven and commissioned him to go and walk in the statutes and commandments that the Lord of glory had given him.

Sixth, though pondering these things, he fell into many transgressions and his father's family suffered many persecutions.

Seventh, when Joseph was seventeen, an angel appeared to him pronouncing forgiveness of sins as well as revealing the existence of plates of gold engraved by 'Maroni' and his fathers, ancient records about inhabitants of the earth, that were deposited in the town of Manchester, New York. On 22 September 1822, three times the angel appeared that night and once the next day.

Eighth, Joseph's three attempts to retrieve the plates were rebuffed by the angel owing to the fact that Joseph had not kept the commandments and had sought to obtain the plates for the purpose of riches.

Ninth, on 22 September 1827, when twenty-one and married to Emma Hale, he obtained the plates.

Tenth, assisted by a fifty-dollar gift from Martin Harris, Smith, Emma, and Harris moved to Susquehanna, Pennsylvania from where Harris took certain characters transcribed from the plates to New York City to have a learned person examine them.

Eleventh, the Lord prepared spectacles for Joseph to read the book.

Twelfth, after translating about 116 pages, Harris 'lost' the pages, having taken them to Palmyra, New York.

Thirteenth, later the Lord showed in a vision the plates to Oliver Cowdery who came to help Smith with the translation.

This initial extant account introduces many of the basic details that would come to be associated with the standard story. Over the years, as other accounts came forward – including some by Smith himself,[4] differences between this first account and later accounts

---

[4] One of the best known being the 'History of Joseph Smith', which appeared in *Times and Seasons* 3.10 (15 March 1842), pp. 726-28; 3.11 (1 April 1842), pp. 748-49; 3.12 (15 April 1842), pp. 753-54. For a survey of the various accounts cf. Dean C. Jessee, 'The early accounts of Joseph Smith's First Vision', *BYU Studies* 9.3 (1969), pp. 275-94.

would begin to emerge.[5] For example, 'the wilderness' in which the bright light appeared would become a 'silent grove' and then 'the woods'. The Lord of the first account becomes two personages: God the Father and his Son, Jesus. The year of the vision begins as 1822 and becomes 1823. The unnamed angel of the first recounting becomes 'Nephi' and then 'Moroni'. The 'inhabitants of the earth' become the Indians who are the literal descendants of Abraham. The intensity of Smith's suffering owing to his vision becomes greater in the later accounts. His spectacles for translating become a breastplate with the Urim and Thummim attached. Smith's three-fold attempt to acquire the plates and his success four years later – when he was twenty-one – becomes an annual trip to the place of their burial, the fourth of which results in the plates' retrieval. In addition, Smith's telling of the story becomes more mature and theologically nuanced in the later accounts.

[5] For an analysis of the differences and similarities amongst these accounts cf. Richard P. Howard, 'An Analysis of Six Contemporary Accounts Touching Joseph Smith's First Vision', in M.L. Draper and C.D. Vlahos (eds.), *Restoration Studies I: A Collection of Essays About the History, Beliefs, and Practices of the Reorganized Church of Jesus Christ of Latter Day Saints* (Independence, MO: Herald Publishing House, 1980), pp. 95-117.

37

COMPLICATIONS TO THE STANDARD STORY

Aside from the complications generated by the differences between the earliest and later accounts of Book of Mormon origins, several aspects from the earliest standard story introduce complications on their own. Several of these will be considered.

Translation

One might get the idea from the standard story that Smith acquired the ability to translate the plates of gold from 'Reformed Egyptian' into English, leaving the impression that he has the gift of translation. Normally, a translation renders words from one language known by the translator into a second language known by the translator. But according to various eyewitnesses, and Smith himself, this was not the way in which the Book of Mormon was 'translated'. Rather, in the beginning of the period of composition, Smith made use of the 'Urim and Thummim' – two smooth stones set as spectacles that were attached to a breastplate. He would dictate from behind a blanket that had been hung dividing him from his scribe, Martin Harris. By the time Oliver Cowdery took over as scribe translation by means of the 'Urim and Thummim' had given way to translation by means of Smith looking into a seer stone placed in his hat – his face hidden in the hat to keep out any light that might distract him. Often during these times the plates themselves were covered on the table, their characters not visible even to Smith as he 'translated'.[1] Words would appear in the seer stone, sentence by sentence, and Smith would read them out to his scribe for copying, often spelling difficult names.[2]

Perhaps something more of the translation process might be inferred from words spoken by Smith to Oliver Cowdery, who had tried to translate a section of the plates but had failed. According to revelation dictated by Smith in *Book of Commandments* 8.3, Jesus Christ instructed Cowdery that when called upon to translate in the future – though not from the plates –

> ... behold I say unto you, that you must study it out in your mind; then you must ask me if it be right, and if it is right, I will cause that your bosom to burn within you: therefore, you shall feel that it is right; but if it be not right, you shall have no such feelings, but you shall have a stupor of thought, that shall cause you to forget the thing which is wrong: therefore, you cannot write that which is sacred, save it be given to you from me.[3]

If these revelatory words of instruction were given by Smith to Cowdery with the expectation that the latter would one day find them useful in his own future translation work, it is possible that they reflect something about the nature of Smith's own translation experience.

Although what can be known about the 'translation' process means that 'translation' terminology should be understood more as transcription or dictation than translation,[4] it did not keep Smith from being widely regarded as a seer who could translate all manner of foreign languages. But this reputation introduces another complication. While claims about Joseph Smith's translation of the Book of Mormon are unverifiable – aside from characters written

---

[1] As John Turner nicely observes, 'They served as an object of inspiration, not as a textual basis for translation'. Turner, *Mormon Jesus: A Biography*, p. 27. On the whole matter of Book of Mormon translation cf. Richard van Wagoner and Steve Walker, 'The Gift of Seeing', *Dialogue: A Journal of Mormon Thought* 15.2 (Summer 1982), pp. 48-68.

[2] Cf. Bushman, *Joseph Smith: Rough Stone Rolling*, pp. 66-73 and Scherer, *The Journey of a People: The Era of Restoration, 1820 to 1844*, pp. 88-92.

[3] On the relevance of these words to the Book of Mormon translation process cf. Scherer, *The Journey of a People: The Era of Restoration, 1820 to 1844*, pp. 101-102.

[4] So Bushman, *Joseph Smith: Rough Stone Rolling*, p. 72.

down and taken to Professor Anthon – as the plates were not available for an independent examination, some of Smith's other attempts at translation are open to such verification. Three notable examples illustrate the complications that such 'translation' work presents.

Book of Abraham

On 3 July 1835, one Michael H. Chandler arrived in Kirtland, Ohio with four mummies and several rolls of papyrus, Egyptian artifacts that he had exhibited in Cleveland, Ohio before coming to Kirtland, owing to Smith's translation abilities. After inspecting the papyri Smith declared that both of the rolls were of importance as one contained the writings of Abraham of Ur, while the other contained the writings of Joseph of Egypt. Smith would work on them over the next several years with a 'translation' of the former appearing in the *Times and Seasons* in 1842, while a 'translation' of the latter would never appear.[5] When the Book of Abraham began to be published in the *Times and Seasons* 3.9 (1 March 1842), Smith introduced the translation's appearance with the words

> A Translation – Of some ancient Records that have fallen into our hands, from the Catecombs [*sic*] of Egypt, purporting to be the writings of Abraham, while he was in Egypt, called the BOOK OF ABRAHAM, written by his own hand, upon papyrus.

The Book of Abraham would be judged for a few years mainly on the basis of the contents of the 'translation'. On the one hand, only in 1837 would the secrets of Egyptian hieroglyphics via the Rosetta Stone's analysis be publicized, taking some time to make its way across the Atlantic. On the other hand, owing to the later sale of the papyri by the Smith family, the papyri were widely thought to have perished in the great Chicago fire, with only three facsimiles in existence.[6] But before long Smith's 'interpretation' would face extraordinary scrutiny.

The first challenge would appear in 1860, when French traveler Jules Remy passed through Salt Lake City, saw the facsimiles, and called them to the attention of Coptic student Theodula Deveria at

---

[5] Bushman, *Joseph Smith: Rough Stone Rolling*, pp. 286, 291.

[6] Brodie, *No Man Knows My History*, pp. 169-75.

the Louvre. Remy would place Smith's interpretation next to Deveria's in parallel columns in Remy's *A Journey to Great Salt-Lake City* published in 1861, underscoring the differences between Smith's interpretation and Deveria's translation, showing what an actual translation of the papyri looks like.[7]

In 1912, J.S. Spalding, the Episcopal Bishop of Utah, produced the most serious assessment to that point of the papyri in facsimile form.[8] Taking up the challenge as to whether or not the Book of Mormon had been correctly translated, Spalding used the Book of Abraham as a test case, owing to the fact that the gold plates were no longer available to assess Smith's Book of Mormon 'translation' but that facsimiles of the papyri from which Smith produced the Book of Abraham were available. Spalding's short monograph then gives the text of Smith's interpretation (pp. 20-22). This is followed by the comments of the world's leading Egyptologists (pp. 23-24) including A.H. Sayce (Oxford University), Arthur Mace (New York Metropolitan Museum of Art), W.M. Flinders Petrie (London University), and J.H. Breasted (University of Chicago), all of whom categorically deny that Smith's interpretation has any basis in the text of these papyri. Rather, these Egyptologists concluded that the papyri consisted of ordinary funerary texts.

Over fifty years later – in 1967 – the story would take an unexpected turn, as word came that the New York Metropolitan Museum of Art actually had eleven fragments of the original papyri. These were returned to the LDS Church in Salt Lake City at which point translations of the Egyptian hieroglyphics contained therein offered by established scholars would be published.[9] Of these developments Bushman would observe,

> Some Mormons were crushed when the fragments turned out to be rather conventional funerary texts placed within mummified bodies, in this case Hôr, to assure continuing life as an immortal

---

[7] Jules Remy and Julius Brenchley, *A Journey to Great Salt-Lake City* (London: W. Jeffs, 1861) II, pp. 536-46.

[8] F.S. Spalding, *Joseph Smith Jr. as a Translator: An Inquiry Conducted* (Salt Lake City: The Arrow Press, 1912).

[9] Cf. *Dialogue: A Journal of Mormon Thought* 3 (Summer 1968), pp. 67-105.

god. According to the Egyptologists, nothing on the fragments resembled Joseph's account of Abraham.[10]

Such results have led most non-LDS readers to the conclusion that Smith's production of the Book of Abraham was not a translation of the papyri in any conventional sense, with no correlation between the papyri's hieroglyphs and Smith's dictated words.

The Greek Psalter

In April 1842, near the time of the publication of the Book of Abraham 'translation', another 'translation' opportunity seems to have presented itself to Joseph Smith. Henry Caswall, a British academic cleric, who had taught at Kemper College near St Louis, paid Smith a visit in Nauvoo, bringing with him an ancient Greek Psalter. Caswall, who would write a number of books on religion – including two on Mormonism, gives two accounts of his encounter with Smith and his examination of the Greek Psalter. In the shorter he writes,

> When an ancient Greek manuscript of the Psalms was exhibited to him as a test of his scholarship, he boldly pronounced it to be a *'Dictionary of Egyptian hieroglyphics.'* Pointing to the capital letters at the commencement of each verse, he said, 'Them figures is Egyptian hieroglyphics, and them which follows is the interpretation of the hieroglyphics, written in the *reformed Egyptian* language. Them characters is like the letters that was engraved on the golden plates.' He afterwards proceeded to show his papyrus, and to explain the inscriptions, but probably suspecting that the author designed to entrap him, he suddenly left the apartment, leaped into his light wagon, and drove away as fast as possible.[11]

The longer account is found in his earlier book where it is revealed that upon his arrival in Nauvoo from Montrose he was greeted in a shop by its keeper, whom Caswall informed of his desire to see the remarkable Egyptian curiosities in Smith's possession and in ex-

---

[10] Bushman, *Joseph Smith: Rough Stone Rolling*, p. 291. For the most recent edition of the papyri cf. Robert K. Reitner, *The Joseph Smith Egyptian Papyri: A Complete Edition* (Salt Lake City: Signature Books, 2014).

[11] Henry Caswall, *The Prophet of the Nineteenth Century; or, the Rise, Progress, and Present State of the Mormons, or Latter Day Saints* ... (London: J.G.F. & J. Rivington, 1843), pp. 223-24.

change Caswall would show Smith a very wonderful book that had recently come into his possession. The shopkeeper and other interested onlookers who had assembled begged to see the book that Caswall had brought with him. Upon viewing it they assured him that he had brought the book to the right place for the prophet would be able to reveal its contents. After refusing to stay in Nauvoo for the evening but before leaving, Caswall was taken to the home of Lucy Smith, to whom he showed his book and where, in turn, he was shown the mummies – as well as sold an 1830 edition of the Book of Mormon. Upon making his way to the printing office a number of Mormon authorities offered to purchase Caswall's ancient book – an offer he declined. Upon his return to Nauvoo Caswall was meet by Smith, who took him to the Mansion House where a conversation about Caswall's book took place. Caswall records the event in the following fashion:

> I handed the book to the prophet, and begged him to explain its contents. He asked me if I had any idea of its meaning. I replied, that I believed it to be a Greek Psalter; but that I should like to hear his opinion. 'No,' he said; 'it ain't Greek at all; except, perhaps, a few words. What ain't Greek, is Egyptian; and what ain't Egyptian, is Greek. This book is very valuable. It is a dictionary of Egyptian hieroglyphic.' Pointing to the capital letters at the commencement of each verse, he said: 'Them figures is Egyptian hieroglyphics; and them which follows, is the interpretation of the hieroglyphics, written in the reformed Egyptian. The characters is like the letters that was engraven on the golden plates.'[12]

After this exchange, Smith then took Caswall to the store and showed him his papyrus. However, Smith was reticent to explain the papyrus, not responding to Caswall's questions, abruptly leaving Caswall. When confronting Mormon apostle Dr Willard Richards with Smith's misidentification of the text and its contents Richards, not explicitly denying Smith's misidentification, responded to Caswall, 'Sometimes Mr. Smith speaks as a prophet, and sometimes

---

[12] Henry Caswall, *The City of the Mormons: Or Three Days at Nauvoo in 1842* (London: J.G.F. & J. Rivington, 1842), pp. 35-36.

as a mere man. If he gave a wrong opinion respecting the book, he spoke as a mere man.'[13]

In these written accounts, Smith was deemed to have been unsuccessful in his attempt at 'translation'.[14]

---

[13] Caswall, *The City of the Mormons*, p. 43.

[14] For a discussion of this event cf. Grant H. Palmer, *An Insider's View of Mormon Origins* (Salt Lake City: Signature Books, 2002), pp. 34-36, and Scherer, *The Journey of a People: The Era of Restoration, 1820 to 1844*, p. 413. Cf. also the 'The Mormon Prophet and the Greek Psalter' in the *Warsaw (IL) Message* 1.45 (1843).

We lately heard a story, which while it may make us mourn over the depravity of Human Nature, serves to show, among many similar facts, the low artifices and cunning tricks, to which the Mormon Prophet will resort, in order to impose upon the gullibility of his followers. The story is in this wise; and can be substantiated by respectable witnesses.

Some time since, Professor Caswell, late of Kemper College, near St. Louis, an Episcopal Clergyman of reputation, being about to leave this country for England, paid a visit to Smith and the Saints, in order that he might be better able to represent the imposture to the British people. It so happened that the Professor had in his possession a Greek Psalter, of great age – one that had been in the family for several hundred years. This book, as a relic of antiquity, was a curiosity to any one – but to some of the Saints, who happened to see it, it was a marvel and wonder. Supposing its origin to have been as ancient, at least, as the Prophet's Egyptian Mummy, and not knowing but the Professor had dug it from the bowels of the same sacred hill in Western New York whence sprung the holy Book of Mormon, they importuned him to allow 'brother Joseph' an opportunity of translating it!

The Professor reluctantly assented to the proposal; and accompanied by a number of the anxious brethren, repaired to the residence of the Prophet. The remarkable book was handed him. Joe took it – examined its old and worn leaves – and turned over its musty pages. Expectation was now upon tip-toe. The brethren looked at one another – at the book – then at the Prophet. It was a most interesting scene!

Presently the spirit of prophecy began to arise within him; and he opened his mouth and spoke. That wonderful power, which enables him to see as far through a mill-stone as could Moses or Elijah of old, had already in the twinkling of an eye, made those rough and uncouth characters as plain to him as the nose on the face of the Professor. 'This Book,' said he, 'I pronounce to be a Dictionary of Ancient Egyptian Hieroglyphics!'

The brethren present were greatly astonished at this exhibition of their Prophet's power of revealing hidden things. After their exaltation had somewhat subsided, the Professor coolly told them that their Prophet was a base impostor! – and that the book before them was but a plain Greek Psalter! – Joe 'stepped out.'

Such is the manner in which this arrant knave imposes upon his followers! and such is the manner in which his knavery is sometimes exposed! Yet, strange that people continue to believe him!

The Kinderhook Plates

In April 1843 yet another 'translation' opportunity presented itself to Joseph Smith in the form of six bell-shaped brass plates that had been dug up from a Native American burial mound in a place called Kinderhook, Pike County, Illinois. One of the 'discoverers', Robert Wiley, claimed to have dreamt of their discovery for three nights running before taking several other individuals including two Mormons, to dig for the plates. An article in the *Times and Seasons* 4.12 (1 May 1843) quickly announced their discovery in three separate articles. The first entitled, 'Ancient Records', notifies the readers that Smith has had, and will have the plates in his possession, though his disposition regarding them is not yet known.[15] The second, which comes in the form of a letter to the editor, recounts the story.

> On the 16th of April last a respectable merchant by the name of Robert Wiley, commenced digging in a large mound near this place: he excavated to the depth of 10 feet and came to rock; about that time the rain began to fall, and he abandoned the work. On the 23d he and quite a number of the citizens with myself, repaired to the mound, and after making ample opening, we found plenty of rock, the most of which appeared as though it had been strongly burned; and after removing full two feet of said rock, we found plenty of charcoal and ashes; also human bones that appeared as though they had been burned; and near the eciphalon a bundle was found that consisted of six plates of brass, of a bell shape, each having a hole near the small end, and a ring through them all, and clasped with two clasps, the ring and claps [clasps] appeared to be of iron very much oxidated [oxidized], the plates appeared first to be copper, and had the appearance of being covered with characters. It was agreed by the company that I should cleanse the plates: accordingly I took them to my house, washed them with soap and water, and a woolen cloth; but finding them not yet cleansed I treated them with dilute sulphuric [sulfuric] acid which made them perfectly clean, on which it appeared that they were completely covered

---

Professor Caswell, since his sojourn in England, has published a work entitled 'Three Days at Nauvoo,' in which this rich scene is represented in an engraving.

[15] *Times and Seasons* 4.12 (1 May 1843), pp. 185-87.

with hieroglyphics that none as yet have been able to read. Wishing that the world might know the hidden things as fast as they come to light, I was induced to state the facts, hoping that you would give it an insertion in your excellent, paper for we all feel anxious to know the true meaning of the plates, and publishing, the facts might lead to the true translation. They were found, I judged, more than twelve feet below the surface of the top of the mound.

The following certificate was forwarded for publication, at the same time.

We the citizens of Kinderhook, whose names are annexed do certify and declare that on the 23d April, 1843, while excavating a large mound, in this vicinity, Mr. R. Wiley took from said mound, six brass plates of a bell shape, covered with ancient characters. Said plates were very much oxidated [oxidized] – the bands and rings on said plates mouldered into dust on a slight pressure. The above described plates we have handed to Mr. Sharp for the purpose of taking them to Nauvoo.

Rob't Wiley, W. P. Harris,
G. W. F. Ward, W. Longnecker,
Fayette Grubb, Ira S. Curtis,
Geo. Deckenson, W. Fugate.
J. R. Sharp.[16]

The third article, entitled 'Singular Discover-Material for Another Mormon Book', comes in the form of a reprint from the *Quincy Whig*, essentially retelling the story, though challenging Smith to translate the newly 'discovered' plates.

By whom these palates [*sic*] were deposited there must ever remain a secret, unless some one skilled in deciphering hieroglyphics, may be found to unravel the mystery. Some pretend to say, that Smith the Mormon leader, has the ability to read them. If he has, he will confer a great favor on the public by removing the mystery which hangs over them. We learn there was a Mormon present when the plates were found, who it is said, leaped for joy

---

[16] *Times and Seasons* 4.12 (1 May 1843), p. 186.

at the discovery, and remarked that it would go to prove the authenticity of the Book of Mormon – which it undoubtedly will.[17]

According to William Clayton, Joseph Smith's scribe, Smith had begun working on a translation of the plates when he first saw them. Clayton writes:

> I have seen 6 brass plates which were found in Adams County by some persons who were digging in a mound ... They are covered with ancient characters of language containing from 30 to 40 on each side of the plates. Prest J. has translated a portion and says they contain the history of the person with whom they were found and he was a descendant of Ham through the loins of Pharaoh king of Egypt, and he received his kingdom from the ruler of heaven and earth.[18]

The idea that Smith had begun a provisional translation appears to be confirmed in a letter from Parley P. Pratt to his cousin a few days later, who claims that the engravings are in the Egyptian language and that they 'contain the genealogy of one of the ancient Jaredites back to Ham the son of Noah'. He further notes that the plates were brought to Smith for an examination and translation and that various citizens have been comparing them to the Egyptian papyri.[19] According to a letter by Charlotte Haven, a non-Mormon Nauvoo resident,

> Mr. Joshua Moore ... last Saturday ... brought with him half a dozen thin pieces of brass, apparently very old, in the form of a bell about five or six inches long. They had on them scratches that looked like writing, and strange figures like symbolic characters. They were recently found, he said, in a mound a few miles below Quincy. When he showed them to Joseph, the latter said that the figures or writing on them was similar to that in which the Book of Mormon was written, and if Mr. Moore could leave

---

[17] *Times and Seasons* 4.12 (1 May 1843), pp. 186-87.

[18] William Clayton, *An Intimate Chronicle: The Journals of William Clayton* (ed. George D. Smith; Salt Lake City: Signature Books, 1991), p. 100.

[19] For an analysis and content of the letter, cf. Brian M. Hauglid, '"Come & Help Build the Temple & City": Parley P. and Orson Pratt's May 1843 Letter to John Van Cott', *Mormon Historical Studies* 11.1 (Spring, 2011), pp. 149-58.

them, he thought that by the help of revelation he would be able to translate them.[20]

The fact that several pages of the *History of the Church* (5.372-79) are devoted to the Kinderhook Plates, including facsimiles of them suggests that Smith at least took them seriously enough to begin translating them. In fact, a broadside from the *Nauvoo Neighbor* dated 24 June 1843 may suggest that he did more than just begin, for it carried facsimiles of the plates promising, 'The contents of the Plates, together with a Fac-Simile of the same, will be published in the "Times and Seasons," as soon as the translation is completed'.[21] The entire translation never appears to have been completed.[22]

Unfortunately for those who believed that Smith was accurately 'translating' the Kinderhook Plates, the entire episode proved to be a hoax, conceived by individuals seeking to entrap Smith – as these individuals later admitted over the course of the next few decades.[23] In 1980, tests on the sole remaining plate would verify that the origin of the plates was the nineteenth century.[24]

These examples from the Book of Abraham, the Greek Psalter, and the Kinderhook Plates do not do much to engender confidence in Smith's abilities as a translator but rather complicate the issue. In point of fact, there appears to be no extant verifiable evidence that Smith ever successfully translated any documents into English, outside of the Hebrew assignments he completed in the Hebrew class offered in the School of the Prophets in Kirtland.

---

[20] Charlotte Haven, 'A Girl's Letters from Nauvoo', *Overland Monthly* (December 1890), p. 630. The letter itself is dated May 2, 1843.

[21] For a copy of the broadside cf. Palmer, *An Insider's View of Mormon Origins*, p. 32.

[22] For the idea that by this point Smith's interest in the Kinderhook Plates was purely academic cf. Brian M. Hauglid, 'Did Joseph Smith Translate the Kinderhook Plates?', in Robert L. Millet (ed.), *No Weapon Shall Prosper: New Light on Sensitive Issues* (Provo, UT: Religious Studies Center, Brigham Young University; Salt Lake City: Deseret Book, 2011), pp. 93–103.

[23] Cf. 'A Hoax: Reminiscences of an Old Kinderhook Mystery', *Journal of the Illinois State Historical Society* 5 (July 1912), pp. 271-73, and Welby W. Ricks, 'The Kinderhook Plates', *Improvement Era* 65 (Sept. 1962), pp. 656-58.

[24] Givens, *By the Hand of Mormon*, p. 105.

A Historical Account

Another complication resulting from the traditional story involves its inference (and contemporary claims by Smith and others) that the book is a historical record of the ancient inhabitants of the Americas. Such unbridled claims created an extraordinarily high level of expectation and optimism on the part of early Mormons that the earth would soon unveil discoveries that would confirm the historical authenticity of the Book of Mormon.[25] Owing to the fact that much of the vast literature devoted to the Book of Mormon touches upon this broad topic, no more than a sampling of the relevant topics may be offered. Four categories of evidence that contribute to this complication are briefly described in what follows: archaeology, DNA analyses, historical anachronisms, and signs of nineteenth century composition.

Archaeology

The results of archaeological research has been on the radar screen of those for whom the Book of Mormon functions as Scripture since as early as 1841 when the work of John Lloyd Stephens entitled *Incidents of Travel in Central America, Chipas and Yucatan* (New York, 1841) appeared on the scene, causing such a stir that the *Times and Seasons* (1 October 1842) announced that Zarahemla had been found. From this point, readers of early Mormon literature would regularly be treated to accounts of archaeological developments and discoveries throughout the Americas and beyond. However, it was not until around 1900 that the LDS church formally sanctioned an initial archaeological exploration in an attempt to prove the truthfulness of the Book of Mormon. The team consisted primarily of Benjamin Cluff, Jr, President of Brigham Young Academy, and a number of students. But the expedition encountered problems from the beginning, including the eventual decision by the church to rescind its endorsement of the project. Losing members along the way, the final six remaining explorers would return after two years unable to penetrate into Columbia, their intended destination, owing to the country's internal chaos.[26]

---

[25] Givens, *By the Hand of Mormon*, pp. 96-106.
[26] Givens, *By the Hand of Mormon*, pp. 107-108.

Not long after this attempt, RLDS writer Louis E. Hills would generate studies that stand near the beginning of what has been called the 'Book of Mormon Geography' movement.[27] Though not a working archaeologist – being dependent on the work of others – Hills would be one of the first to change the focus of attention to the Isthmus of Tehuantepec instead of the Isthmus of Panama as the narrow strip of land mentioned in the Book of Mormon, shifting the geographical attention northward.[28]

In 1946 a post in archaeology would be established at Brigham Young University filled by M. Wells Jakeman, who held a PhD in history with some training in anthropology.[29] Jakeman would lead expeditions in an attempt to confirm the location of Bountiful and Zarahemla. His greatest influence amongst Mormon archaeologists would be his identification of Mesoamerica as the region in which Book of Mormon events most likely took place.[30] Thomas Stuart Ferguson, a trained lawyer and amateur archaeologist, who was friends with Jakeman – having accompanied him to Mexico on early archaeological trips, played a pivotal role in establishing the Middle America Archaeological Foundation, later the New World Archaeological Foundation (NWAF), an organization that would do a great deal of well assessed archaeological work. Ferguson secured funding (much of it from the church) and included numerous non-Mormons in the organization. He was enthusiastic as to how the results could vindicate the Book of Mormon and its claims. Though the NWAF gained a good reputation outside Mormon circles, the results of these approaches did not generate the kinds of discoveries with regard to the Book of Mormon for which believers may have hoped. In fact, eventually Ferguson's optimism gave way to despair about the possibility of ever placing the Book of Mormon within a Mesoamerican context and he would apparently lose his faith in the

---

[27] Michael Coe, 'Mormons and Archeology: An Outside View', *Dialogue: A Journal of Mormon Thought* 8.2 (1973), pp. 42-43.

[28] Cf. Lewis E. Hills, *A Short Work on the Geography of Mexico and Central America from 2234 B.C. to 421 A.D.* (Independence, MO: L.E. Hills, 1917) and *Historical Data from Ancient Records and Ruins of Mexico and Central America* (Independence, MO: L.E. Hills, 1919).

[29] John L. Sorenson, 'Voices from the Dust', *Dialogue: A Journal of Mormon Thought* 1.1 (1966), p. 145.

[30] Dee F. Green, 'Book of Mormon Archaeology: The Myths and the Alternatives', *Dialogue: A Journal of Mormon Thought* 4.2 (1969), p. 73.

Book of Mormon and Joseph Smith concluding, 'You can't set Book of Mormon geography down anywhere – because it is fictional and will never meet the requirements of the dirt-archaeology'.[31]

During the same period that some of this work was going on a number of unsubstantiated archaeological claims on the part of overzealous members of the LDS community were being made, including that the Book of Mormon was being used as a field guide for archaeologists at the Smithsonian Institution in Washington, DC. So much so that as early as 1951 the Smithsonian Institution's Office of Anthropology issued a 'Statement Regarding the Book of Mormon' that they would regularly mail to those making enquiries about the matter. The statement would evolve over the years, with each version making many of the same points though sometimes nuanced slightly differently. A couple of points in each version should perhaps be mentioned here. All the versions begin with the following statement:

> The Smithsonian Institution has never used the Book of Mormon in any way as a scientific guide. Smithsonian archeologists see no direct connection between the archeology of the New World and the subject matter of the book.

They would also include something like the following:

> Reports of findings of ancient Egyptian, Hebrew, and other Old World writings in the New World in pre-Columbian contexts have frequently appeared in newspapers, magazines, and sensational books. None of these claims has stood up to examination by reputable scholars. No inscriptions using Old World forms of writing have been shown to have occurred in any part of the Americas before 1492 except for a few Norse rune stones which have been found in Greenland.[32]

---

[31] Stan Larson, 'The Legacy of Thomas Stuart Ferguson', *Dialogue: A Journal of Mormon Thought* 23.1 (1990), p. 79. Cf. esp. Ferguson's statement on problems with the archaeological record and the Book of Mormon in Stan Larson, *Quest for the Gold Plates: Thomas Stuart Ferguson's Archaeological Search for the Book of Mormon* (Salt Lake City: Freethinker Press, 1996), pp. 235-68.

[32] For the 1965 version cf. Jerald and Sandra Tanner, *Archaeology and the Book of Mormon* (Salt Lake City: Modern Microfilm Company, 1969), p. 2; for the 1979 version cf. Givens, *By the Hand of Mormon*, pp. 115-16.

Such proclamations would seem to speak for themselves. Skepticism about Book of Mormon claims was the order of the day for those outside the LDS family of churches.

A similar frustration with unrestrained claims can also be found amongst scholars for whom the book functions as Scripture. For example, in a footnote, John L. Sorenson remarks, 'Most L.D.S. literature on "archeology and the Book of Mormon" ranges from factually and logically unreliable to truly kooky. In general it appears that the worse the book, the more it sells ...'[33]

One of the strongest critiques of Book of Mormon archaeology has come from Mormon archaeologist Dee F. Green who writes:

The first myth we need to eliminate is that Book of Mormon archaeology exists. Titles on books full of archaeological half-truths, dilettanti on the peripheries of American Archaeology calling themselves Book of Mormon archaeologists regardless of their education, and a Department of Archaeology at BYU devoted to the production of Book of Mormon archaeology do not ensure that Book of Mormon archaeology really exists. If one is to study Book of Mormon archaeology, then one must have a corpus of data with which to deal. We do not. The Book of Mormon is really there so one *can* have Book of Mormon studies, and archaeology is really there so one can study archaeology, but the two are not wed. *At least they are not wed in reality since no Book of Mormon location is known with reference to modern topography.* Biblical archaeology can be studied because we do know where Jerusalem and Jericho were and are, but we do not know where Zarahemla and Bountiful (nor any other location for that matter) were or are. It would seem then that a concentration on geography should be the first order of business. But we have already seen that twenty years of such an approach has left us empty-handed ... Rest assured that we are not accumulating a great flood of 'evidence' which will in a few years burst the dam of secular resistance to the Book of Mormon and flood Zion with hordes of people demanding baptism ... We are not about to

---

[33] John L. Sorenson, 'Ancient America and the Book of Mormon Revisited', *Dialogue: A Journal of Mormon Thought* (1969), p. 81 n. 2.

uncover a sign tomorrow or the next day or a year or ten years from now pointing the way to Zarahemla.[34]

While less scathing than Green, non-Mormon archaeologist Michael Coe concludes:

The bare facts of the matter are that nothing, absolutely nothing, has ever shown up in any New World excavation which would suggest to a dispassionate observer that the Book of Mormon, as claimed by Joseph Smith, is a historical document relating to the history of early migrants to our hemisphere.[35]

He advises,

Forget the so-far fruitless quest for the Jaredites, Nephites, Mulekites, and the lands of Zarahemla and Bountiful: there is no more chance of finding them than of discovering the ruins of the bottomless pit described in the Book of Revelations [sic].[36]

Despite the extensive work done by Mormon archaeologists over the last several decades, and his high praise for the work of archaeologists who happen to be Mormon but work on mainstream archaeology projects, Coe's assessment of Book of Mormon archaeology was very much the same thirty-three years later when it comes to the lack of evidence that would convince anyone but the faithful about the claims of the Book of Mormon. Coe says as much in an interview conducted on 16 May 2006 for part of the PBS 'The Mormons' project. His response is sought to the statement, 'There are people at FARMS [Foundation for Ancient Research and Mormon Studies] who believe important archaeological discoveries are in the making. These are very intelligent people. What is it they are resting their hopes on?' Coe responds,

To make Book of Mormon archaeology at all kind of believable, my friend John Sorenson has gone this route: He has compared, in a general way, the civilizations of Mexico and Mesoamerica with the civilizations of the western part of the Old World, and he has made a study of how diffusion happens, really very good

[34] Green, 'Book of Mormon Archaeology: The Myths and the Alternatives', pp. 77-80.
[35] Coe, 'Mormons and Archeology: An Outside View', p. 46.
[36] Coe, 'Mormons and Archeology: An Outside View', p. 48.

diffusion studies. He's tried to build a reasonable picture that these two civilizations weren't all that different from each other. Well, this is true of all civilizations, actually; there's nothing new under the sun.

So he has built up what he hopes is a convincing background in which you can put Book of Mormon archaeology, and he's a very serious, bright guy. But I'm sorry to say that I don't really buy more than a part of this. I don't really think you can argue, no matter how bright you are, that what's said in the Book of Mormon applies to the peoples that we study in Mexico and Central America. That's one way of doing it – to build up a kind of convincing background, a kind of stage set to this – but there's no actors. That's the problem.[37]

In response to the question, 'How would you describe the attitude of most professional historians to orthodox Mormon archaeology?' Coe responds,

One might wonder how my profession in general, the profession of archaeology, has used Book of Mormon archaeology – or let's say archaeology done by Mormons; I always separate these two things out. I think that for the Book of Mormon, even though they [non-Mormon archaeologists] don't know much about the Book of Mormon or Mormonism, they take the whole thing as a complete fantasy, that this is a big waste of time. Nothing can ever come out of it because it's just impossible that this could have happened, because we know what happened to these people. We can read their writings: They're not in reformed Egyptian; they're in Maya.[38]

Even Mormon apologists appear to concede the point that the archaeological record does not bear witness to the Book of Mormon with regard to its claims about the Americas. The words of Givens on this point are representative, '... as Mormons readily

---

[37] 'Interview Michael Coe' (16 May 2006) http://www.pbs.org/mormons/interviews/coe.html. Coe apparently has in mind John Sorenson's *An Ancient American Setting for the Book of Mormon* (Salt Lake City: Deseret Book Co., 1985).

[38] 'Interview Michael Coe' (16 May 2006 http://www.pbs.org/mormons/interviews/coe.html.

admit, not one single archaeological artifact has been found that conclusively establishes a direct connection between the record and any actual culture or civilization of the Western Hemisphere'.[39]

It appears that the issue of archaeology remains a complication to the standard story.[40]

DNA

Near the turn of the twenty-first century, DNA explorations began to be brought to bear on the authenticity of the Book of Mormon. In 2000, Molecular Genealogy Research Group was established, with the backing of philanthropists Ira Fulton and James Sorenson,

---

[39] Givens, *By the Hand of Mormon*, p. 155.

[40] The intense desire for the identification of archaeological evidence for the Book of Mormon may be gauged by the impact of the so-called 'Nahom' discovery on some apologists – a discovery lauded by some as constituting 'the first actual archaeological evidence for the historicity of the Book of Mormon' (Givens, *By the Hand of Mormon*, p. 120). According to 1 Nephi 16.34, Nahom was the name of a place where Ishmael was buried on the Lehite journey and where the direction of the Lehite journey changed course. The archaeological evidence in question comes in the form of three altar inscriptions in South Arabian Script that mention their benefactor, Bi'athar, identified as the grandson of Naw'um, called the Nihmite. Though the place name, Nahom, does not appear in the inscriptions, the mention of the Nihmite tribe is thought to be sufficient evidence to assume that the location itself was called Nahom. Convenient for this view is the fact that a cemetery was found not far from the temple where the altars were located. The date of the finds, thought to be seventh-sixth century BCE, is deemed to be further corroboration for the identification of this site with the Book of Mormon's Nahom. Philologically, it is suggested that the Hebrew word NHM (נחם) lies behind this South Arabian word thus matching the Book of Mormon location Nahom. While several Mormon writers have been quite encouraged and even excited about such evidence [cf. for example, W.P. Aston, 'Newly Found Altars from Nahom', *Journal of Book of Mormon Studies* 10.2 (2001), pp. 56-61 and S.D. Ricks, 'On Lehi's Trail: Nahom, Ishmael's Burial Place', *Journal of Book of Mormon and Other Restoration Scripture* 20.1 (2011), pp. 66-68], not all Book of Mormon students are convinced of this identification. Specifically, the relatively common occurrence of NHM (נחם) in the Hebrew Bible is noted, often in conjunction with an observation about the similarity of Nahom to King James Version Bible names like Nahum, suggesting that the similarity is owing to coincidence more than anything else. It is also noted that since Hebrew vowels are not written in ancient Hebrew, but must be supplied by the reader, and that the consonants NHM (נחם) are at the root of a variety of Hebrew words, one cannot be at all certain if Nihmite and Nahom are actually from the same word. For these interpreters such evidence is more circumstantial or coincidental than real. The idea that this 'Nahom' is 'the first actual archaeological evidence for the historicity of the Book of Mormon' has not generated any traction amongst those for whom the Book of Mormon does not function as Scripture and even for a significant number of individuals for whom it does function in this manner.

in order to connect present and past people groups. Led by BYU Professor Scott Woodward, this multi-million dollar study sought to provide evidence on the relationship between those of Middle Eastern descent and Native America populations. But just as with the archaeological attempts to vindicate the Book of Mormon, the DNA explorations were terribly disappointing to those interested in establishing such a connection.[41] In the words of Professor of Anthropology Thomas W. Murphy,

> So far, DNA research lends no support to the traditional Mormon beliefs about the origins of Native Americans. Instead, genetic data have confirmed that migrations from Asia are the primary source of American Indian origins. This research has substantiated the archaeological, cultural, linguistic, and biological evidence. While DNA shows that ultimately all human populations are rather closely related, to date no intimate genetic link has been found between ancient Israelites and the indigenous peoples of the Americas, much less within the time frame suggested by the Book of Mormon. Therefore, after considering the research in molecular anthropology summarized here, I have concluded that Latter-day Saints should not realistically expect to find validation for the ancient historicity of the Book of Mormon in genetics. My assessment echoes that of geneticist and former LDS Bishop Simon Southerton whose survey of the literature 'failed to find anything that supported migration of Jewish people before Columbus' and 'no reliable scientific evidence supporting migrations from the Middle East to the New World.' [Simon Southerton, 'DNA Genealogies of American Indians and the Book of Mormon' *Salt Lake Tribune* (17 March 2000).][42]

The disappointing nature of the results of such DNA testing has resulted in a tendency among some LDS readers to devalue the importance of such testing and even to dismiss the possibility, suggesting that such testing is virtually impossible to carry out[43] despite the millions of dollars spent to do just that. Despite the disclaimers to

---

[41] Gutjahr, *The Book of Mormon*, pp. 144-45.

[42] Thomas W. Murphy, 'Lamanite Genesis, Genealogy, and Genetics', in Dan Vogel and Brent Lee Metcalfe (eds.), *American Apocrypha: Essays on the Book of Mormon* (Salt Lake City: Signature Books, 2002), pp. 47-48.

[43] Givens, *The Book of Mormon: A Very Short Introduction*, p. 118.

the contrary, such results complicate claims for the Book of Mormon being a historical narrative.

Historical Anachronisms

The presence in the Book of Mormon of a number of historical anachronisms presents another complication to the claims that the book is an ancient historical narrative. The existence of these rather well known challenges were noticed already by 1922 when LDS Church leader and apologist Brigham H. Roberts presented his manuscript, 'Book of Mormon Difficulties: A Study', to the General Authorities of the Church of Jesus Christ of Latter Day Saints. In this work, written in response to a letter received by the Church from a faithful member, Roberts writes an entire chapter entitled, 'Were Domestic Animals – Horses, Asses, Oxen, Cows, Sheep, Swine; Iron and Steel; Swords and Scimeters; Silk, Wheat, Barley, and Wheel Vehicles Known to Native American Races in Pre-Columbian, and within Historic Times?'[44] After carefully working through each of these issues the implications for Roberts are clear in the questions he raises and observations he makes as he closes this portion of his study.

> There can be no question but what the Book of Mormon commits us to the possession and use of domestic animals by both Jaredite and Nephite peoples; and to the age and civilization of iron and steel and of the wheel, and of a written language, by both these peoples ...
>
> What shall our answer be then? Shall we boldly acknowledge the difficulties in the case, confess that the evidences and conclusions of the authorities are against us, but notwithstanding all that, we take our position on the Book of Mormon and place its revealed truths against the declarations of men, however learned, and await the vindication of the revealed truth? Is there any other course than this? And yet the difficulties to this position are very grave. Truly we may ask 'who will believe our report?' in that case ... Will not the hoped for proof deferred indeed make the heart sick?[45]

---

[44] B.H. Roberts, *Studies on the Book of Mormon* (ed. B.D. Madsen; Salt Lake City: Signature Books, 2nd edn, 1992), pp. 95-115.

[45] Roberts, *Studies on the Book of Mormon*, p. 115.

From these words it appears that Roberts felt the weight of the complications such issues present to Book of Mormon claims about being a historical narrative. In the years since Roberts' rather anguished plea for the LDS church to give concerted attention to these vexing issues, the situation has not changed considerably. Though much attention has been focused on these anomalies, the various responses do not appear to have convinced any but the already convinced, as Givens' conclusion seems to reveal, 'While Book of Mormon historicity may be no less controversial now than it was before, the scholars of FARMS and Brigham Young University have at least raised the level of the debate on the subject …'[46]

Signs of Nineteenth-Century Composition

A variety of aspects of the Book of Mormon appear to reveal nineteenth-century thought, language, and content. If such nineteenth-century concerns are found within the Book of Mormon, it suggests that despite claims to the contrary, the Book of Mormon was composed in the nineteenth century and was not an ancient record of events that transpired between 600 BCE and 400 CE. While numerous nineteenth-century details have been identified by a variety of scholars, the section that follows seeks simply to provide an overview of various categories that arise from these investigations.

Theology

Perhaps the first person to point out the way in which nineteenth-century theological concerns are present within the Book of Mormon is the critique offered of the book by Alexander Campbell at the time of the book's appearance. Specifically, amongst his many points of critique Campbell says:

> This prophet Smith, through his stone spectacles, wrote on the plates of Nephi, in his book of Mormon, every error and almost every truth discussed in N. York for the last ten years. He decides all the great controversies – infant baptism, ordination, the trinity, regeneration, repentance, justification, the fall of man, the atonement, transubstantiation, fasting, penance, church government, religious experience, the call to the ministry, the general resurrection, eternal punishment, who may baptize, and even the

---

[46] Cf. the discussion and quote in Givens, *By the Hand of Mormon*, pp. 141-42.

question of freemasonry, republican government, and the rights of man.[47]

In other words, Campbell accuses the Book of Mormon of containing discussions designed to settle contemporary theological controversies of the nineteenth century. Other evangelical nineteenth century theological concerns would later be identified including the nature of 'man', dissenting Anti-Christs, and the relationship between feelings and truth.[48] Still other nineteenth-century theological issues that are said to appear sometimes just under the narrative's surface include Deism, Revivalism, and sectarian discord.[49]

Conversions

As early as 1922, the similarity between Book of Mormon conversion experiences and the conversion experiences of Joseph Smith and fellow Mormons in the 1830s was recognized by B.H. Roberts. Offering a comprehensive survey of the Book of Mormon conversions, Roberts observes:

> Thus throughout the Book of Mormon, from first to last, and among both its distinct peoples both Jaredites and Nephites, and in widely separated periods of time and of place, are to be found these hysterical religious extravagancies of both speech and action. Traces of the same may be found in the experiences of Joseph Smith.[50]

Roberts goes on to trace these experiences amongst the faithful in Kirtland (pp. 295-98) and then in the life and ministry of Jonathan Edwards in particular (pp. 298-306). Additionally, he surveys episodes from the ministry of John Wesley and George Whitfield among others (pp. 309-19) asking the question, and providing some reflection on, whether it is likely that the influence of these 'ultra-Protestant leaders' would be reflected in the Book of Mormon as well. In the reflection that followed on this question the answer to the question would suggest it be offered in the affirmative.

---

[47] *Millennial Harbinger* (February 7, 1831).

[48] Palmer, *An Insider's View of Mormon Origins*, pp. 119-33

[49] Luffman, *The Book of Mormon's Witness to Its First Readers*, pp. 63-68.

[50] Roberts, *Studies of the Book of Mormon*, p. 295.

A careful comparison of conversion in the nineteenth-century Methodist camp meetings, their conversion styles, and even their preaching styles with specific Book of Mormon texts reveals remarkable similarities. Among the more prominent Book of Mormon texts that seem to fit this pattern are: Enos 4; Mosiah 1-6, 27; Alma 17-19; 21-22; 36; and Helaman 5.[51]

Literary Forms

It is sometimes argued that the Book of Mormon reveals literary features that would be picked up on by a nineteenth-century audience, with the implication being that such devices would be intentionally used by a nineteenth-century author. These literary features normally include the following: narrator commentary (which underscores the historical reliability of the author's account), spiritualizing the narratives (as opposed to a very literalistic interpretation), typology (the language of 'type and shadow' being characteristic of nineteenth century interpretation), conventional narrative forms (the presence of formulaic expressions as well as a set of sequence events within the plot), biblical parallels.[52] According to Luffman, these are used to address issues of concern amongst disaffected nineteenth-century religious seekers and readers.[53]

The Enchanted World

As is widely acknowledged the Book of Mormon was written in the context of belief in an 'Enchanted World' in which magical practices were often seen as residing within the broader world of religion and contact with the supernatural.[54] As noted earlier, much of the Book of Mormon was 'translated' by means of a seer stone, a stone that Smith had earlier used in his attempt to find buried treasure, as

---

[51] Cf. esp. Thomas, *Reclaiming Book of Mormon Narratives: Digging in Cumorah*, pp. 123-47; Palmer, *An Insider's View of Mormon Origins*, pp. 96-118; and Luffman, *The Book of Mormon's Witness to Its First Readers*, pp. 164-77.

[52] Thomas, *Reclaiming Book of Mormon Narratives: Digging in Cumorah*, pp. 5-19, and Luffman (*The Book of Mormon's Witness to Its First Readers*, pp. 46-58) who builds off Thomas' work.

[53] Luffman, *The Book of Mormon's Witness to Its First Readers*, p. 35.

[54] Givens (*The Book of Mormon: A Very Short Introduction*, p. 115) notes, '... it is undeniably the case that folk magic, slippery treasures, and emotionally extravagant reactions to conversion all make their appearance in the Book of Mormon and in the popular culture of Joseph Smith's day'.

well as the plates themselves.[55] Much has been written on the magical world in which the Book of Mormon appeared.[56] In this section attention will be given to places within the Book of Mormon that are said to contain or imply this nineteenth-century phenomenon.

Three categories of evidence of the enchanted world from the Book of Mormon are here offered. First, it might not come as a complete surprise to find within the Book of Mormon a reference to a stone of revelation within the context of Alma's words to Helaman about the twenty-four plates of the Jaredites (Alma 37.23). Specifically, of this stone it is said,

> And the Lord said, I will prepare unto my servant Gazelem, a stone, which shall shine forth in darkness unto light, that I may discover unto my people which serve me, that I may discover unto them the works of their brethren; yea, their secret works, their works of darkness, and their wickedness and abominations. And now my son, these directors [later 'interpreters'] were prepared, that the word of God might be fulfilled ...

It is suggested that the function of this stone is similar to the use of the stone of scrying in magic.[57]

In words spoken in the context of the discovery of the twenty-four plates, reference is made to instruments called 'interpreters' which are considered a gift from God to be used only by the seer whom God choses. As Ammon explains to the king,

> I can assuredly tell thee, O king, of a man that can translate records; for he has wherewith that he can look, and translate all records that are of ancient date; that it is a gift from God. And the things are called interpreters and no man can look in them except he be commanded, lest he should look for that he ought not and he should perish. And whosoever is commanded to look in them, the same is called seer (Mosiah 8.13-14).

---

[55] Luffman, *The Book of Mormon's Witness to Its First Readers*, p. 82.

[56] For the most comprehensive work on this topic cf. D. Michael Quinn, *Early Mormonism and the Magic World View* (Salt Lake City: Signature Books, rev. and enlarged edn, 1998). Cf. also Luffman, *The Book of Mormon's Witness to Its First Readers*, pp. 77-88.

[57] Quinn, *Early Mormonism and the Magic World View*, p. 174.

Mosiah will go on to transfer these interpreters to Alma (Mosiah 28.20).[58]

A second feature of the enchanted world found in the Book of Mormon has to do with the idea that hidden treasures in the earth could become slippery and though one could be near to its location, the treasure could actually slip away. This understanding of slipperiness is exhibited in Samuel's prophecy about those who fail to repent.

> Yea, in that day ye shall say: O that we had remembered the Lord our God in the day that he gave us our riches, and then they would not have become slippery that we should lose them; for behold our riches are gone from us. Behold, we lay a tool here and tomorrow it is gone; and behold, our swords are taken from us in the day we have sought them for battle. Yea, we have hid up our treasures and they have slipped away from us, because of the curse of the land. O that we had repented in the day that the word of the Lord came unto us; for behold, the land is cursed, and all things are become slippery, and we cannot hold them (Helaman 13.33b-36).

The fulfillment of the Helaman passage just cited appears to occur in Mormon 1.18.

> And these Gadianton robbers, who were among the Lamanites, did infest the land, insomuch that the inhabitants thereof began to hide up their treasures in the earth; and they became slippery, because the Lord had cursed the land, that they could not hold them, nor retain them again.[59]

In both passages this slipperiness comes because the Lord had cursed the land.

A third category of evidence of the enchanted world in the Book of Mormon comes with reference to what scholars have called 'second sight', to see with visionary or spiritual eyes.[60] References to aspects of such 'second sight' are found at various places in the Book of Mormon. One of the examples of such a phenomenon is

---

[58] Luffman, *The Book of Mormon's Witness to Its First Readers*, p. 83.

[59] On this idea cf. Quinn, *Early Mormonism and the Magic World View*, p. 196.

[60] Scherer, *The Journey of a People: The Era of Restoration, 1820 to 1844*, p. 109.

expressed by the words 'me thinks' or 'me thought' to mean something like 'it seemed to me', 'I thought I saw', or 'it seems that I saw'. Such expressions indicate a distinction between spiritual sight and natural sight.[61] These words are found in at least three places in the Book of Mormon. A description of Lehi's initial visionary experience includes the phrase:

> and being thus overcome with the spirit, he was carried away in a vision, even that he saw the Heavens open; and he thought he saw God sitting upon his throne, surrounded with numberless concourses of angels in the attitude of singing and praising their God (1 Nephi 1.8).

Later in 1 Nephi 8.4, in a description of Lehi's dream of the tree, a similar expression occurs, 'for, behold, me thought I saw a dark and dreary wilderness'. When Alma recounts his conversion to his son Helaman, the expression occurs again, with reference to his own visionary experience.

> yea, and methought I saw even as our father Lehi saw, God sitting upon his throne, surrounded with numberless concourses of angels, in the attitude of singing and praising our God; yea, and my soul did long to be there (Alma 36.22).

The visionary dimension of such sight is clear to detect, as is the reference back to Lehi's foundational vision.

Other aspects of spiritual sight in the Book of Mormon are conveyed by the phrase an 'eye of faith', which in Alma 5.14-25 appears to be paired with an imaginative viewing of the future day of judgment and in Alma 32.40-41 to looking forward to the future fruit of faith. The 'eye of faith' also occurs near the end of the Book of Mormon (Ether 12.19-20) where it is used to distinguish between the 'eye of faith' and sight in a vision.

> And there were many whose faith was so exceeding strong even before Christ came, which could not be kept from within the veil, but truly saw with their eyes the things which they had beheld with an eye of faith, and they were glad ... one of these was the brother of Jared: for so great was his faith in God, that when God put forth his finger, he could not hide it from the sight of

[61] Thomas, *Reclaiming Book of Mormon Narratives: Digging in Cumorah*, p. 56.

the brother of Jared, because of his word which he had spoken unto him, which word he had obtained by faith.[62]

Such nineteenth century language and thought found within the Book of Mormon presents another complication to the standard story.[63]

Literature

Various pieces of literature appearing in or around the nineteenth century have sometimes been identified as being found or reflected in some sense in the Book of Mormon. It almost goes without saying that the most obvious complication with regard to the presence of nineteenth-century literary references within the Book of Mormon is the clear influence and multiple direct quotations of the KJV Bible. Not only does the KJV influence the language of the Book of Mormon narrative, but extensive quotations of the KJV also raise a host of questions about its presence in an ancient document that claims to have its origins in records that predate the KJV anywhere from just over one to just over two millennia. This conundrum illustrates something of the complication presented by nineteenth-century literary references within the book.[64]

Prominent among nineteenth-century literature that may have influenced the composition of the Book of Mormon to one intent or another is Ethan Smith's *A View of the Hebrews; or the Tribes of Isra-*

---

[62] On all this cf. Thomas, *Reclaiming Book of Mormon Narratives: Digging in Cumorah*, pp. 56-60. With regard to varying aspects of vision within the Book of Mormon, Thomas notes, 'In practice, mundane vision, visionary vision, imaginary vision, and metaphorical vision are each present and tend to blend together in the Book of Mormon'.

[63] The issue of 'second sight' has been utilized by some in assessing the testimony of the three and eight witnesses found within the Book of Mormon. Cf. esp. Palmer, *An Insider's View of Mormon Origins*, pp. 175-213.

[64] For some of the complications presented by the appearance of KJV quotations in the Book of Mormon cf. Hardy, *Understanding the Book of Mormon*, pp. 69, 194, 255, 261, 291 n. 26 and n. 31, 303 n. 38, 313 n. 24 and n. 25, and 323 n. 5. Cf. also David P. Wright, 'Isaiah in the Book of Mormon: Or Joseph Smith in Isaiah', in Dan Vogel and Brent Lee Metcalf (eds.), *American Apocrypha: Essays on the Book of Mormon* (Salt Lake City: Signature Books, 2002), pp. 157-234, and Wunderli, *An Imperfect Book*, pp. 68-77. As acknowledged by Hardy (p. 323 n. 5), 'the most comprehensive list in print of biblical phrases in the Book of Mormon' continues to be the work of Jerald and Sandra Tanner, *Joseph Smith's Plagiarism of the Bible in the Book of Mormon* – Includes *Covering Up the Black Hole in the Book of Mormon* (Salt Lake City: Utah Lighthouse Ministry, rev. and exp. edn, 2010).

el in America, which was published in 1823 with a second edition appearing two years later in 1825. Reverend Smith was pastor of a Congregationalist Church in Poultney, VT, where Oliver Cowdery, Joseph's scribe, lived for over twenty years leaving in 1825. In point of fact, Cowdery's stepmother and three of his sisters were members of Ethan Smith's church from 1821-1826. In 1827 it appears that Rev. Smith even visited Palmyra where he apparently received mail at the Palmyra Post Office (according to the *Wayne Sentinel* January 5, 1827).[65]

Concerns over the relationship between Ethan Smith's *View of the Hebrews* and the Book of Mormon were so pervasive that by 1927, B.H. Roberts had developed an extensive 'parallel' between these works. According to Roberts the eighteen parallels he identifies could have been multiplied by a factor of four. These parallels include: similarities between their places of publication, the place of the American Indians in the title, attention to the origins of the American Indians, the similarities between a lost book and a revealed one (respectively), the transmission of sacred records, the presence of Urim and Thummim as well as a breastplate, the presence of Egyptian Hieroglyphics, the inclusion of two classes of people – barbarous and civilized, the destruction of Jerusalem, the scattering and restoration of Israel, the importance of the Book of Isaiah, the great American Gentile nation that will save Israel, the love of riches and pride, the foolishness of polygamy, Native American virtues, civilization in America, and the presence of the Messiah or Quetzalcotle in the Americas.[66] Roberts concluded that this book among others was 'either possessed by Joseph Smith or certainly known by him' and that this 'common knowledge' was set forth for him 'in almost handbook form in the little work of Ethan Smith *View of the Hebrews*'.[67] Roberts goes on to observe,

> It will appear in what is to follow that such 'common knowledge' did exist in New England; that Joseph Smith was in contact with it; that one book, at least, with which he was most likely acquainted, could well have furnished structural outlines for the

[65] Roberts, *Studies of the Book of Mormon*, pp. 27-28. Interestingly, here Roberts identifies Cowdery as Smith's cousin.

[66] Roberts, *Studies of the Book of Mormon*, pp. 323-44.

[67] Roberts, *Studies of the Book of Mormon*, pp. 153-54.

Book of Mormon, and that Joseph Smith was possessed of such creative imaginative powers as would make it within the lines of possibility that the Book of Mormon could have been produced in that way.[68]

The issue here is not one of plagiarism,[69] but rather possible evidence of the presence of nineteenth-century literature in the Book of Mormon.

Though other pieces of nineteenth-literature are sometimes identified, *View of the Hebrews* is a helpful representative of this phenomenon.[70]

Concluding Remarks on Complications

As any one familiar with the literature knows, this chapter merely scratches the surface of this issue. Entire volumes have been and continue to be written on the origins of the Book of Mormon. A more extensive survey would reveal other categories of complications as well as numbers of studies that seek to answer and/or engage specific aspects of the complications described, as well as those that offer whole theories of origins by insiders and outsiders alike. It should also be observed that not all of these complications are of equal weight nor are they equally problematic for the stand-

---

[68] Roberts, *Studies of the Book of Mormon*, p. 154.

[69] Part of the argument against plagiarism is the fact that a 1842 article in the *Times and Seasons*, of which Smith would have had editorial oversight, quoted *View of the Hebrews* in support of the authenticity of the Book of Mormon, though the quote came from a 1833 version, which appeared three years after the Book of Mormon. Cf. Givens, *By the Hand of Mormon*, p. 161.

[70] Grant Palmer has more recently pointed to E.T.A. Hoffmann's 'The Golden Pot' as another nineteenth-century piece of literature with tantalizing parallels to the Book of Mormon story of origin. 'The Golden Pot' first appeared in German in 1814 and in English in 1827. Palmer suggests that it is possible that one of Joseph Smith's associates, Luman Walters, introduced Smith to the work. Similarities include angelic visitations, the call to translate ancient texts, multiple visits by the messenger, being distracted by the thought of riches, the messenger being his people's last archivist, being chastised for disobedience, visits to the archives at the time of the Fall Equinox, access to the appointed place, being given automatic access, viewing of Egyptian artifacts, encountering a seer's device, the reception of the ancient records on the Fall Equinox, describing the records the characters of which are unknown, translation by inspiration, and the production of a most perfect book. For a discussion of these parallels cf. Palmer, *An Insider's View of Mormon Origins*, pp. 135-74.

ard story of origins. The categories presented here are those that appear to be amongst the most significant complications to the standard story with regard to the book's origins. It is an attempt to acquaint the readers of this volume with various dimensions of this knotty problem. What has been presented is not an attempt to have the final word on any one of these issues but rather to raise them for the reader to indicate something of the starkness of the complications to the standard story they represent. Hopefully, their rehearsal here will generate helpful conversations amongst those interested in this topic regardless of their dispositions on its resolution.

38

A TAXONOMY OF RESPONSES TO THE COMPLICATIONS OF THE STANDARD STORY

This somewhat brief final chapter is designed to trace the different genre of responses to the complications of the standard story that has emerged over the past few years. No attempt is made here to answer the questions raised by the complications, but rather the chapter's purpose is to acquaint the reader with how various students of the book have responded in general to the issues of origins and the Book of Mormon itself in the light of these complications. At least one example of each genre is cited for illustrative purposes.

The Book of Mormon Is What It Claims to Be Despite any Complications and Will Be Vindicated as Such

Despite the complications to the standard story with regard to Book of Mormon origins, numerous individuals and groups have continued to argue that the book is indeed the translation of an ancient historical record and that ultimately the book will be vindicated as such. One of the better-known groups to advocate such a position and response was the Foundation for Ancient Research and Mormon Studies (FARMS). This institute emerged at a time when more liberal approaches and attitudes toward the Book of Mormon were being advocated by a variety of individuals, which coincided with an emerging openness on the part of some in the LDS Church to historical enquiry related to the book's and church's origins. This openness was typified, to a certain extent, by LDS church historian

Leonard Arrington. Unfortunately for Arrington – and others who shared his attitude of transparency with regard to historical documents, the LDS leadership responded by initiating a program of retrenchment with regard to issues of historicity and literalistic interpretation as it related to the Book of Mormon. Arrington would lose his position, or be promoted out of it. FARMS would emerge as a great ally in the church's response to the perceived threat of liberalism. FARMS was founded in 1979 by Jack Welch, a recent addition to the Brigham Young University Law Faculty. By 1997 FARMS would become a formal part of Brigham Young University. The Foundation would be transformed from a stand-alone entity into part of what would become the Maxwell Institute on the campus of Brigham Young University in 2006. Eventually the work of FARMS would be assimilated into the Maxwell Institute, with its imprint retired over time. According to one admirer, the Foundation 'unabashedly operates on the assumption that the Book of Mormon presents us with a historical record'.[1]

The Foundation's approach to the complications with regard the standard story, as well as other complications for the Book of Mormon, was both to respond to any academic (and some popular) work that might reflect negatively upon the Book of Mormon and its historical claims and to address a variety of issues related to the book. Topics of FARMS publications were wide ranging including Book of Mormon archaeology, geography, system of law, Smith's approach to the translation of the Golden Plates, and all manner of individual points of the book's interpretation. Parallels of all sorts were identified in the pages of the Foundation's extraordinarily large corpus of work. Something of the commitment of FARMS contributors to the historicity of the Book of Mormon can be gauged by the tone exhibited in some of its publications with the work of scholars who were perceived to have made interpretive moves deemed to be outside the boundaries of acceptable views. Whether such views came from insiders or outsiders, the tone of some of these responses was hard-hitting, even inflammatory. Though the publications of the Foundation (and its heirs) are voluminous and far-reaching in addressing an enormous array of issues related to the historicity of the Book of Mormon, its influence

---

[1] Givens, *By the Hand of Mormon*, p. 125.

has seldom reached beyond the world of its primarily LDS readership to convince many of those who have explored a variety of the
aforementioned complications to the standard story. Despite its
limited outside influence, the work of the Foundation is a prime
example of readers who have not been convinced that the complications call for a modification of the primary tenets laid out in the
standard story.

Perhaps the most well known individual example of this response to the complications with the standard story is the work of
Terryl L. Givens, Bostwick Professor of English and Professor of
Religion at the University of Richmond in Virginia.[2] Despite being a
professor of literature, Givens' work is primarily historical in orientation. While raising a number of tough questions with regard to the
Book of Mormon, Givens offers an unrelenting apology for the
book and its 'translator', often drawing heavily on the work of
FARMS as evidence that this or that problematic aspect of the book
has been convincingly resolved. Not only does Givens respond to
the various tough questions he raises, but he also offers criticism –
on occasion rather scathing criticism – of scholars who propose
other ways of responding to such questions. Even those who propose more literary approaches to the book as a way forward are
sometimes criticized for a perceived de-emphasis of the book's historicity. For Givens, the Book of Mormon stands or falls with the
author and 'translator', Joseph Smith; there is simply no way around
the historical issues. According to Givens, one must align oneself
with Joseph Smith and his claims about the book in order to read it
properly. Other approaches are seen as diversions that encourage a
de-emphasis of understanding the book as a translation of an ancient record. Though Givens laments the fact that relatively few
scholars, inside or outside of Mormonism, have given attention to
the actual content of the Book of Mormon, he eventually observes
that he believes only those who agree with Mormon claims with
regard to Smith's role in the reception, translation, and production
of the book have a right, or should be in a position to offer such
comment.[3] In the end, despite his laments with regard to content,

---

[2] Cf. Givens, *By the Hand of Mormon* and *The Book of Mormon: A Very Short Introduction*.

[3] Cf. esp. his discussion in Givens, *By the Hand of Mormon*, pp. 175-84.

Givens makes clear that the Book of Mormon's function as sacred sign – to be believed – is more significant than its content. In Givens, those who do not believe the complications to the standard story of origins raise to the level of demanding a modification their reading strategy of the book have a leading spokesperson. More literarily sophisticated than many of the FARMS contributors, Givens' work as an apologist for the Book of Mormon makes use of numerous FARMS studies in his unwavering advocacy for the book.

The Book of Mormon as 'Non'-historical

A recent proposal from one whose work consistently assumes the historicity of the Book of Mormon suggests that a pre-occupation with the Book of Mormon as either historical or unhistorical is a smoke screen of sorts that obscures the more basic nature of the book. According to Joseph M. Spencer,

> On my argument, the Book of Mormon must be regarded as neither historical nor unhistorical, but as *non-historical*. This is not to suggest that the events it records did not happen. On the contrary, it is to claim that it must be subtracted from the dichotomy of the historical/unhistorical because the faithful reader testifies that the *events* – rather than the *history* – recorded in the book not only took place, but are of infinite, typological importance. Any enclosure of the Book of Mormon within a totalized world history amounts to a denial of the book's unique claim on the attention of the whole world. In the end, then, to take the Book of Mormon as *either* historical or unhistorical may be to miss the nature of the book entirely. Both positions in the debate about Book of Mormon historicity – whether critical or apologetic – are founded on a common, backwards belief. The historicity *of the Book of Mormon* is not in question. Rather, as Alma makes clear, it is the Book of Mormon that calls the historicity *of the individual* into question.[4]

Such a proposal is based in part on Spencer's typological investigation of the book where he finds that again and again conversion

---

[4] Spencer, *An Other Testament: On Typology*, p. 28.

realizes itself '*precisely in the act of reading*'. For Spencer, 'In the end, scriptural reading – serious, typological reading of scripture – *is* conversion'[5] in that the Book of Mormon is viewed as a gift of grace the acceptance of which is that 'one is already converted as one begins to read it, precisely in that one begins to read it'.[6] To read the Book of Mormon convertingly is to read it typologically, which makes a place for both a Nephite reading of the book that focuses on the eschatological fulfillment of the Abrahamic covenant and an Abinadite reading that focuses on more of a devotional typology. Spencer concludes, 'The Book of Mormon, read this way, will typologically and salvifically rewrite not only the reader's individual history, but the history of the whole world'.[7] Thus the task ahead is 'to read the Book of Mormon for what it says it is. This strange book – this other testament – still remains, for the most part, to be read'.[8] Thus, Spencer advocates a reading strategy that in some sense sets aside the historical questions to focus on the way the book defines itself and suggests the way(s) in which it should be read.

The Book of Mormon Bears the Marks of the Nineteenth Century and Must Be Explained – at least in part – in that Light

A growing number of individuals find the evidence of a nineteenth-century provenance for the Book of Mormon as too great to ignore and have sought to explore the book in this light. Significantly, a great deal of variety exists in such approaches spanning from those which continue to affirm the place of the Book of Mormon as Scripture to those who are convinced that the book is a nineteenth-century fiction. Four of these explorations are considered in what follows.

---

[5] Spencer, *An Other Testament: On Typology*, p. 27.

[6] Spencer, *An Other Testament: On Typology*, p. 28.

[7] Spencer, *An Other Testament: On Typology*, p. 175.

[8] Spencer, *An Other Testament: On Typology*, p. 175.

Identification of the Role of Joseph Smith in the Production of the Book of Mormon – Redaction Criticism

One of the conclusions that some interpreters have drawn about the Book of Mormon in the light of its apparent nineteenth-century provenance is that if the book is to be regarded as Scripture then one must account for the presence of nineteenth-century elements found within the book. One of the more prominent approaches is the attempt to explore the book in such a way so as to identify Joseph Smith's contribution to the work. Biblical scholars might see similarities between this method and redaction criticism where the role of the editor, or redactor, is the primary focus of attention.

One such approach comes from Dale E. Luffman, Community of Christ scholar and Apostle, who states,

> My prayerful study and reflection on the Book of Mormon text, and on the cultural context in which it was introduced, leads me to the conclusion that Joseph Smith and his environment contributed to both the language and content of this book of scripture ... In referring to Joseph Smith as the author of the Book of Mormon [as does the book's title page], I am recognizing the mix of varied influences that contributed to his development of the text. These include cultural and social influences as well as what is commonly called divine inspiration. Any attempt to describe the entire book or any specific parts of it as being of either divine or human origin is both fruitless and impossible. As with other scriptural texts, it is precisely the combination of the divine and the human that allows the text to speak powerfully to readers in diverse situations.[9]

Luffman is convinced that it is just this combination that spoke so effectively to those who first heard the book's message in the early nineteenth century. It is protest literature designed to speak to those on the margins. By examining its nineteenth-century language, literary forms, sources against which it speaks, and even the enchanted world from which it arises, the meaning of the Book of Mormon becomes even more powerful than in readings that ignore such internal characteristics, or 'spectacles for interpretation'. Such an interpretive approach results in a significant engagement with the

---

[9] Luffman, *The Book of Mormon's Witness to Its First Readers*, pp. 28-29.

theological content of the Book of Mormon. According to Luffman, taking the book's nineteenth-century provenance seriously is essential and enables one to take the Book of Mormon seriously as Scripture. Luffman insists that rather than resulting in a devaluation of the book, this approach allows the book to take its place amongst other writings as Scripture.

Identification of the Role of Joseph Smith in the Production of the Book of Mormon – Intertextuality

One of the more influential attempts to explain the role of Joseph Smith in the composition of the Book of Mormon, while maintaining a view of the book as Scripture, was proposed in 1987 by Blake T. Ostler.[10] He writes,

> It is my purpose ... to offer a theory of the Book of Mormon as Joseph Smith's expansion of an ancient work by building on the work of earlier prophets to answer the nagging problems of his day. In so doing, he provided unrestrictive and authoritative commentary, interpretation, explanation, and clarifications based on insights from the ancient Book of Mormon text and the King James Bible (KJV). The result is a modern world view and theological understanding superimposed on the Book of Mormon text from the plates.[11]

Ostler seeks to accomplish his purpose by arguing for the antiquity of various features of the Book of Mormon whilst acknowledging numerous aspects that appear to be clear signs of a nineteenth century composition. Appealing to form criticism, Ostler concludes that ancient prophetic call forms, ancient Israelite covenant renewal rituals and forms, and formal Hebrew legal procedures represent an ancient source which may be identified as such in the Book of Mormon. By this means he argues that the book cannot simply be considered to be a nineteenth-century composition. At the same time, Ostler acknowledges that there are various nineteenth-century elements evident in the Book of Mormon, elements which Joseph

---

[10] Blake T. Ostler, 'The Book of Mormon as a Modern Expansion of an Ancient Source', *Dialogue: A Journal of Mormon Thought* 20.1 (1987), pp. 66-123. Cf. also Blake T. Ostler, 'Updating the Expansion Theory', *Times and Seasons*. http:// timesandseasons.org/index.php/2005/04/updating-the-expansion-theory/.

[11] Ostler, 'The Book of Mormon as a Modern Expansion of an Ancient Source', p. 66.

Smith knowingly and unknowingly brought to the text, including quotations of the KJV. Through what Ostler describes as a creative co-participatory model of revelation, 'Joseph Smith gave us not merely the words of the Book of Mormon prophets, but also the true meaning of the text within a nineteenth-century thought-world'.[12] Ostler's proposal appears wrongly understood if it is thought to be an attempt to separate tradition from redaction – that is to separate the ancient elements from what Smith brings to the text. Rather, Ostler seems to anticipate an 'intertextual' interpretive approach by viewing Smith's revelatory experience as a transformational one that draws upon all the experiences that Joseph Smith brings to those revelatory moments resulting in 'the true meaning of the text within a nineteenth-century thought-world' in more of a seamless fashion.

The Book of Mormon as Prophetic Parable
A different kind of response stakes out a position that retains a belief in the Book of Mormon as Scripture whilst taking seriously the signs that the book is a product of the nineteenth century. Rejecting the idea that the Book of Mormon is to be understood as a work of ancient history, this view proposes that the book is intended to be taken as a prophetic parable, a move that allows one's testimony about the Book of Mormon to remain in tact despite a variety of 'historical' complications. On this view the Book of Mormon is identified as an example of the utopian vision literary genre. Community of Christ author Andrew Bolton has proposed,

> Instead of conservative and liberal preoccupations with origins of the Book of Mormon I want to advocate for a third way – that of taking seriously the Book of Mormon in terms of its evangelistic proclamation of Christ, and its teachings on faithful discipleship and radical social justice. I want to suggest that the Book of Mormon describes glimpses of the kingdom of God on earth, or to put it another way, gives accounts of religiously inspired utopia.[13]

---

[12] Ostler, 'The Book of Mormon as a Modern Expansion of an Ancient Source', p. 107.

[13] Andrew Bolton, 'Utopian Vision and Prophetic Imagination: Reading the Book of Mormon in a Nineteenth-century Context', in Peter A. Judd (ed.), *Restoration Studies: Theology and Culture in the Community of Christ and the Latter Day Saint*

On this view, 'The Book of Mormon, whilst set in the past – like a historical novel, is not about ancient history: rather it is about criticizing the present by dreaming of a better world in the future'.[14] For example, in Smith's story, native peoples of America through the characters of the Lamanites are deemed worthy of respect, in stark contrast to the 'genocidal practices of most European descendants as the frontier moved west'.[15] Similarly, the utopia of the Book of Mormon includes just treatment for the poor.[16] When the utopia envisioned finally comes in the Book of Mormon it only lasts for around 200 years before dystopia of various sorts occur where rival peoples of common ancestry destroy one another, reinforcing the fact that one must follow Jesus or wind up destroying oneself.[17] According to Bolton,

> ... only utopian imagination can help us envision new, more just, less violent, and sustainable ways of living ... In this way the Book of Mormon is a parable, a dream, an inspired prophetic imagination, to help us hope ... and work for a better day. The utopian vision in the Book of Mormon is like an icon that points beyond itself to something more – the possibility of the kingdom of God on earth.[18]

Bolton concludes,

> Nowhere does the Book of Mormon say to dig in archeological sites to find the truth of its message – for truth is not there. The only promise of establishing the spiritual truth of the Book of Mormon is to be found by reading Moroni 10:4-5; that is to pray, having faith in Christ. The answer to openness and prayer is the testimony of the Holy Spirit that following Christ fully is

---

Movement Volume X (Independence, MO: Community of Christ Seminary Press, 2009), p. 144.

[14] Bolton, 'Utopian Vision and Prophetic Imagination', p. 147.

[15] Bolton, 'Utopian Vision and Prophetic Imagination', p. 148.

[16] Bolton, 'Utopian Vision and Prophetic Imagination', p. 149.

[17] Bolton, 'Utopian Vision and Prophetic Imagination', p. 150.

[18] Bolton, 'Utopian Vision and Prophetic Imagination', p. 151. According to Bolton a contemporary utopian vision would include 'full inclusion of women with equal voice and ministry' (p. 152).

the key to a better world – for that is the message of this book of scripture.[19]

For Bolton the Book of Mormon is a prophetic parable that has a self-authenticating nature and to treat it as needing archaeological and historical affirmation is to misunderstand the nature of the Book of Mormon itself at a very deep level.

The Book of Mormon Is the Result of Joseph Smith's Imaginative Mind

Still another genre of responses to the complications with the standard story is found amongst those who by-pass the need to re-gard the Book of Mormon as Scripture altogether and regard Smith as the author, not the translator of the book. Among the many, var-ied attempts to explain the phenomenon of Joseph Smith and the Book of Mormon in this fashion, the example chosen for inclusion here is the work of Dan Vogel, a historian who would leave his LDS faith for atheism, owing in part to the cumulative weight of the complications surrounding Smith and his claims for the Book of Mormon.

Vogel, who has immersed himself in the primary literature of early Mormonism, seeks to explain Smith's Book of Mormon by reading it in the light of Smith's nineteenth-century context. Es-chewing supernatural explanations given for the book's origins, Vo-gel concentrates on what can be known and/or deduced about Smith's work from a variety of sources. Though others would seek to explain the book on similar grounds, Vogel's attempt appears to be the most ambitious one. Set forth in his award winning biog-raphy, *Joseph Smith: The Making of a Prophet*,[20] Vogel offers one of the more extensive readings of the Book of Mormon to date, a reading in which he seeks to explicate the book's contents in the light of Smith's life experience and nineteenth-century environment. In many ways, this analysis might be characterized as a 'historical-critical' reading. In his own words Vogel says,

In writing this biography, I did not want to provide a simple chronological narrative of Smith's early life. Rather, I intended to consider the psychological implications of Smith's actions and

---

[19] Bolton, 'Utopian Vision and Prophetic Imagination', p. 152.

[20] Vogel, *Joseph Smith: The Making of a Prophet*.

beliefs and get as close to the man as possible. Thus, I have written an interpretive biography of an emotional and intellectual life.[21]

Regarding the Book of Mormon as a 'pious fraud', Vogel attempts to take seriously Smith's religious convictions whilst explaining Smith's own development – and that of the Book of Mormon itself – in naturalistic terms. For example, Vogel argues that for Smith there was a fine line – and connection – between his use of a seer stone to find hidden treasures and his use of the same stone in his work of translation and spiritual discernment. Sometimes Smith's work involved misleading customers and/or readers for their own benefit. Thus, Vogel adopts the language 'pious deceiver' or 'sincere fraud'.

Of special significance for Vogel's analysis are the many contemporary theological topics being debated during Smith's lifetime. Specifically, the doctrine of universalism, which held sway over many, receives a great deal of attention in particular, owing to the fact that it seems to have divided the Smith family at various points. Vogel points to the many Book of Mormon passages that 'correct' or at least disagree with such a theological orientation, as well as arguing for compromise positions taken in an attempt to speak to individuals in his life who were on different sides of this issue. This includes especially his father's religious and theological differences with the rest of the family.

Another issue of significance in Vogel's assessment is the complicated nature of the Smith family dynamics more generally. Utilizing family systems theory, Vogel describes the way in which a variety of Book of Mormon characters are influenced by and constructed in the light of various Smith family members, among others. Throughout his work Vogel alerts the readers to the historical development of Smith's life during the time the Book of Mormon is being composed, often pointing to the way in which he believes the former influenced the latter. Vogel notes,

I am in fact interested in the cultural and environmental influences on the Book of Mormon, and I will bring them to the

---

[21] Vogel, *Joseph Smith: The Making of a Prophet*, p. xvii.

reader's attention whenever applicable, but I am mostly interested in Smith's state of mind.[22]

Thus for Vogel, the prophet puzzle of Joseph Smith and his writing of the Book of Mormon must be approached in a fashion that gives attention to Smith's context from which the book emerges. As such, Vogel is an example of one of the contemporary responses to the complications with the standard story with regard to the origin of the Book of Mormon.

A Final Word on Responses to the Complications to the Standard Story of Book of Mormon Origins

In the taxonomy of responses to the complications to the standard story of Book of Mormon origins surveyed above, the focus has been on responses from those for whom the book functions, or at one time functioned, as Scripture. The chapter has not sought to evaluate the various reading strategies adopted owing to the complications encountered, but rather to acquaint the reader with the diversity of reading options. As such, responses to the individual complications themselves have not received specific attention. Rather, the focus has been on the genre of responses to the complications.[23] My hope is that individual readers will find themselves somewhere in this taxonomy and further that they will feel the description offered of their own approach has been accurate.

It does not appear to be going too far to observe that there are no scholars (or serious students of the book), who hold to the standard story of origins, who do not also believe that the book is Scripture. One's belief in, or testimony of, the truth of the Book of Mormon appears intricately connected to whether or not one believes or holds to the standard story with regard to the book's origins. Since those who believe the standard story of origins all seem to regard the book as Scripture it appears that such belief with regard to the standard story of origins inevitably leads to belief in the

---

[22] Vogel, *Joseph Smith: The Making of a Prophet*, p. xix.

[23] There, of course, are numerous responses made by those for whom the book has never functioned as Scripture that could have been included, all of which would argue that the book is the product of Joseph Smith to one degree or another. Their articulation does not seem to be required here as such is not the intent of the chapter.

book's scriptural status. But this reasoning does not always work in reverse for there are those who continue to regard the book as Scripture while rejecting or seriously questioning some or all of the details of the standard story of origins.

It should also perhaps be noted that a testimony of the truth of the Book of Mormon – technically a phenomenon external to the text, though called for by the text – often plays a determinative role in one's openness to other external evidences with regard to the book's origins and truth claims. In other words, for some, a testimony of the Book of Mormon as Scripture becomes a default position from which all other external evidence is evaluated. This default position can mean that owing to the interpreter's belief in the scriptural status of the Book of Mormon, any complicating evidences must of necessity be assumed to be wrong or not to be as they appear. For others, such complicating external evidences cause a re-assessment of one's reading strategy for the Book of Mormon and the development of other strategies that are deemed to be consistent with a view of the book as Scripture. For still others, such complications result in a re-examination of the external phenomenon upon which a scriptural view of the Book of Mormon is based in the first place. Though the connection between one's testimony of the truth of the Book of Mormon and one's assessment of complicating evidence is often not articulated, it is important for those outside the LDS families of readers to understand the way in which a testimony of the Book of Mormon can have an impact on the scholarly – and or serious – engagement with the book by those who hold it to be Scripture.

AFTERWORD – CONFESSIONS OF A PENTECOSTAL READER

When I began this journey through the Book of Mormon I was uncertain of what I would find, both in the pages of the book and the individuals with whom I would dialogue – or whether there would even be any individuals interested in such dialogue. I knew nothing about the book's structure, little about its content – aside from the fact that it did not contain evidence for some key LDS doctrines, and even less about its theology, reception history, and relationship to Pentecostalism or if there even be a relationship. The aspect of the Book of Mormon with which I was most familiar was the narrative of its coming forth – which came mainly from a graduate course on LDS history and from missionaries with whom I conversed – and some of the problematic aspects surrounding the book's origins, which I learned mainly from those who responded to claims about the book by those who consider it to be Scripture. So I decided that if I were to explore the book formally, the only way I could approach the book is along the lines that I explore biblical texts with which I deal on a daily basis. Given my own journey as an interpreter, I began with the text itself, working my way out as it were, taking up issues of origins only near the journey's end. While this approach will prove confusing to some for whom the book stands or falls with conclusions reached about origins, this strategy makes perfect sense to me as it enabled me to offer a sympathetic treatment of the book along the way, allowing me to read with the grain if you will. For it seems to me that whoever wrote the book or whatever the issues that explain its origins, there are any number of interesting and important issues that insiders and outsiders should be able to discuss about its structure, content, theology, reception, and relationship to other faith traditions without being derailed from the start by the divisive issue of origins.

In point of fact, for a long time during the period of researching and writing I was not certain that I was even going to include a section on origins. But most every one who read various drafts of my work made it clear to me that I owed such a section to my readers. So then the question was, how should I proceed? In the end, I settled on an approach that seemed consistent with my training in biblical studies and sought to be descriptive rather than prescriptive. In short, I tried to expose the reader to the earliest story of the book's origins, take a hard look at the complications to the standard story – complications that nearly everyone with whom I spoke acknowledged as the major issues, and offer an overview of the way individual readers have constructed reading strategies in the light of the complications. While I know some readers for whom the book functions as Scripture will be disappointed that I have not offered a survey of responses to the individual complications, the truth is that the territory is simply too vast to cover in any comprehensive sense, coverage of those responses is readily available in a variety of other places, and of course there is no unanimity amongst interpreters about the best way to respond to the complications. So instead, I have offered a survey of reading strategies as a way of indicating something of the various responses to the complications. I felt that my role as an interpreter at this point was to expose my readers to the issues, not necessarily to settle them or even argue for a specific solution or theory of origins.

As noted above, when I began this journey I was also uncertain about whether there would be anyone interested in entering into dialogue with me as an outsider. But it did not take long to learn that there were many individuals spread across the LDS family of churches interested in hearing about my project and in helping me in any way possible. While there were a few folk who looked upon me with some suspicion – and a couple who did their best to convert me (!), for the most part when I made my intentions known nearly everyone made me feel very welcome and encouraged me in the process. I was especially impressed by the candid conversations I had with numbers of people, many of whose names I do not even know, who expressed to me their understanding of a variety of Book of Mormon issues, which went well beyond any standard talking points evolving into frank and open conversations. These conversations transcended boundaries within the LDS family of churches, conversations that I was surprised to discover were often not taking place between the individuals with whom I was engaging. These times of dialogue included individuals in the Community of Christ, the Church of Christ Temple Lot, the Church of Jesus Christ of Latter Day Saints, the Church of Jesus Christ (Monongahela, PA), other smaller groups within the movement, and even some who no longer considered the Book of Mormon to be Scripture. Such diversity of dialogue partners proved to be enormously helpful to me and I am thankful for them all.

In the Preface to this study I mentioned that I felt called to this project in a way similar to the way I have felt the Spirit call me to the other major research projects I have undertaken during my academic life. When I share this sense of calling with individuals for whom the book functions as Scripture they often get a look in their eyes reminiscent of the look in the eyes of the characters in the Chronicles of Narnia when it is periodically observed that 'Aslan is on the Move!' At the same time, when I share this sense of calling with many of my Pentecostal friends they often look at me with a sense of surprise and even a little bewilderment, while others respond with a real sense of interest as to why I feel I have been called to this task. In fact, I sometimes get the question, what do you think the Lord is up to in all this? And the honest answer to that question is, 'I really don't know!' As my friends in the LDS family of churches know, I am still not numbered amongst those who consider the Book of Mormon to be Scripture and as my Pentecostal family knows I do not have mass conversions to report from my efforts!

So what *do* I know about the reason for this project – aside from satisfying my personal curiosities about the Book of Mormon? I know that conversations are important and that there are many individuals who welcome such conversations provided they are respectful and honest. I know that the response to this project by those who hold the book to be Scripture has far exceeded any expectations I had when I began. It seems that at every stage yet another door would open presenting still another opportunity for serious dialogue about the project, but also dialogue about my own faith tradition and spirituality. I know that I have made many new friends, some of whom are now good and trusted friends, as a result of this journey. And I now know a bit more about the Book of Mormon as a Pentecostal Reader than I did before setting out on this journey.

Thus, this book, which began as a short introduction, is offered as a sympathetic, critical reading of the Book of Mormon that focuses on a variety of issues that for the most part have been underrepresented in the literature currently available. It seeks to acquaint readers for whom the book does not function as Scripture with the book, readers who desire to know more about the book but prefer an approach that is not overtly apologetic for or against the book and its claims. At the same time, it is my hope that readers for whom the book functions as Scripture will gain some insight into the book they treasure, insights that result from a reading that comes outside their tradition. As such, I have sought to maintain an irenic, constructive tone in researching and writing the kind of book I wished had been available to me when I began this journey. Owing to the fact that I have focused on the Book of Mormon and not on any of the churches that hold it to be Scripture, I have not intentionally privileged one stream of interpretive tradition over another but sought to learn from any who have written on the topics covered in this study.

It is my hope that this work will serve both to acquaint readers with the Book of Mormon and to encourage candid, thoughtful, and irenic conversations about the book between those who hold it to be Scripture and those who do not.

BIBLIOGRAPHY

A Book of Commandments for the Government of the Church of Christ Organized according to Law, on the 6th of April 1830 (Zion: W.W. Phelps & Co., 1833).

'A Hoax: Reminiscences of an Old Kinderhook Mystery', *Journal of the Illinois State Historical Society* 5 (July 1912), pp. 271-73.

Addams, R.J., 'The Church of Christ (Temple Lot), Its Emergence, Struggles and Early Schisms', in N.G. Bringhurst and J.C. Hamer (eds.), *Scattering of the Saints: Schism within Mormonism* (Independence, MO: John Whitmer Books, 2007), pp. 206-23.

Alexander, K.E., 'Boundless Love Divine: A Re-evaulation of Early Understandings of the Experience of Spirit Baptism', in S.J. Land, R.D. Moore, and J.C. Thomas (eds.), *Passover, Pentecost & Parousia: Studies in Celebration of the Life and Ministry of R. Hollis Gause* (JPTSup 35; Blandford Forum: Deo, 2010), pp. 145-70.

—*Pentecostal Healing: Models in Theology and Practice* (JPTSup 29; Blandford Forum: Deo, 2006).

Archer, K.J., *The Gospel Revisited: Towards a Pentecostal Theology of Worship and Witness* (Eugene, OR: Pickwick, 2011).

Archer, M.L., *'In the Spirit on the Lord's Day': A Pentecostal Engagement with Worship in the Apocalypse* (Cleveland, TN: CPT Press, 2015).

Ashton, C., A.B. Cadman, and W.H. Cadman (compliers), *A Brief History of the Church of Jesus Christ* (Monongahela, PA: The Church of Jesus Christ Headquarters, 2005).

Aston, W.P., 'Newly Found Altars from Nahom', *Journal of Book of Mormon Studies* 10.2 (2001), pp. 56-61.

Augustine, D., *Pentecost, Hospitality, and Transfiguration: Toward a Spirit-inspired Vision of Social Transformation* (Cleveland, TN: CPT Press, 2012).

Avery, V.T., *From Mission to Madness: Last Son of the Mormon Prophet* (Urbana and Chicago: University of Illinois Press, 1998).

Axelgard, F.W., '1 and 2 Nephi: An Inspiring Whole', *BYU Studies* 26.4 (1986), pp. 53-66.

Bell, E.N., 'What is Mormonism?', *The Pentecostal Evangel* 330/331 (March 6, 1920), p. 5.

Bennion, F.R. 'Women and the Book of Mormon: Tradition and Revelation', in M. Cornwall and S. Howe (eds.), *Women of Wisdom and Knowledge* (Salt Lake City: Deseret, 1990), pp. 169-78.

Black, S.E., *Finding Christ through the Book of Mormon* (Salt Lake City: Deseret Book, 1987).

Blumhofer, E.L., 'Dowie, John Alexander', in S.M. Burgess, G.B. McGee, and P.H. Alexander (eds.), *Dictionary of Pentecostal and Charismatic Movements* (Grand Rapids: Zondervan, 1988), pp. 248-49.

Boddy, A.A., 'Christian Science', *Confidence* 4.7 (July, 1911), p. 165.

—'Towards the Rockies', *Confidence* 5.12 (December, 1912), p. 282.

Bolton, A., 'Anabaptism, the Book of Mormon, and the Peace Church Option', *Dialogue: A Journal of Mormon Thought* 37.1 (2004), pp. 75-94.

—'Is the Book of Mormon an Asset or Liability for Becoming a Peace Church?', *John Whitmer Historical Association Journal* 19 (1999), pp. 29-42.

—'Utopian Vision and Prophetic Imagination: Reading the Book of Mormon in a Nineteenth-century Context', in P.A. Judd (ed.), *Restoration Studies: Theology and Culture in the Community of Christ and the Latter Day Saint Movement* Volume X (Independence, MO: Community of Christ Seminary Press, 2009), pp. 144-53.

Brodie, F.M., *No Man Knows My History: The Life of Joseph Smith* (New York: Vintage, 1995).

Bruening, A.D. and David L. Paulsen, 'The Development of the Mormon Understanding of God: Early Mormon Modalism and Other Myths', *FARMS Review of Books* 13.2 (2001), pp. 109-69.

Bundy, D.D., 'Irving, Edward', in S.M. Burgess, G.B. McGee, and P.H. Alexander (eds.), *Dictionary of Pentecostal and Charismatic Movements* (Grand Rapids: Zondervan, 1988), pp. 470-71.

Bushman, R.L., *Joseph Smith: Rough Stone Rolling* (New York: Vintage Books, 2005).

Cadman, W., J.L. Ambrust, and W.D. Wright (compliers), *Faith and Doctrine of the Church of Jesus Christ* (Greensburg, PA: The Church of Jesus Christ – Print House, 1983).

Callahan, L.D., 'Fleshly Manifestations: Charles Fox Parham's Quest for the Sanctified Body' (PhD dissertation, Princeton University, 2002).

Campbell, A., *Millennial Harbinger* (Bethany, VA, February 7, 1831).

Cannon, D.Q., 'In the Press: Early Newspaper Reports on the Initial Publication of the Book of Mormon', *Journal of Book of Mormon Studies* 16.2 (2007), pp. 4-15, 92-93.

Caswall, H., *The City of the Mormons: Or Three Days at Nauvoo in 1842* (London: J.G.F. & J. Rivington, 1842).

—*The Prophet of the Nineteenth Century; or, the Rise, Progress, and Present State of the Mormons, or Latter Day Saints* ... (London: J.G.F. & J. Rivington, 1843).

Charles, M.M., 'Book of Mormon Christology', in B.L. Metcalfe (ed.), *New Approaches to the Book of Mormon: Explorations in Critical Methodology* (Salt Lake City: Signature Books, 1993), pp. 81-114.

Clayton, W., *An Intimate Chronicle: The Journals of William Clayton* (ed. George D. Smith; Salt Lake City: Signature Books, 1991).

Coe, M., 'Mormons and Archeology: An Outside View', *Dialogue: A Journal of Mormon Thought* 8.2 (1973), pp. 42-48.

Cowdery, O., *Defense in a Rehearsal of My Grounds for Separating Myself from the Latter Day Saints* (Norton, Ohio: 1839).

Davidson, K.L., D.J. Whittaker, M. Ashurst-McGee, and R.L. Jensen (eds.), *Joseph Smith Histories, 1832-1844.* (Vol. 1 of the Histories series of The Joseph Smith Papers I; D.C. Jessee, R.K. Esplin, and R.L. Bushman [eds.]; Salt Lake City: Church Historian's Press, 2012).

Dayton, D.W., *The Theological Roots of Pentecostalism* (Peabody, MA: Hendrickson, 1991).

Dialogue: A Journal of Mormon Thought 3 (Summer 1968), pp. 67-105.

'Did Dowie Preach Polygamy in Zion?', *Salt Lake City Telegram* (April 2, 1906).

Dowie, J.A., 'Opening of Zion's Hall of Seventies', *Leaves of Healing* 5.14 (January 28, 1899), p. 255.

—'Travel Plans', *Leaves of Healing* 1.5, 6, 7 (1890), p. 1.

'Dowie is Coming', *The Chicago Record-Herald* (September 2, 1903), p. 2.

'Dowieites Are Coming', *Salt Lake City Herald* (February 11, 1904), p. 2.

Duffy, J.-C., 'Mapping Book of Mormon Historicity Debates: A Guide for the Overwhelmed – Part I and Part II', *Sunstone Magazine* http://www.sunstonemagazine.com/category/mapping-mormon-issues/.

Earley, P., *Prophet of Death; The Mormon Blood-Atonement Killings* (New York: William Morrow and Co., 1991).

Easton, S.W., 'Names of Christ in the Book of Mormon', *Ensign* (July 1978), pp. 60-61

'False Doctrine', *The Bridegroom's Messenger* 4.84 (April 15, 1911), p. 1.

Faupel, D.W., *The Everlasting Gospel: The Significance of Eschatology in the Development of Pentecostal Thought* (JPTSup 10; Sheffield: Sheffield Academic Press, 1996).

—'Theological Influences on the Teachings and Practices of John Alexander Dowie', *Pneuma* 29.2 (2007), pp. 226-53.

Faulconer, J.E., *Faith, Philosophy, Scripture* (Provo, UT: Neal A. Maxwell Institute; Brigham Young University, 2010).

Flint, Apostle B.C., *An Outline History of the Church of Christ (Temple Lot)* (Independence, MO: Board of Publications The Church of Christ [Temple Lot], 1953 [3rd edn, 1979].

Fraser, A.L., 'Marriage and Divorce', *The Latter Rain* 8.1 (October, 1915), p. 8.

Frederick, N.J., 'Line Within Line: An Intertextual Analysis of Mormon Scripture and the Prologue of the Gospel of John' (PhD dissertation, Claremont Graduate School, 2013).

Fronk, C., 'Desert Epiphany: Sariah and the Women in 1 Nephi', *Journal of Book of Mormon Studies* 9.2 (2000), pp. 5–15.

Gardner, B.A., *Second Witness: First Nephi* (ACCBM 1; Salt Lake City: Greg Kofford, 2007).

—*Second Witness: Second Nephi-Jacob* (ACCBM 2; Salt Lake City: Greg Kofford, 2007).

—*Second Witness: Enos through Mosiah* (ACCBM 3; Salt Lake City: Greg Kofford, 2007).

—*Second Witness: Fourth Nephi-Moroni* (ACCBM 6; Salt Lake City: Greg Kofford, 2011).

Givens, T.L., *By the Hand of Mormon: The American Scripture that Launched a New World Religion* (Oxford: Oxford University Press, 2002).

—*The Book of Mormon: A Very Short Introduction* (Oxford: Oxford University Press, 2009).

'God's Word versus Man's Word', *The Latter Rain Evangel* (December, 1912), pp. 14-15.

Goff, J.R., *Fields White Unto Harvest: Charles F. Parham and the Missionary Origins of Pentecostalism* (Fayetteville, AR: The University Press of Arkansas, 1988).

—'Parham, Charles Fox', in S.M. Burgess, G.B. McGee, and P.H. Alexander (eds.), *Dictionary of Pentecostal and Charismatic Movements* (Grand Rapids: Zondervan, 1988), pp. 660-61.

Green, C.E.W., *Toward a Pentecostal Theology of the Lord's Supper: Foretasting the Kingdom* (Cleveland, TN: CPT Press, 2012).

Green, D.F., 'Book of Mormon Archaeology: The Myths and the Alternatives', *Dialogue: A Journal of Mormon Thought* 4.2 (1969), pp. 71-80.

Gutjahr, P.C., *The Book of Mormon: A Biography* (Lives of Great Religious Books; Princeton: Princeton University Press, 2012).

Hardy, G., *Understanding the Book of Mormon: A Reader's Guide* (Oxford: Oxford University Press, 2010).

Harrell, C.R., *'This Is My Doctrine': The Development of Mormon Theology* (Salt Lake City: Greg Kofford Books, 2013)

Hartshorn, C.B., *A Commentary on the Book of Mormon* (Independence, MO: Herald Publishing House, 1964).

Hauglid, B.M., '"Come & Help Build the Temple & City": Parley P. and Orson Pratt's May 1843 Letter to John Van Cott', *Mormon Historical Studies* 11.1 (Spring, 2011), pp. 149-58.

—'Did Joseph Smith Translate the Kinderhook Plates?', in R.L. Millet (ed.), *No Weapon Shall Prosper: New Light on Sensitive Issues* (Provo, UT: Religious Studies Center, Brigham Young University; Salt Lake City: Deseret Book, 2011), pp. 93–103.

Haven, C., 'A Girl's Letters from Nauvoo', *Overland Monthly* (December 1890), p. 630.

Hills, L.E., *A Short Work on the Geography of Mexico and Central America from 2234 B.C. to 421 A.D.* (Independence, MO: L.E. Hills, 1917).

Hills, L.E., *Historical Data from Ancient Records and Ruins of Mexico and Central America* (Independence, MO: L.E. Hills, 1919).

Hilton III, J. and J. Johnson, 'Who Uses the Word Resurrection in the Book of Mormon and How Is It Used?', *Journal of the Book of Mormon and Other Restoration Scripture* 21.2 (2012), pp. 30-39.

'History of Joseph Smith', *Times and Seasons* 3.10 (15 March 1842), pp. 726-28; 3.11 (1 April 1842), pp. 748-49; 3.12 (15 April 1842), pp. 753-54.

Howard, R.P., 'An Analysis of Six Contemporary Accounts Touching Joseph Smith's First Vision', *Restoration Studies I: A Collection of Essays About the History, Beliefs, and Practices of the Reorganized Church of Jesus Christ of Latter Day Saints* (ed. M.L. Draper and C.D. Vlahos; Independence, MO: Herald Publishing House, 1980), pp. 95-117.

Howard, R.P., *Restoration Scriptures: A Study of their Textual Development* (Independence, MO: Herald Publishing House, 1969).

Huggins, R.V., 'Did the Author of 3 Nephi Know the Gospel of Matthew?', *Dialogue: A Journal of Mormon Thought* 30.3 (Fall, 1997), pp. 137-48.

Hyde, J., '1984 Lafferty Case Still Haunts: 2 Brothers Show no Remorse for Brutal Killings', *Deseret News* (Tuesday July 27 2004).

'Importance of Doctrinal Teaching', *The Bridegroom's Messenger* 4.83 (April 1, 1911), p. 2.

Jensen, R.S., 'Gleaning the Harvest: Strangite Missionary Work, 1846-1850' (MA thesis, Brigham Young University, 2005).

—'Mormons Seeking Mormonism: Strangite Success and the Conceptualization of Mormon Ideology, 1844-50', in N.G. Bringhurst and J.C. Hamer (eds.), *Scattering of the Saints: Schism within Mormonism* (Independence, MO: John Whitmer Books, 2007), pp. 115-40.

Jessee, D.C., 'The early accounts of Joseph Smith's First Vision', *BYU Studies* 9.3 (1969), pp. 275-94.

Journal of Discourses, vols. 9 and 16 (Salt Lake City: Deseret Book Co., 1967).

Kärkkäinen, V.-M., 'A Full Gospel Ecclesiology of *Koinonia*: Pentecostal Contributions to the Doctrine of the Church', in S.D. Moore and J.M. Henderson (eds.), *Renewal History & Theology: Essays in Honor of H. Vinson Synan* (Cleveland, TN: CPT Press, 2014), pp. 175-93.

Kern, K.C., 'Willing to Bear My Name: Nominal Appropriation, Atonement, and Salvation in Latter-day Saint Theology', a paper presented to the Tenth Annual Meeting of the Society for Mormon Philosophy and Theology at Utah Valley University, 2013.

Krakauer, J., *Under the Banner of Heaven: A Story of Violent Faith* (New York: Anchor Books, 2004).

Land, S.J., *Pentecostal Spirituality: A Passion for the Kingdom* (JPTSup 1; Sheffield: Sheffield Academic Press, 1993).

Larson, S., *Quest for the Gold Plates: Thomas Stuart Ferguson's Archaeological Search for the Book of Mormon* (Salt Lake City: Freethinker Press, 1996).

—'The Legacy of Thomas Stuart Ferguson', *Dialogue: A Journal of Mormon Thought* 23.1 (1990), pp. 55-92.

Luffman, D.E., *The Book of Mormon's Witness to Its First Readers* (Independence, MO: Community of Christ Seminary Press, 2013).

Luz, U., *Matthew in History* (Minneapolis, MN: Fortress, 1994).

Macchia, F.D., *Baptized in the Spirit: A Global Pentecostal Theology* (Grand Rapids: Zondervan, 2006).

—*Justified in the Spirit* (Grand Rapids: Eerdmans, 2010).

—'Sighs too Deep for Words: Toward a Theology of Glossolalia', *Journal of Pentecostal Theology* 1 (1992), pp. 47-73.

—'Tongues as a Sign: Towards a Sacramental Understanding of Pentecostal Experience', *Pneuma: The Journal of the Society for Pentecostal Studies* 15.1 (Spring, 1993), pp. 61-76.

Madson, J., 'A Non-Violent Reading of the Book of Mormon', in P.Q. Mason, J.D. Pulsipher, and R.L. Bushman (eds.), *War and Peace in Our Time: Mormon Perspectives* (Salt Lake City: George Kofford Books, 2012), pp. 9-28.

Madson, J., 'With God on Our Side' (unpublished paper).

Marshall, J.G., *A Biographical Sketch of Richard G. Spurling, Jr.* (Cleveland, TN: Pathway Press, 1974).

Matthews, R.J., 'What the Book of Mormon Tells Us about Jesus Christ', in P.R. Cheesman (ed.), *The Book of Mormon: The Keystone Scripture* (Provo, UT: Religious Studies Center, Brigham Young University, 1988), pp. 21–43.

McQueen, L.R., *Toward a Pentecostal Eschatology: Discerning the Way Forward* (JPTSup 39; Blandford Forum: Deo, 2012).

'Mormonism!: A Survey of Its Blasphemous Pretentions and Evil Practices', *The Latter Rain Evangel* 12.5 (February, 1920), pp. 20-22.

Mounce, W.D., *Pastoral Epistles* (WBC 46; Nashville: Thomas Nelson, 2000).

Murphy, T.W., 'Lamanite Genesis, Genealogy, and Genetics', in D. Vogel and B.L. Metcalfe (eds.), *American Apocrypha: Essays on the Book of Mormon* (Salt Lake City: Signature Books, 2002), pp. 47–77.

Newell, L.K. and V.T. Avery, *Mormon Enigma: Emma Hale Smith* (Urbana and Chicago: University of Illinois Press, 2nd edn, 1994).

O'Dea, T.F., *The Mormons* (Chicago: University of Chicago Press, 1957).

Ostler, B.T., 'The Book of Mormon as a Modern Expansion of an Ancient Source', *Dialogue: A Journal of Mormon Thought* 20.1 (1987), pp. 66-123.

—'Updating the Expansion Theory', *Times and Seasons* http://timesandseasons.org/index.php/2005/04/updating-the-expansion-theory/.

Palmer, G.H., *An Insider's View of Mormon Origins* (Salt Lake City: Signature Books, 2002).

Parker, T., R. Lopez, and M. Stone, *The Book of Mormon Script Book: The Complete Book and Lyrics of the Broadway Musical* (New York: HarperCollins, 2011).

Poulton, D.L., *Reuben Kirkham: Pioneer Artist* (Springville, UT: Cedar Fort, Inc., 2011).

Pratt, J.R., 'Book of Mormon Chronology', in *Encyclopedia of Mormonism* (New York: MacMillan, 1992), I, pp. 169-71.

'Questions Concerning Tongues', *The Bridegroom's Messenger* 1.14 (May 15, 1908), p. 2.

Quinn, D.M., *Early Mormonism and the Magic World View* (Salt Lake City: Signature Books, rev. and enlarged edn, 1998).

Reed, D.A., *'In Jesus' Name': The History and Beliefs of Oneness Pentecostals* (JPTSup 31; Blandford Forum: Deo, 2008).

Reitner, R.K., *The Joseph Smith Egyptian Papyri: A Complete Edition* (Salt Lake City: Signature Books, 2014).

Remy J., and Julius Brenchley, *A Journey to Great Salt-Lake City* (London: W. Jeffs, 1861) II, pp. 536-46.

Reynolds, N.B., 'Nephi's Outline', *BYU Studies* 20.2 (1980), pp. 131-49.

Ricks, S.D., 'On Lehi's Trail: Nahom, Ishmael's Burial Place', *Journal of Book of Mormon and Other Restoration Scripture* 20.1 (2011), pp. 66-68.

Ricks, W.W., 'The Kinderhook Plates', *Improvement Era* 65 (Sept. 1962), pp. 656-58.

Roberts, B.H., *Studies on the Book of Mormon* (ed. B.D. Madsen; Salt Lake City: Signature Books, 2nd edn, 1992).

Rochester Daily Advertiser and Telegraph Volume 4 No. 1057 (April 2, 1830).

Russell, W.D., 'The Remnant Church: An RLDS Schismatic Group Finds A Prophet of Joseph's Seed', *Dialogue: A Journal of Mormon Thought* 38.3 (Fall, 2005), pp. 75-106.

Rust, R.D., *Feasting on the Word: The Literary Testimony of the Book of Mormon* (Salt Lake City: Deseret Book Co and FARMS, 1997).

Saints' Herald 54 (20 May 1907), pp. 229-30.

Scherer, M.A., *The Journey of a People: The Era of Restoration, 1820 to 1844* (Independence, MO: Church of Christ Seminary Press, 2013).

—*The Journey of a People: The Era of Reorganization, 1844 to 1946* (Independence, MO: Community of Christ Seminary Press, 2013).

Smith, E. (Selector), *A Collection of Sacred Hymns for the Church of the Latter Day Saints* (Kirtland, OH: F.G. Williams & Co., 1835).

Smith, J.R., 'Scattering of the Hedrickites', in N.G. Bringhurst and J.C. Hamer (eds.), *Scattering of the Saints: Schism within Mormonism* (Independence, MO: John Whitmer Books, 2007), pp. 224-46.

Sorenson, J.L., 'Ancient America and the Book of Mormon Revisited', *Dialogue: A Journal of Mormon Thought* (1969), pp. 80-94.

—'Voices from the Dust', *Dialogue: A Journal of Mormon Thought* 1.1 (1966), pp. 144-49.

Southerton, S., 'DNA Genealogies of American Indians and the Book of Mormon' *Salt Lake Tribune* (17 March 2000).

Spalding, F.S., *Joseph Smith Jr. as a Translator: An Inquiry Conducted* (Salt Lake City: The Arrow Press, 1912).

Speek, V.C., 'From Strangites to Reorganized Latter Day Saints: Transformations in Midwestern Mormonism, 1856-79', in N.G. Bringhurst and J.C. Hamer (eds.), *Scattering of the Saints: Schism within Mormonism* (Independence, MO: John Whitmer Books, 2007), pp. 141-60.

Spencer, J.M., *An Other Testament: On Typology* (Salt Lake City: Salt Press, 2012).

Spurling, R.G., *The Lost Link* (Turtletown, TN: self-published, 1920).

Stephens, J.L., *Incidents of Travel in Central America, Chipas and Yucatan* (New York, 1841).

Stott, G. St. John, 'Talking to Angels; Talking of Angels: Constructing the Angelology of the Book of Mormon', *Theology and Religion* 19 (2012), pp. 92-109.

Strachan, G., *The Pentecostal Theology of Edward Irving* (Peabody, MA: Hendrickson, 1988).

Stronstad, R., *The Prophethood of All Believers* (Cleveland, TN: CPT Press, 2010).

Sturgess, G.L., 'The Book of Mosiah: Thoughts about Its Structure, Purposes, Themes, and Authorship', *Journal of Book of Mormon Studies* 4.2 (1995), pp. 107-35.

Swanson, V.G., 'The Development of the Concept of a Holy Ghost in Mormon Theology', in G.J. Bergera (ed.), *Line upon Line Essays on Mormon Doctrine* (Salt Lake City: Signature Books, 1989), pp. 89-98.

Tanner, J. and S., *Archaeology and the Book of Mormon* (Salt Lake City: Modern Microfilm Company, 1969).

—*Joseph Smith's Plagiarism of the Bible in the Book of Mormon* – Includes *Covering Up the Black Hole in the Book of Mormon* (Salt Lake City: Utah Lighthouse Ministry, rev. and exp. edn, 2010).

Taylor, G.F., 'Mormons', *The Pentecostal Holiness Advocate* 2.6 (June 6. 1918), p. 4.

'The Growth of Mormonism', *The Bridegroom's Messenger* 6.121 (November 15, 1912), p. 4.

The Latter Rain Evangel 2.9 (June, 1910), p. 17.

'The Mormon Prophet and the Greek Psalter', in the *Warsaw (IL) Message* 1.45 (1843).

'The Uncovering of the Mormon Fraud', *Weekly Evangel* 106 (September 4, 1915), p. 100.

Thomas, J.C., 'Biblical Reflections on Women in Ministry', in L.R. Martin (ed.), *Toward a Pentecostal Theology of Preaching* (Cleveland, TN: CPT Press, 2015), pp. 135-40.

—*Footwashing in John 13 and the Johannine Community* (Cleveland, TN: CPT Press, 2nd edn, 2014).

—*The Apocalypse: A Literary and Theological Commentary* (Cleveland, TN: CPT Press, 2012).

—*The Devil, Disease, and Deliverance: Origins of Illness in New Testament Thought* (Cleveland, TN: CPT Press, 2010).

—(ed.), *Toward a Pentecostal Ecclesiology: The Church and the Five-fold Gospel* (Cleveland, TN: CPT Press, 2010).

—'Women, Pentecostals, and the Bible: An Experiment in Pentecostal Hermeneutics', in *The Spirit of the New Testament* (Blandford Forum: Deo, 2005), pp. 233-47.

Thomas, M.D., *Digging in Cumorah: Reclaiming Book of Mormon Narratives* (Salt Lake City: Signature Books, 1999).

Times and Seasons 3.9 (1 March 1842).

Times and Seasons (1 October 1842).

Times and Seasons 4.12 (1 May 1843), pp. 185-86.

'Try the Spirits', *Times and Seasons* (April, 1842), pp. 743-47.

Turner, J.G., *Brigham Young: Pioneer Prophet* (Cambridge, MA: Belknap Press, 2012).

—*Mormon Jesus: A Biography* (Cambridge, MA: Belknap Press, 2016).

Twain, M., *The Innocents Abroad and Roughing It* (The American Library; New York, NY: Penguin Putnam, 1984).

Underwood, G., 'The Book of Mormon Usage in Early LDS Theology', *Dialogue: A Journal of Mormon Thought* 17.3 (1984), pp. 35-74.

—*The Millenarian World of Early Mormonism* (Urbana and Chicago: University of Illinois Press, 1993).

Van Orden, Bruce A., 'Anglo-Israelism and Its Impact on Mormon Theology', a paper presented to the 1984 Meeting of the Mormon History Association.

Van Orden, Bruce A., *The Life of George Reynolds: Prisoner for Conscience' Sake* (Salt Lake City: Deseret Book Company, 1992).

Van Noord, R., *King of Beaver Island: The Life and Assassination of James Jesse Strang* (Urbana and Chicago: University of Illinois Press, 1988).

Van Wagoner, R., and Steve Walker, 'The Gift of Seeing', *Dialogue: A Journal of Mormon Thought* 15.2 (Summer 1982), pp. 48-68.

Vogel, D,. *Joseph Smith: The Making of a Prophet* (Salt Lake City: Signature, 2004).

Waddell, R.C., *The Spirit of the Book of Revelation* (JPTSup 30; Blandford Forum: Deo, 2006).

Wardle, M.E., *Minerva Teichert: Pageants in Paint* (Provo, Utah: BYU Press, 2007).

Wangsgard, D.A., 'Washing of Feet', in D.H. Ludlow (ed.), *Encyclopedia of Mormonism* (New York: Macmillan, 1992), IV, p. 1550.

Watson, L., 'The Church of Jesus Christ (Headquartered in Monongahela, Pennsylvania), Its History and Doctrine', in N.G. Bringhurst and J.C. Hamer (eds.), *Scattering of the Saints: Schism within Mormonism* (Independence, MO: John Whitmer Books, 2007), pp. 190-205.

Wayne Sentinel January 5, 1827.

Welch, J.W., 'Chiasmus in the Book of Mormon', in N.B. Reynolds (ed.), *Book of Mormon Authorship: New Light on Ancient Origins* (Provo, UT: BYU Religious Studies Center, 1982), pp. 33-52.

Welch J.W., and Doris R. Dant, *The Book of Mormon Paintings of Minerva Teichert* (Provo and Salt Lake City, Utah: BYU Studies and Bookcraft, 1997).

Widmer, K., *Mormonism and the Nature of God: A Theological Evolution, 1830-1915* (Jefferson, NC: McFarland, 2000).

Wilde, A., 'Fundamentalist Mormonism: Its History, Diversity and Stereotypes, 1886-Present', in N.G. Bringhurst and J.C. Hamer (eds.), *Scattering of the Saints: Schism within Mormonism* (Independence, MO: John Whitmer Books, 2007), pp. 258-89.

Williams, C.S., 'Women in the Book of Mormon: Inclusion, Exclusion, and Interpretation', *Journal of Book of Mormon Studies* 11.1 (2002), pp. 66-79, 111-14

Wilson, L.S.H., 'Joseph Smith's Doctrine of the Holy Spirit Contrasted with Cartwright, Campbell, Hodge, and Finney' (PhD dissertation, Marquette University, 2010).

Wright, D.P., 'Isaiah in the Book of Mormon: Or Joseph Smith in Isaiah', in D. Vogel and B.L. Metcalf (eds.), *American Apocrypha: Essays on the Book of Mormon* (Salt Lake City: Signature Books, 2002).

INDEX OF BIBLICAL AND BOOK OF MORMON REFERENCES

16.2	374	*2 Nephi*		4.15-35	42
16.3	278	1.1-4.12	39	4.24	250
16.6	36	1.1	40	4.25	215
16.7-8	337	1.3	40	4.32	289, 290
16.8	36	1.4	40	5.3-4	278, 279
16.9	36	1.5	40	5.6	42
16.10-16	36	1.6	40	5.8-9	42
16.20	36, 278	1.8	40	5.10-18	42
16.24-25	36	1.9	40, 235	5.14	42
16.25	278	1.10-23		5.21-23	42, 236
16.33-34	36	1.10-11	40	5.26-28	42
16.34	418	1.10	43	5.28	16
16.35-39	36	1.14	40	5.29-33	42
16.38	250	1.15	289	5.34	16, 43
17.1-6	36	1.20	92, 235	6.1-10.25	39, 43, 47
17.2	55, 284	1.21	40	6.1-8.25	43
17.3	278	1.22	40	6.2	43
17.4-5	16	1.24	40	6.3	43
17.4	17	1.27	40	6.10	43
17.7-16	36	1.28-32	40	6.11	251, 274
17.13	235	1.31	235	7.1-8.25	43
17.17-22	36, 278	1.32	235	7.8	374
17.23-47	36	2.1-2	40	9.1-54	43
17.41	381	2.3	40	9.1-16	43
17.45	250	2.5	374	9.1-2	274
17.47	213	2.11-13	40	9.2	246, 274
17.48-55	36	2.11	40	9.6	223
17.49	278	2.14-30	40	9.7	227
17.52	212	2.14-28	223	9.10-36	290
18.1-8	36	2.17	252	9.11	43
18.9-25	36	2.18	223	9.12	43, 272
18.16	278	2.25	41	9.15	273
19.1-7	36, 264	2.27	41	9.17-19	43
19.8-21	37	2.29	290	9.18	43, 54
19.8	16, 17, 21,	3.1-25	41	9.19	43, 54
	134	3.2	43	9.21	282
19.10-21	49	3.3-25	265	9.22	272, 273
19.21-22	264	3.5	212	9.23-24	231
19.22-21.26	37	4.1-2	41	9.23	44
20.1	231	4.3-9	41	9.24	44
22.1-31	37	4.4	235	9.25-38	44
22.2	220	4.7	41	9.25	44, 226
22.13-14	242	4.10-12	41	9.26	44
22.23	242	4.13-5.34	39, 41	9.34	290
22.31	31, 37	4.13-14	41	9.36	290

45.10	21, 211	51.37	19	59.5-13	118
45.15-19	109	52.1-62.52	113	60.1-36	118
45.19	215	52.1-4	113	60.4	279
45.20-24	109	52.1	19, 20	61.1-21	119
45.20	19	52.5-14	113	61.33-34	119
46.1-62.41	254	52.14	19, 20	62.1-11	119
46.1-51.37	109	52.15-40	114	62.8-9	254
46.11-27	109	52.15	19, 20	62.12-29	119
46.14-15	229	52.18	19, 20	62.12	19
46.23	235	52.19	19, 20	62.29	254
46.28-41	109	53.1-7	114	62.30-38	120
47.1-36	110	53.8-23	114	62.39-52	120
48.1-10	110	53.8-22	255	62.39	19
48.11-20	110, 254	53.13-15	257	62.51	235
48.13	254	53.23	19, 20	63.1-17	88, 120
48.15	235	54.1-14	114	63.1-3	120
48.16	254	54.1	20	63.1	19
48.17	254	54.7	289	63.3	19
48.21-25	110	54.11	290, 374	63.4-9	120
48.25	235	54.15-24	114	63.4	19
49.1-30	111	54.22	289	63.6	19
49.1	19	55.1-35	115	63.7	19
49.29	19	55.19	254	63.9	19
49.30	235	55.22-27	254	63.10-13	120
50.1-16	111	55.35	19	63.10	19
50.1	19	56.1-58.41	115	63.14-16	120
50.16	19	56.1-19	115, 255	63.16	19
50.17-22a	111	56.1	20		
50.17	19	56.7	20	*Helaman*	
50.20	235	56.9	20	1.1-2.14	121
50.22b	111	56.20-57	116	1.1-2.10	122
50.23	19, 111, 156	56.20	20	1.1-13	122
50.24	18, 19, 111	56.54-57	255	1.1	19
50.25-36	112	57.1-5	116	1.13	19
50.25	19	57.5	20	1.14	19
50.30-31	287	57.6-27	255	1.22-33	122
50.35	19	57.6-23	117	1.34	19
50.37-40	112	57.6	19, 20	2.1-13	122
50.40	19	57.26-36	117	2.1-4	122
51.1-8	112	58.1-12	117	2.1	19
51.1	19	58.13-31	117	2.12	19
51.9-12	112	58.32-41	118	3.1-6.41	121, 123
51.9	112	58.35	279	3.1-4.26	123
51.12	19, 112	58.38	19, 20	3.1-12	123
51.13-21	113	58.39	255	3.1-3	18
51.22-27	113	59.1-4	118	3.1	19, 247
51.28-37	113	59.1	19, 20	3.2	18, 19

12.1-2	142, 233	17.4	197	21.23-24	274
12.1	144, 221	17.7	381	21.26-23.5	150
12.2	221	17.8	381	21.22	247
12.3-14.27	143	17.9	381	23.5	233
12.3-12	143	17.10	377, 381	23.6-13	150
12.6	143	17.11-25	146	23.6-7	265
12.9	374	18.1-16	146	24.1-25.5	150
12.13-16	143	17.24	250	24.2	269, 383
12.20	235	18.11	233, 248	25.2	381
12.21-22	257	18.13	289, 290	26.1-5	150
12.22	290	18.14	235	26.3-5	269, 272
12.23	257	18.16	233, 247	26.3	150, 271
12.24	144	18.17-25	146	26.4-5	273
12.30	290	18.19	197	26.4	271
12.39	257	18.26-35	146	26.6-14	147
12.43-45	258	18.30	233	26.8-13	13
12.45	374	18.32	381	26.8-10	265
12.46-47	144	18.36-39	147	26.15-30.2	134, 150
13.1-4	144	19.1-14	147	26.15	381
13.5-15	144	19.13	221	26.20	151
13.16-18	144	19.14	250	27.1-12	151
13.19-20	144	19.15	250	27.2	152
13.25-34	144	19.15-26.5	147	27.4	279
13.25	144	19.15-36	148	27.13-22	151
14.1-6	144	19.19-20	197	27.16-17	270, 272, 383
14.1	144	19.25-30	238	27.16	233
14.7-12	144	19.25	147	27.20	233, 251, 376
14.13	144	19.31-34	219	27.23-27	151, 265
14.14	144	20.1-9	148	27.28-33	152
14.15-23	144	20.9	213	28.1-12	152
14.24-27	144	20.10b-29	148	28.11	221
15.1-19.14	145	20.16-17	149	28.13-23	152
15.1-10	145	20.22	274	28.18	233
15.1	197	20.26	197	28.24-30.2	152
15.5-10	145	20.27	214	28.24-40	152
15.10	235	20.31	197	28.24-26	153
15.11-16.3	145	20.44	267	28.27-35	153
15.14	197	21	149	28.30	251
15.21	145	21.1-10	267	28.36-40	153
15.24	197	21.2	149, 212	28.39	376
15.36-37	182	21.6	233	29.1-30.2	153
16.4-20	145	21.9	197	29.1-9	153
16.6	221	21.10	381	29.2	270, 383
16.10	244	21.14a	149	29.6	212, 217, 221, 381
16.16	197	21.19	244		
17.1-10	146	21.22-25	149	30.1-2	153

1.6b-33	171	12.2	214	6.5-9	183, 248
1.34-6.18	169, 170, 171	12.6-13.12	177	6.9	212
1.34-43	170, 172	12.6-41	170, 171	7.1-48	14, 181, 184
2.1-8	170, 172	12.6	177	7.1-14	184
2.8-10	235	12.10-21	177	7.3-4	260
2.9-12	170, 172	12.14	221, 239	7.15-19	184
2.13-3.5	170	12.19-20	426	7.16	229
2.13-16a	173	12.23	178	7.17	252
2.16b-25	173	12.25	178	7.19	374
3.1-5	173	12.26-28	178	7.20-39	184
3.6-20	202	12.29-37	178	7.25	229
3.6-16	170, 174	12.38-41	178	7.32	229
3.14	206, 207	12.38	177	7.34	233
3.17-20	170, 174	13.1-15.34	260	7.39	229
3.21-28	170, 174	13.1-12	171, 178	7.41	227, 273
4.1-5.6	170	13.2-3	274	7.44	212
4.1-19	175	13.5	275	7.47-48	184
4.7	206, 376	13.9-10	275	8.1-9.26	181
4.12d	198	13.13-22	171, 178	8.1-30	15, 185
5.1-6	175	13.23-31	178	8.1-26	185
6.1-13	170, 175	13.23-14.31	171	8.7	213
6.14-18	170, 175	14.1-2	179, 235	8.9	220
6.19-11.23	169, 170, 175	14.3-30	179	8.10	233
6.19-27	175	15.1-15	171	8.12	196
6.19-26	170	15.1-14	179	8.14	290, 291
6.27-8.19	170	15.3	235	8.18	185, 196
7.23-26	176	15.15-32	179	8.20	227
7.26	235	15.16-32	171	8.21	290, 291
8.7-19	176	15.19	221	8.23	213
8.8	287	15.33-34	171	8.31	289
8.10	287	15.33	179	8.35	233
8.20-26	170, 176	15.34	179	8.27-30	185
8.20	176			8.28	221
8.26	176	*Moroni*		9.1-26	15, 185
9.1-11.23	170, 176	1.1-6.9	14, 181	9.4	221
9.16	176	1.1-4	265	9.26	197
9.22	176	2.1-3	182, 354	10.1-34	181, 185
9.28	176	2.3	214	10.4-7	213
10.3	177	3.1-4	182	10.4-5	186, 268,
10.11	177	3.3	247		300, 363, 368
10.28	177	3.4	212	10.4	229
11.1-2	177	4.1-3	183	10.8-19	186
11.5-6	177	4.3	235, 248, 376	10.9-18	221
11.12-13	177	5.1-2	183	10.10	21
11.20-22	177	5.2	248, 376	10.11	381
12.1-15.34	170, 171, 177	6.1-4	183, 233	10.14	251
12.1-5	171, 177	6.4	212	10.15-16	218

10.20-23	186	10.32	376	*Book of Commandments*	
10.24-29	187	10.33	376	8.3	402
10.30-33	187	10.34	15, 187	24.7-11	297

INDEX OF AUTHORS

Made in the USA
Las Vegas, NV
14 January 2022

41326812R00272